CHEMICAL BONDING *for*

JEE Main & Advanced/ NEET

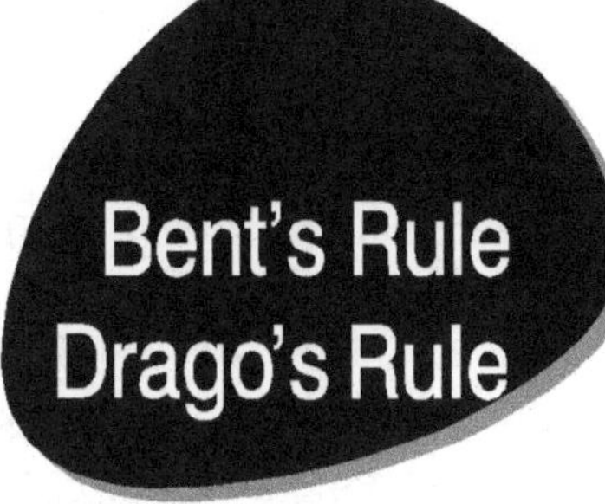

Newly added

HYDROLYSIS OF INORGANIC COVALENT COMPOUNDS

Vaibhav Trivedi

ACKNOWLEDGMENT

To my teachers : I owe an enormous debt of thanks to my teachers, especially to Mr. Gurdev Bharadwaj & Dr Ram Kuntal Hazra who always blessed & supported me during my entire student life.

To my family : I express special thanks to my parents, bhaiya bhabhi & my wife who constantly motivated me to write this book & also to my sweet daughter Parlika who smile has been a constant source of motivation for me.

I am indebted to **Archana Grover** for her help in doing editing and proof reading.

I would like to thank my publisher for his faith in me & for brilliant editing over designing of this book. I would also mention sincere efforts of my computer operator Mr. Sunil Kumar & wish a joyous time to all the readers of this book.

This book is dedicated to my mother who always inspired me to go high but I couldn't touch.

Published by :

DISHA PUBLICATION

Corporate Office : 45, 2nd Floor,
Maharishi Dayanand Marg,
Corner Market, Malviya Nagar,
New Delhi-110017
Tel. : 011-26692293 / 26692294
Tel. : 26692293 / 26692294
email : info@aiets.co.in
Web : www.aiets.co.in

Printed at : Repro Knowledgecast Limited, Thane

Preface

I wish to express my gratitude and indebtedness to all students and teachers who have been using the earlier editions. The book has been improved a lot as a result of their valuable suggestions and comments.

The present edition of this book has been thoroughly revised in accordance with the latest competitive trends while retaining the salient features and strengths of the previous editions.

In this edition, a new chapter entitled 'Hydrolysis of covalent compound' has been introduced. Further the book has been updated with the past questions of NEET,JEE Mains and Advance along with their solutions at the end of the book in the form of 3 new chapters. Errors in previous editions have also been rectified. Requisite modifications in some chapters and addition of problems in every chapter has been done keeping in mind the requirements of IIT-JEE aspirants.

A separate section comprising of true-false exercises has also been introduced at the end of the book with the primary aim of enabling the students to check their conceptual base and strengthen it accordingly.

I shall feel highly obliged, if the students and their fellow teachers send their constructive criticism and suggestions which we will be using in the publication of future editions.

I hope that the readers will enjoy and benefit from the experience of learning

'Chemical bonding' as is presented in this revised edition.

VAIBHAV TRIVEDI

M.Sc IIT-R, NET

organicvaibhav@gmail.com

Contents

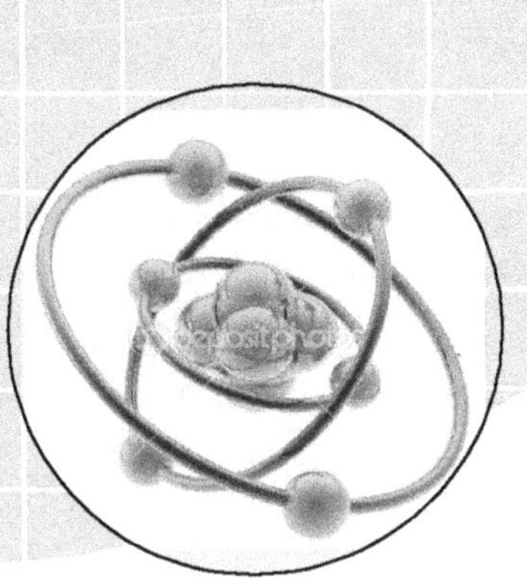

Some Basic Concepts of Atomic Structure & Periodic Properties

It is necessary to understand atomic structure and periodic properties to know the concept of chemical bonding fully.

Every atom has one nucleus inside it and orbits all around or we call them energy levels. These orbits further have sub shell or sub energy levels and these sub energy levels contain orbitals . 1st, 2nd, 3rd …….shells are called K, L, M …………etc. The sub shells are assigned with $s, p, d,$ and f. If 'n' shows number of shell then it must have 'n' sub shell and n^2 orbitals. Since each orbital has maximum capacity of 2 electrons thus, a shell can not hold more than $2n^2$ electrons.

s-sub shell	▢	One orbital ($2e^-$)
p-sub shell	▢▢▢	Three orbitals ($6e^-$)
d-sub shell	▢▢▢▢▢	Five orbitals ($10e^-$)
f-sub shell	▢▢▢▢▢▢▢	Seven orbitals ($14e^-$)

Finally we can say that in 1st energy level only one sub shell (s) is present, in 2nd shell two sub shells (s & p) are present similarly in 3rd & 4th shell three (s, p & d) & four (s, p, d & f) sub shells are present.

No. of shell (n)	Sub shells (n)	Total number orbitals (n^2)	Maximum electrons $2n^2$
1st (K)	s	$1s$ ▢	2
2nd (L)	s & p	$2s$ ▢ $2p$ ▢▢▢	8
3rd (M)	s, p & d	$3s$ ▢ $3p$ ▢▢▢ $3d$ ▢▢▢▢▢	18
4th (N)	s, p, d & f	$4s$ ▢ $4p$ ▢▢▢ $4d$ ▢▢▢▢▢ $4f$ ▢▢▢▢▢▢▢	32

➤ 1.1 Orbital and orbital wave function

"The region around the nucleus where probability of finding electron is maximum is called orbital and the region where probability of finding electron is zero is called node"

In order to find out the probability of finding electron in a given space of volume within the nucleus, we take help of wave function (ψ). Orbital wave function (ψ) can be written in the form of product of two wave functions.

$$\psi \quad = \quad \psi(r) \quad \times \quad \psi(\theta, \phi)$$

(Radial function)   (Angular function)

The radial part of orbital wave function i.e $\psi(r)$ gives the information about the size of orbital and depends on quantum number 'n' & 'l'. On the other hand, the angular part of wave function gives the information of shape of orbital and depends on quantum numbers 'l' & 'm'. The variation of the radial part of the orbital wave function for $1s$ and $2s$ orbitals is given below

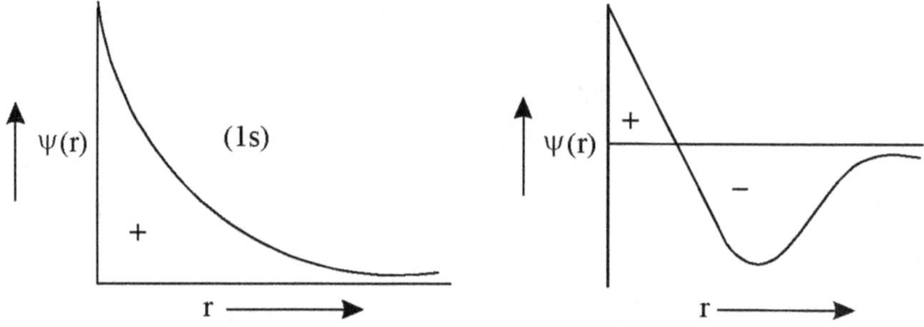

In this figure, +ve and −ve sign indicates that in particular region wave function is +ve and −ve. It has no relation with +ve and −ve charge.

It is observed that the shape of 's' orbital does not depend on angular part of wave function but it only depend upon radial part of wave function. Therefore, all 's' orbitals are spherical because they have no directional dependence.

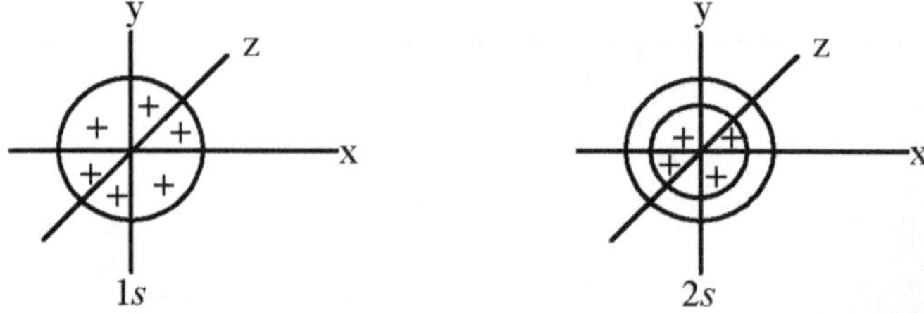

Probability density (ψ^2): - Wave function only shows amplitude of electron wave whereas square of wave function ψ^2 shows the probability of finding electron in a definite region around the nucleus.

The graph between ψ^2 and r (distance from nucleus) denotes probability density curve. Here probability density curves for $1s$ & $2s$ orbitals are shown below

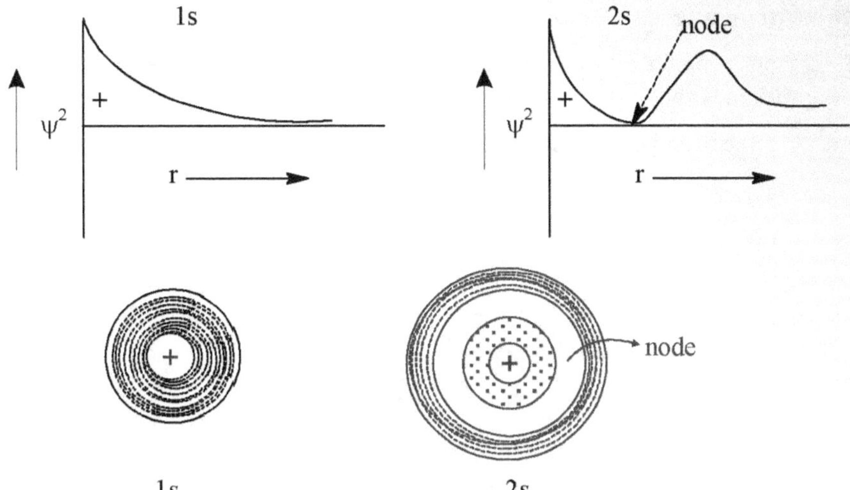

The shapes of the orbitals can be represented quite accurately with the help of boundary surface diagram. The boundary surface diagram for 's' orbitals are spherical in shape. The size of 's' orbital however increases with increase in number of shell. The boundary surface diagram of the three $2p$ orbitals is not spherical. Each 'p' orbital consists of two lobes which are separated by a region of zero probability (node).

In three 'p' orbitals lobes lie on p_x, p_y & p_z axis respectively

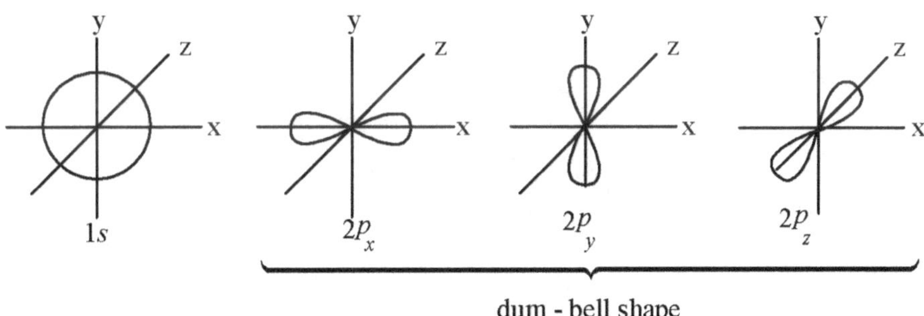

dum - bell shape

Shapes of d orbitals (double dumbell):-

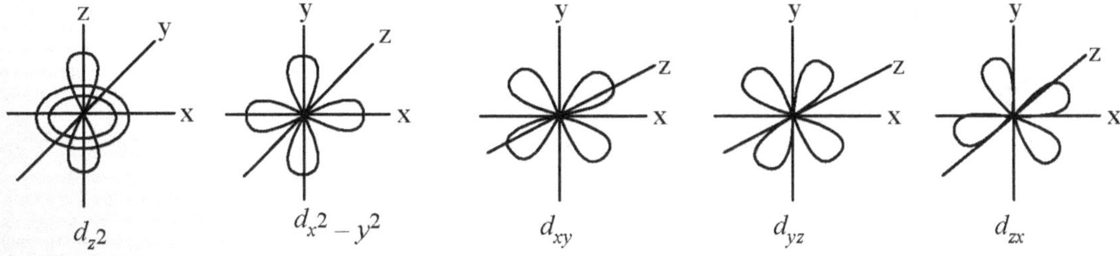

Out of five 'd' orbitals, only two 'd' orbitals d_{z^2} & $d_{x^2-y^2}$ have their lobes on the axis, rest all 'd' orbitals have their lobes in between the axis.

➤1.2 Aufbau principle and electronic configuration

The electrons are added progressively to the various orbitals in their order of increasing energies starting with the orbital of lowest energy.

In order to remember the various orbitals in increasing order of energy, we take help of following diagram

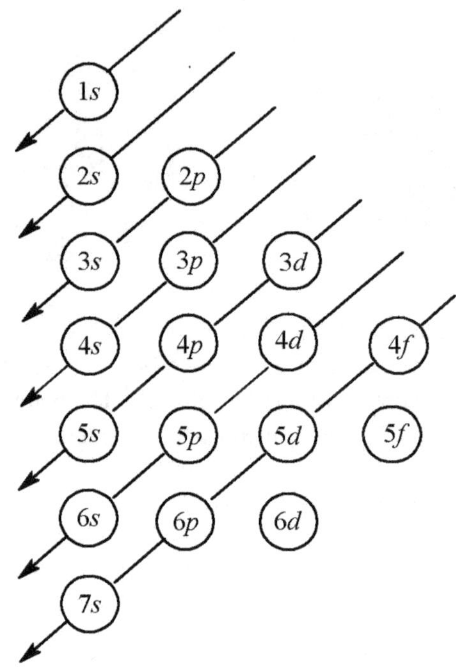

$1s, 2s, 2p, 3s, 3p, 4s, 3d, 4p, 5s, 4d, 5p, 6s, 4f, 5d, 6p, 7s$ ....

Electronic configurations of some elements are given below

$H\,(1e^-)$ $1s^1$

$He\,(2e^-)$ $1s^2$

$Li\,(3e^-)$ $1s^2, 2s^1$

$C\,(6e^-)$ $1s^2, 2s^2, 2p^2$

$V\,(23e^-)$ $1s^2, 2s^2, 2p^6, 3s^2, 3p^6, 4s^2, 3d^3$

➤1.3 Hund's rule of maximum multiplicity

Pairing of electron in degenerate orbitals (orbitals with same energy) belonging to same sub shell does not occur till each orbital of that sub shell is singly occupied with parallel spin.

$N\,(7e^-)$

↑↓	↑↓	↑	↑	↑
$1s^2$	$2s^2$		$2p^3$	

$F\,(9e^-)$

↑↓	↑↓	↑↓	↑↓	↑
$1s^2$	$2s^2$		$2p^5$	

➢ 1.4 Nuclear charge (Z) and effective nuclear charge (Z*) & Screening effect

Nuclear charge (Z) is defined as the number of protons, present in the nucleus, for example the nucleus of H has one electron therefore, its Z = 1 similarly Z = 3 for lithium as it possesses three protons in its nucleus.

The electron in the outermost shell is attracted by the protons present with in the nucleus but it is also repelled by the electrons present in the inner shell as well as from the electrons present in its own shell. The combined effect of this attractive and repulsive force acting on valence electron is that the valence electron experience less attraction from the nucleus. This is called **Shielding or Screening effect.**

Therefore, the net charge with which valence electron feels attraction is called effective nuclear charge (Z*)

$$Z^* = z - \sigma$$

Here σ = screening constant.

The electrons present in different sub shell possess different capacity to shield or screen the nucleus. The electrons present in 's' orbital shield the nucleus maximum as they are closer to nucleus, whereas electrons in 'd' and 'f' sub shells have poor screening effect as they are away from the nucleus. The sequence of shielding capacity by the electron in different sub shell is given as:-

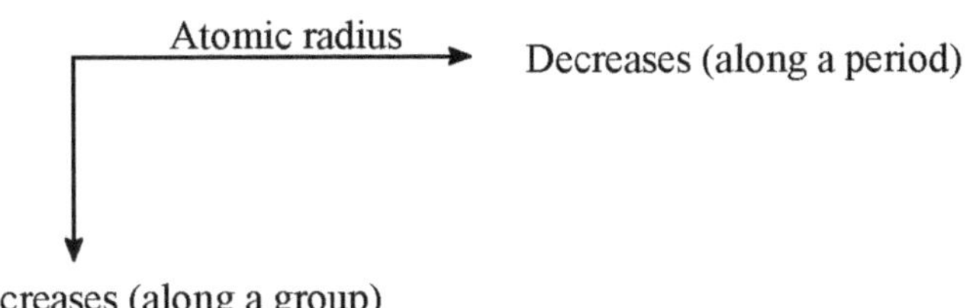

$$s \quad\quad p \quad\quad d \quad\quad f$$

$$s \;>\; p \;>\; d \;>\; f$$

(Good screening)　　　　(Poor screening)

Along with it, if all sub shells are completely filled with electrons, the order of screening will be:-

$$f \;>\; d \;>\; p \;>\; s$$

Effective nuclear charge increases while moving from left to right in a periodic table whereas it remains constant on moving down in a group.

➢ 1.5 Periodic properties and their variations

(a) **Atomic radius:** - It is the distance from the centre of the nucleus of the atom to the valence electron

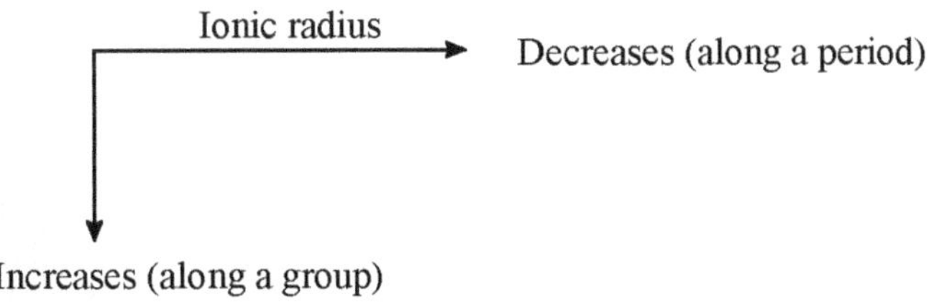

(b) **Ionic radius:** - It is defined as the effective distance from the nucleus of the ion to the point up to which it has an influence (or effect) in the ionic bond.

The radius of cation is smaller than its parent atom because when atom releases an electron to form cation, its effective nuclear charge ($Z^* = p/e$ theoretically) increases and valence electron feels more attraction from the nucleus, consequently radius decreases. On the other hand the radius of anion is more than its parent atom because when an atom gains electron to form anion its effective nuclear charge ($Z^* = p/e$) decreases and valence electron feels less attraction from the nucleus resulting in small ionic radius.

(c) **Ionization energy (I.E) or Ionization potential (I.P):** - It is the amount of energy required to remove an electron from an isolated gaseous atom to produce cation

$$M(g) \xrightarrow{\text{(I.E.)}} M^{(+)}(g) + e^-$$

In general I.E. decreases on moving down the group because on moving down the group atomic size increases & valence electron feels less attraction from nucleus.

If an atom has exactly half filled or completely filled sub shells, then such an atom requires more ionization energy than the atom with partially filled sub shell. For example, first I.E. of nitrogen is greater than oxygen.

N $1s^2$ $2s^2$ $\underbrace{2p^3}$ O $1s^2$ $2s^2$ $\overbrace{2p^4}$

           half filled   Partially filled
           'p' sub shell   'p' sub shell

(d) **Electron gain enthalpy of electron affinity (E.A):-** It is the energy released when an electron is added to a neutral gaseous atom to convert it in to an anion

$$X(g) \ + \ e^- \longrightarrow X^{(-)}(g) \ + \ E.A.$$

E.A. $\propto$ 1 / atomic size
E.A $\propto$ 1 / screening effect

(e) **Electronegativity (E.N)**

Electronegativity is a measure of the tendency of an element to attract electrons towards it self in a covalently bonded molecules

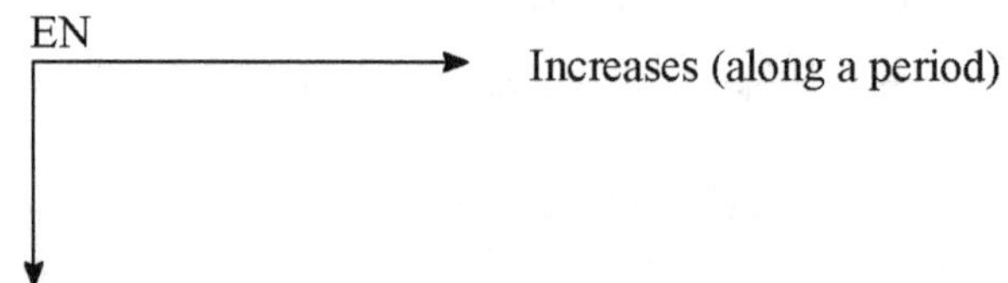

There is no direct method to measure the value of electronegativity; however there are some scales like Pauling scale, Mulliken scale & Allred - Rochow scale, to measure its value. In chemical bonding, we often use Pauling scale Electronegativity of some elements on Pauling scale is given below.

Li	**Be**	**B**	**C**	**N**	**O**	**F**
(1.0)	(1.5)	(2.0)	(2.5)	(3.0)	(3.5)	(4.0)
Na						**Cl**
(0.9)						(3.0)
K						**Br**
(0.8)						(2.8)
Rb						**I**
(0.8)						(2.5)
Cs						
(0.7)						

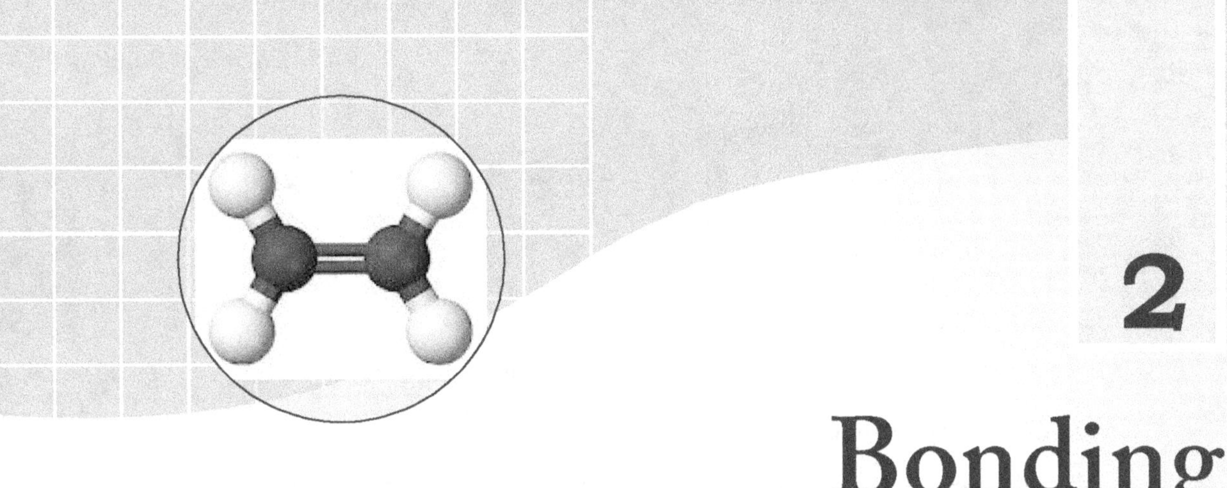

Bonding

2

What is a chemical bond?

If energy released by the attraction of two atoms is more than 42 KJ / mol then it is considered as chemical bond.

$$A + B \longrightarrow AB + \text{Energy (more than 42 KJ / mol)}$$

The attractive force which holds together the atoms or groups of atoms in a chemical species is known as chemical bond.

But the question arises that why elements combine with each other. Various facts have been put forward to understand it; finally Kossel and Lewis successfully presented the fact in 1916. They made electronic configuration as base and explained that atoms of inert gas possess least probability to combine with other elements. It means that the electronic configuration of inert gases is more stable; therefore, they do not react with other atoms (Except Xenon)

Outer most shell of all inert gas elements is completely filled. Except 'He' electronic configuration of all inert gas atoms is ns^2, np^6, it means, there are 8e in their outermost shell. Except noble gas, no other elements possess 8e in their outermost shell. Therefore, the other elements combine together or with other elements in order to complete their octet. This gives birth to octet rule. **According to octet rule:-**

"Atoms combine together to complete their outermost shell and to attain the configuration of noble gas which is a stable configuration."

Based on modes of combination chemical bonds are classified as:-

(a)	Ionic bond	(b)	Covalent bond
(c)	Coordinate bond	(d)	Metallic bond

➤2.1 Ionic bond or Electrovalent bond

We all know that sodium reacts with chlorine readily to form NaCl. The outermost shell of Na has one electron (2, 8, 1) whereas chlorine has 7- electrons in valence shell (2, 8, 7) so, 'Na' transfers its one electron to 'Cl' and forms NaCl. This allows 'Na' and 'Cl' to complete their octet. These oppositely charged ions (Na^+ and Cl^-) are held together by an electrostatic force of attraction called ionic bond or electrovalent bond

Thus, **ionic bond** can be defined as:-

"It is electrostatic force of attraction between two oppositely charged ions"

Conditions for formation of ionic compounds:-

(1)　The electronegativity difference between combining atoms should be large

(2)　The atom which makes cation should have greater size and low ionization energy so that it can easily loose its outermost electron. Nearly all elements of s - block owing to their large sizes and low ionization energies form ionic compounds. For e.g. $NaCl$, KCl, $CaCl_2$, and $CsCl$ etc.

(3)　The atom which forms anion should have small size and more electron affinity. Non metals owing to their small size and more electron affinity form ionic compounds with 's' block elements like Na_2O, MgO, $CaSO_4$, $CaCl_2$ ....etc

(4)　Ionic crystals have high lattice energy (discussed later)

General properties of ionic compounds

(1)　Ionic compounds are soluble in polar solvents like water but insoluble in non polar solvents like benzene.

(2)　Due to the strong electrostatic forces of attractions between oppositely charged ions, ions are tightly bound with each other and this result in high melting point and thermal stability.

(3)　They exist in solid or liquid state at room temperature but not in gaseous state.

(4)　Ionic solids are almost non conductor and conducts very small magnitude of current due to crystal defect.

　　In solid state they do not conduct electricity because ions are not mobile whereas in molten state ionic compounds conduct electricity because ions are mobile and can easily conduct current from one place to another. The aqueous solution of these compounds are good conductor of electricity because ions remain mobile in this form.

(5)　They show isomorphism (see section 4.10 in chapter - 04)

Note: - All the physical properties of ionic compounds have been discussed in chapter - 05 with detailed discussion & clear explanation.

➤2.2 Lattice energy

Ionic compound not only forms by the combination of cation and anion but ionic compound requires considerable electrostatic forces of attractions between cation and anion.

When these cations and anions in large number and in equal number come closer, they arrange themselves in regular pattern and attain a closed packed structure; during this arrangement energy is released to stabilize the system. This released energy is called lattice energy.

$$Na^{(+)} + Cl^{(-)} \longrightarrow Na^{(+)}Cl^{(-)} + lattice\ energy$$
$$crystal\ lattice$$

Structure of NaCl crystal is shown below

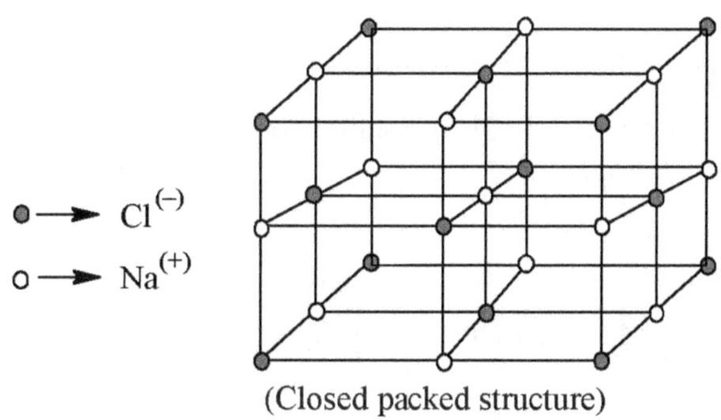

(Closed packed structure)

Thus, **lattice energy can be defined as:-**

"Energy released when 1 mol of an ionic compound is formed by its constituent ions in gaseous state"

Or

"Energy required to break 1 mol of an ionic compound in to its constituent ions in gaseous state"

$$Na^{(+)}_{(g)} + Cl^{(-)}_{(g)} \longrightarrow NaCl + 185.2\,Kcal/mol$$

It means that if 1 mol NaCl is to be broken in gaseous ions $Na^{(+)}$ & $Cl^{(-)}$ then 185.2 Kcal energy is required.

➢ **Determination of lattice energy: -** There are two methods to determine lattice energy.

(a) Born Haber cycle (indirect method)

(b) Kapustunskii equation (direct method)

(a) **Born Haber cycle: -** This method is based on Hess law. For example NaCl is formed by two methods

Path - I $Na + 1/2Cl_2 \longrightarrow NaCl + \Delta H_f$ (heat of formation)
(s) (g)

Path - II $Na_{(s)} \xrightarrow{\triangle H\ sublimation} Na_{(g)}$

$Na_{(g)} \xrightarrow{I.E.} Na^+ + e^-$ I.E = Ionisation energy
(g)

$1/2Cl_2 \xrightarrow{\triangle H\ dissociation} Cl$
(molecule) (atom)

$$Cl_{(g)} + e^{(-)} \xrightarrow{\text{E.A.}} Cl^{(-)}_{(g)} \qquad\qquad EA = \text{Electron affinity}$$

$$Na^{(+)}_{(g)} + Cl^{(-)}_{(g)} \xrightarrow{\text{E.A.}} NaCl + \text{lattice energy}$$

By Hess law (the law of conservation of energy) the total heat change from path I & path II will be same

$$\Delta H_f = \Delta H (\text{sublimation}) + I.E + \Delta H (\text{dissociation}) + E.A. + \text{lattice energy} \ldots\ldots\ldots(1)$$

If we know the values of ΔH_f, I.E, E.A, sublimation & dissociation energy, we can calculate lattice energy by the help of equation (1)

(b) Kapustunskii equation

$$L.E. = \frac{120200 \ \gamma \ |Z^+||Z^-|}{r}\left(1 - \frac{34.5}{r}\right) \ KJ/mol$$

γ = No. of ions per mol for example for Na_2SO_4, $\gamma = 3$ for $BaSO_4$, $\gamma = 2$, Z^+ & Z^- are the charges present on cation and anion respectively.

r = Inter ionic distance = radius of cation (r^+) + radius of anion (r^-) (in pm)

➢ **Factor affecting lattice energy :-**

From Kapustunskii relation we have

$$L.E. \propto |Z^+| \ |Z^-| \quad \text{or} \quad q_1 q_2$$

$$L.E. \propto 1/(r^+ + r^-)$$

For example

NaCl	KCl	RbCl	CsCl

$\xleftarrow{\hspace{5cm}}$

Increasing lattice energy

	MgCl$_2$	MgO	Mg$_3$N$_2$
$q_1 q_2 \ =$	2×1	2×2	2×3

$\xrightarrow{\hspace{5cm}}$

Increasing lattice energy

➢2.3 Covalent bond

According to Lewis, "Covalent bond is formed from the sharing of same number of electron between two atoms"

The atoms which take part in sharing complete their octet by sharing one two or three electrons. If one electron is shared between two atoms then it forms single bond. Similarly double & triple bonds are formed by the sharing of two and three electrons. For example:-

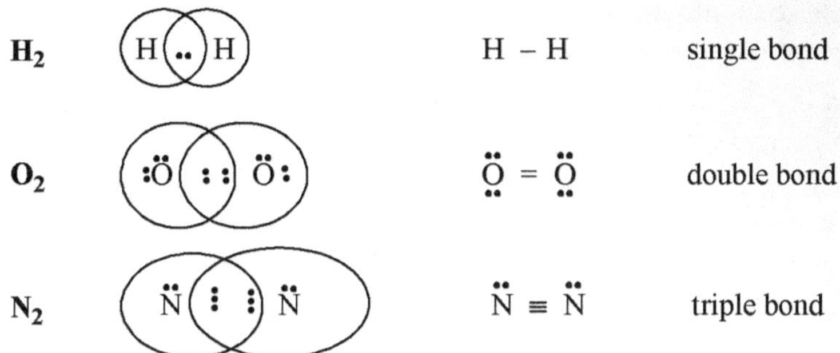

H_2	H(··)H	H – H	single bond
O_2	:Ö(::)Ö:	Ö = Ö	double bond
N_2	Ñ(⋮⋮)Ñ	Ñ ≡ Ñ	triple bond

➢ Only the electrons of valence shell take part in sharing. The electrons of valence shell which do not take part in chemical bonding are called lone pair or non bonding electrons. For example in O_2 six valence electrons of oxygen atom (2, 6) can take part in bonding. Out of six electrons two electrons are shared by one oxygen atoms thus after bond formation each oxygen possesses four electrons (or two lone pairs)

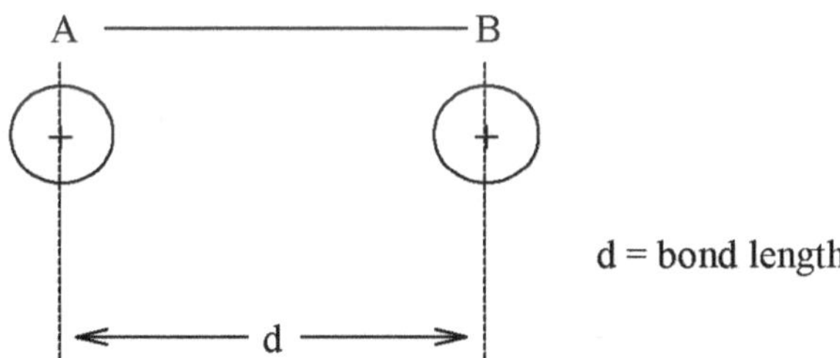

➢ **Bond length :-** It is defined as the inter nuclear distance between two covalently bonded atoms

$$ A \text{———} B $$

d = bond length

$$\text{Bond length} \propto \frac{1}{\text{Bond order}} \propto \frac{1}{\text{Stability}}$$

➢ **Bond order (B.O.) :-** The number of bonds present between two covalently bonded atoms is called bond order

$$F - F \qquad \text{B.O.} = 1, \qquad O = O \qquad \text{B.O.} = 2$$

$$\text{Bond order} \propto \text{Stability} \propto \frac{1}{\text{Bond length}}$$

If the number of bonds is more between two atoms, more energy is required to break those bonds, thus, it increases the stability

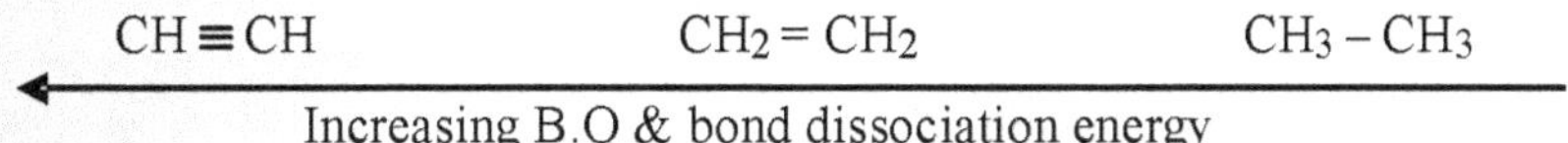

$$CH \equiv CH \qquad\qquad CH_2 = CH_2 \qquad\qquad CH_3 - CH_3$$

Increasing B.O & bond dissociation energy

This clears the concept why N_2 behaves like inert gas at room temperature. The reason is that in N_2, nitrogen atoms are joined with each other by the help of triple bond which is difficult to break at room temperature.

Due to increase in number of bonds (B.O), bonding atoms come close to each other and bond length decreases

$$CH \equiv CH \qquad\qquad CH_2 = CH_2 \qquad\qquad CH_3 - CH_3$$

$$\longleftarrow \text{Decreasing bond length}$$

➢ 2.4 Lewis structure drawing

For this we have to follow following rules

Rule - 1 :-

Calculate n_1 = Total number of valence shell electron + (negative charges) – (positive charges)

Calculate n_2 = 2 (number of H – atoms) + 8 (number of other atoms)

Calculate $n_3 = (n_2 - n_1)$

Number of bonded electrons i.e. number of bond pair = $n_3 / 2$

Calculate $n_4 = (n_1 - n_3)$

Number of lone pair of electrons = $n_4 / 2$

Rule - 2 :-

Find out central atom either more electro positive or least in number for example in H_2SO_4, 'S' is considered as central atom similarly P is considered as central atom in PCl_5 & H_3PO_4

Rule - 3 :-

Arrange the surrounding atoms around central atom and join them with the help of bond pair calculated $(n_3 / 2)$ verify octet of each atom. If octet is not found to be completed then utilize the lone pair to fulfill the octet.

Rule - 4 :-

To understand the bonding properly we shall calculate formal charge for each atom (discussed later)

Let us consider some examples

1. $H - CN$:

$$n_1 \quad = \quad 1 + 4 + 5 \quad = \quad 10$$
$$n_2 \quad = \quad 2 \times 1 + 8 \times 2 \quad = \quad 18$$
$$n_3 \quad = \quad n_2 - n_1 \quad = \quad 18 - 10 \quad = \quad 8$$
$$\text{Bond pair} \quad = \quad 8 / 2 \quad = 4$$
$$\text{Lone pair} \quad = \quad 10 - 8 / 2 \quad = 1, \quad \text{i.e} \quad H - C \equiv \overset{\cdot\cdot}{N}$$

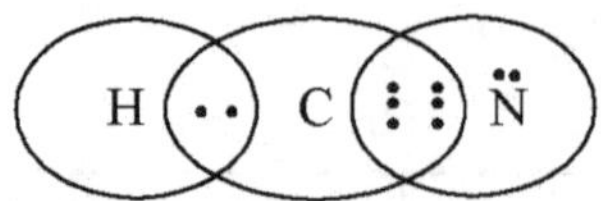

2. CO_2:

$$n_1 = 4 + 6 + 6 = 16$$
$$n_2 = 3 \times 8 = 24$$
$$n_3 = 24 - 16 = 8$$
$$\text{bond pair} = 8/2 = 4$$
$$n_4 = n_1 - n_3 = 16 - 8 = 8$$
$$\text{lone pair} = n_4/2 = 8/2 = 4 \quad \text{i.e} \quad \ddot{O} = C = \ddot{O}$$

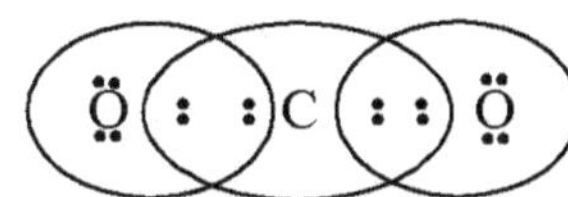

3. NO_3^-:

$$n_1 = 5 + (6 \times 3) + 1 = 24$$
$$n_2 = 8 \times 4 = 32$$
$$n_3 = 32 - 24 = 8, \quad \text{bond pair} = 8/2 = 4$$
$$n_4 = n_1 - n_3, = 24 - 8 = 16$$
$$\text{lone pair} = 16/2 = 8$$

Calculation of formal charge (F.C)

F.C = (valence shell electrons of atom) –(number of bonds associated with that atom) –(number of unshared electrons by it)

(1) $:\ddot{O} - \overset{(2)}{N} = \ddot{O}:$ (3)   Now formal charges on 1, 2, 3 & 4
         $|$ can be calculate as
        $:\ddot{O}:$ (4)

1st atom: -   F. C = 6 – 1 – 6 = –1
2nd atom: -   F. C = 5 – 4 – 0 = +1
3rd atom: -   F. C = 6 – 2 – 4 = 0
4th atom: -   F. C = 6 – 1 – 6 = –1

Hence NO_3^- can be represented as:- $(-) :\ddot{O} - \overset{(+)}{N} = \ddot{O}:$
                                                    $|$
                                                  $:\ddot{O}:$
                                                   $(-)$

Lewis dot structures of some species are given below:-

H_2O_2 $H \cdot\cdot \ddot{O} \cdot\cdot H$ or $H - \ddot{O} - \ddot{O} - H$

PH_3 $H \cdot\cdot \ddot{P} \cdot\cdot H$ or $H - \ddot{P} - H$
              H H

CO_3^{2-} $\left[:\ddot{O} : : \ddot{O} \cdot\cdot \ddot{O}: \right]^{-2}$ or $:\ddot{O} = \ddot{C} - \ddot{O}:^{(-)}$ with $\ddot{O}:^{(-)}$ on top

H_3O^+

$$\left[\; H \;\cdot\cdot\; \ddot{O} \;\cdot\cdot\; H \atop H \; \right]^+ \qquad \text{or} \qquad H-\overset{(+)}{\underset{H}{O}}-H$$

HNO_3

$$:\!\ddot{O}\!: \;\;:\!N\!: \;\; \ddot{O}\!: H \atop :\ddot{O}\!: \qquad \text{or} \qquad :\!\ddot{O} = \overset{(+)}{N} - \underset{:\underset{(-)}{\ddot{O}}\!:}{\ddot{O}} - H$$

H_3PO_4

$$H\cdot\cdot\ddot{O}\!: \quad P \quad \cdot\cdot\ddot{O}\cdot\cdot H \qquad \text{or} \qquad H-\ddot{O}-P-\ddot{O}-H$$

(with $:\ddot{O}:$ above and below P in the left structure; $H-\ddot{O}$ with O double-bonded below and $:\ddot{O}:$ above P in the right structure)

SO_4^{-2}

$$\left[:\!\ddot{O}\cdot\cdot\!\overset{:\ddot{O}:}{\underset{:\ddot{O}:}{S}}\!\cdot\cdot\ddot{O}\!: \right]^{-2} \qquad \text{or} \qquad \left[:\!\ddot{O}-\overset{:\ddot{O}:}{\underset{:\ddot{O}:}{S}}-\ddot{O}\!: \right]^{-2}$$

➤2.5 Limitations of the octet rule

It is useful for understanding the structures of most of the organic compounds and it applies mainly to the second period elements of the periodic table. There are three types of exceptions to the octet rule.

(a)   The expanded octet or super octet (Hypervalent compounds):-

There are many stable molecules in which central atom have more than $8e^-$ in its valence shell for e.g. IF_7 ($14e^-$ in valence shell), PCl_5 ($10e^-$), SF_6($12e^-$)

For such kind of molecules central atom should have 'd' orbitals for bonding

(b)   The incomplete octet of central atom (Hypovalent compounds):-

In some compounds, the number of electrons surrounding the central atom is less than 8. This is specially the case with elements having less than four valence electrons.

For e.g. $BeCl_2$, BCl_3, $LiCl$

$$:\ddot{C}l - Be - \ddot{C}l: \qquad \overset{:\ddot{C}l}{\underset{:\ddot{C}l}{\diagdown}} B - \ddot{C}l:$$

(4 valence e^-)   (6 valence e^-)

(c) **Odd electrons molecules :** There are some species which have odd number of electrons, like KO_2, RbO_2, NO, NO_2 and CsO_2. In these cases, octet rule is not obeyed by all the elements of species

$$\dot{\ddot{N}} = \ddot{O} \qquad\qquad O \leftarrow \dot{N} = \ddot{O}$$

(Nitric oxide)

These species are coloured and paramagnetic in nature because of presence of unpaired electron.

Apart from these, octet rule does not give any information about the shape of species as well as it can not explain that why Xe (inert gas elements) forms variety of compounds like XeF_6, $XeOF_2$ & XeF_4 etc.

➢ 2.6 Polar and non polar covalent molecules

If the two bonded atoms have equal values of electronegativites, the bonded pair of electrons is equally shared between them, i.e. shared pair of electrons remains in the middle (just in between the atoms). Such a bond is called non polar covalent bond.

For example $H - H$, $O = O$, $N \equiv N$, $C - C$, $F - F$ ....etc bonds. However, if the bonded atoms differ in their elecronegativities, the bonded pair of electrons is attracted more towards at atom with the larger electronegativity, resulting in the development of partial negative charge over this atom and equal but opposite charge over the other bonded atom. Such a covalent bond is called polar covalent bond. For e.g. $I - Cl$, $C - Cl$, $C = O$, $H - F$

$$H \underline{\quad\quad\infty\quad\quad} H \qquad\qquad \overset{\delta^+}{H} \underline{\quad\quad\infty}\text{-}\overset{\delta^-}{F}$$

(non polar molecule)   (polar molecule)

Extent of polarity in a bond is measured in terms of dipole moment (discussed later in chapter - 05)

➢ 2.7 General properties of covalent molecules

➢ **Solubility :** These compounds are usually insoluble or less soluble in water and in other polar solvents. Polar covalent molecules are more soluble in water in comparison to that of non polar covalent molecules.

➢ **Low melting point and boiling point:** - The intermolecular forces of attractions between the molecules of covalent compounds are generally weak. As a result, lesser amount of energy is needed to overcome these intermolecular forces. Thus, these compounds usually have low melting point and boiling point than ionic compounds.

➢ **Conducting nature:** - These are generally poor conductors of electricity in the fused or dissolved state due to non existence of ions.

➤ **Molecular reactions:-** These compounds generally do not produce ions in aqueous medium. There fore, their reactions are not ionic in nature. These reactions involve the breaking of covalent bonds in reaction molecules and forming new bonds to give molecules of the products. Therefore, these reactions are quite slow because energy is required to break covalent bonds.

➤ **State of existence:** - There are weak intermolecular forces between the molecules and hence, they exist as liquids or gases at room temperature. However, a few covalent compounds also exist in the solid state for e.g. glucose, urea, thiourea & sugar etc.

➤ 2.8 Coordinate bond (Dative bond)

In this type of bonding, one atom donates its electron pair to the other. In other words electron sharing takes place between two atoms but sharing involves one atom only. The atom which receives electron pair is known as receiver whereas the one which donates electron pair is known as donor atom.

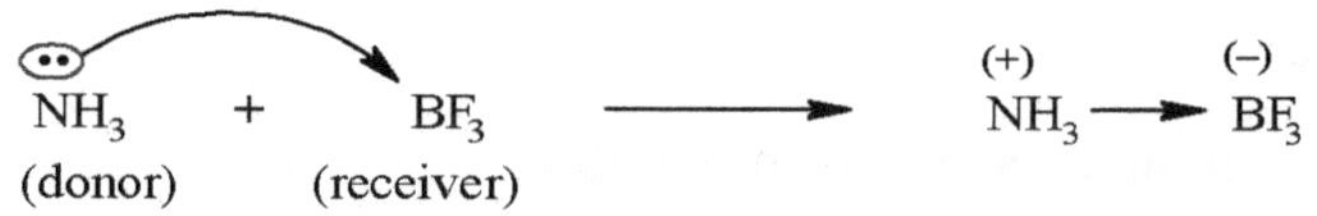

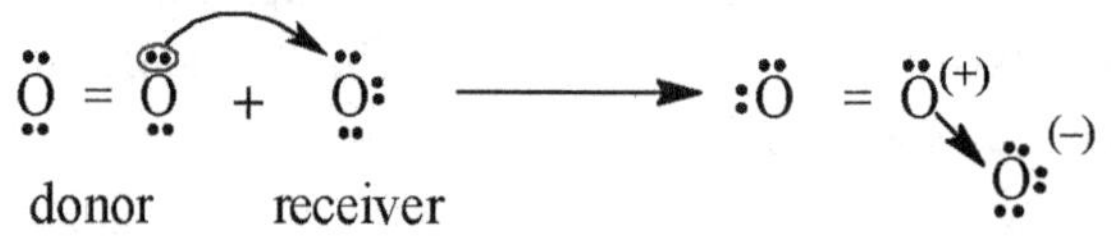

$$NH_3 \; + \; BF_3 \longrightarrow \overset{(+)}{NH_3} \longrightarrow \overset{(-)}{BF_3}$$

(donor)   (receiver)

$$\ddot{O} = \ddot{O} \; + \; \ddot{O}: \longrightarrow :\ddot{O} = \overset{(+)}{\ddot{O}} \searrow \overset{(-)}{\ddot{O}:}$$

donor   receiver

The nature of coordinate bond is semi ionic or semi covalent. This is explained as:-

There are two steps involved in the formation of coordinate bond between A and B.

Step - I: - Firstly, atom A gives its electron to atom B

$$\ddot{A} \; + \; B \longrightarrow \overset{+}{A} \quad \overset{-}{B}$$

Step - II: - Now both A + and B- share one electron with each other

$$\overset{+}{A} \cdot \; + \; \cdot \overset{-}{B} \longrightarrow \overset{+}{A} - \bullet\bullet - \overset{-}{B}$$

Thus, coordinate bond has semi ionic nature. Therefore physical properties of these compounds like solubility, melting point, boiling point and electrical conductance lies between covalent and ionic compounds (For more discussion see chapter - 05)

Subjective Exercise

Q.1 Draw Lewis dot structures for the following species:-

CO_3^{2-}, $HCO_3^{(-)}$, SO_2, SO_3, Na_2CO_3, N_2O_4

Q.2 Calculate formal charges on bold elements

(a) $H-\ddot{N}-\overset{\overset{\textstyle :O:}{\|}}{C}-\ddot{\underset{..}{O}}-H$

(b) $H-\underset{\underset{\textstyle H}{|}}{\overset{\overset{\textstyle H}{|}}{N}}-CH_2-\ddot{\underset{..}{O}}-H$

(c) $H_2\ddot{C}-NH-\ddot{S}\diagup^{H}_{\diagdown H}$

Q.3 Arrange the following in decreasing order of electrical conductance.

(a) $NaCl(l)$ $MgCl_2(l)$ $K_2SO_4(l)$

(b) $NaCl(l)$ $MgCl_2(l)$ $NaCl(s)$

(c) $MgCl_2(s)$ $NaCl(l)$ $MgCl_2(l)$

Q.4 NaCl is soluble in water but not in benzene explain.

Q.5 Use Lewis symbols to show electron transfer between the following atoms to form cations & anions

(a) K and O

(b) Ca & S

Q.6 Predict the nature of bond in each case formed between atoms

(a) P & H

(b) N & Cl

(c) Mg & O

(d) K & O

(e) Sr & F

Q.7 Draw Lewis dot structure of the molecule in which three 'C' atoms are present, total atoms are 5 and total double bonds are '4'

Q.8 Calculate number of double bonds in following species

(a) $HCOOH$

(b) $COOH-COOH$

(c) N_2H_4

(d) $CH_3COCOOH$

Q.9 Calculate L.E. of CaF_2 by using following data ΔH sublimation (Ca) = 48 K Cal / mol

$(I.E.)_1$ = 141 K Cal / mol

$(I.E.)_2$ = 274 K Cal / mol

ΔH dissociation (F_2) = 34 K Cal / mol

E.A. = -83 K Cal / mol

$\Delta H^\circ_f (CaF_2) = -296$ K Cal / mol (Ans = -627 k Cal / mol)

Q.10 Write partial positive and negative charges on each atom in following molecules

(a) H_2O (b) F_2O (c) NH_3 (d) NF_3

Objective Exercise

Q.1 Which among the following possesses ionic as well as covalent bonds?

(a) $MgCO_3$

(b) NH_4Cl

(c) HBF_4

(d) All of these

Q.2 The type of bond present in N_2O_4

(a) Only covalent

(b) Only ionic

(c) Ionic and covalent

(d) Covalent & Coordinate

Q.3 Which of the following does not contain coordinate bond?

(a) SO_3

(b) H_2SO_4

(c) $H_3O^{(+)}$

(d) All of these contains coordinate bond

Q.4 Which of the following is an example of super octet rule?

(a) CO_2

(b) PCl_3

(c) ClF_3

(d) NF_3

Q.5 Which of the following is an example of super octet rule?

(a) XeF_6

(b) IF_7

(c) SF_6

(d) All of these

Q.6 One mol of phosphate ion reacts with two moles of $H^{(+)}$ ion to produce 'X'. The formula of compound formed by $Na^{(+)}$ & X is

(a) Na_2X

(b) NaX

(c) Na_3X

(d) Na_3X_2

Q.7 How many double bonds are present in C_3O_2:-

(a) 1

(b) 2

(c) 3

(d) 4

Q.8 Highest electrical conductance will be found in:-

(a) $LiCl(l)$

(b) $NaCl(l)$

(c) $KCl(l)$

(d) $RbCl(l)$

Q.9 Highest electrical conductance will be found in:-

(a) $Na_3AlF_6(l)$

(b) $MgCl_2((l)$

(c) $MgSO_4(l)$

(d) $KNO_3(l)$

Q.10   **Column - I**   **Column - II**

    (A) Na_3AlF_6 (1)   Contains '4' double bonds

    (B) AgCl   (2)   Contains Coordinate bond

    (C) Na_2SO_4 (3)   Least electrical conductance in molten state

    (D) C_3S_2 (4)   Produce 4 ions when dissolve in water

Correct matching code is:-

    (a) $A \rightarrow 4, B \rightarrow 2, C \rightarrow 3, D \rightarrow 1$

    (b) $A \rightarrow 4, B \rightarrow 3, C \rightarrow 2, D \rightarrow 1$

    (c) $A \rightarrow 3, B \rightarrow 2, C \rightarrow 4, D \rightarrow 1$

    (d) $A \rightarrow 1, B \rightarrow 2, C \rightarrow 3, D \rightarrow 4$

Q.11   Which will not produce ions in aqueous medium

    (a) $MgCl_2$ (b) $BeCl_2$

    (c)   NaCl   (d)   CsCl

Q.12   In $NO_3^{(-)}$ ion, number of bond pair and lone pair of electron on nitrogen atom are?

    (a)   2, 2   (b)   3, 1

    (c)   1, 3   (d)   4, 0

Q.13   Which of the following is the electron deficient molecule?

    (a) C_2H_6 (b) B_2H_6

    (c) SiH_4 (d) PH_3

Q.14   Which of the following types of bonds are present in $CuSO_4.5H_2O$?

    (1)   electrovalent   (2)   covalent   (3)   coordinate

    Select the correct answer using the code given below.

    (a)   1 and 2 only   (b)   1 and 3 only

    (c)   1, 2 and 3   (d)   2 and 3 only

Q.15   Lattice energy of an ionic compound depends upon

    (a)   packing of ions only   (b)   size of the ion only

    (c)   charge on the ion and size of the ion (d)   charge on the ion only

Q.16   In OF_2, number of bond pairs and lone pairs of electrons are respectively

    (a)   2, 6   (b)   2, 8

    (c)   2, 10   (d)   2, 9

Q.17   The ion which is ioselectronic with CO is

    (a) $CN^{(-)}$ (b) $O_2^{(-)}$

    (c) $N_2^{(+)}$ (d) $O_2^{(+)}$

Q.18   The octet rule is not valid for which of the following molecule?

(a) CO_2 (b) H_2O

(c) O_2 (d) CO

Q.19   Out of the following pair of species which one is most likely to combine by co-ordinate bond?

(a) $H_2 + I_2$ (b) $Mg + 1/2O_2$

(c) $Cl\,(g) + Cl\,(g)$ (d) $H^{(+)}$ and H_2O

Q.20   The most polar bond is:-

(a) $Cl - F$ (b) $Br - F$

(c) $I - F$ (d) $F - F$

Q.21   In an ionic compound $X^{(+)}Y^{(-)}$ the degree of covalent bonding will be maximum when

(a)   Both cation & anion are small

(b)   cation is small & anion is large

(c)   Both cation & anion are of approximately same size

(d)   anion is small & cation is large

Q.22   The formal charge on the nitrogen atom of nitrite ion is

(a) $+1$ (b) -1

(c) 0 (d) $+3$

Q.23   The total number of electrons involved in double bonds in 0.5 mol of nitrate ions (according to its Lewis structure) is:

(a) $4N_A$ (b) $2N_A$

(c) N_A (d) $3N_A$

Q.24   The number of pi electrons present in 2.6 g of ethyne is

(a) 2.408×10^{24} (b) 2.408×10^{25}

(c) 2.408×10^{23} (d) 1.204×10^{23}

Q.25   Which is the correct Lewis arrangement of S_2^{2-} ion?

(a) $[\ddot{\underset{..}{S}} = \ddot{S}\colon]^{2-}$ (b) $[\colon\overset{..}{\underset{..}{S}} = \overset{..}{\underset{..}{S}}\colon]^{2-}$

(c) $[\colon\overset{..}{\underset{..}{S}} - \overset{..}{\underset{..}{S}}\colon]^{2-}$ (d)   None of these

Q.26   Electronic structure of four elements is X, Y, Z, W are given below

$X : 2s^2$; $Y : 1s^2 2s^2 2p^2$

$Z : 1s^2 2s^2 2p^5$; $W : 1s^2 2s^2 2p^6$

The tendency to form covalent bond is maximum in

(a)   W   (b)   Y

(c)   Z   (d)   X

Q.27   Which of the following bond is most ionic?

(a) $Cs - Cl$ (b) $Al - Cl$

(c) $I - Cl$ (d) $H - Cl$

Q.28   Ionic reaction take place mainly in:–

(a)   Liquid state   (b)   Solution in benzene

(c)   aq. solution   (d)   Gaseous State

Q.29 Of the following solvents, the one most likely to dissolve ionic compound is:-

(a) Carbon tetrachloride   (b) Methanol

(c) Liquid NH_3 (d) Dibutyl ether

Q.30 Odd electron bonds are present in:-

(a) NO   (b) NO_2

(c) ClO_2 (d) All the above

Q.31 Which compounds do not have all three types of bonds?

(a) $Na_2S_2O_3$ (b) $BF_4^{(-)}$

(c) NH_4CN (d) Al_2Cl_6

Q.32 Dative bond is present in:-

(a) $N_2H_5^{(+)}$ (b) $H_3O^{(+)}$

(c) CO   (d) All of these

Q.33 The compound with highest lattice energy is:-

(a) LiI   (b) NaF

(c) MgO   (d) Na_2O

Q.34 The bonds present in N_2O_5 are:-

(a) Ionic   (b) Covalent and co-ordinate

(c) Covalent   (d) Ionic and covalent

Q.35 Octet rule is not valid for the molecule:-

(a) HCN   (b) PCl_3

(c) N_2 (d) HNC

Q.36 Which combination is best explained by the co-ordinate covalent bond?

(a) $H_2 + I_2$ (b) $Ca + S$

(c) $F + F$ (d) $H^{(+)} + H_2O$

Q.37 The internuclear distance in H_2 and Cl_2 molecules are 74 and 198 pm respectively the bond length of HCl may be:-

(a) 272 pm   (b) 70 pm

(c) 136 pm   (d) 248 pm

Q.38 Which one of the following is not isoelectronic with the rest three?

(a) $NO^{(-)}$ (b) $CN^{(-)}$

(c) N_2 (d) $O_2^{2(+)}$

Q.39 Hypervalent compound is:-

(a) $MgSO_4$ (b) NH_3

(c) $BeCl_2$ (d) $MgCO_3$

Q.40 Which of the following does not contain co-ordinate bond?

(a) $BH_4^{(-)}$ (b) $NH_2^{(-)}$

(c) $CO_3^{2(-)}$ (d) O_3

Q.41 Br_2 has lesser boiling point than ICl. This is because of:-

(a) Radius of I is greater than Br   (b) I. E. of I is lesser than Br

(c) ICl is polar while Br_2 is non polar   (d) ICl has large size in comparison to Br_2

HINTS & SOLUTIONS

SUBJECTIVE EXERCISE

2.   (a) $-1, 0, 0$ (b) $+1, +1$ (c) $-1, +1$

3.   (a) $MgCl_2 > K_2SO_4 > NaCl$ (b) $MgCl_2(l) > NaCl(l) > NaCl(s)$

      (c) $MgCl_2(l) > NaCl(l) > MgCl_2(s)$

4.   NaCl is an ionic compound & hence it will not dissolve in benzene as benzene is a non polar solvent (like dissolves like)

6.   (a) Covalent   (b) Covalent   (c) ionic   (d) ionic   (e) ionic

7. $O = C = C = C = O$ i.e. C_3O_2

8.   (a) 1   (b) 2   (c) 0   (d) 2

10.
$$\overset{\delta^+}{H} - \overset{\delta^-}{O} - \overset{\delta^+}{H} \qquad\qquad \overset{\delta^-}{F} - \overset{\delta^+}{O} - \overset{\delta^-}{F}$$

$$\overset{\delta^+}{H} - \overset{\delta^-}{N} - \overset{\delta^+}{H} \qquad\qquad \overset{\delta^-}{F} - \overset{\delta^+}{N} - \overset{\delta^-}{F}$$
$$\underset{H^{\delta^+}}{|} \qquad\qquad\qquad\quad \underset{F^{\delta^-}}{|}$$

OBJECTIVE EXERCISE

1. (d)   2. (d)   3. (d)

4. (c) There are 10 e in valence shell of chlorine atom

5. (d)

6. (b) $PO_4^{3-} + 2H^+ \longrightarrow H_2PO_4^- \xrightarrow{Na^+} NaH_2PO_4 (NaX)$

7. (d)

8. (a) small size of Li^+ provides lithium ion more velocity and more electrical conductance.

9. (a) It gives four ions   10. (b)   11. (b)   12. (d)   13. (b)

14. (c)   15. (c)   16. (b)   17. (a)

18. (d) Carbon has incomplete octet & it completes its octet by receiving electrons with oxygen by the help of coordinate bond.

19. (d)   20. (c)   21. (b)   22. (a)

23. (b)   24. (c)   25. (c)   26. (b)   27. (a)

28. (c) In ionic compound ions are bonded by strong electrostatic forces of attractions, thus, to break these forces a polar medium is required thus ions react with one another in polar medium like water & not in benzene.

29. (c)   30. (d)   31. (d)   32. (d)   33. (c)

34. (b)   35. (b)   36. (c)   37. (c)   38. (a)

39. (a) $Mg^{2+}\left[O - \overset{\overset{\textstyle O}{\|}}{\underset{\underset{\textstyle O}{\|}}{S}} - O \right]^{2-}$ 40. (c)   41. (c)

Valence Bond Theory & Resonance

➤ 3.1 Valence bond theory (V.B.T)

In order to explain the nature of covalent bond, Heitler and London proposed a theory in 1927 which is known as valence bond approach, later extended by Pauling and Slater in 1931. According to this theory:-

(a) Covalent bond between two atoms is formed by the partial overlap of atomic orbitals.

(b) Each overlapping orbital should have one electron with opposite spin for the formation of covalent bond or one overlapping orbital should have a pair of electron & other overlapping orbital should be empty.

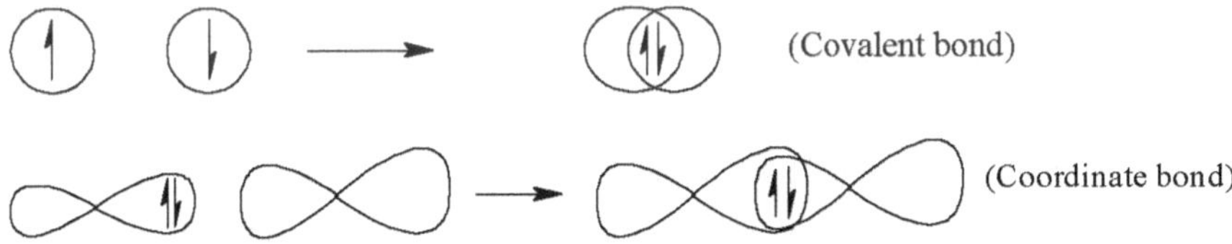

(c) Covalent bonds are of two type viz. Sigma bond & Pi bond

(d) **Sigma bond (σ bond):-** It is the bond formed by the head on overlapping of orbitals i.e. overlapping orbitals along molecular axis or internuclear axis. Suppose 'z' is molecular or internuclear axis then various sigma bonds can be formed as:-

(i) s - s sigma bond :- (For e.g. H_2, Li_2)

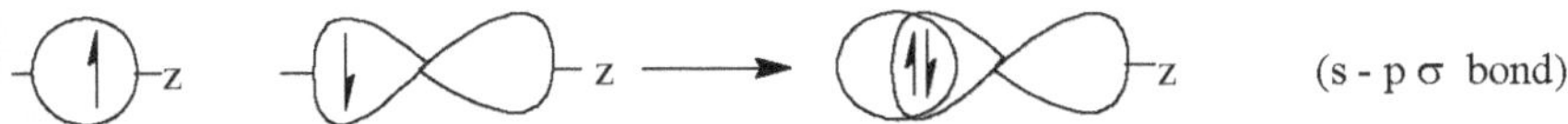

(ii) s - p sigma bond :- (For e.g. HF, H_2O)

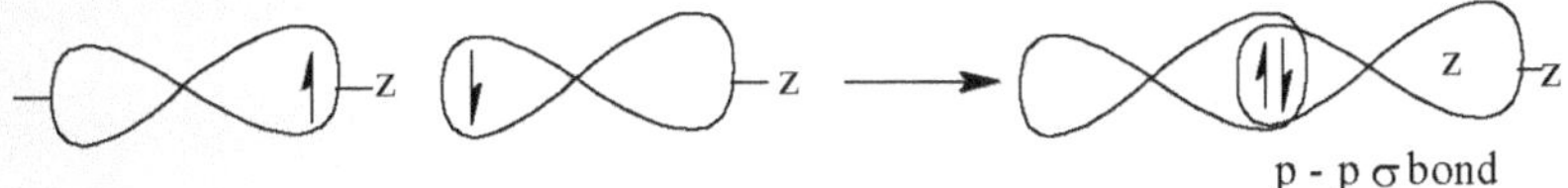

(iii) p - p sigma bond :- (For e.g. F_2, N_2, O_2.........etc)

(e) **Pi bond (π bond):-** The bond formed by the lateral overlapping of atomic orbitals is called Pi bond. This overlapping takes place on the axis perpendicular to molecular axis. If 'z' is molecular axis then π bond forms either on 'y' axis or on 'x' axis. Various types of pi bonds are shown below.

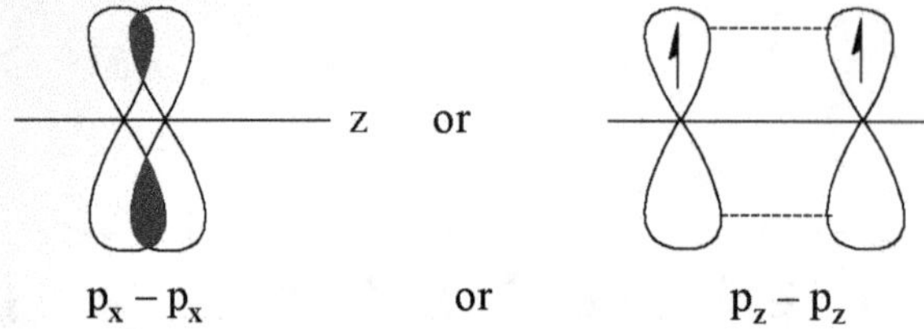

$p_x - p_x$ or $p_z - p_z$

This kind of pi bond is called $p\pi$ - $p\pi$ bond, 'd' orbitals can also form π bonds with 'd' & 'p' orbitals.

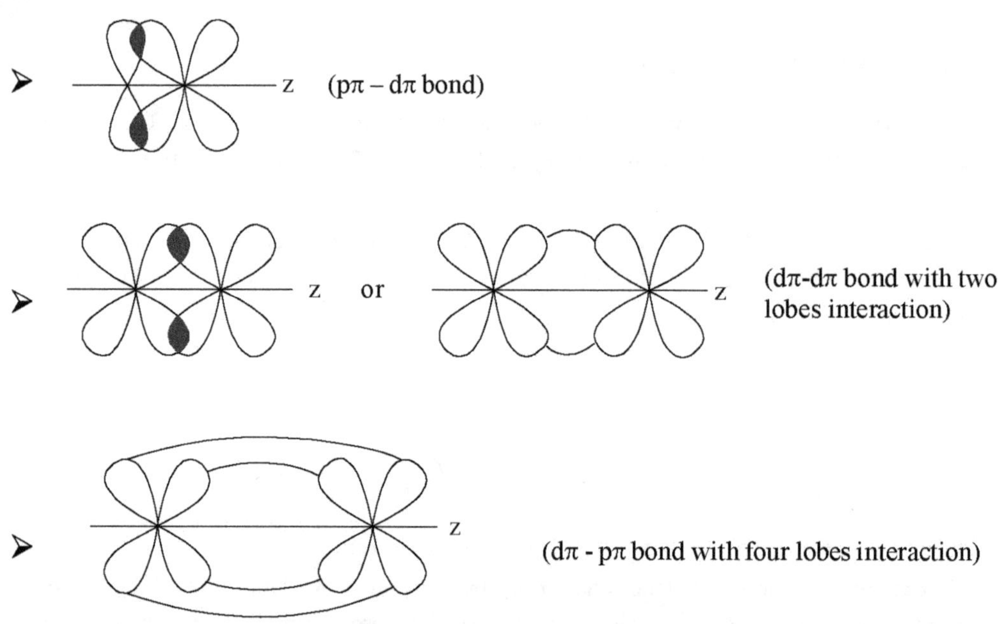

➤   z   ($p\pi - d\pi$ bond)

➤   z   or   z   ($d\pi$-$d\pi$ bond with two lobes interaction)

➤   z   ($d\pi$ - $p\pi$ bond with four lobes interaction)

$p\pi$ - $p\pi$ bond with four lobe interaction is called delta bond (δ - bond).

(f) Sigma bond is stronger bond than pi because in sigma bond overlapping area of orbitals is large in comparison to pi bond.

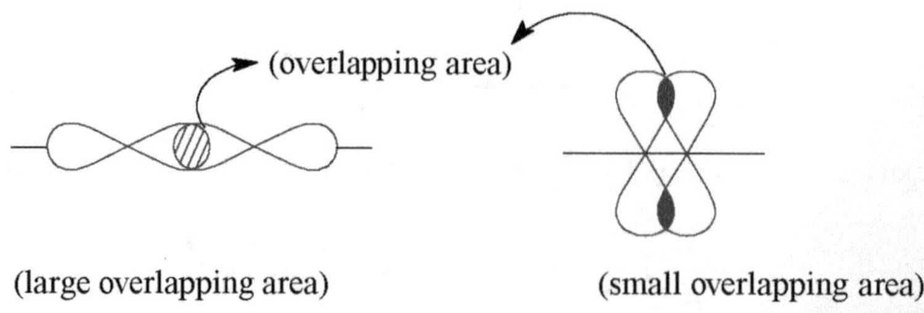

(large overlapping area)   (small overlapping area)

(g)   Following overlappings of atomic orbitals are not allowed:-

➢   If the wave function of two overlapping atomic orbitals is different then bond formation is not possible.

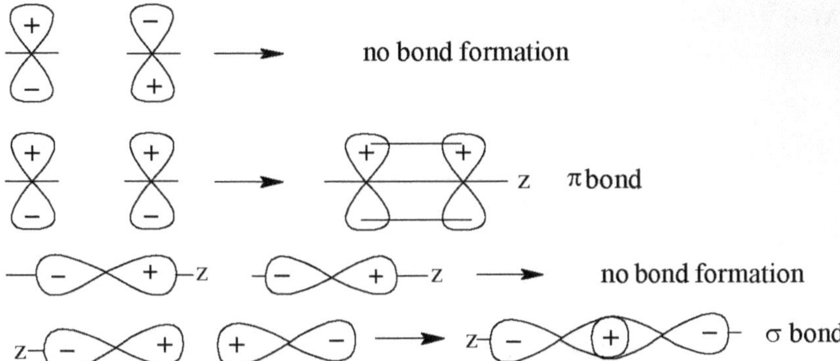

➢   It is not possible to form bond with 'p' orbitals having their lobes on different axis

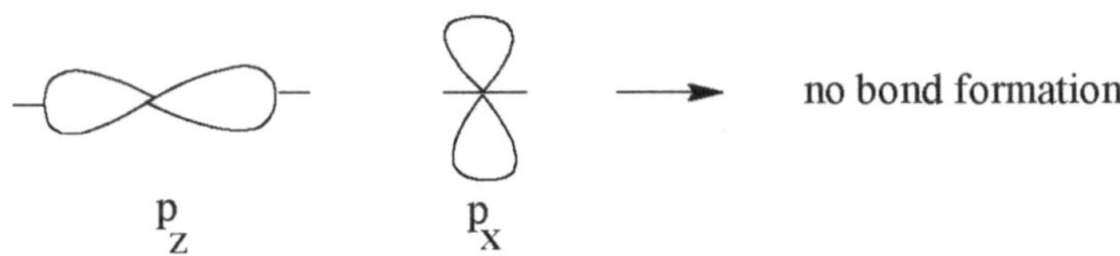

➢   's' orbital does not form π bond.

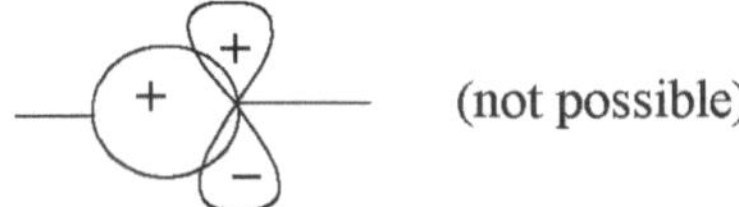

(h)   Strength of σ bonds: - Higher is the extent of overlap, higher will be the strength

   p - p > s - p > s - s (descending order of strength)

   F_2 can be supposed to be formed by two ways

(A)	(B)
F (ground state)	F (ground state)

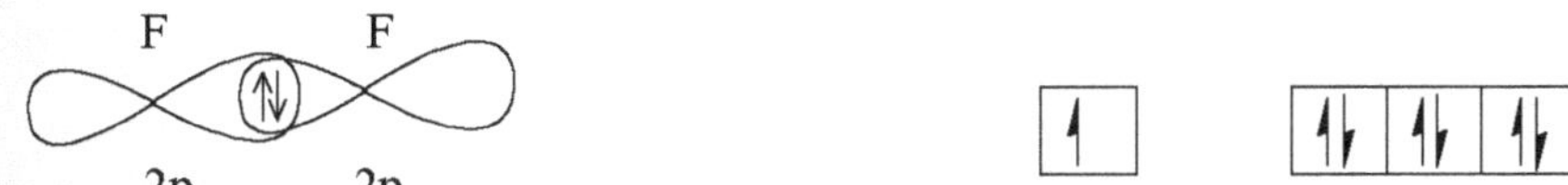

F —— F (p - p σ bond)   i.e.   F —— F (s - s σ bond)

Out of A & B, former has more probability than later because in (A) p – p σ bond formation occurs which is stable than s – s σ bond of (B)

Strength of π - bond: - Strength of π bond depends on the closeness of overlapping orbitals

Stability of π bond $\propto$ 1 / distance between overlapping orbitals

2pπ - pπ   >   3pπ - pπ

(More stable)   (Less stable)

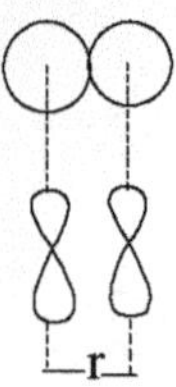
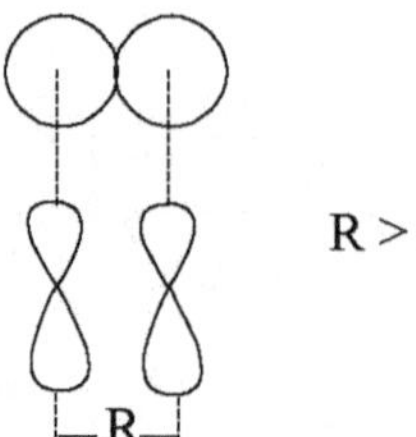

R > r

3pπ - 2pπ   <   3dπ - 2pπ

(Less stable)   (More stable)

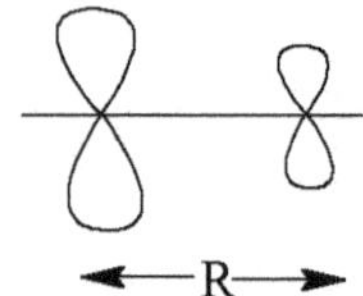
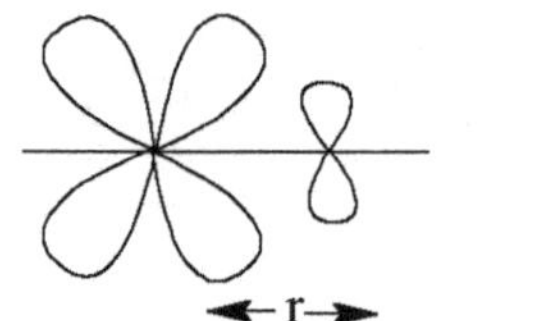

R > r

This is the reason that compounds with $2p\pi – 2p\pi$ bonds are much abundant while compounds with $3p\pi – 2p\pi$ bonds are rare

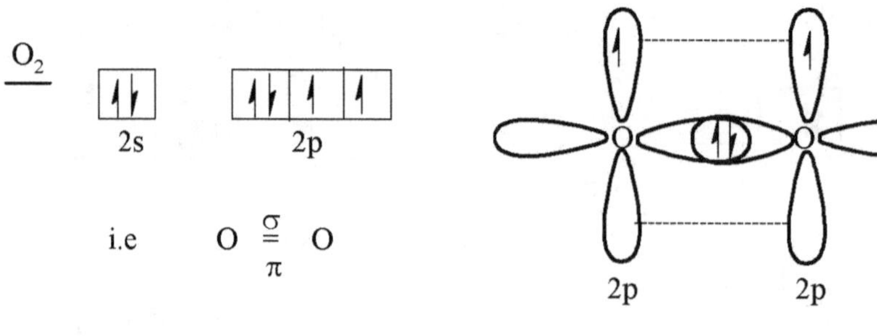

$$\text{>}C = C\text{<}$$ $$\text{>}Si = Si\text{<}$$

(Many compounds)   (Rare)

Let us discuss the structures of some molecules by the help of V.B.T

$\underline{O_2}$

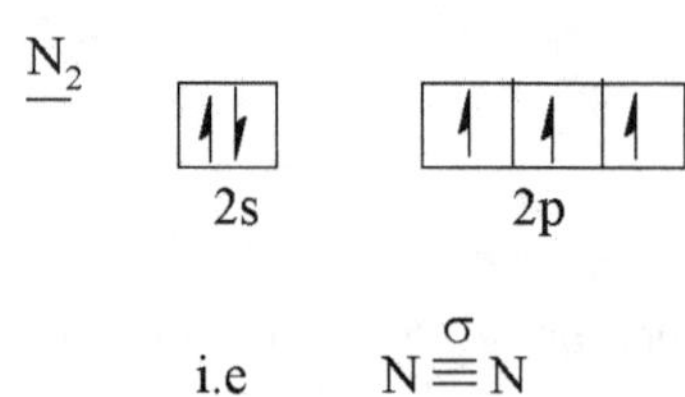

i.e $O \overset{\sigma}{\underset{\pi}{=}} O$

2p   2p

$\underline{N_2}$

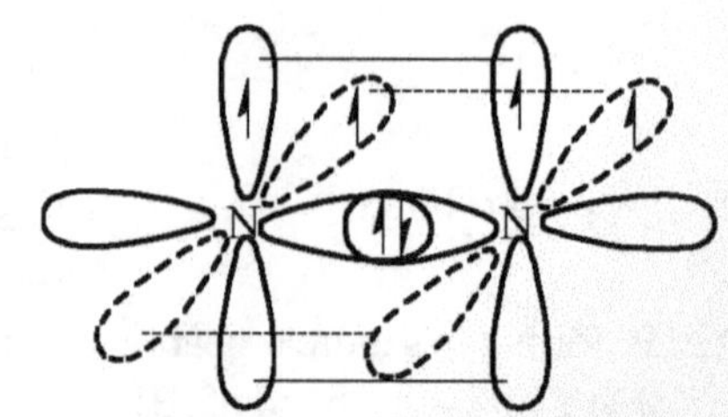

i.e $N \overset{\sigma}{\underset{2\pi}{\equiv}} N$

From these two examples it is evident that in between two atoms σ bond forms only one time, rest all bonds are π bonds.

B.O.	=	1	(one sigma bond)
B.O.	=	2	(one sigma + one pi bond)
B.O.	=	3	(one sigma + two pi bonds)

The valence bond theory introduced an idea about the directional property of covalent bond

For e.g. In H_2O oxygen contains two lone pair, out of which one is present in 2s orbital and second lone pair is present in 2p orbital. Rest two p orbitals possess one unpaired electron which can form two σ bonds with two 'H' atoms. Since all the 'p' orbitals are mutually perpendicular to one another hence the two σ bonds (O — H bonds) in water should be perpendicular to each other.

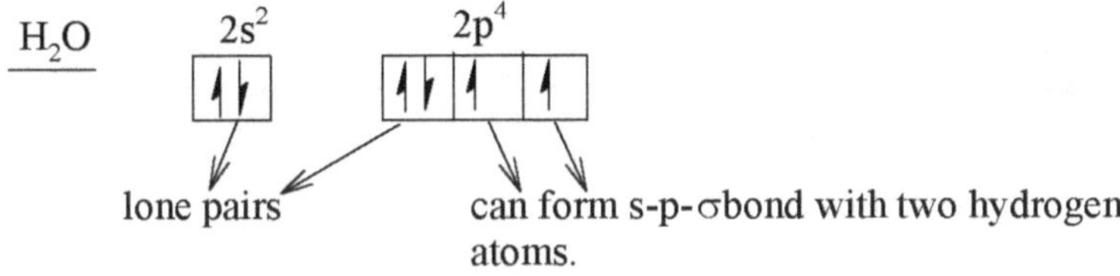

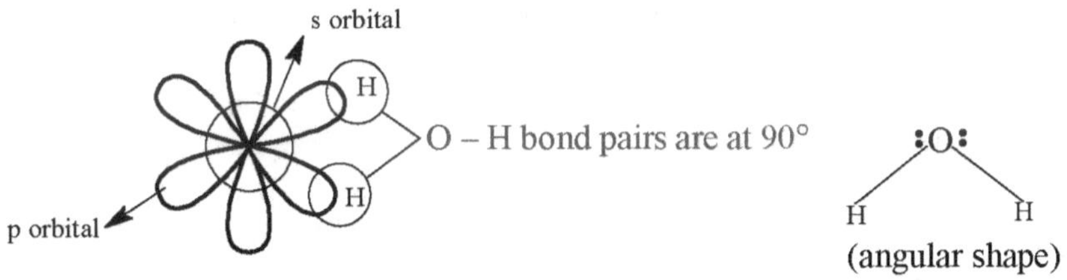

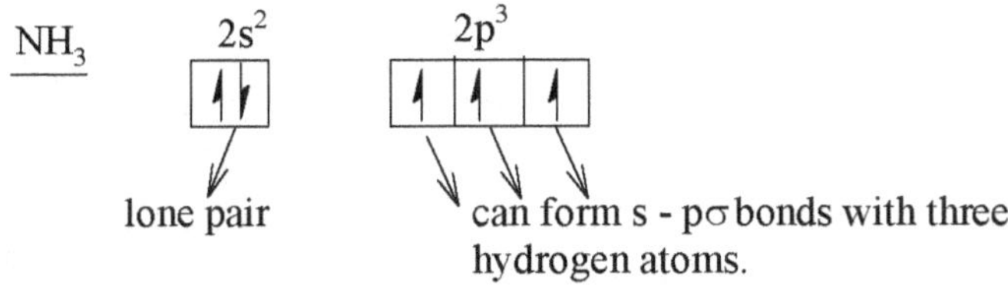

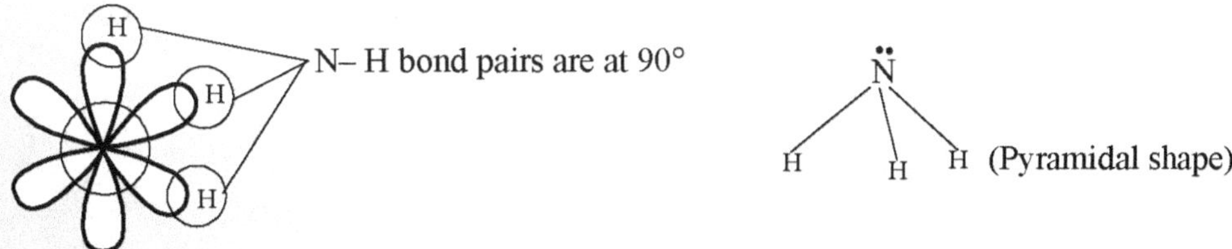

➤ 3.2 Limitations of V.B.T

In CH_4, carbon forms 4 sigma bonds

$$C \qquad 2s^2 \qquad\qquad 2p^2$$

(Ground state)

(Excited state)

Carbon can form three sigma bonds with three hydrogen atoms by s-p overlapping. These three bonds are mutually perpendicular to one another but there is no certainty of position of 4th C – H bond which is formed by s – s overlapping because infinite direction of approaches are there in s – s overlapping.

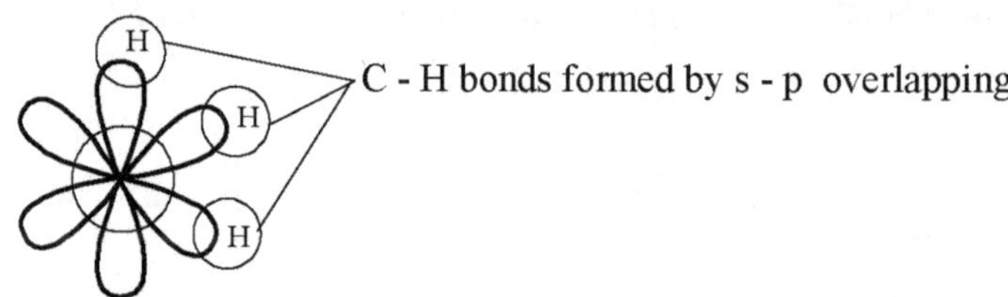

Since s – p bond is stronger than s – s σ bonds hence in CH_4 three sigma bonds should be stronger than fourth sigma bond but in actual practice it is found that all C – H bonds are identical. They have equal bond lengths & same bond energies. Also in CH_4 all the H – C – H bond angles are 109° 28'. Thus, in order to explain these facts phenomenon of hybridization of atomic orbitals has been proposed (discussed in chapter - 04)

➤ 3.3 Resonance (Modification of V.B.T)

In V.B.T it is assumed that bonded atoms share electron pair equally in covalent bonding. The number of bonds formed between bonded atoms must be integral always.

F — F	B.O.	=	1	(Single bond)
O = O	B.O.	=	2	(Double bond)
N ≡ N	B.O.	=	3	(Triple bond)

Whereas experimental studies revealed that bond order is fractional in some species.

For e.g. in CO_3^{2-}, bond order is 1.33 between C & O, on the contrary in PO_4^{3-}, bond order is 1.25.

The V.B.T does not provide any direct method for treating such species. In other words, it is not possible to represent structure that would correctly account for the properties of the species concerned. It is possible, however, to explain properly the properties of many species in terms of a combination hybrid of two or more valence bond structures. In such cases we can say that species is a resonance hybrid of two or more valence bond structures. These structures are called resonating structures for e.g. CO_3^{2-} can be represented by three resonating structures as follows :

These three are resonating structures. It reveals that double bond and negative charge has no fixed location. Therefore, in order to explain actual structure of this carbonate ion, a hybrid is shown (formed) with the help of these resonating structures. This hybrid is called resonance hybrid.

Similarly in phosphate ion four resonating structures are possible

(Resonance hybrid)

Fractional bond order can be calculated by the formula

B.O. = No. of bonds taking part in resonance / No. of resonating structures

For e.g. in CO_3^{2-} four bonds are participating in resonance & it has '3' resonating structures, there fore,

B.O. = $4/3$ = 1.33

Similarly in phosphate ion   B.O. = $5/4$ = 1.25

Conditions for resonance: - A molecule or an ion undergoes resonance when it shows the following conditions:-

(i)   Identical arrangement of atoms in various resonating (or canonical) forms.

(ii)   Each resonating structure must have same number of unpaired electrons.

(iii) Each resonating structure must have nearly same energy content.

(iv) The species must have planar structure.

(v)   It usually involves delocalization of π - electrons.

Characteristics of resonance:-

(i)   Due to resonance bond order & bond length of species get changed. Resonance gives rise to identical bond lengths in molecule.

e.g., All the three bonds in $CO_3^{2(-)}$ are of same length with bond order 1.33

(ii) Resonance give rise to extra stability to a molecule. The resonance hybrid possesses less energy in comparison to canonical forms and thus gains extra stability.

Resonance energy = Experimental heat of formation of molecule

– Theoritical heat of formation of molecule

R.E. of C_6H_6 = $-1039 - (-999)$ = -40 kcal.

and   R.E. of CO_2 = $-336 - (-300)$ = -36 kcal.

(iii) Greater the resonance energy of the molecule more is its stability.

(iv) More is the number of covalent bonds is canonical forms, more is its stability.

Subjective Exercise

Q.1 Explain why compounds with $Si = Si$ linkages are rare.

Q.2 CO_2 has discrete unit while SiO_2 has long chain structure.

Q.3 Phosphorous exists as P_4 while nitrogen exist as N_2

Q.4 H_2 is more reactive than F_2 explain.

Q.5 Arrange $p - p$, $s - s$ & $s - p$ covalent bonds in order of extent of overlapping.

Q.6 $(CH_3)_2 C (OH)_2$ is unstable & produce water along with CH_3COCH_3 but $(CH_3)_2Si (OH)_2$ does not loose water to produce CH_3SiOCH_3. Explain.

Q.7 Out of $CH_2 = CH - S^{(-)}$ & $CH_2 = CH - O^{(-)}$ former is less stabilized by resonance in comparison to later.

Q.8 Calculate bond order of $C - O$ bond in carbonate ion.

Q.9 In sulphate ion, all $S - O$ bonds are identical explain.

Q.10 Explain why $\alpha = \beta = \gamma$

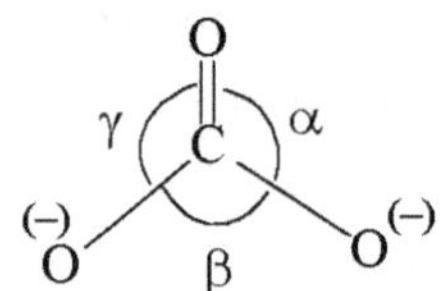

Objective Exercise

Q.1 Correct order of stability is:-

(a) $HF > H_2 > F_2$ (b) $H_2 > F_2 > HF$

(c) $F_2 > H_2 > HF$ (d) $F_2 > HF > H_2$

Q.2 Which of the following gives rise to formation of bond?

(a) 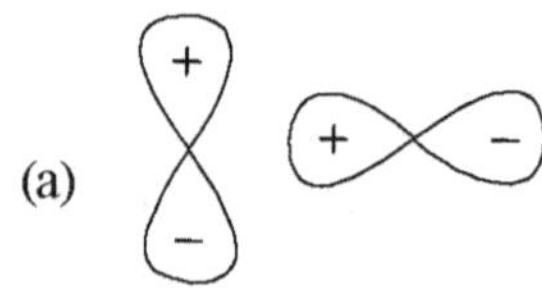

(b) 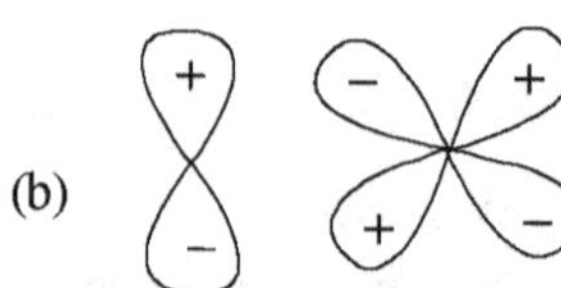

(c) 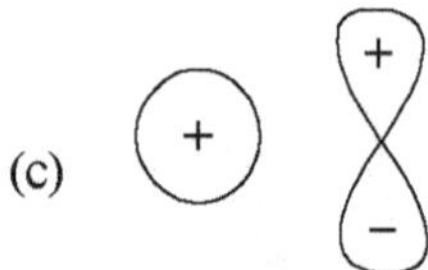

(d) None of these

Q.3 Least stable ion is:-

(a) SO_4^{2-} (b) PO_4^{3-}

(c) HCO_3^- (d) CO_3^{2-}

Q.4 Highest bond order will be present in:-

(a) CO_3^{2-} (b) SO_4^{2-}

(c) PO_4^{3-} (d) All have same bond order

Q.5 In which case 1st overlap is more effective than 2nd one:-

(a) $3d\pi - 2p\pi, 3p\pi - 2p\pi$ (b) $3p\pi - p\pi, 2p\pi - 2p\pi$

(c) $s - p\ \sigma$ bond, $p - p\ \sigma$ bond   (d) $\pi -$ bond, sigma bond

Q.6 According to V.B.T which is correct about CH_4

(a) All the four $C - H$ bonds are different

(b) All the four $C - H$ bonds are identical

(c) Two $C - H$ bonds are different from the other two $C - H$ bonds

(d) One $C - H$ bond is different than rest of the three $C - H$ bonds

Q.7 Weakest bond is:-

(a) $H - F$ (b) $H - Cl$

(c) $H - Br$ (d) $H - I$

Q.8 In which case π bond will form if x is bonding axis.

(a) $p_x - p_y$ (b) $p_y - p_y$

(c) $p_x - p_x$ (d) $p_x - p_z$

Q.9 In which of the following case σ bond will form:-

(a) $s - p_x$ (b) $p_y - p_y$ (bonding axis 'x')

(c) $p_y - p_z$ (bonding axis 'z')   (d) $p_z - p_z$ (bonding axis 'y')

Q.10 In which case σ bond will form

(a) $p_x - p_y$ (bonding axis z)   (b) $p_y - p_y$ (bonding axis y)

(c) $p_y - p_z$ (bonding axis y)   (d) $p_z - p_z$ (bonding axis x)

Q.11 Which among the following diatomic molecule will require least bond dissociation energy?

(a) B_2 (b) Cl_2

(d) N_2 (d) O_2

Q.12 Which combination will not lead to the formation of sigma bond?

(a) 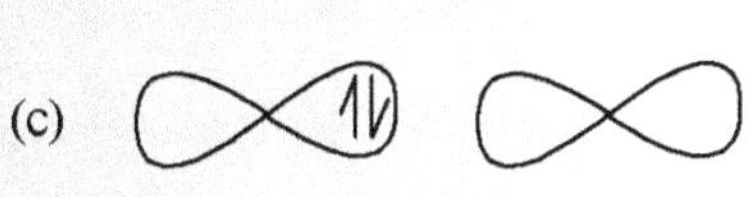   (b) 

(c)    (d)

Q.13   In $\overset{1}{CH_2} = C \overset{2}{=} C \overset{3}{=} CH_2$ double bonds are numbered as 1, 2 & 3, pick out the correct statement

(a)   1, 2 & 3 are in same plane

(b)   1, 2 & 3 are in different plane

(c)   1 & 3 are in same plane and perpendicular to 2nd double bond

(d)   1 & 2 are in same plane and perpendicular to 3rd double bond

Q.14   In $\overset{1}{CH_2} = C \overset{2}{=} C \overset{3}{=} C \overset{4}{=} CH_2$ double bonds are numbered as 1, 2, 3 & 4 pick out the correct statement

(a)   1, 2 are in same plane and perpendicular to the plane in which 3 & 4 are present

(b)   1 & 3 are in same plane and perpendicular to the plane in which 2 & 4 are present

(c)   1, 2, 3 & 4 all are present in same plane

(d)   1, 2, 3 & 4 all are present in different plane

Q.15   In which of the following case both the bonds have same strength assuming that 'y' is bonding axis.

(a) $s - p_y, p_x - p_x$ (b) $p_x - p_x, p_y - p_y$

(c) $p_x - p_x, p_z - p_z$ (d) $s - p_y, p_y - p_y$

Q.16   In which of the following case 1st bond is stronger than 2nd one.

(a) $s - s, p_x - p_x$ (x is bonding axis)   (b) $p_y - p_y, p_x - p_x$ (z is bonding axis)

(c) $p_y - p_y, p_z - p_z$ (z is bonding axis)   (d) $p_y - p_y, p_z - p_z$ (y is bonding axis)

Q.17   Among the following ions the $p\pi - d\pi$ overlap could be present in

(a) $NO_2^{(-)}$ (b) $NO^{(-)}$

(c) PO_4^{2-} (d) CO_3^{2-}

Q.18   Which of the following has $p\pi - d\pi$ bonding?

(a) $NO_3^{(-)}$ (b) SO_3^{2-}

(c) BO_3^{3-} (d) $HCO_3^{(-)}$

Q.19   What is the number of sigma and pi bonds present in a molecule of sulphuric acid?

(a) $6\sigma, 2\pi$ (b) $6\sigma, 0\pi$

(c) $2\sigma, 4\pi$ (d) $2\sigma, 2\pi$

Q.20   In which of the following species the bonds are non-directional?

(a) NCl_3 (b) $RbCl$

(c) $BeCl_2$ (d) BCl_3

Q.21   The number of sigma (σ) and pi (π) bonds present in tetracyanoethylene $[(CN)_2C = C(CN)_2]$ molecule are respectively

(a) 5σ and 9π (b) 5σ and 8π

(c) 9σ and 9π (d) 9σ and 7π

Q.22 Which of the following resonating structure is not correct for CO_2?

(a) 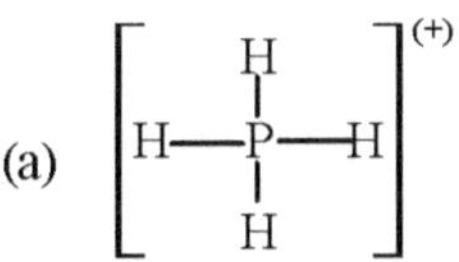

(b) $:\overset{(-)}{\underset{..}{O}}-C\equiv\overset{(+)}{O}:$

(c) $\overset{(+)}{\underset{..}{:O}}-C\equiv\underset{..}{O}:^{(-)}$

(d) 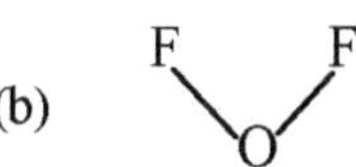

Q.23 How many resonating forms can be written for nitrate and chlorate ions respectively?

(a) 3, 2

(b) 2, 3

(c) 3, 3

(d) 2, 4

Q.24 Which of the following formula does not correctly represent the bonding capacities of the atoms involved?

(a) $\left[\begin{array}{c} H \\ | \\ H-P-H \\ | \\ H \end{array}\right]^{(+)}$

(b) F–O–F (bent structure)

(c) $O\leftarrow\overset{O}{\overset{||}{N}}-O-H$

(d) $H-C=\overset{O}{\overset{||}{C}}-O-H$

Q.25 Among the following the bond with highest bond dissociation energy is:-

(a) Se – Se

(b) Te – Te

(c) S – S

(d) O – O

Q.26 In the lewis formula of O_3, there are

(a) 2σ, 1π bond, 4 lone pairs

(b) 1σ, 2π bonds, 1 lone pairs

(c) 2σ, 2π bonds, 3 lone pairs

(d) 2σ, 1π bond and 6 lone pairs

Q.27 Select the correct statement

(a) According to V.B.T. bond angles in NH_3 & H_2O are same

(b) H_2O is more acidic than H_2S

(c) PH_3 is less acidic than NH_3

(d) According to V.B.T. bond angle is PH_3 is lesser than NH_3

Q.28 V.B.T. fails to explain the bonding in:-

(a) PCl_5

(b) PH_3

(c) PCl_3

(d) N_2

Q.29 Among HF, HCl, HBr & HI strongest acid is:-

(a) HF

(b) HCl

(c) HBr

(d) HI

Q.30 Resonance is possible in:-

(a) $BF_4^{(-)}$

(b) $H_3O^{(+)}$

(c) $N_2H_5^{(+)}$

(d) None of these

HINTS & SOLUTIONS

SUBJECTIVE EXERCISE

1. $3p\pi - 3p\pi$ bond is weak due to more inter nuclear distance (see text)
2. Carbon can form multiple bonds with oxygen ($2p\pi - 2p\pi$ bond) but silicon can not form multiple bonds - with oxygen as $2p\pi - 2p\pi$ bond is stable then that of $3p\pi - 2p\pi$ bond

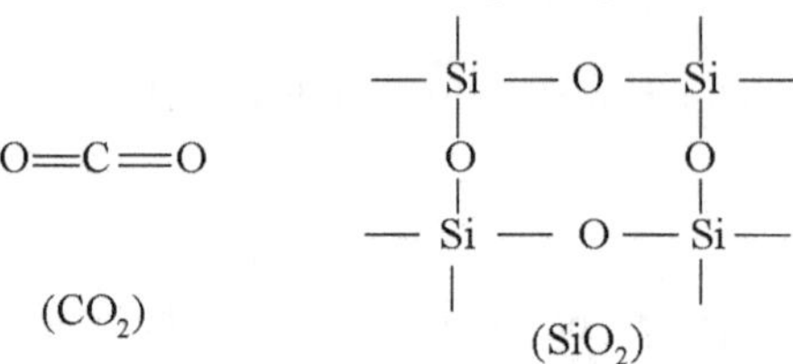

$$O\!=\!C\!=\!O$$

(CO_2)

(SiO_2)

6. Carbon can form stable $2p\pi - 2p\pi$ bond with oxygen while silicon can not form less stable $2p\pi - 3p\pi$ bond

$$(CH_3)_2C(OH)_2 \longrightarrow H_2O + CH_3 - \overset{O}{\overset{\|}{C}} - CH_3 \quad 2p\pi - 2p\pi$$

$$(CH_3)_2Si(OH)_2 \longrightarrow H_2O + CH_3 - \overset{O}{\overset{\|}{Si}} - CH_3 \quad 2p\pi - 3p\pi \ bond$$

(not possible)

7. $\overset{(-)}{CH_2 = CH - S} \longleftrightarrow \overset{(-)}{CH_2 - CH = S}$, $\overset{(-)}{CH_2 = CH - O} \longleftrightarrow \overset{(-)}{CH_2 - CH = O}$

    less stable $2p\pi - 3p\pi$ bond   more stable $2p\pi - 2p\pi$ bond

In 1st case chances of resonance are least due to the formation of less stable $2p\pi - 3p\pi$ bond hence -ve charge is less delocalized and more available for reaction with $H^{(+)}$ (acid)

8. Resonance takes place

9. Resonance makes all the bonds identical

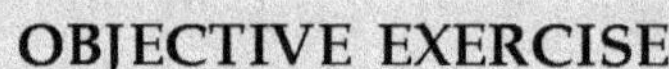

OBJECTIVE EXERCISE

1. (d) $p - p > p - s > s - p$ 2. (d)
3. (d) Less chances of resonance
4. (b)   5. (a)   6. (d)
7. (d) More bond length due to large size of iodine hence less stability
8. (b)   9. (a)   10. (b)   11. (b)   12. (d)
13. (c)   14. (b)   15. (c)   16. (d)
17. (c) 'P' belongs to third period & hence can form $p\pi - d\pi$ bond
18. (b)   19. (a)
20. (b) Except RbCl rest all are covalent compounds while RbCl is ionic
21. (c)   22. (a)   23. (c)
24. (d) Carbon can not form five bonds
25. (c)   26. (d)   27. (a)
28. (a) V.B.T. fails to explain the bonding of hypervalent compounds
29. (d)   30. (d)

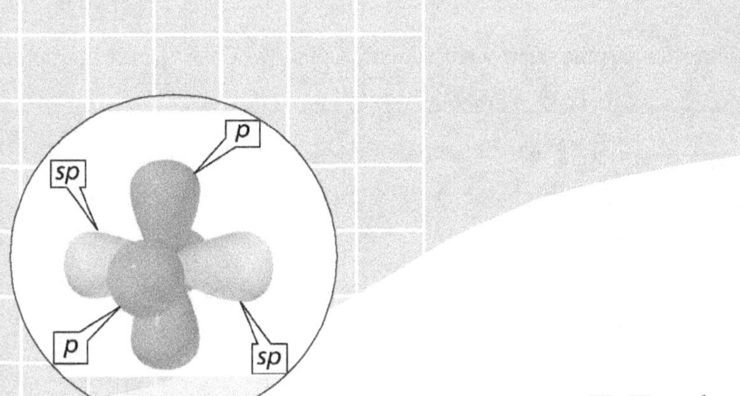

4

Hybridization
(VSEPR, Bent's & Drago's Rule)

➤ 4.1 Hybridization

➤ In hybridization two or more than two atomic orbits having same energies or nearly same energies combine to form two or more than two hybridized orbitals with same energy, same size and identical shape.

➤ 1s, 2s, can not mix

2s, 2p can mix

3s, 4d, 5s can not mix

➤ On the basis of participation of atomic orbitals in hybridization, hybridized orbitals get their names. For e.g. If one s & one p orbitals undergo hybridization they form two hybridized orbitals with the name **'sp'**. Similarly if one s and two p orbitals undergo hybridization then they form three hybridized orbitals with the name **'sp^2'**

Atomic orbitals participating in hybridization	No. of hybridized orbitals produced	Shape of hybridized orbitals
One 's' + one 'p'	Two	sp
One 's' + two 'p'	Three	sp^2
One's + three 'p'	Four	sp^3

➤ All hybridized orbitals have same energy with equal % of s, % of p & % of d character

     sp hybridization   ⟶   50 % 's' character, 50% 'p' character

     sp^2 hybridization   ⟶   33.33% 's' character, 66.66% 'p' character

     sp^3 hybridization   ⟶   25% 's' character, 75% 'p' character

Note: - % s character $\propto$ Electronegativity

With the increase in % s character the bulkiness of hybridized orbital increases where as with increase in % p character it attains longitivity and thinness

%'s' character $\propto$ bulkiness of orbitals

% 'p' character $\propto$ longitivity & thinness

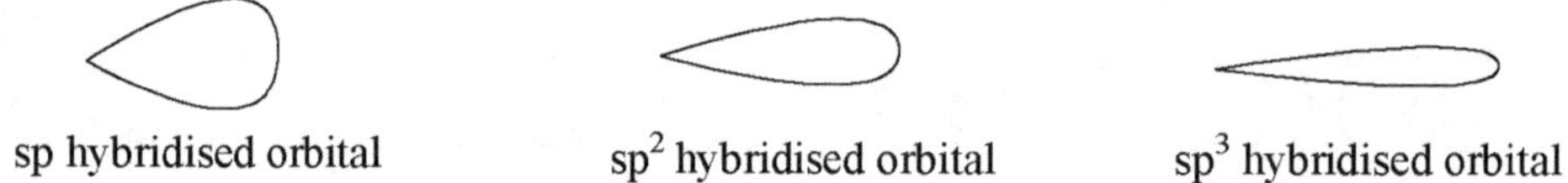

     sp hybridised orbital sp^2 hybridised orbital sp^3 hybridised orbital

As the shape of 's' orbital is spherical therefore, with increase in % 's' character bulkiness of hybridized orbital also increases, where as, due to the increase in % 'p' character the longitivity and thinness in hybridized orbital begins to develop because of thin and long shape of 'p' orbital.

In sp hybridization %'s' character is more therefore, its size is big in comparative to sp^2 and sp^3 hybridized orbitals. Hence sp hybridized orbitals experience more repulsion from each other and due to this bond angle between two 'sp' hybridized orbitals is found to be maximum (180°)

Consider the following examples -

$BeCl_2$ Be $1s^2$ $2s^2$ $2p^o$

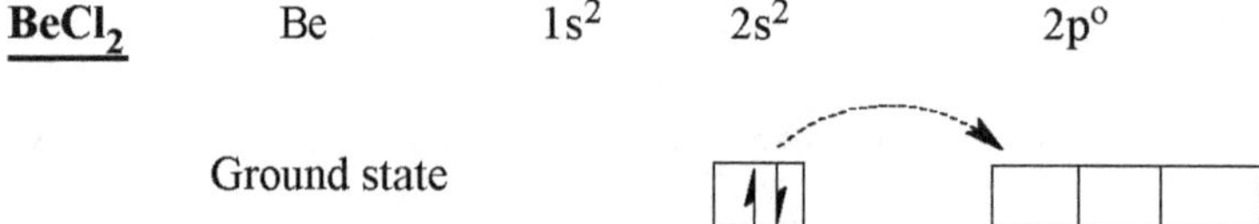

Ground state

For the formation of two sigma bonds Be should have two unpaired electrons

Excited state

sp hybridization

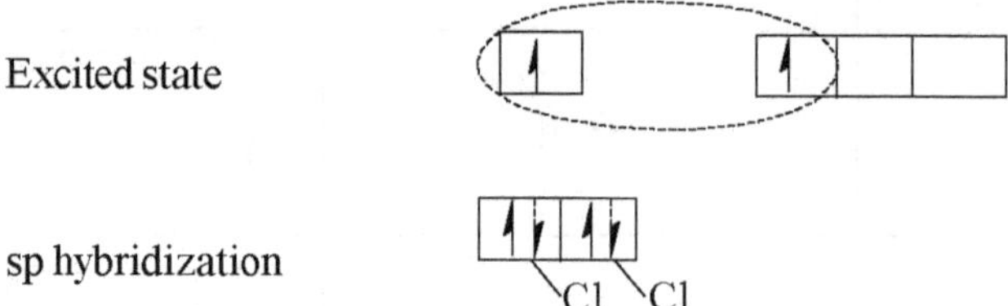

Cl atoms form two σ bonds by overlapping with these hybridized orbitals

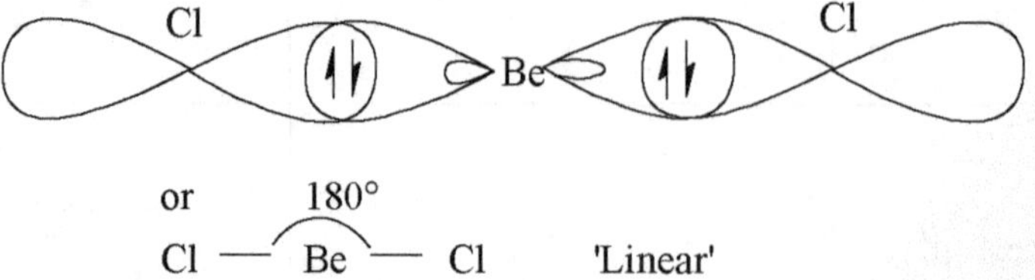

     or   180°

     Cl — Be — Cl   'Linear'

Here Be – Cl bond is sp – p sigma bond

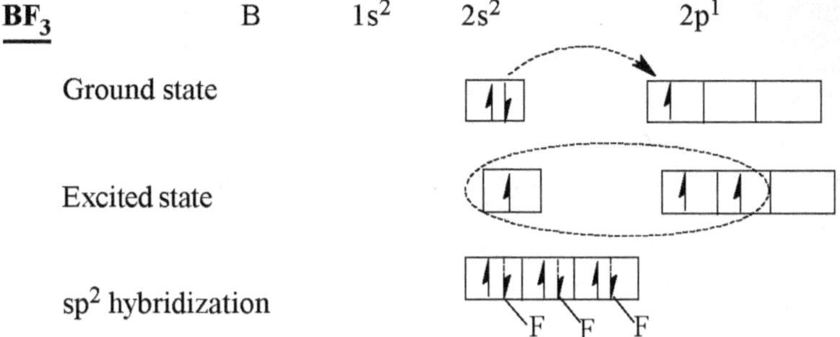

BF_3   B $1s^2$ $2s^2$ $2p^1$

Ground state

Excited state

sp^2 hybridization

F atoms form three σ bonds by overlapping with these sp^2 hybridized orbitals

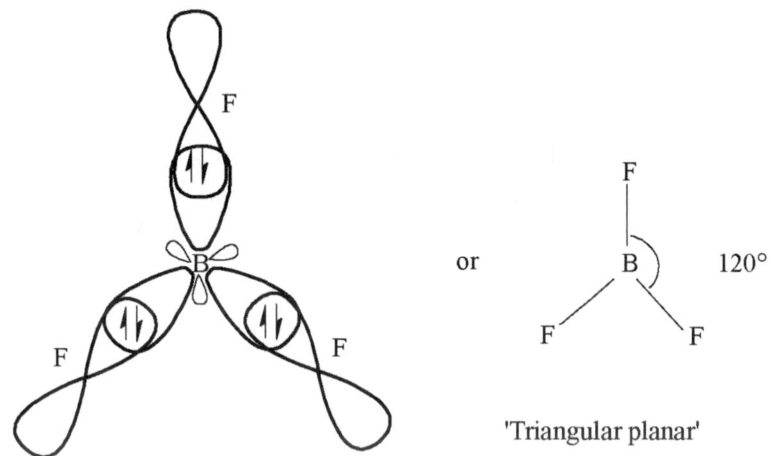

Here B – F bonds are sp^2 – p sigma bonds

CH_4   C $1s^2$ $2s^2$ $2p^2$

Ground state

Excited state

sp^3 hybridization

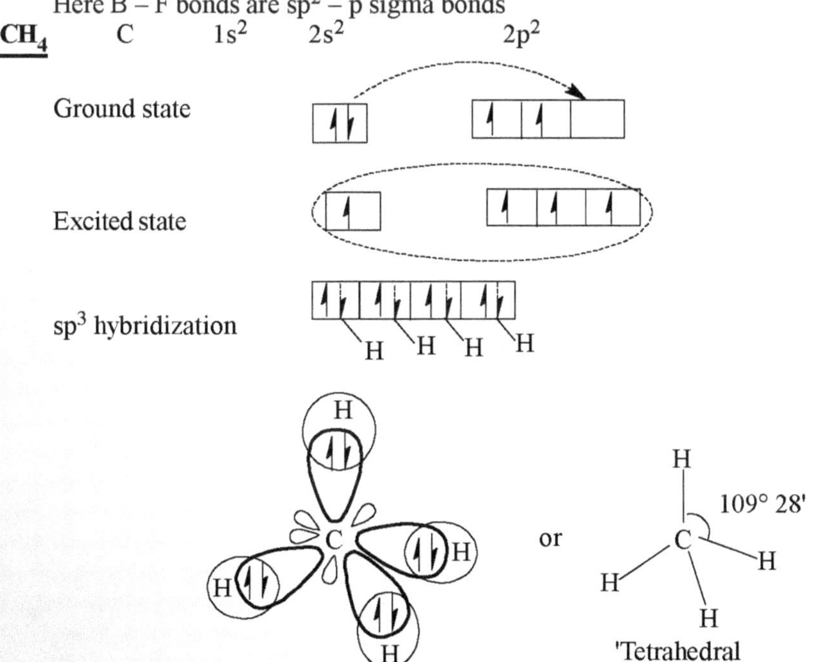

Here, all C – H bonds are sp^3 – s σ bonds

The concept of hybridization reduces the drawbacks of V.B.T. because it gives us the idea about bond angle and shape. It gives the clear explanation why all C – H bonds of CH_4 are identical. In the same manner we can understand the geometries of PCl_5, SF_6 & IF_7

PCl$_5$ Phosphorous wants to make 5 σ bonds with 5 'Cl' atoms, so it needs five hybridized orbitals. Thus, it involves mixing of five orbitals viz. one s, three p and one d orbital.

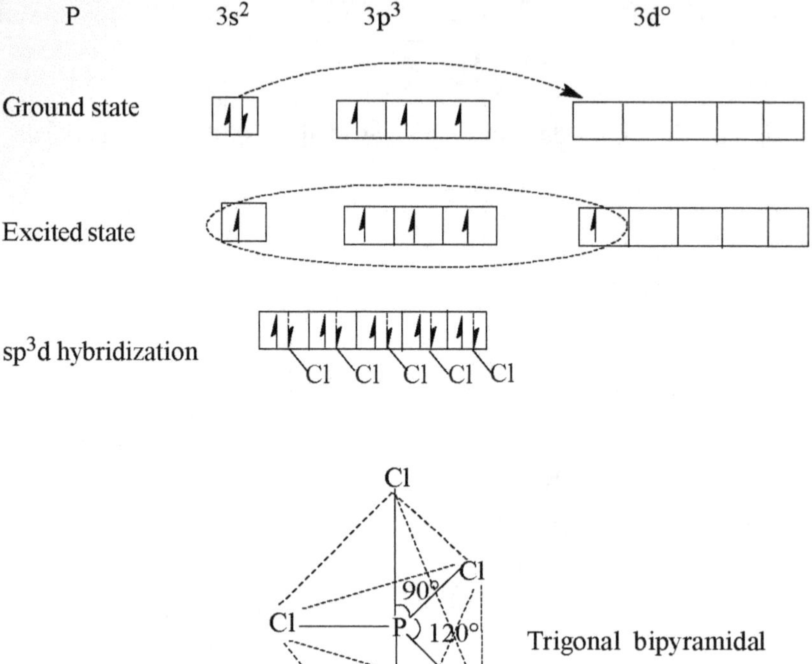

SF$_6$ For the formation of six σ bonds with six F atoms sulphur needs six hybridized orbitals thus, it involves mixing of one s, three p and two d orbitals

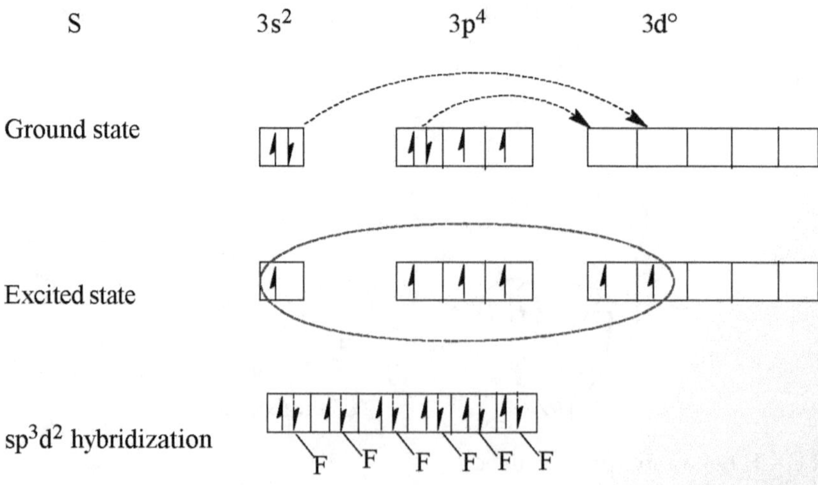

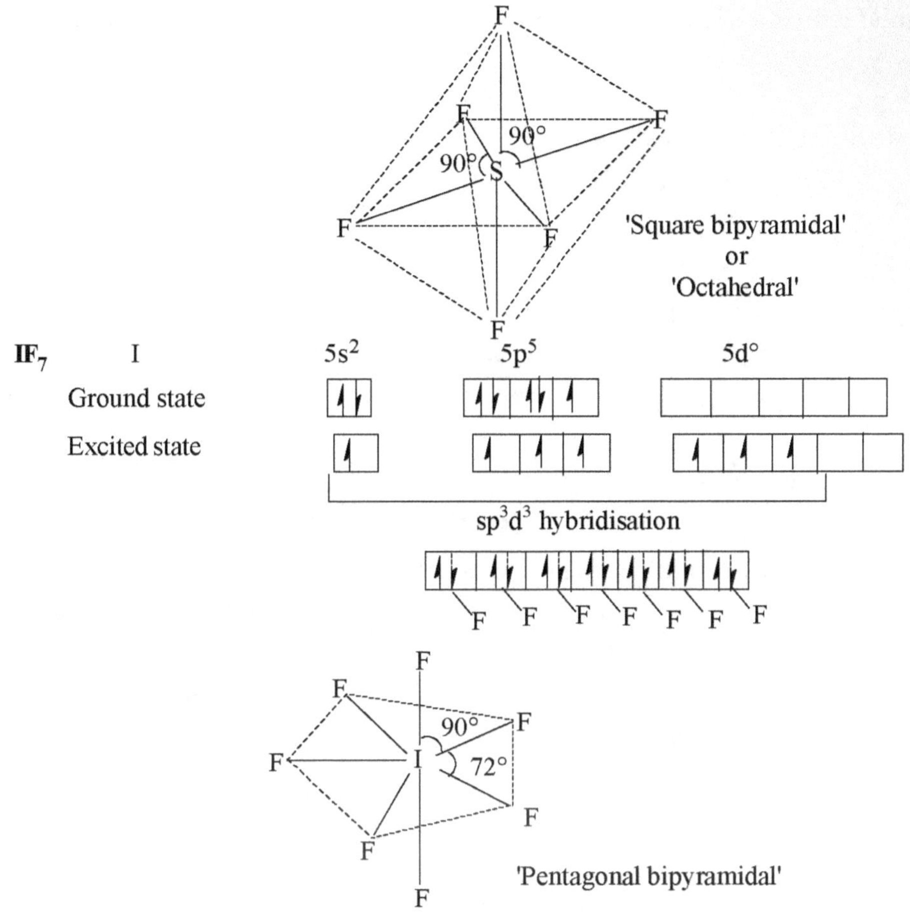

Number of bond pairs or steric number	Geometry	Hybridization	Bond angle	Examples	Orbitals involved in hybridization
2	Linear	sp	180°	$BeCl_2$	s + any 'p' orbital
3	Triangular planar	sp^2	120°	BCl_3, BF_3	s + any two p orbitals
4	Tetrahedral	sp^3	109°.28'	CH_4, CCl_4 $SiCl_4$	$s + p_x + p_y + p_z$
5	Trigonal bipyramidal	sp^3d	90°, 120°	PCl_5	$s + p_x + p_y + p_z + d_{z^2}$
6	Octahedral	sp^3d^2	90°	SF_6	s + all three p orbitals + $d_{z^2} + d_{x^2-y^2}$
7	Pentagonal bipyramidal	sp^3d^3	90°, 72°	IF_7	s + all three p orbitals + $d_{z^2} + d_{x^2-y^2} + d_{xy}$

Evaluation of hybridization:- To find hybridization of central atom either of the two ways can be used.

Ist Method:-

(σ bond pair) + (lone pair) + (–ve charge) = Hybridization

For e.g.

$$Cl-\overset{..}{\underset{|}{P}}-Cl \qquad Cl$$

σ bp = 3

lp = 1   sum = 3 + 1 = 4 (sp³)

$$H-\overset{(-)}{\underset{|}{C}}-H \qquad H$$

σ bp = 3   –ve charge = 1

sum = 3 + 1 = 4 (sp³)

$$O \overset{\sigma}{=} C \overset{\sigma}{=} O$$

σ bp = 2 (sp)

$$F-\overset{..}{\underset{\diagup\quad\diagdown}{S}}-F \qquad F \quad F$$

σ bp = 4   lp = 1

sum = 4 + 1 = 5 (sp³ d)

Here bp & lp are bond pair & lone pair of electrons respectively

2ⁿᵈ Method: -Firstly, valence electrons of all atoms should be counted in the species. If the sum of these valence electrons varies between 2 to 8 then it should be divided by 2 and if sum varies from 9 to 56 then it should be divided by 8 and if sum is found to be greater than 56 it should be divided by 18.

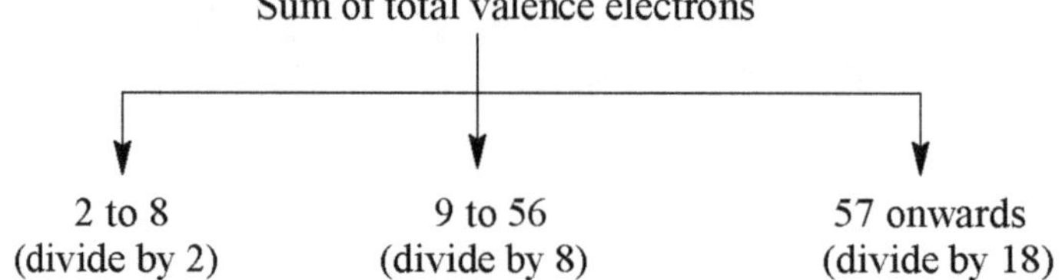

Sum of total valence electrons

2 to 8	9 to 56	57 onwards
(divide by 2)	(divide by 8)	(divide by 18)

The quotient so obtained is called steric number

For e.g.

PCl₅   Total valence electrons

$$= 5 + 7 \times 5 = 40$$

$$= 40 / 5 = 5 \qquad \text{i.e.} \qquad 5 \ (sp^3 d)$$

XeF₄   Total valence electrons = $8 + 7 \times 4 = 36$

$$8 \overline{)36(}4$$
$$\underline{32}$$
$$2\overline{)4(}2$$
$$\underline{4}$$
$$X$$

i.e. $4 + 2 = 6$ $sp^3 d^2$

IF₇   Total Valence electrons = $7 + 7 \times 7 = 56$

$$= 56/8 = 7 \qquad \text{i.e} \quad 7 \quad sp^3 d^3$$

By using both the methods (1ˢᵗ and 2ⁿᵈ) we can evaluate hybridization as well as lone pair of electrons of central atom.

For eg.   **PCl_3**   Total valence electrons
$$= 5 + 7 \times 3 = 26$$

$$
\begin{array}{r}
8)\,\overline{26}\,(3 \\
24 \\
\hline
2)\,\overline{2}\,(1 \\
2 \\
\hline
X \\
\hline
\end{array}
$$

i.e. $3 + 1 = 4$ (sp^3)

In PCl_3, P can form 3 σ bonds with three chlorine atoms

σ bp + lp + (–ve charge) = hybridization

$3 + lp + 0 = 4$

$lp = 1$

Thus, in PCl_3, phosphorous possesses one lp of electrons.

Similarly in **XeF_2**   Total valence electrons $= 8 + 7 \times 2 = 22$

$$
\begin{array}{r}
8)\,\overline{22}\,(2 \\
16 \\
\hline
2)\,\overline{6}\,(3 \\
6 \\
\hline
X \\
\hline
\end{array}
$$

i.e. $2 + 3 = 5$ (sp^3d)

Xenon can form only two σ bonds with two 'F' atoms thus, in XeF_2; Xenon contains three lone pair of electrons.

σ bp + lp + –ve charge = Hybridization

$2 + lp + 0 = 5$

$lp = 3$

➤ 4.2 Shapes of molecules / ions when central atom contains lone pair of electrons

(1)   While observing the shape of species, lone pair should not be considered, however, the presence of lone pair may or may not influence the geometry of species (See VSEPR theory) but lone pair is not the part of geometry.

For e.g. If central atom does not have lone pair in sp^2 hybridization, its shape is always triangular planar but when central atom possesses one lone pair it attains bent shape

Trigonal planar	**Bent**	**Linear**

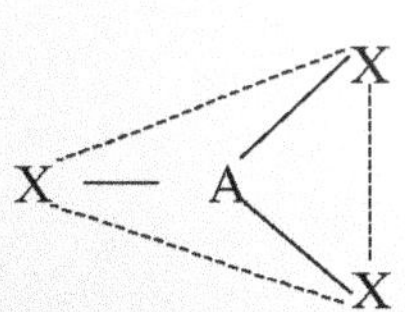
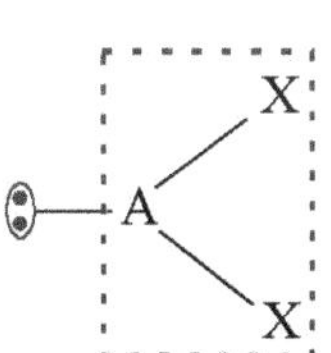

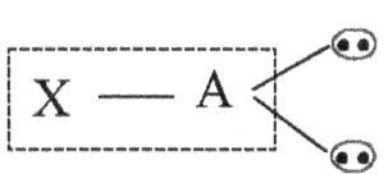

bp = 3	bp = 2	bp = 1
lp = 0	lp = 1	lp = 2

Similarly, if central atom of sp^2 hybridization has two lp then it possesses linear shape.

$$sp^2 \begin{cases} lp = 0, bp = 3 & \text{(Triangular planar)} \\ lp = 1, bp = 2 & \text{(Bent shape)} \\ lp = 2, bp = 1 & \text{(Linear)} \end{cases}$$

$$sp^3 \begin{cases} lp = 0, bp = 4 & \text{(Tetrahedral)} \\ lp = 1, bp = 3 & \text{(Pyramidal)} \\ lp = 2, bp = 2 & \text{(Bent)} \\ lp = 3, bp = 1 & \text{(linear)} \end{cases}$$

(2) sp^3d hybridization holds trigonal bipyramidal shape (TBP). It has two types of bond, axial and equatorial as shown in figure.

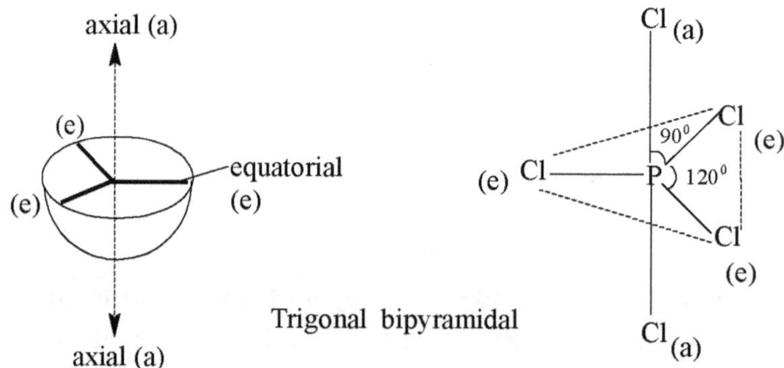

Axial and equatorial bonds have different characteristics (See Bent's rule). Axial bonds are longer and weaker than equatorial bonds. Due to this reason both axial bonds in PCl_5 break while heating.

$$PCl_5 \xrightarrow{\Delta} PCl_3 + Cl_2$$

If lone pair is present in TBP geometry, then on the basis of repulsions in lp & bp, structure of the species is decided.

Descending order of repulsion is :-

$$lp - lp \quad > \quad lp - bp \quad > \quad bp - bp$$
$$\text{(more strong)} \quad\quad \text{(strong)} \quad\quad\quad \text{(weak)}$$

Only those repulsions are considered in which angle between electron pairs is less than or equal to $90°$ rest of the repulsions are ignored. For e.g. three geometries of ClF_3 are possible

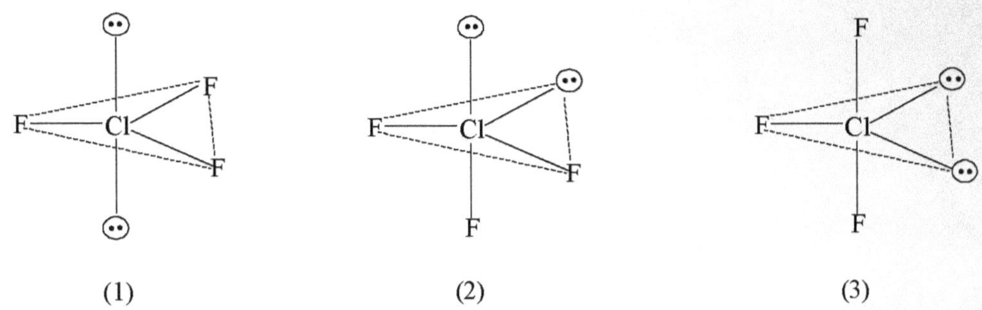

(1)   (2)   (3)

Repulsions

lp – lp = 0	lp – lp = 1 (more strong)	lp – lp = 0
lp – bp = 6 (strong)	lp – bp = 3 (strong)	lp – bp = 4 (strong)
bp – bp = 0	bp – bp = 2 (weak)	bp –bp = 2 (weak)

Among 1, 2 & 3, 3rd has minimum repulsions therefore 3rd shows the correct geometry of ClF_3. Similarly for SF_4

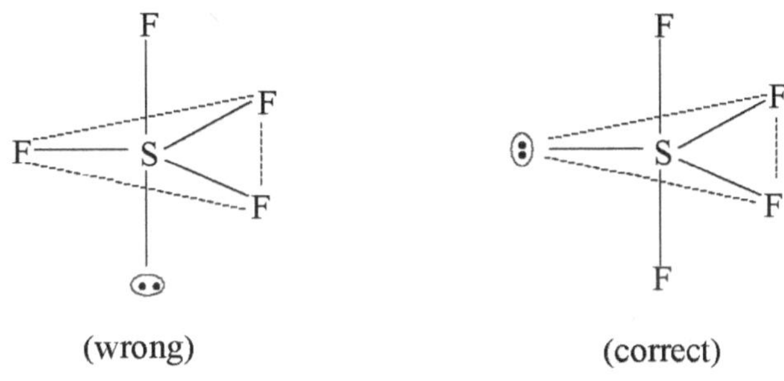

(wrong)   (correct)

Repulsions

lp – lp = 0	lp – lp = 0
lp – bp = 3 (strong)	lp – bp = 2 (strong)
bp – bp = 3 (weak)	bp – bp = 4 (weak)

(3) **Bent's rule (For sp^3d hybridization)**

This rule is applicable to understand TBP geometry According to this rule.

"More electronegative element prefers to stay at axial position whereas lone pair prefers to stay at equatorial location. For e.g.

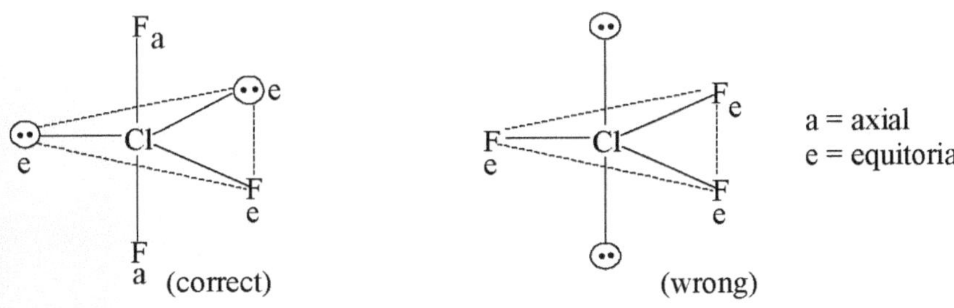

(correct)   (wrong)

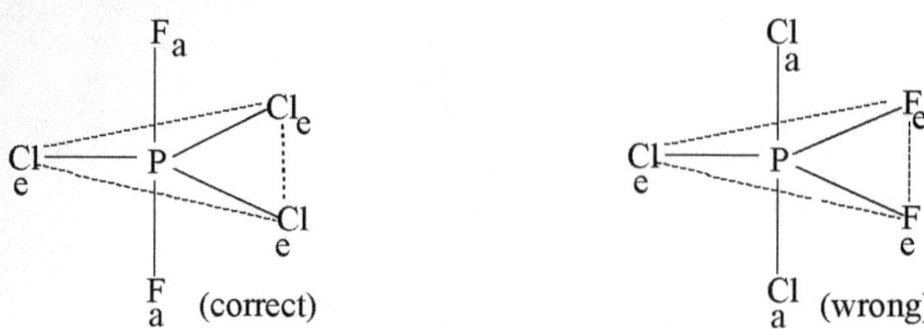

Explanation: - We can split sp³d hybridized orbital in the following manner.

$$sp^3d \quad = \quad \underbrace{sp^2}_{\text{equatorial}} \quad + \quad \underbrace{pd}_{\text{axial}}$$

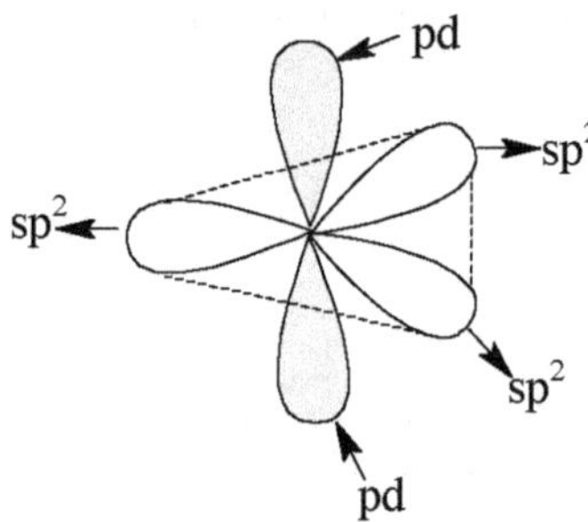

In TBP geometry two 'pd' orbitals are present on axial position; therefore % s character on axial position is zero. This is why central atom has minimum electro negativity at axial position. With the same reason electronegative element prefers to stay at axial location so that the element attracts electrons of bond pair towards it.

Lone pair of electrons is always attracted towards the nucleus of one atom; therefore, they like to stay where they feel close to nucleus. Since's' orbital is closest to the nucleus, so lone pair prefer to stay with those orbital which have more % s character. This allows lone pair of electrons to sit on equatorial location because at equatorial location (sp²) 33.33%'s' character is present while at axial position % s character is zero.

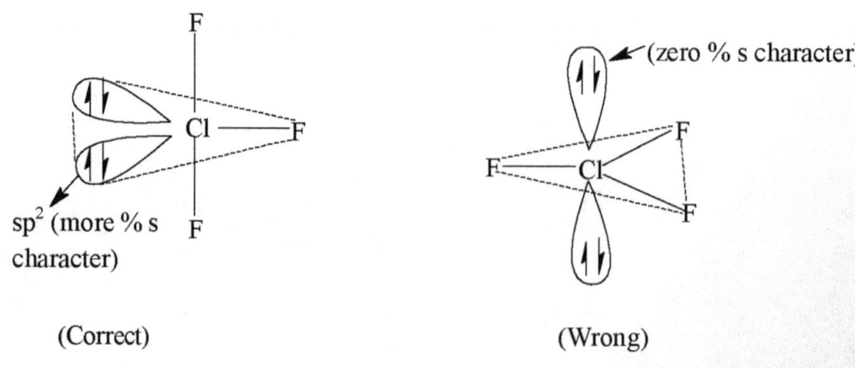

(Correct)   (Wrong)

Since axial bonds have more % p character comparative to equatorial bonds, therefore, axial bonds are longer & less stable than equatorial bonds.

$$\% \text{ p character} \ \propto \ \text{longitivity \& thinness}$$

By using Bent's rule various geometries in sp^3d hybridization can be predicted.

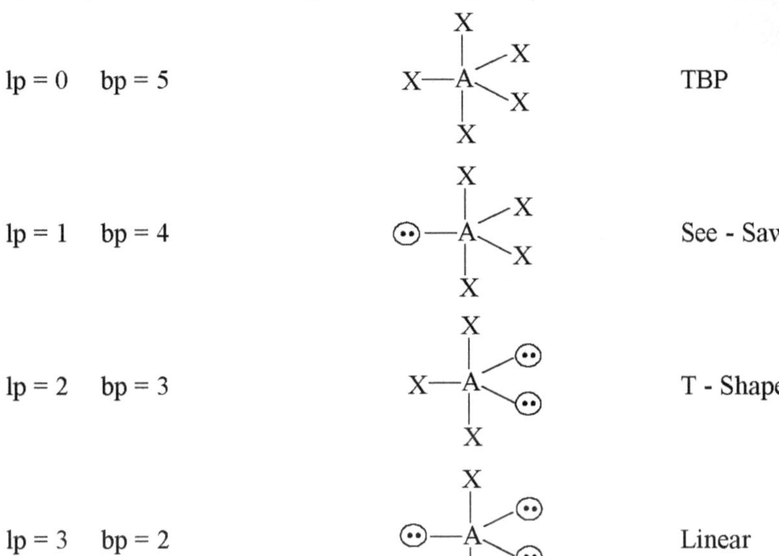

lp = 0   bp = 5 — TBP

lp = 1   bp = 4 — See - Saw

lp = 2   bp = 3 — T - Shape

lp = 3   bp = 2 — Linear

Example: - Discuss the shape of the following

     (a) $XeOF_2$ (b) SF_4 (c) ICl_2^+

Solution: - (a) $XeOF_2$ Total valence electrons

$$= 8 + 6 + 14 = 28$$

$$8\overline{)\,28\,(}3$$
$$\underline{24}$$
$$2\overline{)\ 4\ (}2$$
$$\underline{4}$$
$$\overline{\quad X \quad}$$

      i.e. $3 + 2 = 5\ (sp^3d)$

'Xe' forms three σ bonds, two with 'F' & one with 'O'

$\sigma\ bp + lp + (-ve\ charge) = $ Hybridization

      $3 + lp + 0 = 5,$ $lp = 2$

In TBP geometry lp prefers to stay at equatorial position hence $XeOF_2$ has T shape

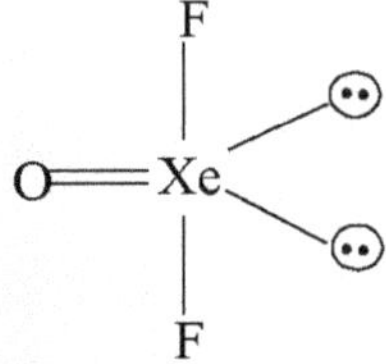

Since in TBP geometry more electronegative element prefers to stay at axial position, thus, F is placed at axial position while oxygen which is less electronegative than F, is placed at equatorial position.

(b) **SF_4:-** Total valence electrons $= 6 + 7 \times 4 = 34$

$$8\overline{)34}(4$$
$$\underline{32}$$
$$2\overline{)2}(1$$
$$\underline{2}$$
$$X$$

i.e. $4 + 1 = 5$ (sp^3d)

σ bp + lp + (−ve charge) = Hybridization

$4 + lp = 5,$ $lp = 1$

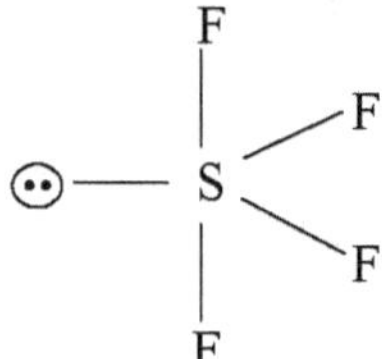

See - Saw

(c) **$ICl_2{}^+$:-** Total valence electrons $= 7 + 7 \times 2 - 1$ (+ve charge) $= 20$

$$8\overline{)20}(2$$
$$\underline{16}$$
$$2\overline{)4}(2$$
$$\underline{4}$$
$$X$$

i.e. $2 + 2 = 4$ (sp^3)

σ bp + lp + (−ve charge) = Hybridization

$2 + lp + 0 = 4,$ $lp = 2$

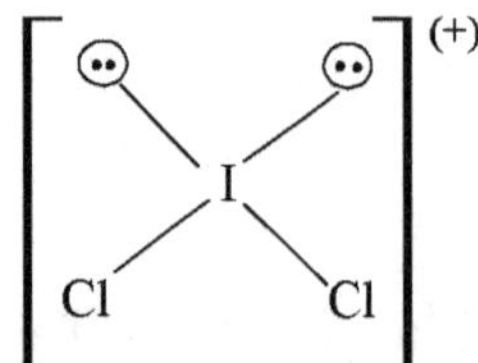

Bent or V Shape

➤ 4.3 Modified Bent's rule

$XeF_5{}^{(−)}$ is the only species which exhibit pentagonal planar shape.

Total valence electrons $= 8 + 7 \times 5 + 1 = 44$

$$8\overline{)44}(5$$
$$\underline{40}$$
$$2\overline{)4}(2$$
$$\underline{4}$$
$$X$$

i.e. $5 + 2 = 7$ (sp^3d^3)

σ bp + lp + (–ve charge) = Hybridization

$5 + lp + 1 = 7,$ $lp = 2$

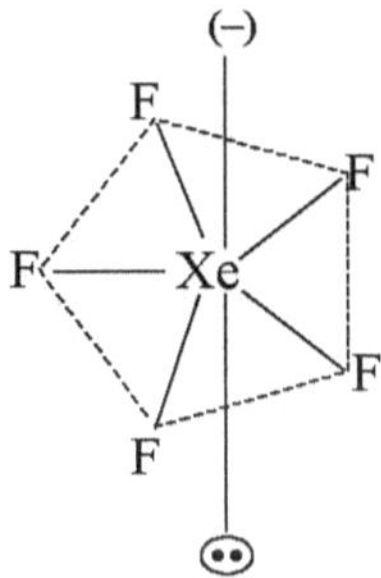

Experimentally it has been observed that $XeF_5^{(-)}$ has pentagonal planar shape. This geometry of $XeF_5^{(-)}$ can not be explained by Bent's rule. To understand above concepts Bent's rule is presented as follows :

"The orbital occupying more space with respect to the central atom will have more % s - character"

In means lone pair and negative charge prefers to stay in the orbital where % s character is more. Such orbitals are big in size because % s character increases the bulkiness of hybridized orbitals. Hence these orbitals require more space and like to stay where bond angle is more.

In TBP geometry bond angle between equatorial and axial bonds is 90° which is lesser than the angle between two equatorial bonds i.e. 120°. Thus, lone pair stays with equatorial bonds because here more space is available.

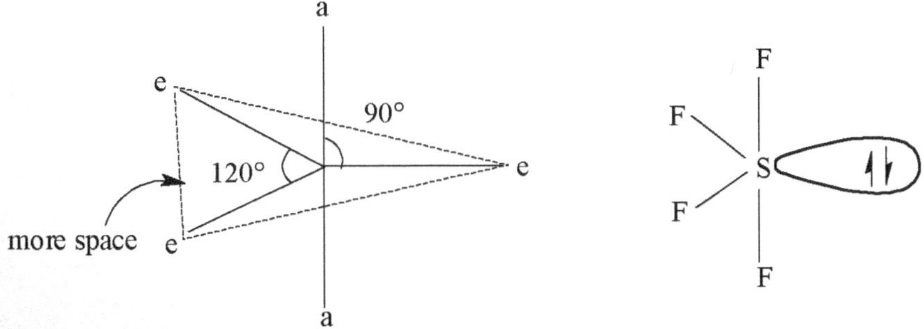

Similarly, in pentagonal bi pyramidal (sp^3d^3) geometry the bond angle between axial and equatorial bonds is 90° whereas it is only 72° in between equatorial - equatorial bonds.

Thus, the bond angle between axial and equatorial bonds is more so lone pair and negative charge stays at axial location as here more space is available.

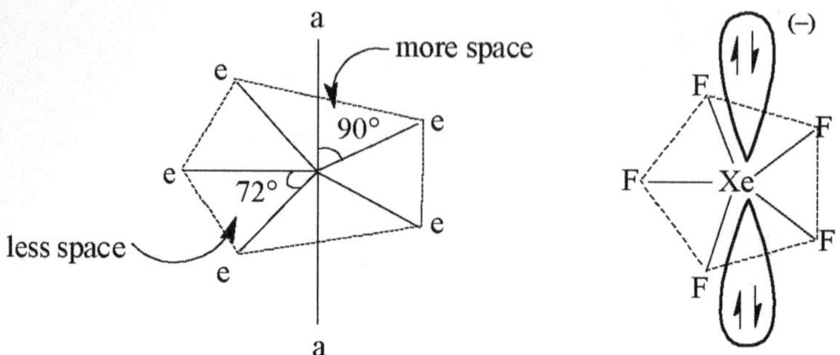

Note: -(a) In sp^3d^2 hybridization lone pair can be placed anywhere because in octahedral geometry all bond angles are 90°.

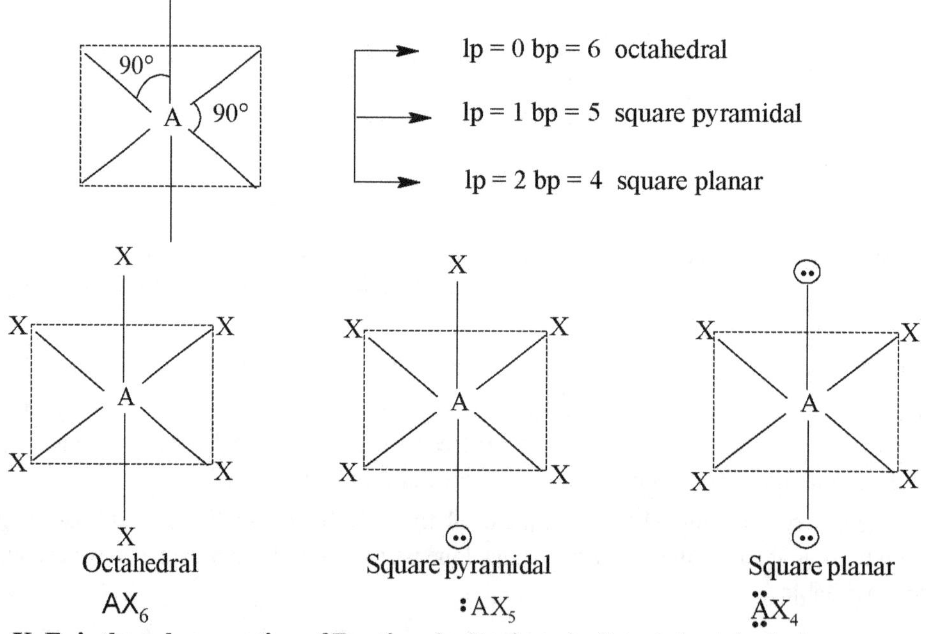

(b)   **XeF_6 is the only exception of Bent's rule.** Its shape is distorted octahedral

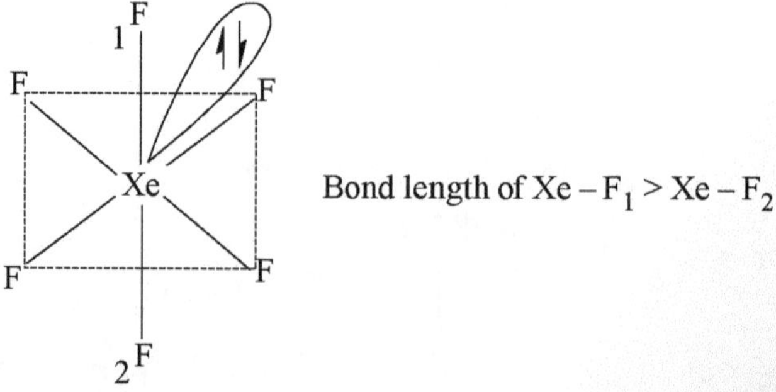

This can not be explained with the help of Bent's rule. The bond length of both axial Xe–F bonds is different due to lp–bp repulsion. The upper Xe–F bond is long where as the lower Xe–F bond is comparatively short.

➤ 4.4 Recent amendments in Bent's rule

The more electronegative element not only prefers to stay in the orbital having more p - character but it can also increases the p - character in its attached orbital of the central atom depending upon the circumstances.

This can be applicable only if all the substituents of central atom are not same

For e.g. In CH_4 or CF_4, this rule is not applicable but in CH_2F_2, CH_2Cl_2 and $CHCl_3$ this principle can be applied.

In CH_2F_2, the % p character of C – F is more because F is an electronegative element therefore, it possibly reduces % s character & increases % p character in C – F bonds.

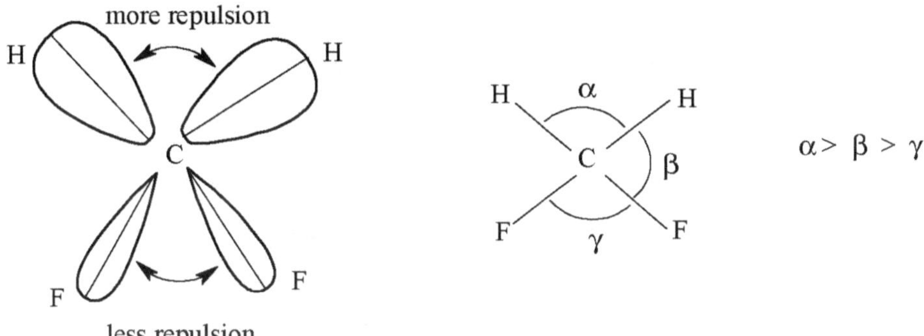

Due to more % p – character in C – F bonds, these orbitals are long and thin, and shows least repulsion while, on the other hand due to more % s character in C – H bonds, these orbitals are bulky and shows maximum repulsion. This clears the concept that bond angle of HCH bond is more than 109° 28' whereas bond angle of FCF bond is less than 109° 28'.

Since C – F bond has more % p character therefore it is longer as compared to C – H bond

(% p character $\propto$ longitivity)

Example: - Compare C – Cl bond length in CF_3Cl and CH_3Cl

Solution:-

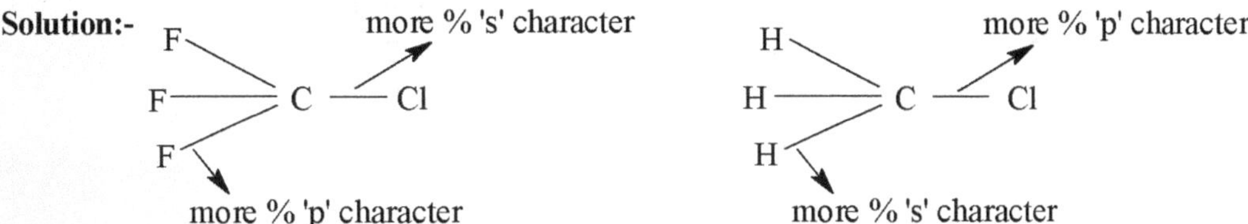

Due to more % p character C — Cl bond of CH_3Cl is longer than C — Cl bond of CF_3Cl

Example: - Discuss the shape of XeO_2F_2 by the help of hybridization. How many pπ - dπ bonds are present in it.

Solution: - Total valence electrons $= 8 + 12 + 14 = 34$

$$8\overline{)34}\,(4$$
$$\underline{32}$$
$$2\overline{)2}\,(1$$
$$\underline{2}$$
$$X$$

i.e. $\quad 4 + 1 = 5 \ (sp^3d)$

σ bp + lp + (–ve charge) = Hybridization

$4 + lp + 0 = 5,$

$lp = 1$

According to Bent's rule it should have See - Saw geometry.

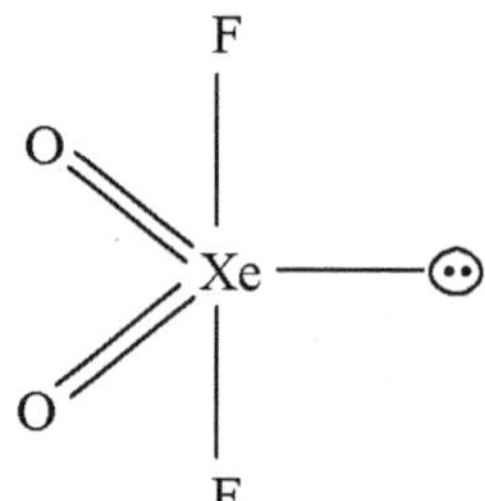

Since 'O' is less electronegative than F hence, F is placed at axial position.

$$Xe \qquad 5s^2 \qquad\qquad 5p^6 \qquad\qquad\qquad 5d^0$$

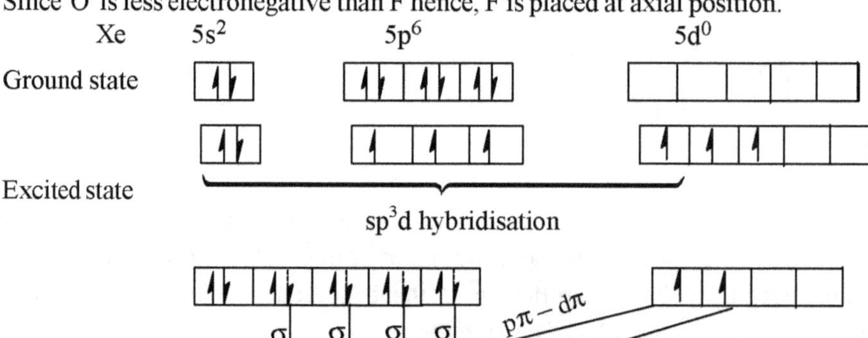

Hence in XeO_2F_2 two pπ - dπ bonds are present.

➤ 4.5 Calculation of % s & % p character

The % s character and % p character can be calculated by using the following formula

$$\cos \theta = s / (s - 1) \qquad \& \qquad \cos \theta = (p - 1) / p$$

Let us calculate % s character of axial bond is TBP geometry

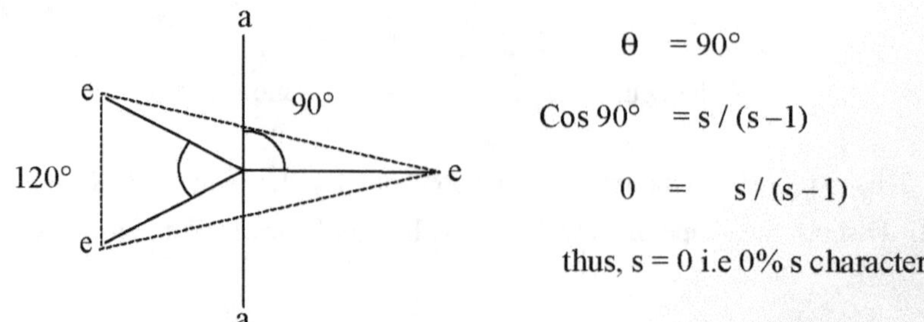

$\theta = 90°$

$\cos 90° = s / (s - 1)$

$0 = s / (s - 1)$

thus, $s = 0$ i.e 0% s character

Similarly for equatorial bonds

$$\theta = 120°$$

$$Cos\,120° = s/s-1, = s = 0.33, \text{ i.e. } 33\%$$

Example: - Calculate % s character in sp^2 hybridized orbitals

Solution:-

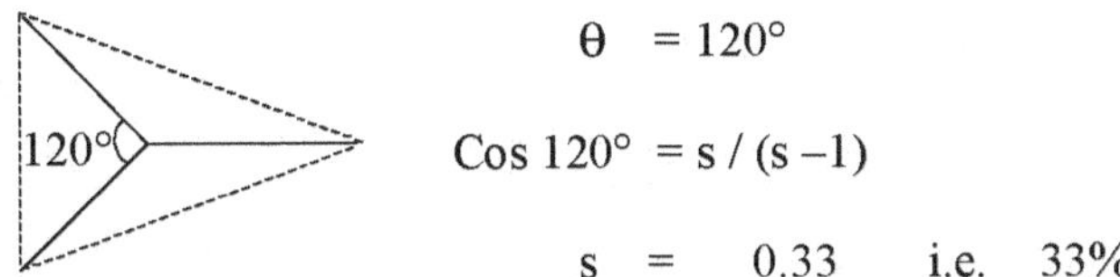

$$\theta = 120°$$

$$Cos\,120° = s/(s-1)$$

$$s = 0.33 \quad \text{i.e.} \quad 33\%$$

➢ 4.6 VSEPR Theory (Valence Shell electron pair repulsion)

Rule - 1   Presence of lone pair on central atom may or may not affect the angle as well as shape of the molecule

Order or repulsion   lp – lp > lp – bp > bp – bp

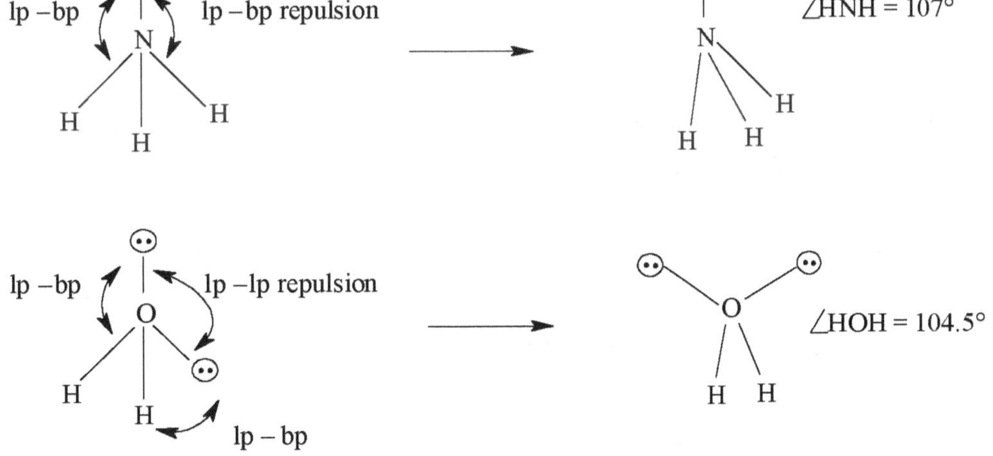

The Structure of SF_4 is not a perfect **See - Saw** because lp – bp repulsion is present in it

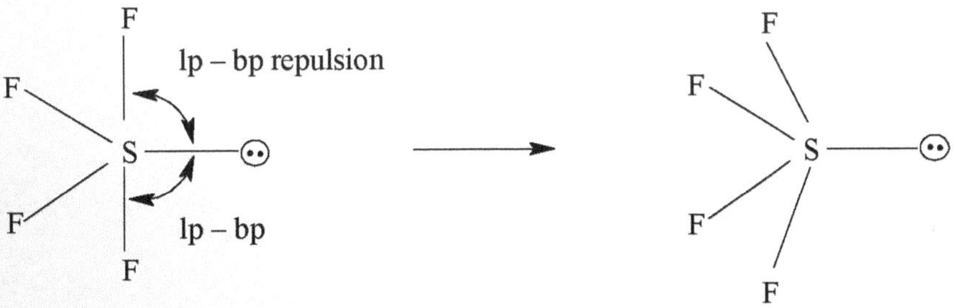

Similarly, ClF_3 does not show perfect 'T' due to the presence of lp – bp & lp – lp repulsions repulsions.

While bond angles are not affected in XeF_4 and XeF_2 due to the presence of lone pair

$\angle FXeF = 180°$

$\angle FXeF = 90°$

Rule - 2   A double bond needs more space than single bond. Descending order of repulsion is:-

db – db > db – sb > sb –sb

Here db = double bond & sb = single bond

For example in HCHO, carbon is sp^2 hybridized but all bond angles are not exactly equal to 120°.

sb – db repulsion

sb – sb repulsion

$\alpha > \beta$

In CO_3^{2-} ion, 'C' is sp^2 hybridized but resonance makes all the bond angles equal

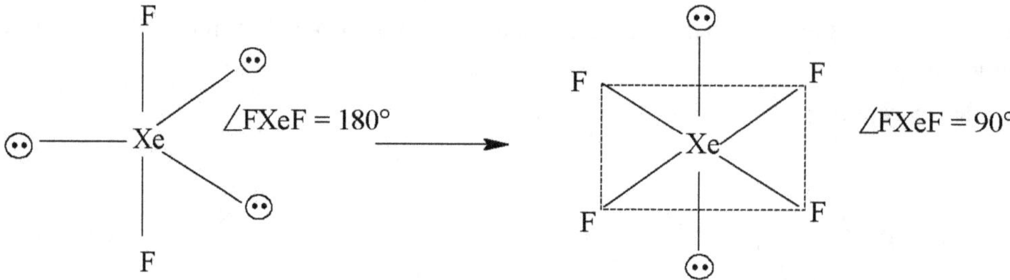

Here $\alpha = \beta$

Rule - 3 : If central atom & number of lone pair present on central atom are same then as the electro negativity of surrounding atom increases, bond angle reduces.

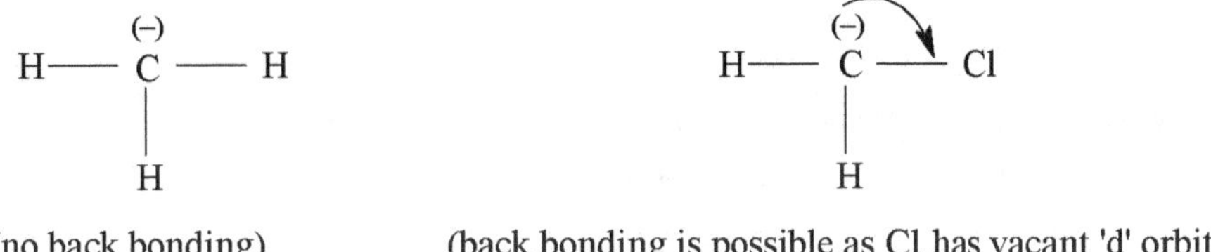

$\angle HNH = 107°$ $\angle FNF = 102°$

It is noted that this rule is applicable if and only if lone pair is present on central atom. This rule is not valid for CH_4, CF_4 & CCl_4 like molecules.

Rule - 4 Back bonding : If two atoms are joined with each other by sigma bond then either of the two can donate its lone pair or negative charge to the other atom when the other has vacant 'p' or 'd' orbital.

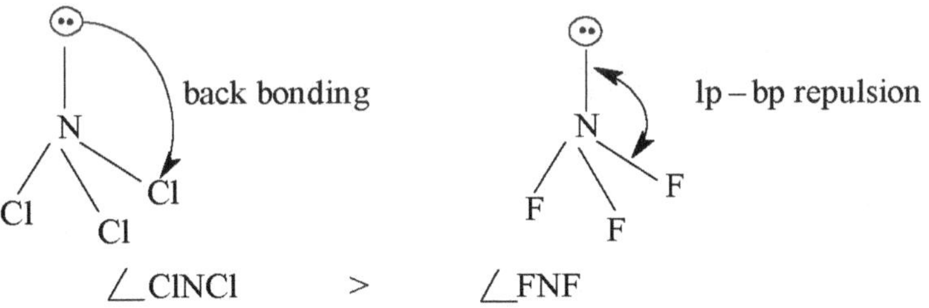

(no back bonding)   (back bonding is possible as Cl has vacant 'd' orbital)

For back bonding one of the two atoms must be from IInd period and other atom should be from IInd or IIIrd period. The back bonding reduces lone pair bond pair repulsions, this increases bond angle.

back bonding   lp – bp repulsion

$\angle ClNCl$ > $\angle FNF$

If we arrange NH_3, NCl_3 and NF_3 on the basis of decreasing order of bond angle, we get the following sequence

$$NCl_3 > NH_3 > NF_3$$

NCl_3 shows largest bond angle because Cl receives the lone pair of nitrogen by back donation which reduces the lp – bp repulsion and increases the bond angle (Rule-4) we know that back donation is not possible in NH_3 & NF_3 therefore, NF_3 has small bond angle comparative to NH_3 (Rule-3)

Similarly

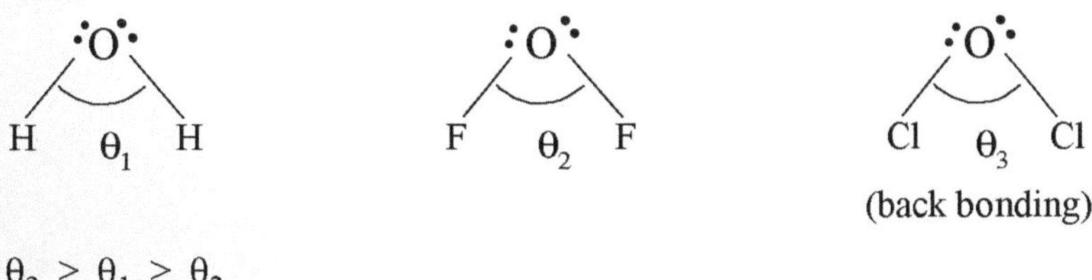

(back bonding)

$$\theta_3 > \theta_1 > \theta_2$$

Rule - 5   Keeping the surrounding atom same if the electronegativity of the central atom (having lone pair) decreases then bond angle decreases

Molecules	NH_3	PH_3	AsH_3	SbH_3
Bond angles	107°	94°	93°	92°

On moving from NH_3 to SbH_3, electro negativity of central atom reduces and thus, bond angle also reduces. This decrease in bond angle is maximum in between NH_3 & PH_3. VSEPR can not explain this sudden change in bond angle. Similarly when we move from H_2O to H_2Te, maximum reduction in bond angle is found in between H_2O & H_2S

H_2O	H_2S	H_2Se	H_2Te
104.5°	92°	91°	90.5°

This rapid change in bond angle can be explained by the help of Drago's rule.

➤ 4.7 Drago's rule

If central atom belongs to 3rd period or onwards and electronegativity of surrounding atom is 2.5 or less, then hybridization is not possible on central atom.

NH_3, H_2O — Shows hybridization

PH_3, AsH_3, SbH_3, H_2S, H_2Se, H_2Te → According to Drago's rule, central atom has no hybridization

In PH_3, P does not show sp^3 hybridization, therefore, three hydrogen overlap with half filled 'p' oribitals and form PH_3.

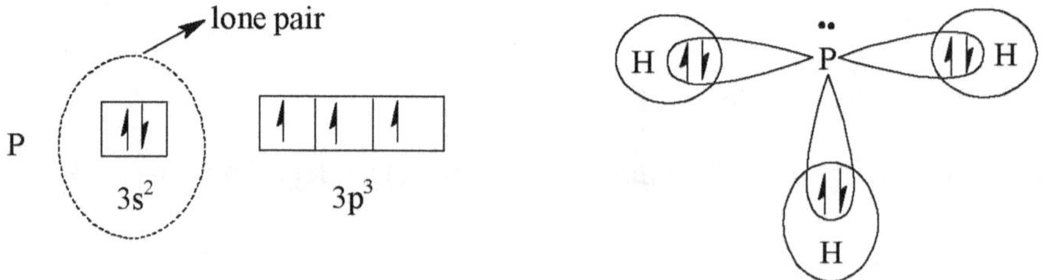

All three 'p' orbitals are perpendicular to one another, there fore bond angle in PH_3 is 94°.

If we compare the basic character of NH_3 and PH_3, then we find that NH_3 is more basic than PH_3, this is because in NH_3 lone pair is present in sp^3 hybridized orbital whereas in PH_3 lone pair is present in pure 's' orbital. Thus, lone pair of PH_3 is more close to the nucleus and less available for the reaction with acid or $H^{(+)}$

For example: - Formation of PH_4^+ is difficult in comparison to NH_4^+

$$NH_3 \text{ (dil)} + HCl \longrightarrow NH_4^{(+)} + Cl^{(-)}$$

$$PH_3 \text{ (conc)} + HCl \longrightarrow PH_4^{(+)} + Cl^{(-)}$$

- Solubility of NH_3 is much higher compared to PH_3 in water

$$NH_3 + H_2O \longrightarrow NH_4^{(+)} + OH^{(-)}$$

$$PH_3 + H_2O \longrightarrow \text{(no reaction)}$$

- NH_3 forms large number of complexes while PH_3 hardly forms complexes

Explanation of Drago's rule

According to Drago's rule, 'P' does not show hybridization in PH_3. This fact can be explained on the basis of calculation of % s character.

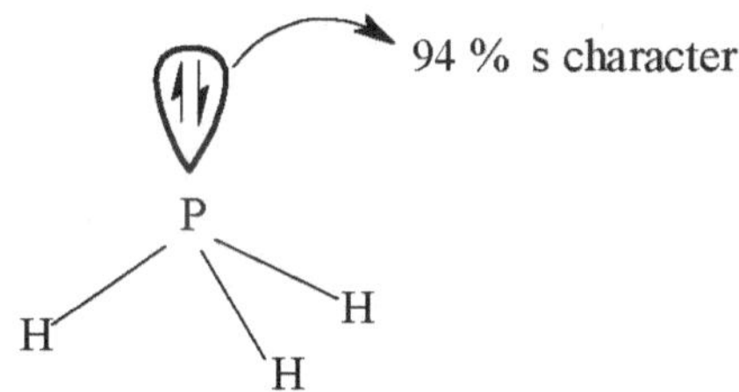

$$\theta = 94° \qquad Cos\,\theta = \frac{s}{s-1}$$

$$Cos\,94° = \frac{s}{s-1}$$

$$s = 0.02$$
$$\text{i.e } 2\%$$

This % s character is of a single 'P – H' bond. The % s character for three P – H bonds will be 6 %, thus, % s character of the orbital containing lone pair will be 94%

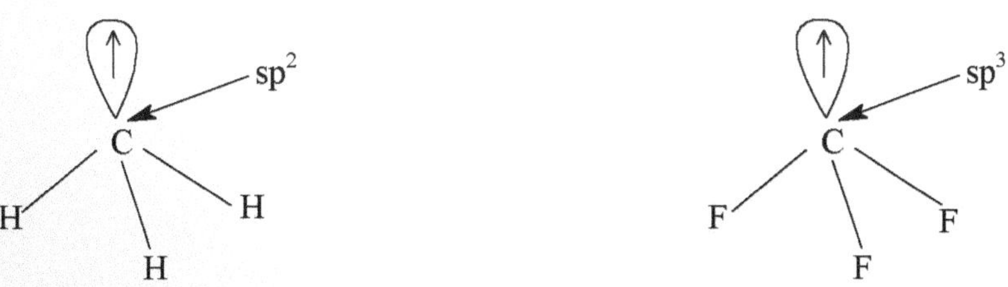

Among sp (50%), sp^2 (33.33%) and sp^3 (25%) hybridized orbitals no one has 94% s character. This shows that lone pair of electrons are present in almost pure's' orbital (94 % s character)

➤ 4.8 Hybridization in odd electron species

The presence of odd electrons in an orbital increases its energy and this restricts its involvement in hybridization. But if surrounding atom is more electronegative, partial positive charge is developed on central atom. This positive charge attracts the orbital containing odd electron towards central atom & hence it participates in hybridization. For example

➤ 4.9 Hybridization of some covalent compounds in solid state

Some covalent compounds dimerise in their solid state. They present in the form of cation and anion in solid state. For e.g. PCl_5 found in the form of dimer in solid state

$$2PCl_5 \longrightarrow [PCl_4]^{(+)} \quad [PCl_6]^{(-)}$$
$$\text{solid} \qquad\qquad sp^3 \qquad\quad sp^3d^2$$

But this dimerisation is not possible in PBr_5 because the size of Br is large and P can not adjust more than 5 Br in its surrounding

$$2PBr_5\ (s) \longrightarrow [PBr_4]^{(+)} \quad [PBr_6]^{(-)} \qquad \text{(not possible)}$$

$$PBr_5 \longrightarrow [PBr_4]^{(+)}\ Br^{(-)}$$
$$\text{solid} \qquad\qquad sp^3$$

In the same way:-

$$N_2O_4 \longrightarrow NO^{(+)}\ NO_3^{(-)}$$
$$\text{solid} \qquad\qquad sp \quad sp^2$$

$$Cl_2O_6 \longrightarrow [ClO_2]^{2+} \quad [ClO_4]^{2-}$$
$$\text{solid} \qquad\qquad\quad sp \qquad\quad sp^3$$

➤ 4.10 Isomorphism

(1) The property of showing same crystal structure by two ionic compounds is called isomorphism For e.g. $FeSO_4.7H_2O$ & $MgSO_4.7H_2O$

(2) Conditions for isomorphism

➤ These compounds have same formula type

➤ The crystal of these substances should have the same shape For e.g. $BaSO_4$, $KMnO_4$.

Both SO_4^{2-} and MnO_4^{2-} ions show tetrahedral geometry but $NaClO_3$ and $NaNO_3$ do not show isomorphism because of sp^2 hybridization in $NaNO_3$ and sp^3 hybridization in ClO_3^- former is trigonal planar while later is pyramidal in shape.

➤ In both the compounds polarizing properties of both cation and anion should be same.

(3) When a solution of two isomorphous substance is concentrated to the point of crystallization we get crystals which are homogeneous and contain both the isomorphous substance in the same ratio in which they were present in the solution.

Subjective Exercise

EXERCISE 4.1

Q.1 Which one of the following has larger bond angle than other in each pair?

(i) NH_3 & BF_3 (ii) C_2H_4 & C_2H_6

(iii) CO_2 & NH_3 (iv) SF_6 & PCl_5

Q.2 Explain the hybridization in:-

(a) $XeOF_2$ (b) IF_5

(c) ICl_2^+ (d) $ICl_2^{(-)}$

(e) $SiCl_4$ (f) PCl_5

(g) PCl_5 (in solid state)   (h) PBr_5 (in solid state)

(i) XeF_4 (j) XeF_6

(k) $(CH_3)_3N$ (l) $I_3^{(-)}$

(m) $XeF_5^{(-)}$ (n) $CO_3^{2(-)}$

(o) $SO_4^{2(-)}$ (p) $ClO_4^{(-)}$

(q) $PO_4^{3(-)}$

Q.3 PCl_5 is possible but PH_5 is not. Explain.

Q.4 PCl_5 is possible but NCl_5 is not. Explain.

Q.5 CCl_4 does not undergo hydrolysis but $SiCl_4$ undergoes hydrolysis easily. Explain.

EXERCISE 4.2

Q.1 Arrange the following in order of bond angle.

(i) H_2O , H_2Se, H_2Te (ii) NH_3, NF_3 , NCl_3

(iii) CH_4 , PH_3 , AsH_3 (iv) BF_3 , NH_3

(v) $(CH_3)_3N$, $(SiH_3)_3N$

Q.2 $CF_3^{(-)}$ is more basic than $CCl_3^{(-)}$ explain

Q.3 Discuss shapes of the following

(a) XeF_4 (b) $XeOF_2$

(c) $ICl_2^{(+)}$ (d) $ICl_2^{(-)}$

(e) XeF_2 (f) $XeF_5^{(-)}$

(g) BrF_3

Objective Exercise

Q.1

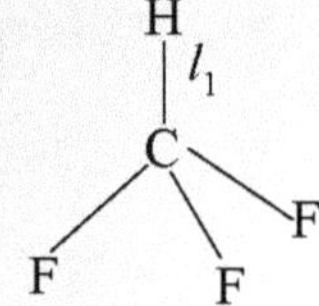

l_1, l_2 and l_3 are the bond lengths of C – H bonds in the given molecules. Correct order of these bond lengths will be:-

(a) $l_1 > l_2 > l_3$ (b) $l_3 > l_2 > l_1$

(c) $l_1 > l_3 > l_2$ (d) $l_1 = l_2 = l_3$

Q.2

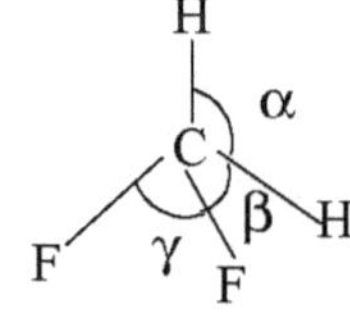

α, β and γ are bond angles then

(a) $\alpha > \beta > \gamma$ (b) $\beta > \gamma > \alpha$

(c) $\alpha > \gamma > \beta$ (d) $\gamma > \beta > \alpha$

Q.3 Which among the following will not produce Cl_2 on heating?

(a) PCl_5 (b) PBr_2Cl_3

(c) PF_3Cl_2 (d) All of these will produce Cl_2 on heating

Q.4 In which case presence of lone pair of electrons on central atom does not influence the geometry.

(a) XeF_2 (b) BrF_3

(c) NH_3 (d) XeF_6

Q.5 Which among the following is not linear?

(a) $XeOF_2$ (b) ICl_2^+

(c) BrF_3 (d) All are non linear

Q.6

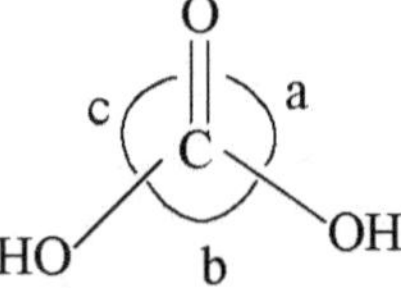 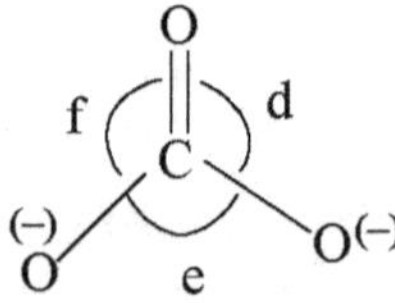

For the following two species following statements are proposed

1. $a > b > c$ 2. $a = b = c$

3. $f = d = e$ 4. $a = c > b$

5. $f = d > e$

Out of these statements, correct statements are:-

(a) 1 & 3

(b) 2 & 4

(c) 3 & 4

(d) 4 & 5

Q.7 Boron forms trivalent halides of the type BX_3. Pick out the wrong statement regarding these halides.

(a) BF_3 is more acidic than BCl_3

(b) Both BF_3 and BCl_3 are electron deficient compounds

(c) In BI_3 boron does not exhibit any hybridization

(d) BCl_3 can not undergo dimerisation to produce B_2Cl_6

Q.8 Which is correctly matched?

	Species	Shape
(a)	BrF_5	Trigonal bipyramidal
(b)	$ICl_4^{(+)}$	Tetrahedral
(c)	$ICl_4^{(-)}$	Tetrahedral
(d)	BrF_3	T - shape

Q.9 Out of SF_4, CF_4 and XeF_4 the molecules with identical shapes are:-

(a) SF_4 & XeF_4

(b) CF_4 and SF_4

(c) CF_4 and XeF_4

(d) all have different geometries

Q.10 In which of the following cases M – F bond has partial double bond character where M is central atom.

(a) OF_2

(b) PF_3

(c) CCl_3F

(d) all of these

Q.11 Which among the following is not linear?

(a) $N_3^{(-)}$

(b) $ICl_2^{(-)}$

(c) XeF_2

(d) all are linear

Q.12 Correct order of size of hybridized orbitals is:-

(a) $sp^3 > sp^2 > sp$

(b) $sp > sp^2 > sp^3$

(c) $sp^3 = sp^2 = sp$

(d) $sp^2 > sp^3 = sp$

Q.13 Hybridization of carbon in C_3O_2 is:-

(a) sp

(b) sp^2

(c) sp^3

(d) both sp and sp^2

Q.14 Which kind of hybridization is present on carbon atoms of Mg_2C_3

(a) sp^3

(b) sp^2

(c) sp

(d) both (a) and (c)

Q.15 You have four alkyl halides

$CH_3 - CF_3$	$CH_2F - CH_2F$	$CHF_2 - CHF_2$	$CF_3 - CF_3$
(1)	(2)	(3)	(4)

Correct order of C – C bond lengths of these halides will be:-

(a) $4 > 3 > 2 > 1$

(b) $1 > 2 > 3 > 4$

(c) $3 > 4 > 2 > 1$

(d) $2 > 4 > 3 > 1$

Q.16 Anionic part of solid N_2O_4 involves --------- hybridization on central atom

(a) sp

(b) sp^2

(c) sp^3

(d) sp^3d

Q.17 Anionic part of solid ICl_3 involves -------- hybridization on central atom.

(a) sp^3

(b) sp^3d

(c) sp^3d^2

(d) sp^2

Q.18 x, y & z are the % s character C – H bonds of the following molecules.

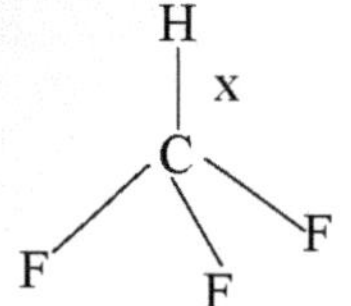 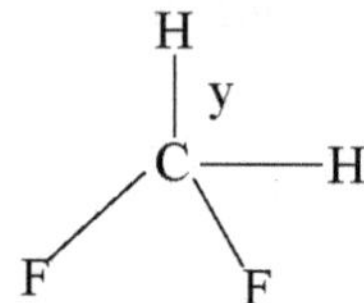 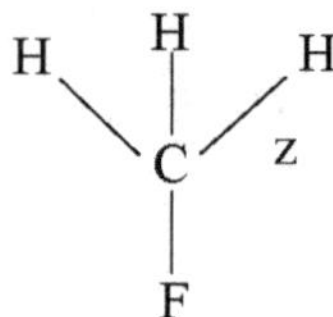

Correct order of % s character is:-

(a) $z > y > x$

(b) $x = y = z$

(c) $x > y > z$

(d) $x = y > z$

Q.19 In which of the following cases cationic part does not involve sp^3 hybridization

(a) PCl_5

(b) PBr_5

(c) XeF_6

(d) Both (b) & (c)

Q.20 Correct statement about PCl_5, IF_7 and SF_6 is:-

(a) All S – F bond lengths in SF_6 are identical.

(b) All I – F bond lengths in IF_7 are identical

(c) All P – Cl bond lengths in PCl_5 are identical

(d) In SF_6 two S – F bonds are shorter than rest four S – F bonds

Q.21 Which will have regular octahedral shape?

(a) XeF_6

(b) $ICl_6^{(-)}$

(c) $IF_6^{(-)}$

(d) None of these

Q.22 Iso structural pair is:-

(a) $PO_4^{3(-)}$ & $NO_3^{(-)}$

(b) $NO_3^{(-)}$ & $ClO_3^{(-)}$

(c) $NH_4^{(+)}$ & XeF_4

(d) None of these

Q.23 The shape of gaseous $SnCl_2$ is:-

(a) Tetrahedral

(b) Linear

(c) Angular

(d) T - shaped

Q.24 Which of the following is planar:-

(a) $XeOF_4$

(b) XeO_3F

(c) XeF_4

(d) XeO_2F_2

Q.25 Which of the following are isoelectronic as well as isostructural

$NO_3^{(-)}$, $\qquad$ $CO_3^{2(-)}$, $\qquad$ $ClO_3^{(-)}$, $\qquad$ SO_3

(a) $NO_3^{(-)}$, $CO_3^{2(-)}$

(b) SO_3, $NO_3^{(-)}$

(c) $ClO_3^{(-)}$, $CO_3^{2(-)}$

(d) $CO_3^{2(-)}$, SO_3

Q.26 Correct order of strength of covalent bond is:-

(a) $sp^2 - sp^2 > sp^3 - sp^3 > sp - sp$

(b) $sp - sp > sp^2 - sp^2 > sp^3 - sp^3$

(c) $sp^3 - sp^3 > sp^2 - sp^2 > sp - sp$

(d) $sp^2 - sp^2 > sp^2 - sp^2 > sp^3 - sp^3$

Q.27 In which of the following cases bond angle is maximum.

(a) $(CN)_2$

(b) BF_3

(c) BrF_3

(d) $NH_4^{(+)}$

Q.28 In which of the following case each carbon atom is sp hybridized.

(a) CH_2CO

(b) $C_2(CN)_4$

(c) C_3O_2

(d) both (b) and (c)

Q.29 $C - C$ bond in $CH_3 - CF_3$ undergoes homolytic dissociation the hybridization on two resulting carbon atoms is / are:-

(a) sp^2, sp^3

(b) sp^3 both

(c) sp^2 both

(d) sp^2, sp^2

Q.30 In which of the following pair both the species has trigonal planar geometry.

(a) BF_3 & NH_3

(b) BF_3 & PCl_3

(c) BF_3 and IF_3

(d) None of these

Q.31 The type of orbital not used by chlorine in ClF_3.

(a) p_x

(b) d_{z^2}

(c) p_z

(d) $d_{x^2 - y^2}$

Q.32 The type of orbital not used by Xe in XeF_6 is

(a) $d_{x^2 - y^2}$

(b) d_{z^2}

(c) d_{xy}

(d) p_z

Q.33 The number of lone pairs on Xe in XeF_4, XeO_3 and XeF_2 are respectively.

(a) 2, 1, 3

(b) 3, 1, 2

(c) 2, 2, 1

(d) 2, 1, 2

Q.34 Which among the following contains longest $P - Cl$ bond?

(a) PCl_3F_2

(b) PF_3Cl_2

(c) PF_4Cl

(d) PCl_5

Q.35 XeO_3 is not isostructural with

(a) NH_3

(b) $CH_3^{(-)}$

(c) ClF_3

(d) both (a) & (b)

Q.36 The linear structure is not assumed by

(a) $SnCl_2$

(b) $NO_2^{(+)}$

(c) HCN

(d) CS_2

Q.37 Which of the following species contains two lone pair and two bond pair around central atom?

(a) CO_2

(b) H_2O

(c) NH_3

(d) BF_3

Q.38 Planar structure is shown by:-

(a) $CO_3^{2(-)}$

(b) BCl_3

(c) $N(SiH_3)_3$

(d) All the above

Q.39 Using VSEPR theory, predict the species having square pyramidal shape:-

(a) XeF_4

(b) BrF_5

(c) SF_4

(d) SO_3

Q.40 The central atom assumes sp^3 hybridisation:-

(a) $S_2O_3^{(2-)}$

(b) SO_3

(c) BF_3

(d) $NO_3^{(-)}$

Q.41 The hybridization of Ag in a $[Ag(NH_3)_2]^{(+)}$ is:-

(a) sp

(b) sp^2

(c) sp^3

(d) dsp^2

Q.42 Which of the following is planar?

(a) XeO_4

(b) XeO_3F

(c) XeO_2F_2

(d) XeF_4

Q.43 In which of the following bond angle is maximum?

(a) NH_3

(b) $NH_4^{(+)}$

(c) PCl_3

(d) SCl_2

Q.44 Among the following, the pair in which the two species are not isostructural, is

(a) SiF_4, SF_4

(b) $IO_3^{(-)}, XeO_3$

(c) $BH_4^{(-)}, NH_4^{(+)}$

(d) $PF_6^{(-)}, SF_6$

Q.45 Maximum number of atoms present in one plane in $PF_2(CH_3)_3$ are

(a) 3

(b) 5

(c) 4

(d) 7

Q.46 Which one of the following compounds has sp^2 hybridization?

(a) CO_2

(b) SO_2

(c) N_2O

(d) CO

Q.47 Which of the following are isoelectronic and isostructural $NO_3^{(-)}, CO_3^{2-}, ClO_3^{(-)}$ & SO_3

(a) $NO_3^{(-)}, CO_3^{-2}$

(b) $SO_3, NO_3^{(-)}$

(c) $ClO_3^{(-)}, CO_3^{-2}$

(d) CO_3^{-2}, SO_3

Q.48 In which one of the following pairs, molecules/ions have similar shape?

(a) CCl_4 and $CH_3CH_2^{(-)}$

(b) NH_3 and BF_3

(c) BF_3 and $CH_3^{(+)}$

(d) CO_2 and H_2O

Q.49 Which are the species in which sulphur undergoes sp^3 hybridization?

(1) SF_4

(2) SCl_2

(3) SO_4^{2-}

(4) H_2S

Select the correct answer using the code given below:-

(a)　1 and 2

(b)　2, 3 and 4

(c)　1, 3 and 4

(d)　1, 2 and 3

Q.50　Which of the following species have undistorted octahedral structures?

(1)　SF_6

(2)　$PF_6^{(-)}$

(3)　SiF_6^{2-}

(4)　XeF_6

(a)　1, 3 and 4

(b)　1, 2 and 3

(c)　1, 2 and 4

(d)　2, 3 and 4

Q.51　Consider the following molecules or ions.

(i)　Chloroform

(ii)　$NH_4^{(+)}$

(iii)　SO_4^{2-}　　　　(iv)　$ClO_4^{(-)}$

(v)　$H_3O^{(+)}$

sp^3 hybridization is involved in

(a)　(i), (ii), (v) only

(b)　(i), (ii) only

(c)　(i), (ii), (iii), (iv)

(d)　(i), (ii), (iii), (iv), (v)

Q.52　The number of lone pairs on Xe in XeF_2, XeF_4 and XeO_2F_2 respectively are:-

(a)　3, 2, 1

(b)　2, 4, 6

(c)　1, 2, 3

(d)　6, 4, 2

Q.53　The correct order of bond angles (smallest first) in H_2S, NH_3, BF_3 and SiH_4 is:-

(a)　$H_2S < SiH_4 < NH_3 < BF_3$

(b)　$NH_3 < H_2S < SiH_4 < BF_3$

(c)　$H_2S < NH_3 < SiH_4 < BF_3$

(d)　$H_2S < NH_3 < BF_3 < SiH_4$

Q.54　In which of the following compounds will the bond angle be maximum?

(a)　NH_3

(b)　Al_2Cl_6

(c)　PCl_5 (solid)

(d)　$SnCl_2$

Q.55　Which of the following two are isostructural?

(a)　XeF_2, $IF^{(-)}$

(b)　NH_3, BF_3

(c)　$HCO_3^{(-)}$, SO_2

(d)　PCl_5, IF_5

Q.56　Which of the following species has a linear shape?

(a)　$NO_2^{(+)}$

(b)　O_3

(c)　$NO_2^{(-)}$

(d)　SO_2

Q.57　What is the hybridization state of the central atom in the conjugate base $H_3O^{(+)}$ ion?

(a)　sp

(b)　sp^2

(c)　sp^3

(d)　dsp^2

Q.58　Which one of the following is a planar molecule?

(a)　NH_3

(b)　SF_4

(c)　Na_2CO_3

(d)　PBr_3

Q.59　Which one of the following molecules has the smallest bond angle?

(a)　H_2O

(b)　NH_3

(c)　H_2Se

(d)　H_2S

Q.60 Which of the following is a linear molecule?

(a) SO_2

(b) $XeOF_2$

(c) $ICl_2^{(+)}$

(d) $BeCl_2$

Q.61 Which of the following statement applies to ClF_3?

I. Geometrical arrangement is pyramidal

II. The molecule is almost T shaped

III. F – Cl – F bond angle is exactly 90°

(a) I and II

(b) II and III

(c) only I

(d) only II

Q.62 Which shape is associated with $ClF_4^{(-)}$ ion?

(a) Tetrahedral

(b) Square planar

(c) T-shape

(d) Square pyramid

Q.63 Among the following the pair in which two species are not iso structure is:-

(a) $Na_2S_2O_3$ and Na_2SO_3

(b) $IO_3^{(-)}$ and XeO_3

(c) SO_4^{2-} and $NH_4^{(+)}$

(d) $I_3^{(-)}$ and $ICl_2^{(-)}$

Q.64 The bond angle around 'S' in H_2S molecule is

(a) $> H_2O$

(b) $< H_2O$ but $> H_2Se$

(c) $> NH_3$

(d) $> H_2O$ as well as NH_3

Matrix match: -

Q.65

Column - I		Column - II
(A) $I_3^{(-)}$	(p)	2 non bonding electron pair around central atom
(B) $H_3O^{(+)}$	(q)	Pyramidal
(C) XeF_2	(r)	Linear
(D) BrF_3	(s)	One lone pair

Q.66

Column - I		Column - II
(A) XeF_6	(p)	Regular structure
(B) $XeF_5^{(-)}$	(q)	Distorted structure
(C) XeF_4	(r)	Two lone pair on central atom
(D) BrF_3	(s)	One lone pair on central atom

Q.67

Hybridisation		Orbitals involved
(A) sp^2	(p)	p_y
(B) sp	(q)	p_z
(C) dsp^2	(r)	$d_{x^2-y^2}$
(D) sp^3d	(s)	d_{z^2}

Q.68

Molecule/ ion		Hybridisation
(A) $Cr_2O_7^{2-}$	(p)	sp^3
(B) MnO_4^-	(q)	sp^2
(C) K_2SO_4	(r)	sp
(D) K_2SO_3	(s)	sp^3d

Q.69

Column - I		Column - II	
(A)	SF_6	(p)	Two axial bonds
(B)	SF_4	(q)	Four equatorial bonds
(C)	XeF_4	(r)	Three equatorial bonds
(D)	PCl_5	(s)	Non planar
		(t)	Two lone pair on central atom

Q.70

Column - I		Column - II	
(A)	S_8	(p)	Exists in dimeric form
(B)	$BeCl_2$ (solid)	(q)	Exists in polymeric form
(C)	P_4 (white)	(r)	sp^3 hybridisation
(D)	$AlCl_3$	(s)	Crown shape

Q.71

Column - I		Column - II	
(A)	NH_3	(p)	Lone pair on sp^3 hybridised atom
(B)	H_2O	(q)	Lone pair on sp^2 hybridised atom
(C)	C_6H_6	(r)	sp^2 hybridised carbon
(D)	Acetylene	(s)	sp hybridised carbon
		(t)	$\mu = 0$

Q.72

Column - I		Column - II	
(A)	PF_3	(p)	Covalent bond
(B)	NH_4Cl	(q)	Dative bond
(C)	$H_3O^{\oplus}$	(r)	δ- bond
(D)	H_2SO_4	(s)	Ionic bond
		(t)	Back bonding

Q.73

Column - I		Column - II	
(A)	S_2F_2	(p)	$\mu = 0$
(B)	H_2O_2	(q)	$\mu \neq 0$
(C)	Ethene	(r)	sp^2 hybridised atom
(D)	CH_3—$CH = CH$—CH_3 (cis)	(s)	Back bonding

Q.74

Column - I		Column - II	
(A)	$XeF_5^{\ominus}$	(p)	Angular shape
(B)	XeF_6	(q)	Pyramidal shape
(C)	$ClF_4^{\ominus}$	(r)	Planar shape
(D)	$BrF_2^{\oplus}$	(s)	One non bonding electron pair on central atom
		(t)	See saw shape

HINTS & SOLUTIONS

SUBJECTIVE EXERCISE

EXERCISE 4.1

1.   (i) BF_3 (120°)   (ii) C_2H_6 (120°)   (iii) CO_2 (180°)   (iv) PCl_5 (90°, 120°)

2.   (a) sp^3d (b) sp^3d^2 (c) sp^3 (d) sp^3d

  (e) sp^3 (f) sp^3d (g) sp^3, sp^3d^2 (h) sp^3

  (i) sp^3d^2 (j) sp^3d^3 (k) sp^3 (l) sp^3d

  (m) sp^3d^3 (n) sp^2 (o) sp^3 (p) sp^3

  (q) sp^3

3. Due to less electronegativity of hydrogen atom, in phosphorous excitation of 3s electron to 3d sub shell does not occur

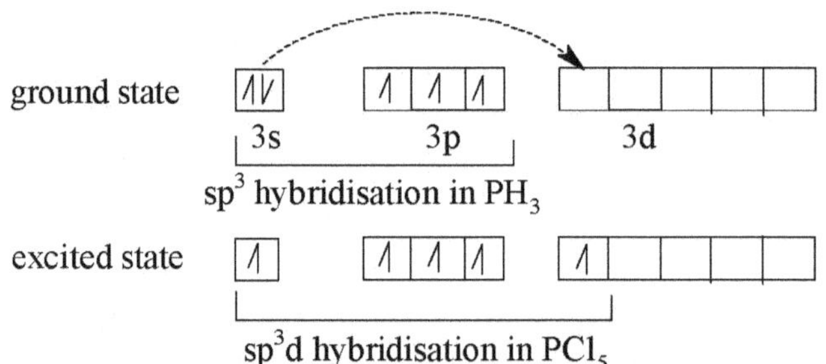

4. For the formation of NCl_5, N should exhibit sp^3d hybridization but N can not show sp^3d hybridization as it does not contain d orbital

5. Si possesses empty d orbital in which Si can receive lone pair of electrons donated by H_2O molecules during hydrolysis which is not possible in CCl_4 as carbon does not contain empty 'd' orbital.

EXERCISE 4.2

1.   (i) $H_2O > H_2Se > H_2Te$ (ii) $NCl_3 > NH_3 > NF_3$ (iii) $CH_4 > PH_3 > AsH_3$

  (iv) $BF_3 > NH_3$ (v) $(CH_3)_3N < (SiH_3)_3N$

2. Due to back bonding negative charge is delocalized in $CCl_3^{(-)}$ & hence, electrons of negative charge are less available for protonation (reaction with H^+ or acid)

3. (a) square planar   (b) T-shaped   (c) Bent   (d) Linear

   (e) Linear   (f) Pentagonal planar   (g) T-shaped

OBJECTIVE EXERCISE

1. (b)   2. (a)   3. (c) It has two axial P–F bonds   4. (a)   5. (d)   6. (c)

7. (a) In BF_3 back donation takes place which reduces electron deficiency of boron

8. (d)   9. (d)   10. (b)   11. (d)   12. (b)   13. (a) $O=C=C=C=O$

14. (d) $Mg_2^{+2}[\overset{-1}{C}\equiv C-\overset{-3}{C}]$ 15. (b)   16. (b)   17. (c)   18. (c)

19. (c)   20. (a)   21. (d)   22. (d)

23. (c) [Sn with two lone pairs, bonded to Cl and Cl]   24. (c)   25. (a)   26. (b)

27. (a) $N\equiv C-C\equiv N$ bond angle $180°$

28. (d) $N\equiv C-C\equiv C-C\equiv N$ $O=C=C=C=O$

29. (a) 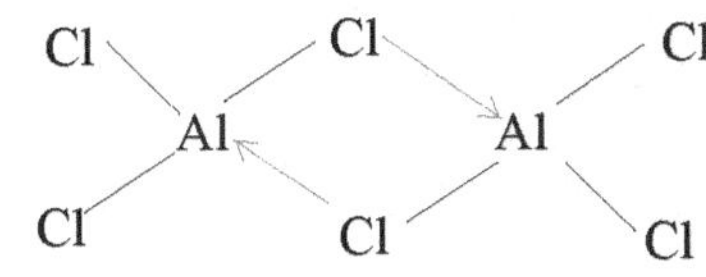 $\overset{\bullet}{CH_3}\ (sp^2)\ +\ \overset{\bullet}{CF_3}\ (sp^3)$

30. (d)   31. (d)   32. (c)   33. (a)   34. (d) as it contains two axial P–Cl bonds

35. (c) Except ClF_3 rest all are pyramidal where as ClF_3 has T-shape   36. (a)   37. (b)

38. (d)   39. (b)   40. (a)   41. (a)   42. (d)   43. (b)   44. (a)   45. (d)

46. (b)   47. (a)   48. (c)   49. (b)   50. (b)   51. (d)   52. (a)   53. (c)

54. (b) In Al_2Cl_6 aluminium is sp^2 hybridized & it occurs as:-

Cl   Cl   Cl
   Al   Al
Cl   Cl   Cl

55. (a)   56. (a)   57. (c)   58. (c) The 'C' of sodium carbonate is sp^2 hybridized

59. (c)   60. (d)   61. (d)   62. (b)   63. (a)   64. (b)

65. A–r   B–q,s   C–r   D–p   66. A–q,s   B–r,p   C–p,r   D–q,r

67. A–p,q   B–p,q   C–p,q,r   D–p,q,s   68. A–p   B–p   C–p   D–q

69. A–s   B–p,s   C–t   D–p,r,s   70. A–r,s   B–q,r   C–q,r   D–p,r

71. A–p   B–p   C–r,t   D–s,t   72. A–p,t   B–p,q,s   C–p,q   D–p,q

73. A–q,s   B–q   C–p,r   D–q,r   74. A–r   B–s   C–r   D–p

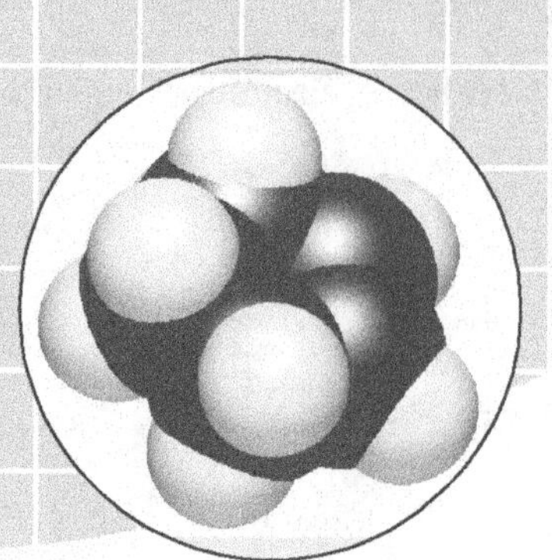

Polarization, Dipole Moment & Hydration Energy

5

We have studied ionic and covalent bonds in chapter - 02. Experiments revealed that no bond is 100% ionic or covalent. Covalent compounds have some ionic character and vice - versa.

In any ionic compound covalent character can be observed by the help of polarization. On the other hand ionic nature in covalent compounds can be observed by either of the two ways.

- Henry - Smith method
- Dipole moment

➤5.1 Henry - Smith method

% ionic character $= 16\Delta + 3.5\,\Delta^2$ ....(1)

Where Δ = Electronegativity difference of the covalently bonded atoms

For example in HF % ionic character is found to be 43 %

$X_F = 4$ $X_H = 2.1$

$$\begin{aligned} \text{% ionic character} \ &= 16(4-2.1) + 3.5(4-2.1)^2 \\ &= 30.40 + 12.63 = 43.03 \end{aligned}$$

In equation (1) Pauling electro negativity (X) is used

Note : % ionic character of homonuclear diatomic molecules like O_2, N_2 and H_2 can not be explained using Henry - Smith method because in these cases electro negativity difference is zero. Their % ionic character can be observed experimentally. For e.g. in H_2 % ionic character is 2% which is developed due to instantaneous induced dipole moment.

➤5.2 Dipole moment

When electro negativity difference between covalently bonded atoms is large shared electron pair is shifted towards more electronegative element and thus, dipole is generated

$$A^{\delta^+} \longrightarrow\!\!\bullet\bullet\, B^{\delta^-} \qquad X_B > X_A$$

Such molecules are called polar molecules.

$$H^{\delta^+}\longrightarrow\!\!\bullet\bullet\, F^{\delta^-} \qquad\qquad F\longrightarrow\!\!\bullet\bullet\, F$$
polar molecule   non polar molecule

Strength of dipole can be measured in terms of dipole moment (μ) which is defined as:-

(1) **"It is equal to the product of the electronic charge and distance 'd' between negative and positive electric centers in the dipole"**

$$\vec{\mu} = q \times d$$

or

$$\vec{\mu} = q \times \text{bond length.}$$

(2) **Dipole moment is a vector quantity it has direction from +ve to −ve**

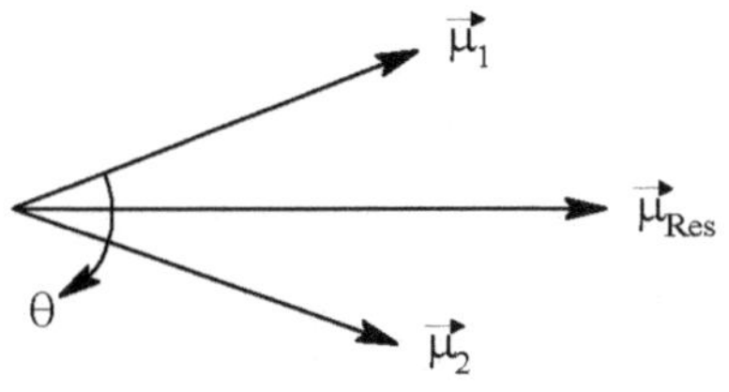

$$= \sqrt{\mu_1^2 + \mu_2^2 + 2\mu_1\mu_2 \cos\theta}$$

$$\vec{\mu}_{Res} \propto \cos\theta \propto \frac{1}{\theta}$$

(3) **Units of dipole moment**

M.K.S $=$ Coulomb meter

C.G.S $=$ e.s.u. cm

Another unit of dipole moment is Debye (D)

1 Debye (D) $= 0.33 \times 10^{-29} \, C \times m$

1 D $= 10^{-18} \, e.s.u \times cm$

1 unit charge $= 1.6 \times 10^{-19} \, c$ or $4.8 \times 10^{-10} \, e.s.u$

(4) **Application of dipole moment**

(a) With its help we can find out % ionic character in a covalent compound.

% ionic character $=$ (observed $\mu \times 100$) / Calculated μ

For example :- Dipole moment of HCl is found to be 1.03 D Bond length of H — Cl bond is 1.27 Å Hence, by the help of these values we can calculate % ionic character in HCl molecule as follows:-

$$\overset{\delta^+}{H} \text{———————} \overset{\delta^-}{Cl}$$

$q = 1 \text{ unit} = 4.8 \times 10^{-10} \, e.s.u.$

$\mu \, (\text{Calculated}) = 4.8 \times 10^{-10} \times 1.27 \times 10^{-8} = 6.10 \times 10^{-18} \, e.s.u. \, cm$

$= 6.10 \times 10^{-18} / 10^{-18} = 6.10 \, D$

% ionic character $= (1.03 \times 100) / 6.10 = 16.89\%$

(b) If the dipole moment of a species is known then its structure can be predicted easily

For eq. Experimental μ of CO_2 is zero, for this reason its shape is linear & not bent

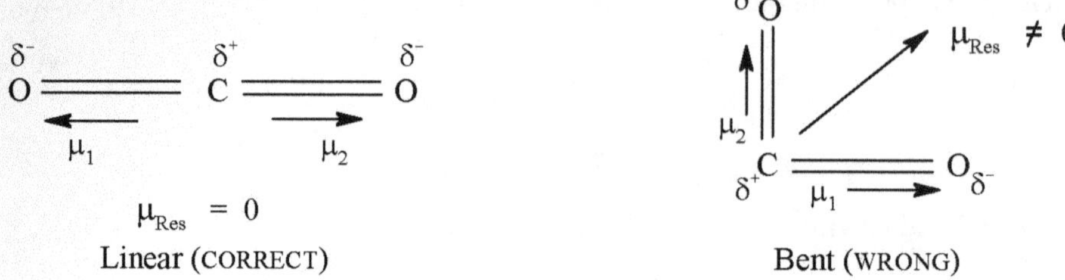

$\mu_{Res} = 0$

Linear (CORRECT)   Bent (WRONG)

Similarly μ_{exp} of BF_3 is zero, thus it acquires triangular planar shape

$\mu_{Res} = 0$

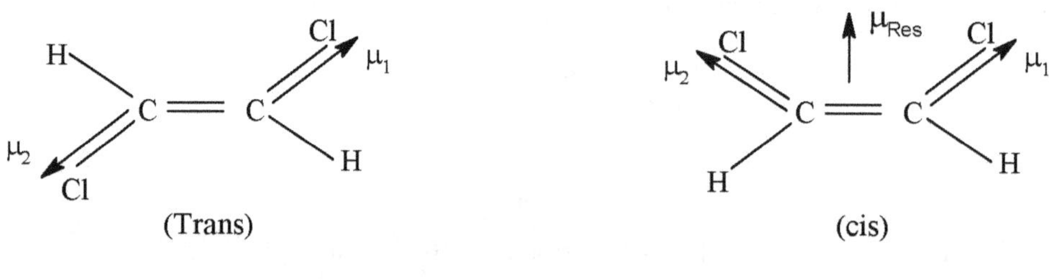

(c) By the help of μ geometrical isomers can be distinguished. In general μ of cis form is found to be greater than that of trans form.

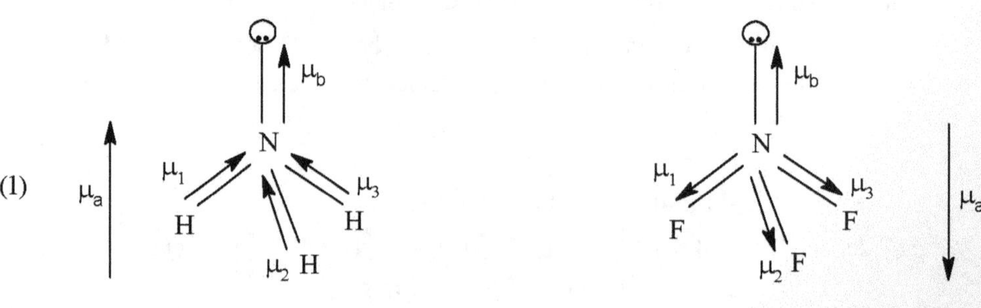

(Trans)   (cis)

$\mu(cis) \; > \; \mu(trans)$

Let us see some miscellaneous examples

(1)

$$\mu_{Res} = \mu_a + \mu_b \qquad\qquad \mu_{Res} = \mu_a \sim \mu_b$$

Here μ_a = Resultant of μ_1, μ_2 and μ_3. From above diagrams it is clear that

μ of $NH_3 \; > \; \mu$ of NF_3

(2)

$$\theta = 60°$$
(A)

$$\theta = 120°$$
(B)

$$\theta = 180°$$
(C)

As we know that resultant dipole moment is reciprocal to 'θ' therefore, $\mu_A > \mu_B > \mu_C$

(3)　　Since CH_3 is an electron repelling group therefore, $\mu_C > \mu_B > \mu_A$

$$\theta = 120°$$
(A)

$$\theta = 60°$$
(B)

$$\theta = 0°$$
(C)

➤ 5.3 Polarization (Covalent character in ionic compound)

(1)　　In an ionic compound, covalent character can be observed with the help of polarization. When cation and anion come close to each other, they form ionic bonds. In isolated conditions both cation and anion are spherical and symmetrical in shape but as they come closer to each other, the electron cloud of anion is attracted by the charge of cation, whereas, electron cloud of cation is attracted by the nucleus of anion. This attraction develops distortion in electron cloud. This distortion is negligible in cation owing to its small size and electron cloud of cation is strongly bonded to its nucleus but electron cloud of anion is loosely bonded to its nucleus owing to its large size which results in to distortion in the size of anion by cation. Thus polarization of anion is defined as

"The distortion in electron cloud of anion by cation and the tendency of cation to distort anion is called polarizing power of cation or ionic potential (ϕ) or degree of covalency or charge density."

(2)　　It must be noted that polarization is favourable if both anion and cation are of incomparable size so that cation can easily polarize anion.

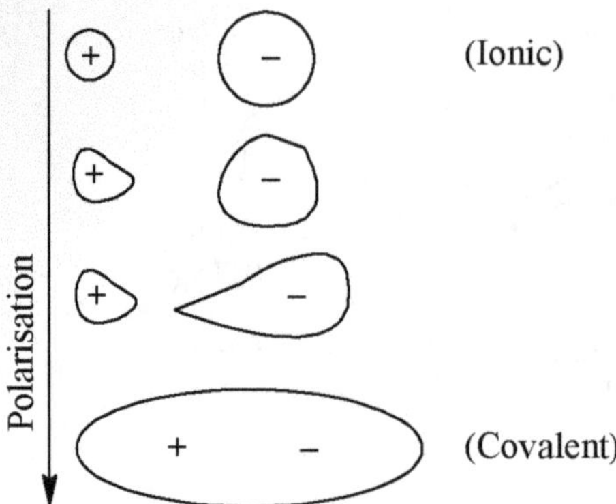

Polarization	$\propto$	Covalent character
Polarization	$\propto$	1 / Ionic character
Polarization	$\propto$	1 / Thermal stability
Polarization	$\propto$	1 / Solubility in polar solvents like water

(3)   **Fajan rule** - Fajan suggested some rules for effective polarization.

➢   Cation should be small and anion should be large in size

➢   Both cation and anion should have high charge

➢   Cations having pseudo inert configurations have more polarizing power than the cations having inert and non inert configurations.

Order of Polarizing power of cations is:-

Pseudo configuration > non - inert configuration > inert configuration

On the basis of polarizing power cations can be categorized in three ways.

(a)   **Cation with inert gas configuration** - These cations have 8 electrons in their valence shell ($ns^2 np^6$)

   For e.g. Na^+, Mg^{+2}, Al^{+3}, Ca^{+2} etc

(b)   **Cations with pseudo inert configuration** - The valence shell of these cations have 18 electrons. Their d sub shell is completely filled ($ns^2 np^6 nd^{10}$)

   For e.g. Zn^{+2} ($3d^{10}$), Cu+ ($3d^{10}$), Ag^+, Cd^{+2}, Hg^{+2} ………..etc

(c)   **Cations with non inert configuration** - These cations hold $20e^-$ in their valence shell. Their general electronic configuration is $ns^2 np^6 nd^{10} (n + 1)s^2$ or $(n-1)s^2 (n-1)p^6 (n-1)d^{10} ns^2$

   For e.g. Tl^+, Pb^{+2}, Bi^{+3}

For more details see inert pair effect

➢5.4 Application of polarization (Fajan rule) & lattice energy

(A) Covalent Character - If polarization increases, covalent character also increases and ionic character decreases

$$\text{Pseudo inert gas configuration} \left\{ \begin{array}{ccc} CuCl & > & NaCl \\ AgCl & > & KCl \\ CdCl_2 & > & CaCl_2 \end{array} \right\} \text{Inert gas configuration}$$

(More Covalent)   (Less Covalent)

$$PdCl_2 \quad > \quad CaCl_2$$
(Non inert configuration)   (Inert configuration)

(B) Nature of Oxides

MO (Base)   + $H^{(+)}$ (acid) $\longrightarrow$ MOH

$\phi \quad \propto \quad$ 1 / Basic character $\propto$ acidic character

On moving from top to bottom in any group the size of cation increases, thus, 'ϕ' decreases and the basic character increases.

$Li_2O < Na_2O < K_2O < Rb_2O < Cs_2O$

(Less basic)   (More basic)

$MgO < CaO < SrO < BaO$

Similarly   ZnO   (Pseudo inert configuration) is less basic than MgO (Inert gas configuration)

$ZnO \quad < \quad PbO \quad < \quad MgO$

(Pseudo)   (Non inert)   (Inert)

➢ All oxides of 's' block elements are basic in nature except BeO which shows amphoteric nature

➢ Oxides of non metal are acidic in nature except N_2O, NO and CO which are neutral.

➢ On moving from left to right along a period, acidic character of non metal oxides increases.

$$MgO \quad < \quad P_2O_5 \quad < \quad SO_3$$
(Less acidic)   (More acidic)

$$\overset{+2}{MnO} \qquad\qquad \overset{+4}{MnO_2} \qquad\qquad \overset{+7}{Mn_2O_7}$$
(Basic)   (amphoteric)   (acidic)

$\longrightarrow$ ϕ increases

➢ $\sqrt{\phi} \quad = \quad$ 2.2 to 3.2   amphoteric oxide

$\sqrt{\phi} \quad < \quad$ 2.2   Basic oxide

$\sqrt{\phi} \quad > \quad$ 3.2   acidic oxide

Amphoteric oxides - As_2O_3, Sb_2O_3, Bi_2O_3, GeO, ZnO, Al_2O_3, BeO, Cr_2O_3, Ga_2O_3, PbO, SnO

(C) Colour or intensity of Colour in Compounds -

Polarization $\propto$ Intensity of Colour.

More polarization increases distortion in electron cloud, which makes electronic transition easy and compound seemed to be coloured.

AgCl	AgBr	AgI	Ag_2S
(White)	(Light yellow)	(Dark yellow)	(Black)

(D) Thermal stability - Here we are discussing thermal stabilities of metal carbonates, sulphates, nitrate, bicarbonates and halides

(1) Metal Carbonates -

$$MCO_3 \xrightarrow{\Delta} MO + CO_2 \uparrow$$

$$\phi \propto \text{Polarisation power} \propto \frac{1}{\text{Thermal Stability}}$$

On moving from top to bottom in any group, the size of cation increases and thermal stability increases

$$BeCO_3 < MgCO_3 < CaCO_3 < SrCO_3 < BaCO_3$$

(More thermally stable)

Thus, to dissociate $BaCO_3$ high temperature is needed, on the other hand $BeCO_3$ needs low temperature for dissociation.

Among alkali metals Li has smallest size hence maximum polarization takes place in Li_2CO_3 due to incomparable sizes of Li^+ (Very small size) and CO_3^{2-} (large size)

Li_2CO_3	Na_2CO_3	K_2CO_3	Rb_2CO_3	Cs_2CO_3

More polarisation
More covalent
Thermally unstable

less chance of plarisation because of comparable sizes of M^+ and CO_3^{2-}

$$Li_2CO_3 < Na_2CO_3 < K_2CO_3 < Rb_2CO_3 < Cs_2CO_3$$

Increasing thermal stability

$$Li_2CO_3 \xrightarrow{\Delta} Li_2O + CO_2$$

Na_2CO_3, K_2CO_3, Rb_2CO_3 and Cs_2CO_3 are ionic in nature due to poor polarization hence these carbonates are thermally stable and do not easily decompose on heating

(2) Metal sulphate -

$$MSO_4 \xrightarrow{T < 1073 \ K} MO + SO_3 \uparrow$$

$$MSO_4 \xrightarrow{T > 1073 \ K} MO + SO_2 \uparrow + 1/2 \ O_2 \uparrow$$

$$\phi \propto \text{Polarizing power} \propto \text{covalent character}$$

$$\propto \frac{1}{\text{Thermal stability}}$$

On moving from top to bottom in any group, the size of cation increases and thermal stability increases

$$BeSO_4 < MgSO_4 < CaSO_4 < SrSO_4 < BaSO_4$$

(Less thermally stable)   (More thermally stable)

Among alkali metal sulphates only Li_2SO_4 is thermally unstable

$$Li_2SO_4 \qquad Na_2SO_4 \qquad K_2SO_4 \qquad Rb_2SO_4 \qquad Cs_2SO_4$$

More polarisation
More covalent
Thermally unstable

less chance of polarisation because of comparable sizes of M^+ and SO_4^{2-}

$$Li_2SO_4 < Na_2SO_4 < K_2SO_4 < Rb_2SO_4 < Cs_2SO_4$$

Increasing thermal stability

$$Li_2SO_4 \xrightarrow{\Delta} Li_2O + SO_3$$

Na_2SO_4, K_2SO_4, Rb_2SO_4, Cs_2SO_4, are ionic in nature due to poor polarization hence, these sulphates are thermally stable and do not easily decompose on heating.

Green vitriol is an exceptional case

$$FeSO_4 . 7H_2O \xrightarrow{\Delta} FeSO_4 + 7H_2O$$

$$2FeSO_4 \xrightarrow{\Delta} Fe_2O_3 + SO_2 + SO_3$$

---

(3)   **Metal nitrate** - Metal nitrate produce metal oxide and NO_2 on heating

$$Metal\ nitrate \xrightarrow{\Delta} NO_2 + Metal\ oxide$$

$$Mg(NO_3)_2 \xrightarrow{\Delta} MgO + 2NO_2 + 1/2O_2$$

$$2LiNO_3 \xrightarrow{\Delta} Li_2O + 2NO_2 + 1/2O_2$$

But nitrates of Na^+, K^+, Rb^+, Rb^+ and Cs^+ give following reactions-

$$2MNO_3 \xrightarrow{\Delta} 2MNO_2 + O_2$$

At high temperature MNO_2 further undergoes dissociation as -

$$2MNO_2 \xrightarrow{\Delta} M_2O + N_2 + 3/2O_2$$

For e.g.

$$2NaNO_3 \xrightarrow[-O_2]{\Delta} 2NaNO_2 \xrightarrow[\text{High T}]{\Delta} Na_2O + N_2 + 3/2O_2$$

Polarization $\propto$ Covalent character

$$\propto \frac{1}{\text{Thermal stability}}$$

$$LiNO_3 < NaNO_3 < KNO_3 < RbNO_3 < CsNO_3$$
$$Be(NO_3)_2 < Mg(NO_3)_2 < Ca(NO_3)_2 < Sr(NO_3)_2 < Ba(NO_3)_2$$

$\longrightarrow$

Increasing thermal stability

Oxides of native metals (Ag, Hg, Pt & Au) are thermally unstable & give O_2 along with metal on heating.

$$Ag_2O \xrightarrow{\Delta} 2Ag + 1/2O_2$$

---

(4) **Metal bicarbonates** - Metal bicarbonate dissociates on heating and get converted in to carbonates

$$MHCO_3 \xrightarrow{\Delta} \text{Metal Carbonate} + H_2O + CO_2$$

For e.g.

$$2LiHCO_3 \xrightarrow{\Delta} Li_2CO_3 + H_2O + CO_2$$
$$\downarrow \Delta$$
$$Li_2O + CO_2$$

But $NaHCO_3$, $KHCO_3$, $RbHCO_3$ and $CsHCO_3$ dissociate as -

$$2NaHCO_3 \xrightarrow{\Delta} Na_2CO_3 + H_2O + CO_2$$
$$\downarrow \Delta$$
$$\text{no reaction}$$

In $LiHCO_3$ polarization occurs effectively due to uncomparable sizes of Li^+ (small) & HCO_3^- (big). Thus, due to better polarization $LiHCO_3$ is more covalent in comparison to rest bicarbonates of alkali metals. Due to more polarization $LiHCO_3$ exists in liquid state

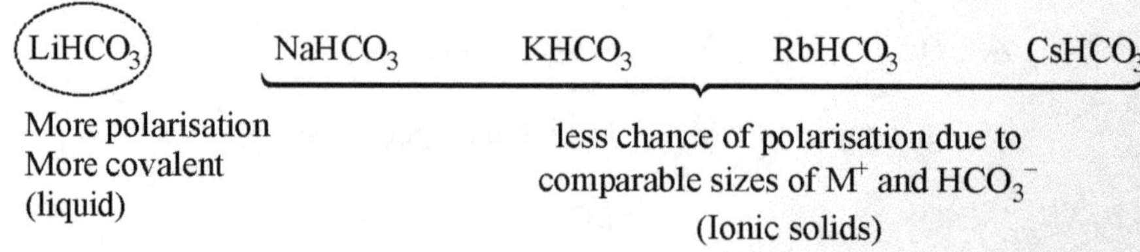

All bicarbonates of alkaline earth metals exist in liquid form due to effective polarization. These metal cations are smaller than the cations of alkali metals and they have +2 charge. This is responsible for effective polarization in bi carbonates of alkali earth metals

$$Be(HCO_3)_2 \qquad Mg(HCO_3)_2 \qquad Ca(HCO_3)_2 \qquad Sr(HCO_3)_2 \qquad Ba(HCO_3)_2$$

(Exist in liquid state)

$$\phi \quad \propto \quad \text{Polarizing power} \quad \propto \quad \frac{1}{\text{Thermal stability}}$$

$$LiHCO_3 < NaHCO_3 < KHCO_3 < RbHCO_3 < CsHCO_3$$
$$Be(HCO_3)_2 < Mg(HCO_3)_2 < Ca(HCO_3)_2 < Sr(HCO_3)_2 < Ba(HCO_3)_2$$

Increasing thermal Stability

(5) **Metal halide** - Thermal stability of metal halides is checked by lattice energy and not by polarization

Lattice energy $\propto$ Thermal stability of metal halide

Lattice energy $\propto$ charge on cation and anion

$$\propto \quad \frac{1}{(r^+)+(r^-)}$$

KF > KCl > KBr > KI

LiF > NaF > KF > RbF > CsF

Decreasing order of Thermal stability

In the same way metal nitrides and metal oxides can be arranged in order of thermal stability.

$$Li_3N > Na_3N > K_3N$$
$$Li_2O > Na_2O > K_2O > Rb_2O$$

Decreasing lattice energy

Decreasing Thermal stability

As we know, lattice energy is proportional to the product of ionic charges therefore, thermal stability increases with increase in ionic charges

$$L.E. \quad = \quad K\, q_1\, q_2 / r_2$$

$$\begin{array}{ccccc} +2\ -1 & & +2\ -2 & & +2\ -3 \\ MgF_2 & < & MgO & < & Mg_3N_2 \end{array}$$

$$q_1 q_2 = 2 \qquad q_1 q_2 = 4 \qquad q_1 q_2 = 6$$

Increasing lattice energy & Thermal stability

➤ 5.5 Hydration energy - (Solvation energy)

When a cation or an anion in the gaseous state reacts with a solvent in the liquid state, energy is liberated. This liberated energy is termed as solvation energy. When the solvent is water the liberated energy is called hydration energy.

$$Li^+ + H_2O \longrightarrow Li^+ + 124.4\,kcal/mol.$$
$$(g) \quad (l) \qquad\qquad (aq)$$

Water is a polar solvent $(\overset{\delta-}{HO}\!\!-\!\!\overset{\delta+}{H})$. A gaseous cation is attracted by the negative oxygen ends of the water molecules while the anion is attracted by the hydrogen ends. The greater the charge density (charge / surface area) of the ion the greater will be the interaction i.e. the greater will be the hydration energy.

Hydration $\quad\propto\quad$ Hydration energy $\quad\propto\quad$ 1 / size of ion

$\qquad\qquad\quad\propto\quad$ Charge on ion $\qquad\propto\quad$ size of hydrated ion

More is the hydration more will be the size of hydrated ion.

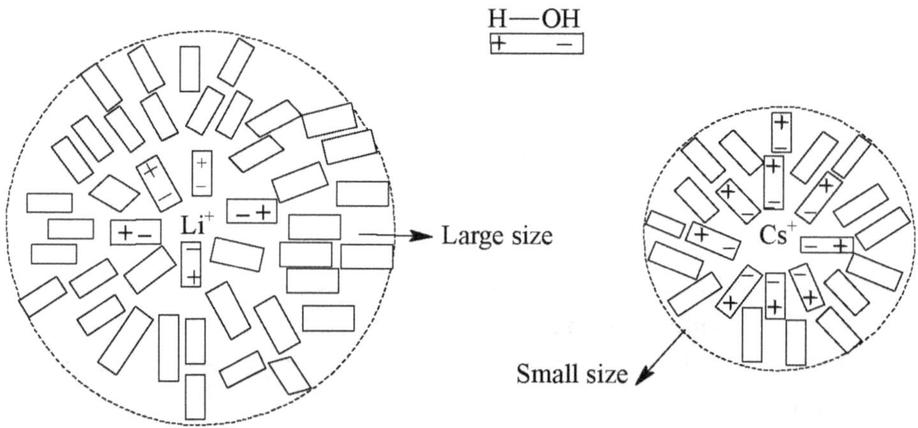

Since $Li^+(aq)$ is bigger in size in comparison to that of $Cs^+(aq)$ hence $Li^+(aq)$ will have less ionic mobility in comparison to $Cs^+(aq)$

Hydration $\quad\propto\quad$ 1 / ionic mobility

Interestingly there is a considerable difference in the hydration energy of $F^{(-)}$ and $K^{(+)}$ ions although they have the same ionic radius (1.36Å). This is due to the fact that $F^{(-)}$ interacts with small H atoms while K^+ interacts with much larger oxygen atom of water. More hydrogen atom can get around a $F^{(-)}$ ion compared to oxygen atoms around the $K^{(+)}$ ions

Ion	Hydration energy	Ion	Hydration energy
Li^+	− 124.4 kcal / mol	$F^{(-)}$	− 121 kcal / mol
Na^+	− 97	$Cl^{(-)}$	− 87
K+	− 77	$Br^{(-)}$	−80

➤ 5.6 Solubility of ionic compounds

It is very popular proverb that 'like dissolves like'. Means polar compounds dissolve in polar medium and non polar compound dissolve in non polar medium. For eq. NaCl is an ionic compound, it dissolves easily in polar medium like water but NaCl does not dissolve in benzene because benzene is a non polar solvent. Similarly, naphthalene ($C_{10}H_8$) is a non polar compound can easily dissolve in benzene but it is insoluble in water. Generally, we check solubility of compounds in water (an universal solvent)

There are three factors for dissolution of a compound in water.

➤ Compound is ionic and undergoes dissociation when dissolved in water to form aqueous ions

$$AB + H_2O \longrightarrow A^{(+)} + B^{(-)}$$
$$\text{(s)} \qquad\qquad\qquad \text{(aq)} \quad \text{(aq)}$$

➤ Compound forms hydrogen bond with water (Disused later in chapter - 07)

➤ The molecules of compound easily accommodate in free space present in water molecules

Here we shall discuss the solubility of ionic compound in water.

Key Point - Those students who have not studied thermodynamics are advised to study the portion written after solubility temperature curve.

When a solute dissolves in a solvent then the value of ΔG in the whole process is always negative ($\Delta G = -ve$) and the value of ΔS remains positive ($\Delta S = +ve$)

Solute + Solvent $\longrightarrow$ Solution or dissolution of solute

When solute is added in a solvent, the heat of dissolution (ΔH) will be +ve or −ve from Gibb's Helmholtz equation.

$$\Delta G = \Delta H - T\Delta S$$

If the value of ΔH is negative, then ΔG is −ve and compound can easily dissolve in solvent but if the value of ΔH is +ve, then to make ΔG negative $T\Delta S$ should have more value. For this we increase temperature in order to increase the value of $T\Delta S$ and ΔG would become −ve.

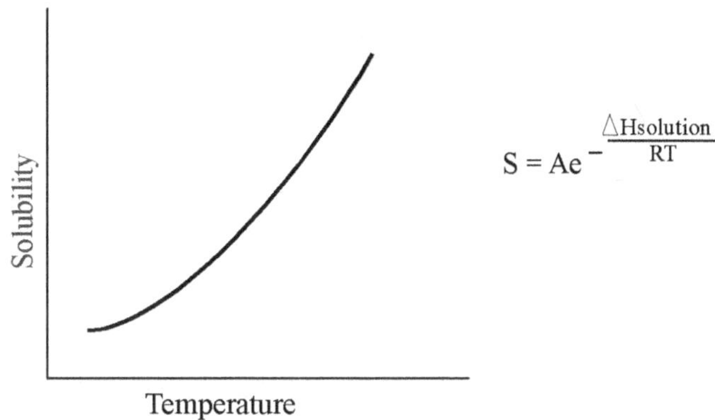

Therefore, on increasing temperature, solubility of a compound increases. Normally, the solubility of ionic compound in water depends on two factors.

➤ Polarization

➤ Lattice energy & hydration energy

As polarization increase, covalent character increases and ionic character decreases. Thus, ionic compounds show less solubility in water on increasing polarization.

Polarization $\propto$ Covalent character $\propto$ 1 / Ionic character

                    $\propto$ 1 / solubility in water

Lattice energy $\propto$ 1 / size of ions $\propto$ charge on ions

Hydration energy $\propto$ 1 / size of ions $\propto$ charge on ions

The factors affecting hydration energy & lattice energy are same. Thus, it is difficult to predict the exact solubility of ionic compound in water because-

Hydration energy (H.E) $\propto$ Solubility in water

Lattice energy (H.E) $\propto$ 1 / solubility in water

An ionic compound dissolves in water only when $|H.E| > |L.E|$

Here we are showing two cases to explain the solubility of the salts of alkali and alkaline earth metals in water

Case - I : When the size of anion is small or we can say if the sizes of both anion and cation are comparable (Like O^{-2}, S^{-2}, $OH^{(-)}$, $F^{(-)}$ & $Cl^{(-)}$ etc), then on moving from top to bottom in a group, there is apparent decrease of H.E and L.E but the decrease in L.E is found to be more than that of H.E and hence solubility of salts increase on moving down the group.

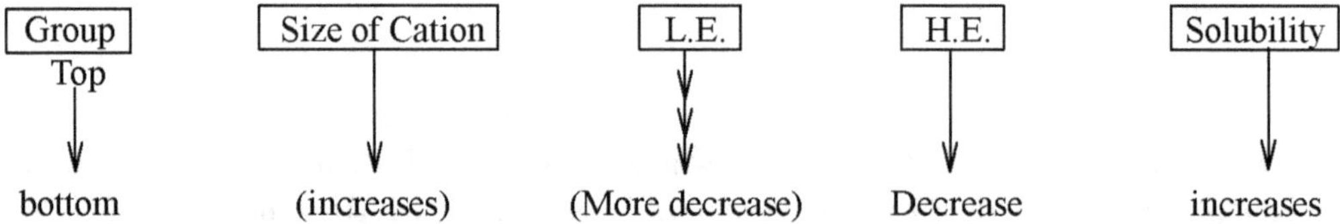

(Less soluble) LiCl < NaCl < KCl < RbCl < CsCl (More soluble)

(Less soluble) MgO < CaO < SrO < BaO (More soluble)

$Br^{(-)}$ & $I^{(-)}$ ions are not an example of this class because these ions have large sizes.

Case - II : When the size of anion is large, its hydration does not occur properly, thus, on moving down the group L.E. & H.E. both show decrease but decrease in H.E. is found to be greater than L.E. Hence solubility decreases.

For eg. SO_4^{-2}, CO_3^{2-}, $NO_3^{(-)}$, $Br^{(-)}$, $I^{(-)}$, PO_4^{3-}

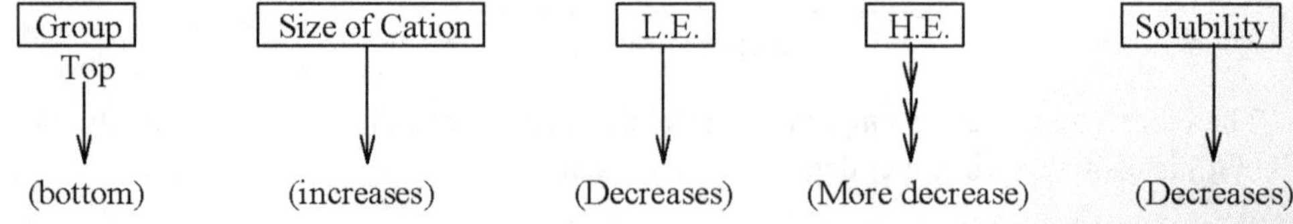

(More soluble)$MgSO_4$ > $CaSO_4$ > $SrSO_4$ > $BaSO_4$(Least soluble)

(More soluble)$NaNO_3$ > KNO_3 > $RbNO_3$ > $CsNO_3$(Least soluble)

Note: **-** Although the size of $HCO_3^{(-)}$ is large yet it is an example of Case - I. i.e. solubility of metal bicarbonates increases on moving down the group (we will discuss it in next chapter).

Let us clear these cases by taking some more examples (descending order of solubility)

$MgSO_3 > CaSO_3 > SrSO_3 > BaSO_3$ (Case - II)

$NaCl > NaBr > NaI$ (Polarization)

$NaBr > KBr > RbBr > CsBr$ (Case - II)

$AgF > AgCl > AgBr > AgI$ (Polarization)

$NaNO_3 > KNO_3 > RbNO_3 > CsNO_3$ (Case - II)

$Na_2O < K_2O < Rb_2O < Cs_2O$ (Case - I)

➤ 5.7 Some exceptional solubility order

$MgF_2 < CaF_2 < SrF_2 < BaF_2 < BeF_2$

$Li_2CO_3 < Na_2CO_3 < K_2CO_3 < Rb_2CO_3 < Cs_2CO_3$

$NaI > LiI > KI > RbI > CsI$

$LiCl > CsCl > RbCl > NaCl > KCl$

$BeX_2 > MgX_2 > CaX_2 > SrX_2 > BaX_2$ (X = Cl, Br, I)

$MgC_2O_4 < CaC_2O_4 < SrC_2O_4 < BaC_2O_4 < BeC_2O_4$

Subjective Exercise

Q.1 $SnCl_2$ is white but SnI_2 is red explain.

Q.2 CH_3Cl has more dipole moment than CH_3F explain.

Q.3 Explain why Li shows diagonal relationship in properties with Mg.

Q.4 Out of Li_2CO_3, Na_2CO_3, K_2CO_3, $RbCO_3$ & $CsCO_3$ only Li_2CO_3 undergoes dissociation to produce CO_2. Explain.

Q.5 AgCl is white AgI is yellow & Ag_2S is black explain.

Q.6 $SnCl_2$ melts at 535°C white, $SnCl_4$ melts at - 15°C explain.

Q.7 Arrange the following in descending order of :-

    (a)   Intensity of colour   AgCl, AgBr, AgI

    (b)   Solubility in water $MgSO_4$, $CaSO_4$, $SrSO_4$ $BaSO_4$

    (c)   Solubility in water MgF_2, CaF_2, SrF_2 & BaF_2

    (d)   Melting point   NaCl KCl   RbCl CsCl

    (e)   Thermal stability   NaCl KCl   RbCl CsCl

    (f)   Thermal stability $NaNO_3$ KNO_3 $RbNO_3$ $CsNO_3$

    (g)   Lattice energy $MgCl_2$ MgO Mg_3N_2

    (h)   Solubility in water   AgCl AgBr AgI

Q.8 For a diatomic molecule dipole moment is 1.2 D and interatomic spacing is 1 A°. What fraction of charge is present on each atom?   **(Ans = 25 %)**

Q.9 Dipole moment in water is 1.85 Debye. If bond length of O – H bond is 0.94 Å and bond angle is 105°. Calculate fraction of charge present on each atom. Given that Cos 52.5° = 0.609   **(Ans 67.29%)**

Q.10 Dipole moment of HBr is 2.6×10^{-30} coulomb meter. Calculate % ionic character if inter atomic spacing is 1.41 Å.   **(Ans = 11.5%)**

Objective Exercise

Q.1   Dipole moment of NH_3 is greater than

(a) PCl_5 (b) CO_2

(c) NF_3 (d)   all of these

Q.2   The correct order of dipole moment is:-

(a) $CF_4 > NF_3 > NH_3 > H_2O$ (b) $H_2O > NH_3 > NF_3 > CF_4$

(c) $H_2O > NH_3 > CF_4 > NF_3$ (d) $CF_4 > NH_3 > NF_3 > H_2O$

Q.3   The % ionic character in LiF if internuclear spacing is 0.156 pm and experimental dipole moment of LiF is 6.32 D, will be:-

(a)   84.5%   (b)   50%

(c)   58.7%   (d)   17%

Q.4   Which statement is incorrect regarding AgCl and NaCl

(a)   Both are colorless   (b)   AgCl is more covalent than NaCl

(c)   Both exhibit isomorphism

(d)   NaCl is more soluble in acetone in comparison to AgCl

Q.5   In which case Ist molecule is more thermally stable than 2nd.

(a) $MgCO_3$, Na_2CO_3 (b) K_3N, Na_3N

(c)   LiF, NaF   (d) $MgSO_4$, $CaSO_4$

Q.6   Which among the following will not exist in liquid form?

(a) $Mg(HCO_3)_2$ (b) $Ca(HCO_3)_2$

(c) $LiHCO_3$ (d) $NaHCO_3$

Q.7   Correct order of solubility in water is:-

(a) $NaHCO_3 > KHCO_3 > RbHCO_3$ (b) $RbHCO_3 > KHCO_3 > NaHCO_3$

(c) $NaHCO_3 = KHCO_3 > RbHCO_3$ (d) $RbHCO_3 = KHCO_3 > NaHCO_3$

Q.8   Correct order of solubility in water

(a) $Na_2SO_4 > K_2SO_4 > Rb_2SO_4 > Cs_2SO_4$ (b) $Cs_2SO_4 > Rb_2SO_4 > K_2SO_4 > Na_2SO_4$

(c) $Cs_2SO_4 > Rb_2SO_4 > Na_2SO_4 > K_2SO_4$ (d)   All have same solubility in water

Q.9   Which will produce SO_3 on heating?

(a) $FeSO_4$ (b) $MgSO_4$

(c) $BeSO_4$ (d) $CuSO_4$

Q.10   Which among the following will produce O_2 on heating?

(a) $AgNO_3$ (b) $NaNO_3$

(c)   HgO   (d)   All of these

Q.11 Correct order of covalent character is:-

(a) $NaF > KF > LiF > RbF > CsF$

(b) $LiF > NaF > KF > RbF > CsF$

(c) $CsF > RbF > KF > NaF > LiF$

(d) $CsF > RbF > KF > LiF > NaF$

Q.12 Correct order of acidity is :-

(a) $PbO > MgO > ZnO$

(b) $MgO > PbO > ZnO$

(c) $ZnO > MgO > PbO$

(d) $ZnO > PbO > MgO$

Q.13 Which among the following is colourless?

(a) $AgCl, AgBr$

(b) ZnS, PbF_2

(c) PbI_2, Ag_2S

(d) MgS, CdS

Q.14 Which has maximum dipole moment?

(a) 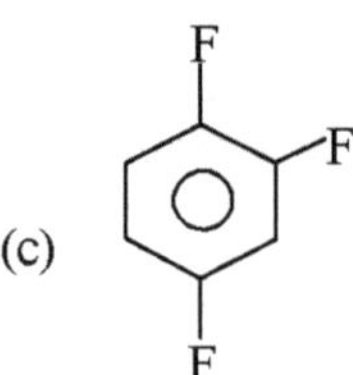

(b)

(c)

(d)

Q.15 In which solvent AgI has maximum solubility?

(a) Diethyl ether

(b) Water

(c) Acetone

(d) C_2H_5OH

Q.16 Which of the following molecule do not have zero dipole moment?

(a) 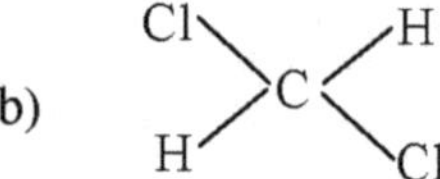

(b)

(c) $CH_3C \equiv CCH_3$

(d) PCl_5

Q.17 Standard heat of formation of an ionic compound 'AB' is –67 k cal/mol, electron affinity of 'B' is 83 k cal/mol, dissociation energy for B_2 is 34 k cal/mol, Ist I.E. for A is 141 k cal/mol & heat of sublimation for A is 48 k cal / mol. Calculate lattice energy of AB.

(a) $-190\,k\,cal\,/\,mol$

(b) $-207\,k\,cal\,/\,mol$

(c) $-627\,k\,cal\,/\,mol$

(d) $-162\,k\,cal\,/\,mol$

Q.18 Which statement is not correct regarding the dipole moments of the following molecules?

$$\text{Cl}\diagdown\atop\text{H}\diagup C = C = C\diagup^{H}_{\diagdown Cl} \quad \& \quad \text{Cl}\diagdown\atop\text{H}\diagup C = C = C = C\diagup^{H}_{\diagdown Cl}$$

(1)   (2)

(a) $\mu_1 = \mu_2 = 0$ (b) $\mu_1 \neq \mu_2 \neq 0$

(c) $\mu_1 > \mu_2$ (d) $\mu_2 > \mu_1$

Q.19 $NCl_3 \longrightarrow NCl_2 + Cl$ $\Delta H = +x\ KJ/mol$

      $NOCl \longrightarrow NO + Cl$ $\Delta H = +y\ KJ/mol$

If x & y are the dissociation energies of N – Cl bond in NCl_3 & $NOCl$ respectively then:-

(a) $x > y$ (b) $x < y$

(c) $x = y$ (d) cannot predict

Q.20 The compound with highest melting point is:-

(a) MgO (b) $NaCl$

(c) KBr (d) BaO

Q.21 Compound with least boiling point is:-

(a) CH_3CH_2F (b) CH_3CHF_2

(c) CF_3CF_3 (d) CH_3CF_3

Q.22 Correct order of dipole moment is:-

(a) $CH_3F > CH_3Cl > CH_3Br > CH_3I$ (b) $CH_3I > CH_3Br > CH_3Cs > CH_3F$

(c) $CH_3Cl > CH_3F > CH_3Br > CH_3I$ (d) $CH_3F = CH_3Cl > CH_3Br > CH_3I$

Q.23

Molecule		**Dipole moment**	
(A)	CH_3F	(P)	$1.82\,D$
(B)	CH_2F_2	(Q)	$1.97\,D$
(C)	CHF_3	(R)	$1.65\,D$
(D)	CF_4	(S)	$0\,D$

Correct matching is:-

(a) $A \longrightarrow Q, B \longrightarrow R, C \longrightarrow P, D \longrightarrow S$

(b) $A \longrightarrow P, B \longrightarrow Q, C \longrightarrow R, D \longrightarrow S$

(c) $A \longrightarrow Q, B \longrightarrow P, C \longrightarrow R, D \longrightarrow S$

(d) $A \longrightarrow R, B \longrightarrow P, C \longrightarrow Q, D \longrightarrow S$

Q.24

Molecule	Dipole moment
(A) CH_3Cl	(P) 1.94 D
(B) CH_2Cl_2	(Q) 1.03 D
(C) $CHCl_3$	(R) 1.60 D
(D) CCl_4	(S) 0 D

Correct matching is:-

(a) A$\longrightarrow$P, B$\longrightarrow$Q, C$\longrightarrow$R, D$\longrightarrow$S

(b) A$\longrightarrow$R, B$\longrightarrow$Q, C$\longrightarrow$P, D$\longrightarrow$S

(c) A$\longrightarrow$S, B$\longrightarrow$R, C$\longrightarrow$P, D$\longrightarrow$Q

(d) A$\longrightarrow$P, B$\longrightarrow$R, C$\longrightarrow$Q, D$\longrightarrow$S

Q.25 In which of the following molecule, the oxygen atom constitutes the positive end of electric dipole?

(a) XeO_3 (b) $NOCl$

(c) F_2O (d) $XeOF_2$

Q.26 Which of the bond is most polar?

(a) $C-O$ (b) $O-F$

(c) $C-F$ (d) $N-F$

Q.27 Which is not polar molecule?

(a) C_2F_2 (b) $CHCl_3$

(c) F_2O (d) CH_2Cl_2

Q.28 AB_3 has non zero dipole moment. A can exhibit ------- hybridization.

(a) sp^3 (b) sp^3d

(c) Both   (d) none

Q.29 Among the following compounds, the one that is polar and has the central atom with sp^2 hybridization is:-

(a) SiF_4 (b) BF_3

(c) $HClO_2$ (d) H_2CO_3

Q.30 Among the following compounds the one that is polar and has the central atom with sp^2 hybridization is:-

(a) HNO_3 (b) SiF_4

(c) B_2H_6 (d) $HClO_4$

Q.31 Which one of the following pairs of molecules will have permanent dipole moments for both members?

(a) SiF_4 and NO_2 (b) NO_2 and CO_2

(c) NO_2 and O_3 (d) SiF_4 and CO_2

Q.32 Select correct statement:-

(a)   When a covalent bond is formed, transfer of electrons takes place

(b)   Pure H_2O does not contain any ion

(c)   A bond is formed when attractive forces over-come repulsive forces

(d)   HF is less polar than HBr

Q.33   Which of the following are non-polar?

(1) SiF_4 (2) XeF_4

(3) SF_4 (4) $BeCl_2$

(5) NCl_3

Select the correct answer using the code given below:-

(a)   1, 2 and 4   (b)   3, 4 and 5

(c)   2, 3 and 4   (d)   1, 3 and 4

Q.34   Which of following has zero dipole moment?

(a)   ClF   (b) PCl_3

(c) SiF_4 (d) $CFCl_3$

Q.35   The electronegativities of F, Cl, Br, I are 4.0, 3.0, 2.8, 2.5 respectively. The hydrogen halide with a highest percentage of ionic character is :-

(a)   HF   (b)   HCl

(c)   HBr   (d)   HI

Q.36   Which of the following statements is true?

(a)   HF is a good acid than HI

(b) CH_4 contains polar bonds but its resultant dipole moment is zero

(c) CO_2 contains polar bonds but its resultant dipole moment is zero

(d)   Dipole moment of CO bond in 'CO' is greater than that of CO bond present in CH_3COCH_3

Q.37   Dipole moment is shown by

(a)   1, 4-dichlorobenzene   (b)   1, 2-dichlorobenzene

(c)   Trans -1, 2-dichloroethene   (d)   Trans -2, 3-dichloro-2-butene

Q.38   Which of the following represents a non-polar molecule with polar bonds?

(a) NCl_3 (b) NF_3

(c) N_2 (d) CCl_4

Q.39   Out of the four planar molecules given below which one has μ (dipole moment)= 0

(a)   cis-ClCH = CHCl   (b)   trans-ClCH = CHCl

(c) $CH_2 = CDCl$ (d) $CD_2 = CBr_2$

Q.40   Which of the following would have a permanent dipole moment?

(a) SiF_4

(b) SF_4

(c) PCl_5

(d) BCl_3

Q.41 The halide having the highest melting point is:-

(a) NaF

(b) NaCl

(c) KBr

(d) LiF

Q.42 The highest dipole moment is of

(a) CCl_4

(b) CH_3OH

(c) CS_2

(d) CH_3F

Q.43 The most polar bond is:-

(a) $C-F$

(b) $F-O$

(c) $C-Br$

(d) $C-N$

Q.44 The molecule having largest dipole moment among the following is:-

(a) CHI_3

(b) CH_4

(c) $CHCl_2$

(d) CCl_4

Q.45 Which of the following is least soluble in water?

(a) BaF_2

(b) SiF_4

(c) CaF_2

(d) MgF_2

Q.46 Ionic reactions take place mainly in:-

(a) Liquid state

(b) Solid state

(c) aq. solution

(d) Gaseous state

Q.47 Among the following iso structural compounds, identify the compound which has the highest lattice energy:-

(a) LiF

(b) LiI

(c) NaBr

(d) MgO

Q.48 Which of the following ions has the highest polarizing power:-

(a) $K^{(+)}$

(b) Ca^{+2}

(c) Al^{+3}

(d) Si^{+4}

Q.49 Low solublility of $BaSO_4$ in water is due to:-

(a) Low dissociation energy

(b) Ionic bond

(c) High value of lattice energy

(d) None of the above

Q.50 The order of decreasing polarity in compounds:-

CaO, CsF, KCl, MgO is

(a) CaO, CsF, KCl, MgO

(b) MgO, KCl, CaO, CsF

(c) KCl, CaO, CsF, MgO

(d) CsF, KCl, CaO, MgO

Q.51 Which of the following is least ionic?

    (a)   KCl   (b)   AgCl

    (c) $MgCl_2$ (d) $FeCl_2$

Q.52 Among $LiCl$, BCl_3, $BeCl_2$, CCl_4, the covalent characteristics follow the decreasing order:-

    (a) $LiCl > BCl_3 > BeCl_2 > CCl_4$ (b) $CCl_4 > BCl_3 > BeCl_2 > LiCl$

    (c) $LiCl > BeCl_2 > CCl_4 > BCl_3$ (d) $BeCl_2 > LiCl > BCl_3 > CCl_4$

Q.53 The strongest hydrogen bonding is present:-

    (a) NH_3 & CH_3NH_2 (b) $H_2O + NH_3$

    (c) $CH_3NH_2 + C_2H_5OH$ (d) $HF + H_2O$

Matrix Match

Q.54   **Column - I**   **Column - II**

    (A) $AB_2\ (\mu = 0)$ (p)   Linear geometry

    (B) $AB_3\ (\mu = 0)$ (q)   Planar geometry

    (C) $AB_2\ (\mu \neq 0)$ (r)   One lone pair on central atom

    (D) $AB_3\ (\mu \neq 0)$ (s)   Two lone pair on central atom

Q.55   **Column - I**   **Column - II**

    (A) BrF_3 (p) $\mu = 0$

    (B) PCl_5 (q) $\mu \neq 0$

    (C) IF_7 (r)   Two axial bonds

    (D) NH_3 (s)   One equatorial bond

Q.56   **Column - I**   **Column - II**

    (A) SF_4 (p)   Polar

    (B) $B_3N_3H_6$ (q)   Non polar

    (C) C_6H_6 (r)   Planar

    (D) XeF_4 (s)   Non planar

HINTS & SOLUTIONS

SUBJECTIVE EXERCISE

7. (a) $AgI > AgBr > AgCl$ (b) $MgSO_4 > CaSO_4 > SrSO_4 > BaSO_4$

(c) $MgF_2 < CaF_2 < SrF_2 < BaF_2$ (d) $NaCl > KCl > RbCl > CsCl$

(e) $NaCl > KCl > RbCl > CsCl$ (f) $CsNO_3 > RbNO_3 > KNO_3 > NaNO_3$

(g) $Mg_3N_2 > MgO > MgCl_2$ (h) $AgCl > AgBr > AgI$

8. $\mu = q \times d, \quad 1.2 \times 10^{-18} = q \times 10^{-8}, \qquad q = 1.2 \times 10^{-10}$

Thus, fraction of charge present on each atom $= (1.2 \times 10^{-10}) \times 100 / (4.8 \times 10^{-10}) = 25\%$

9.

$$OB = 0.94 \cos 52.5 = 0.572\text{Å}$$
$$\text{Dipole moment} = q \times d, \quad q = \frac{1.85 \times 10^{-18}}{0.572 \times 10^{-8}}$$
$$q = 3.23 \times 10^{-10}$$

Fraction of charge $= (3.23 \times 10^{-10}) \times 100 / 4.8 \times 10^{-10} = 67.29$

OBJECTIVE EXERCISE

1. (d) **2.** (b) **3.** (a)

4. (d) NaCl is more ionic than AgCl & it is more soluble in water in comparison to acetone.

5. (c) **6.** (d) **7.** (b) **8.** (a) **9.** (a) **10.** (d)

11. (a) **12.** (d) Extent to polarization $\propto$ acidic character **13.** (b) **14.** (a)

15. (a) Due to polarization AgI has covalent character so it will have highest solubility in non polar medium (diethyl ether).

16. (b) CH_2Cl_2 has tetrahedral shape. **17.** (a) Use born Haber cycle.

18. (c)

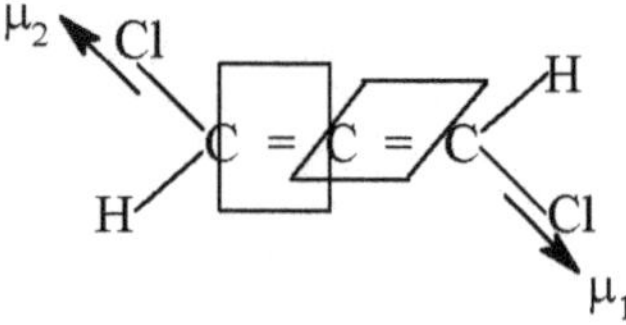

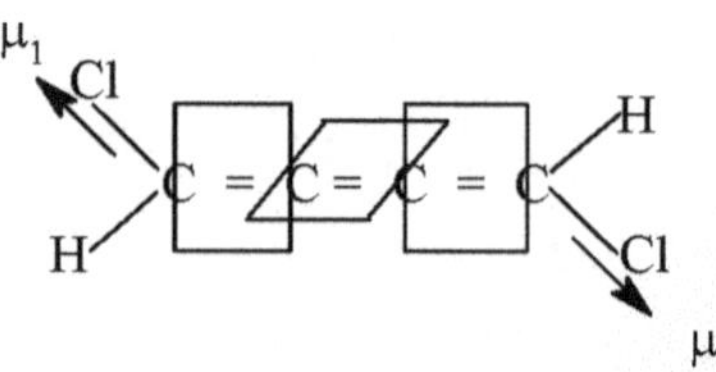

19. (a) 20. (a) MgO has highest lattice energy 21. (c) 22. (c)

23. (c) 24. (d) 25. (c) Because fluorine is more electronegative than oxygen

26. (c) 27. (a) 28. (c) 29. (d) 30. (a) 31. (c)

32. (c) 33. (a) 34. (c) 35. (a) 36. (c) 37. (b)

38. (d) 39. (b) 40. (b) 41. (d) as it has highest lattice energy

42. (d) 43. (a) 44. (c) 45. (b)

46. (c) in ionic compound ions are bonded by strong electrostatic forces of attractions, thus, to break these forces a polar medium is required thus ions react with one another in polar medium like water.

47. (d) 48. (d) 49. (c) 50. (d) 51. (b) 52. (b)

53. (d)

54. A - p ; B - q ; C - r, s ; D - r, s

55. A - q, r, s ; B - p, r ; C - p, r ; D - q

56. A - p, s ; B - p, r; C - r, q ; D - p, r

Molecular Orbital Theory & Metallic Bonding

Before we discuss molecular orbital theory it is necessary to understand the term paramagnetism and diamagnetism.

Paramagnetic substances are those substances which attract towards magnetic field if they are placed in a magnetic field whereas diamagnetic substances are repelled by magnetic field.

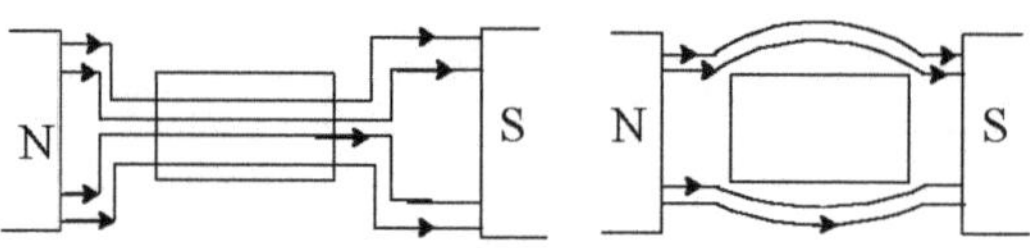

(Paramagnetic substance)   (Diamagnetic substance)

The magnetic behavior of a substance is measured by the term magnetic moment (μ)

$$(\mu) = \sqrt{n(n+2)} \ \text{B.M}$$

Where   n = number of unpaired electrons present in the substance

B.M. = Bohr magneton (unit of magnetic moment)

It means that if unpaired electrons are present in a substance its magnetic moment (μ) will be non zero and it well be a paramagnetic substance.

Similarly it substance does not contain unpaired electrons its magnetic moment will be zero and substance will be diamagnetic. For e.g. Fe^{+2} ($3d^6$) and Zn^{+2}($3d^{10}$), former is paramagnetic and later is diamagnetic.

Fe^{+2} ($3d^6$)

n = unpaired electrons = 4

$\mu = \sqrt{n(n+2)} = \sqrt{2(2+4)} = 2\sqrt{6}$ B.M. (Paramagnetic)

Zn^{+2}($3d^{10}$)

n = 0, μ = 0 (Diamagnetic)

➢6.1 Molecular orbital theory (M.O.T.)

This theory was proposed by Robert Mulliken and he explained the paramagnetic behavior of O_2 with the help of this theory which is diamagnetic according to valence bond theory.

Several important features of M.O.T. are given below.

(1.) Atomic orbitals (A.O.) of the individual atoms can be combined to give rise to molecular orbitals (M.O.). The number of molecular orbitals formed is equal to the number of atomic orbitals involved in combination. It should be noted that the energies of the atomic orbitals of the combining atoms must be close to each other.

(2.) Two atomic orbitals produce two molecular orbitals, one of which has energy lower than the energy of combining atomic orbital and the other has energy higher than the energy of combining atomic orbitals. The lower energy molecular orbital is called **bonding molecular orbital (B.M.O.)** and the higher energy orbital is called **anti bonding molecular orbital (ABMO).**

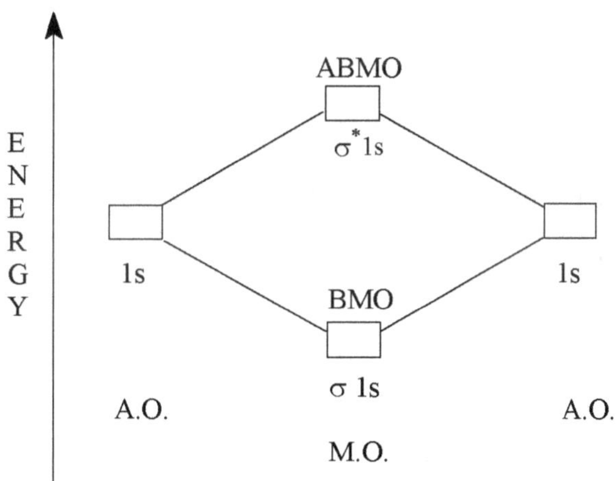

(Linear combination of atomic orbitals)

(3) B.M.O. is formed by addition of wave function whereas ABMO is formed by subtraction of wave function.

$$A \quad + \quad B \quad \longrightarrow \quad AB$$

Wave functions $\quad \Psi_A \qquad\qquad \Psi_B$

$\qquad$ (Atom) $\qquad\qquad$ (Atom) $\qquad\qquad$ (Molecule)

B.M.O. are formed by constructive interference of wave functions (in phase)

$$\Psi_A \; + \; \Psi_B$$

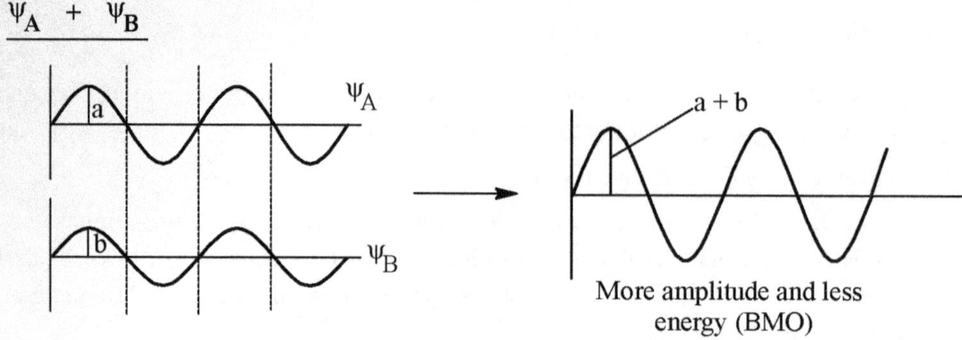

ABMO are formed by destructive interference (out of phase)

$$\Psi_A \; - \; \Psi_B$$

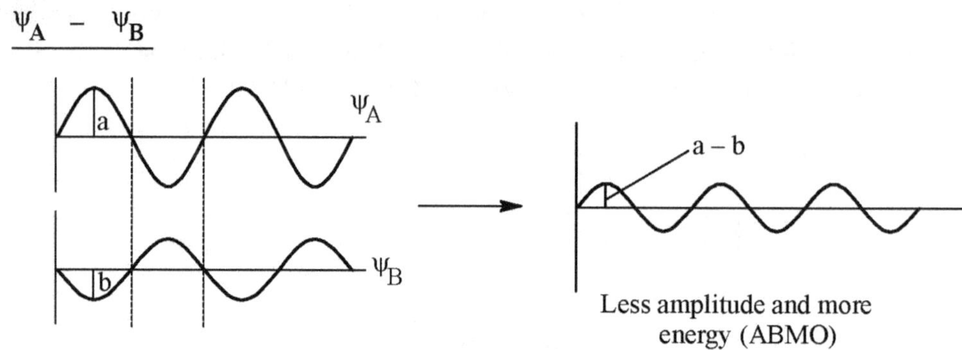

(4.) In B.M.O. electron density increases in the internuclear region whereas in ABMO electron density decreases in inter nuclear region.

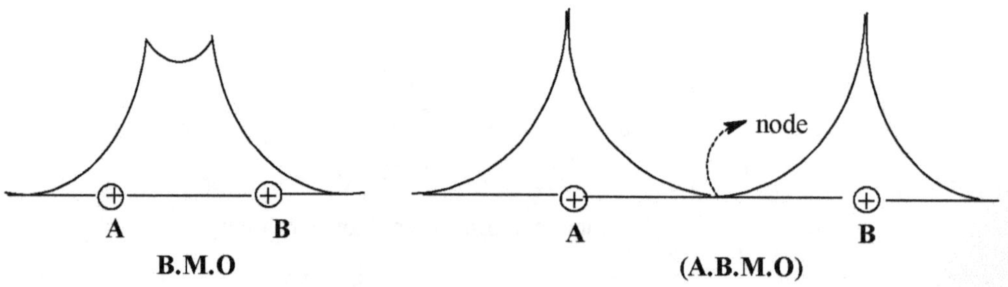

(5.) In ABMO there is one nodal plane bisecting perpendicularly the internuclear axis.
(6.) BMO stabilizes the molecule whereas ABMO destabilizes the molecule.
(7.) Head on overlap or mixing of atomic orbital generates σ **molecular orbital** whereas side wise or lateral overlap of atomic orbital generates π molecules orbital.

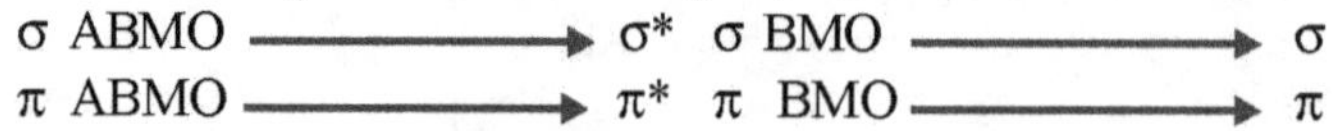

(8) Shapes of molecular orbitals -

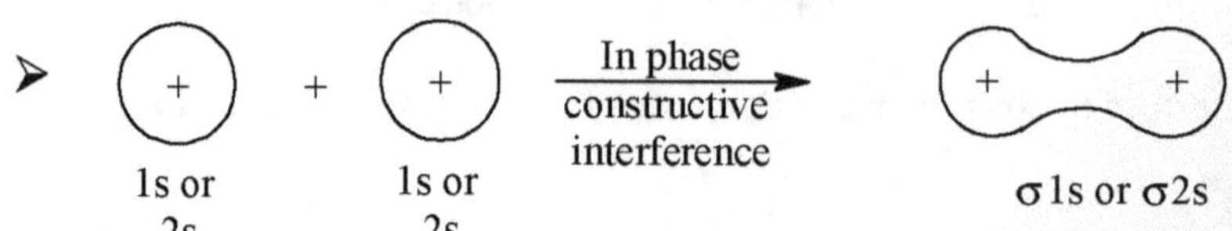

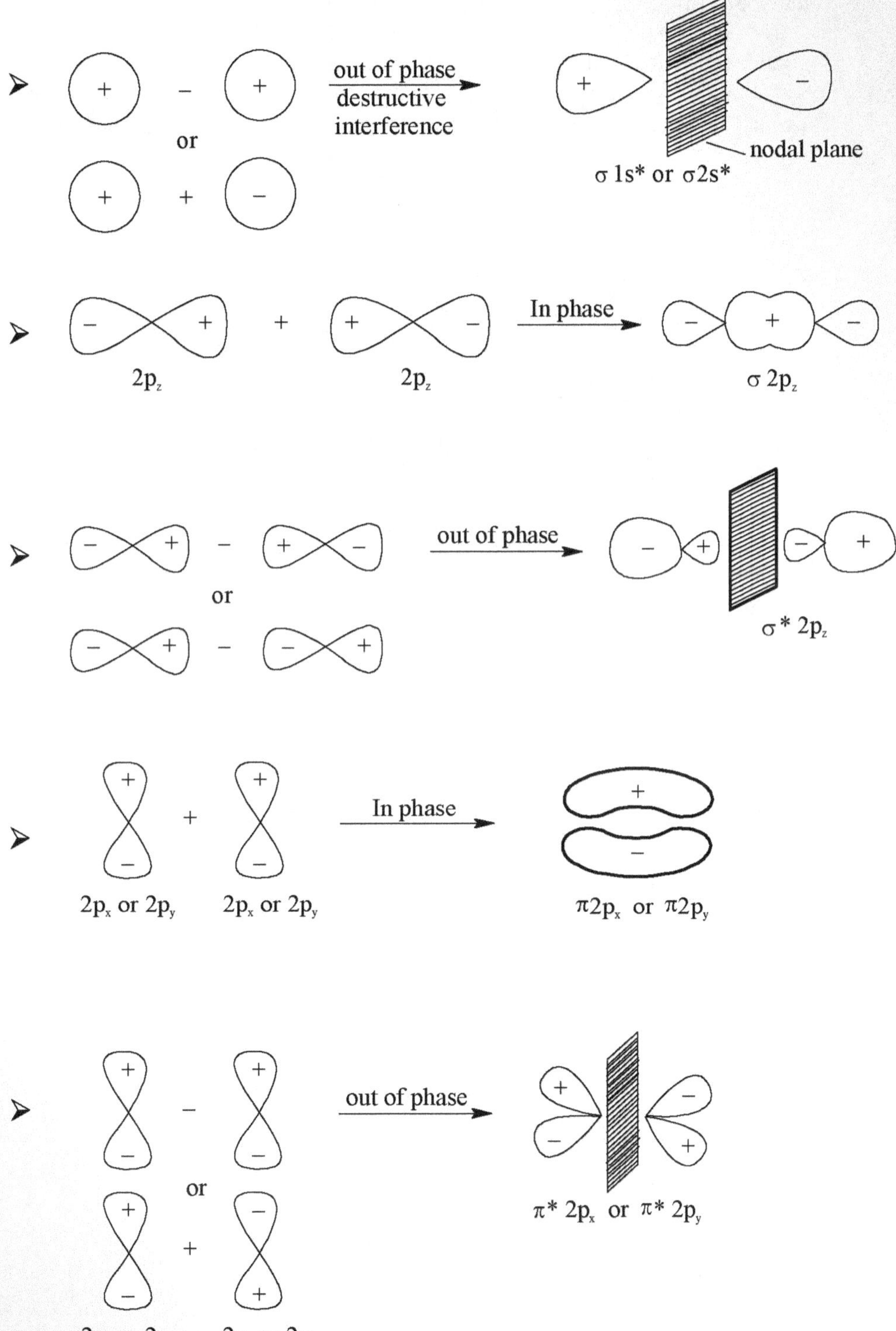

out of phase
destructive
interference
or
nodal plane
σ 1s* or σ2s*
2p_z   2p_z   σ 2p_z
In phase
out of phase
or
σ* 2p_z
2p_x or 2p_y   2p_x or 2p_y   π2p_x or π2p_y
In phase
out of phase
or
π* 2p_x or π* 2p_y
2p_x or 2p_y   2p_x or 2p_y

(9.) Filling of molecular orbitals

Sequence (A) When total electrons are more than 14

$\sigma 1s$, $\sigma^* 1s$, $\sigma 2s$, $\sigma^* 2s$, $\sigma 2p_z$, $\pi 2p_x = \pi 2p_y$, $\pi^* 2p_x = \pi^* 2p_y$, $\sigma^* 2p_z$

Sequence (B) When total electrons are less than equal to 14

$\sigma 1s$, $\sigma^* 1s$, $\sigma 2s$, $\sigma^* 2s$, $\pi 2p_x = \pi 2p_y$, $\sigma 2p_z$, $\pi^* 2p_x = \pi^* 2p_y$, $\sigma^* 2p_z$

These molecular orbitals can be represented by the following molecular orbital diagram.

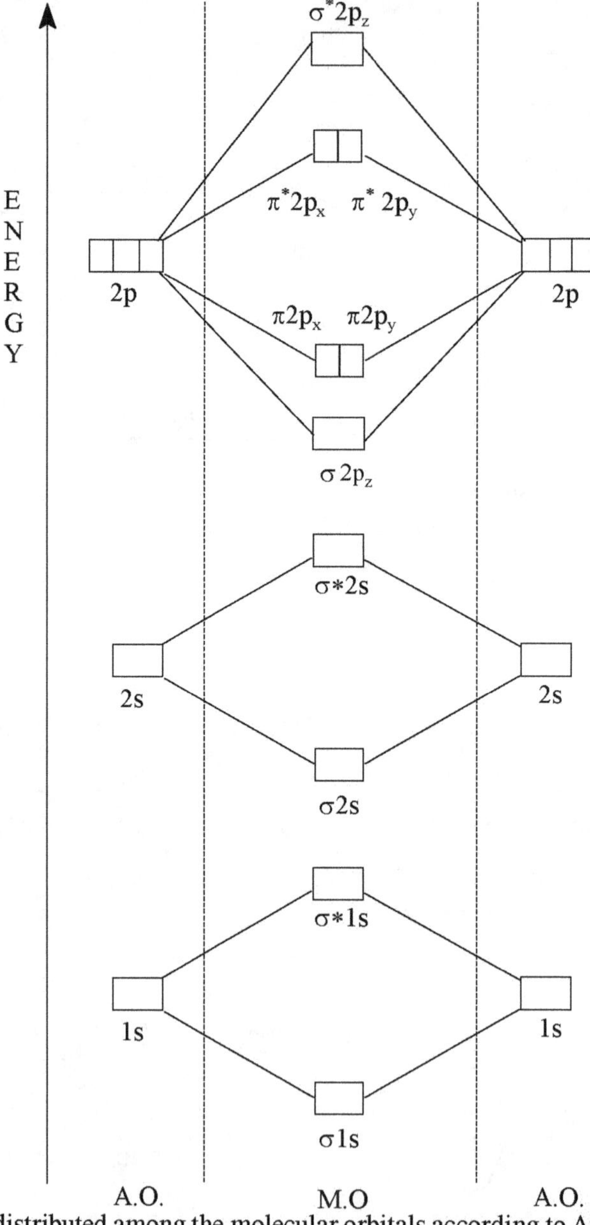

Electrons are distributed among the molecular orbitals according to Aufbau's, Hund's and Pauli's Principle i.e.

➢ Each molecular orbital can accommodate a maximum of two electrons of opposite spins

➢ Electrons occupy lowest energy molecular orbital. Higher energy orbitals will not be filled as long as low energy orbitals are available.

(10) Bond order $\quad=\quad 1/2\,(n_b - n_a)$

Where $n_b \quad=\quad$ electrons in BMO and

$\qquad n_a \quad=\quad$ electrons in ABMO

Bond order $\quad\propto\quad$ Bond dissociation energy

$\qquad\qquad\propto\quad$ Stability $\propto$ 1 / Bond length

If two species have same bond order then that species will be more stable in which more number of electrons are present in BMO

Bond order (B.O.) $=\quad$ 1 (single bond)

$\qquad$ B.O. $\quad=\quad$ 2 (double bond)

$\qquad$ B.O. $\quad=\quad$ 3 (Triple bond)

$\qquad$ B.O. $\quad=\quad$ 0 (Molecule does not exist)

(11) Any species is found to be coloured if it possesses unpaired electrons.

Let us take some examples to clear above points

(a) $\quad H_2 \qquad$ Total electrons $\quad=2$

$\qquad\qquad \sigma 1s^2 \quad \sigma^* 1s^0$

$\qquad\qquad$ Bond order $\quad=\quad 1/2\,(2-0)=1$

i.e. two H atoms are joined together by single bond

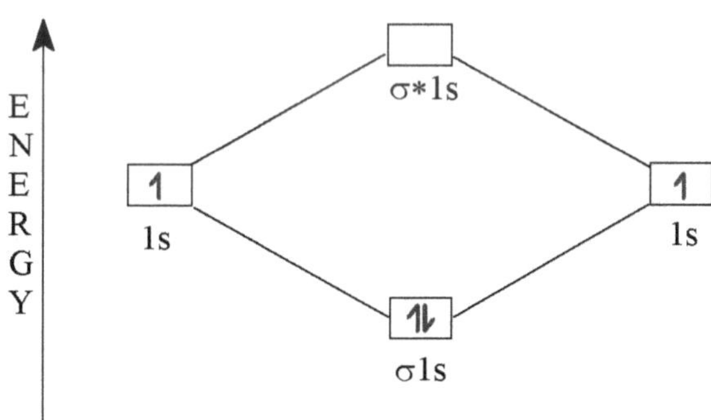

Since unpaired electron is absent in H_2 thus it is colorless and diamagnetic

$\qquad n \;=\; 0 \to \mu \;=\; \sqrt{n(n+2)} \;=\; 0 \qquad$ B.M.

(b) Be_2 Total electrons $=\;8 \qquad$ thus, sequence B will be used

$\sigma 1s^2, \sigma^* 1s^2, \sigma 2s^2, \sigma^* 2s^2 \;$ or $\qquad KK\, \sigma 2s^2, \sigma^* 2s^2,$

B.O. $=\;1/2\,(4-4)\;=\;0 \qquad$ It indicates that Be_2 does not exist in nature

(c) $O_2 \quad$ Total electrons $=\;16 \qquad$ thus, sequence A will be used

$\sigma 1s^2, \sigma^* 1s^2, \sigma 2s^2, \sigma^* 2s^2, \sigma 2p_z^2, \pi 2p_x^2 = \pi 2p_y^2, \pi^* 2p_x^1 = \pi^* 2p_y^1$

or $\quad KK\, \sigma 2s^2, \sigma^* 2s^2, \sigma 2p_z^2, \pi 2p_x^2 = \pi 2p_y^2, \pi^* 2p_x^1, = \pi^* 2p_y^1$

B.O. $=\;1/2\,(10-6)=\;4/2\;=\;2,$ i.e. $\qquad$ double bond

Since unpaired electrons are present in π^*2p_x and π^*2p_y molecular orbitals thus, O_2 is paramagnetic in nature.

$$\mu = \sqrt{n(n+2)} = \sqrt{2(2+2)} = 2.828 \text{ B.M}$$

Presence of unpaired electron makes O_2 coloured. In liquid state O_2 has blue colour.

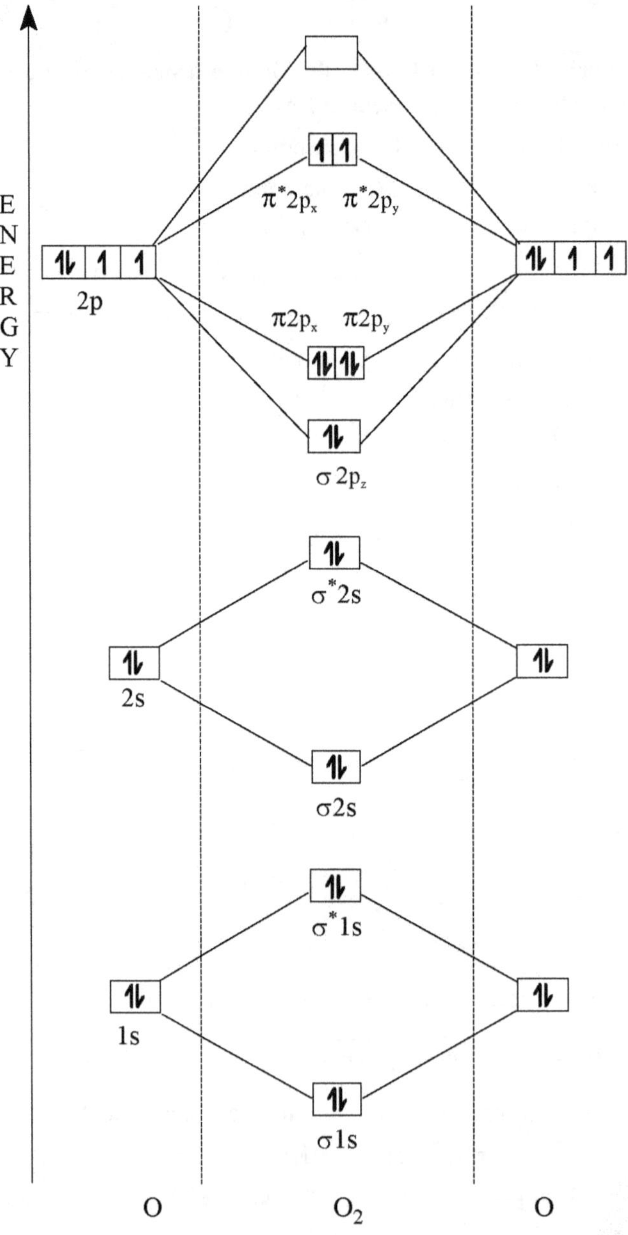

(d) CO Total electrons $= 6 + 8 = 14$

Thus, sequence 'B' will be used.

$\sigma 1s^2, \sigma^*1s^2, \sigma2s^2\, \sigma^*2s^2, \pi2p_x^2 = \pi2p_x^2, \sigma2p_z^2$

KK $\sigma 2s^2\, \pi^*2s^2\, \pi 2p_x^2 = \pi 2p_y^2,\, \sigma 2p_z^2$

B.O. $= 1/2\,(10-4) = 6/2 = 3$, i.e. $\quad C \equiv O$

Since unpaired electrons are absent hence, it is diamagnetic and colourless.

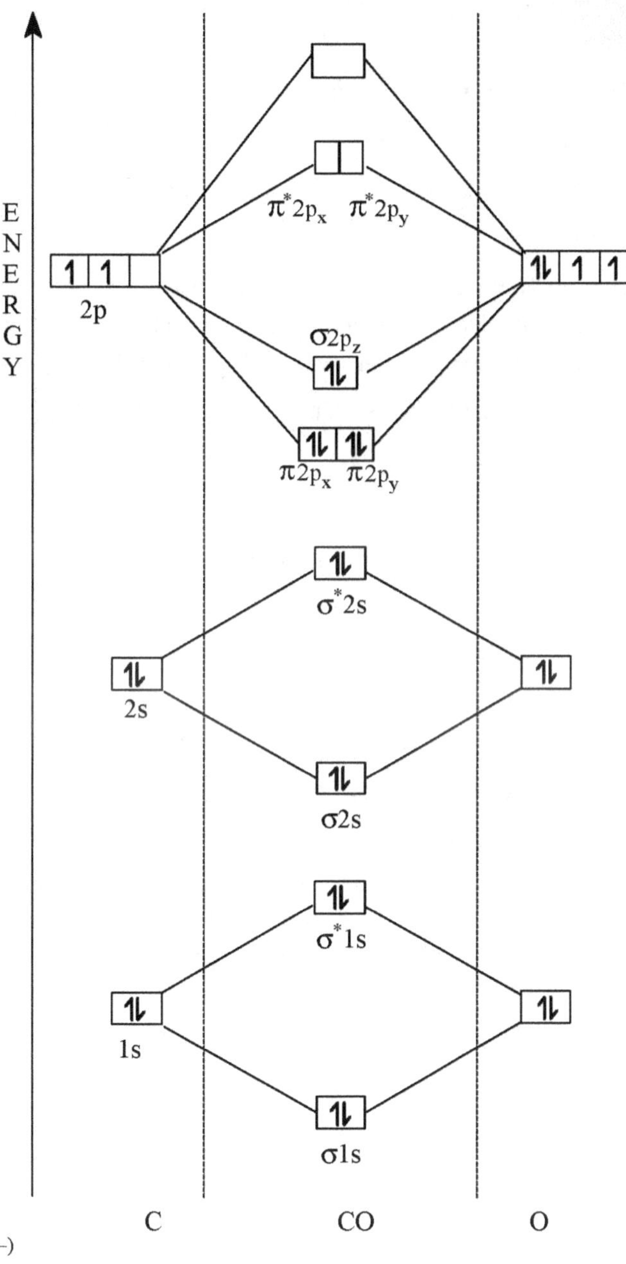

(e) $O_2,\ O_2^+,\ O_2^{(-)}$

$O_2\ (16e^{(-)})\quad \sigma 1s^2\ \sigma^*1s^2\ \sigma 2s^2\ \sigma^*2s^2\ \sigma 2p_z^2,\ \pi 2p_x^2 = \pi 2p_y^2,\ \pi^*2p_x^1 = \pi^*2p_y^1$

B.O. $= 1/2\,(10-6) = 2$

$O_2+\ (15e^{(-)})\quad \sigma 1s^2\ \sigma^*1s^2\ \sigma 2s^2\ \sigma^*2s^2\ \sigma 2p_z^2\ \pi 2p_x^2 = \pi 2p_y^2,\ \pi^*2p_x^1 = \pi^*2p_y^0$

B.O. $= 1/2\,(10-5) = 2.5$

$O_2^{(-)}\ (17e^{(-)})\quad \sigma 1s^2\ \sigma^*1s^2\ \sigma 2s^2\ \sigma^*2s^2\ \sigma 2p_z^2\ \pi 2p_x^2 = \pi 2p_y^2,\ \pi^*2p_x^2 = \pi^*2p_y^1$

$B.O. = 1/2\,(10-7) = 1.5$

$B.O.\quad O_2^+ > O_2 > O_2^{(-)}$

Sequence for stability & bond dissociation energy is $O_2^+ > O_2 > O_2^{(-)}$

Sequence for bond length is $O_2 < O_2 < O_2^{(-)}$

(f) $N_2, N_2^+, N_2^{(-)}$

$N_2(14e^-)\quad \sigma 1s^2\ \sigma^* 1s^2\ \sigma 2s^2\ \sigma^* 2s^2\ \pi 2p_x^2 = \pi 2p_y^2, \pi 2p_z^2$

$B.O. = 1/2\,(10-4) = 3$

$N_2{+}(13e^-)\quad \sigma 1s^2\ \sigma^* 1s^2\ \sigma 2s^2\ \sigma^* 2s^2\ \pi 2p_x^2 = \pi 2p_y^2,\ \pi 2p_z^1$

$B.O. = 1/2\,(9-4) = 2.5$

$N_2^{(-)}$ has 15 electrons but we do not use sequence A because the selection of sequence (A or B) is based on the number of electrons which are present in the molecular state of species. Since N_2 contains $14e^-$ thus sequence B will be used for $N_2{+}$ and $N_2^{(-)}$

$N_2^{(-)}\,(15e^-)\quad \sigma 1s^2\ \sigma^* 1s2\ \sigma 2s^2\ \sigma^* 2s^2\ \pi 2p_x^2 = \pi 2p_y^2\ \pi 2p_z^2\ \pi^* 2p_x^1 = \pi^* 2p_y$

$B.O. = 1/2\,(10-5) = 2.5$

$B.O. = N_2 > N_2^{(+)} = N_2^{(-)}$

Since $N_2^{(-)}$ has more electrons in its BMO in comparison to that of N_2^+ thus, $N_2^{(-)}$ will be more stable than N_2^+

Stability : $\qquad\qquad N_2 > N_2^{(-)} > N_2^{(+)}$

Bond length : $\qquad\quad N_2^{(+)} > N_2^{(-)} > N_2$

Similarly we can arrange C_2, C_2^+ and $C_2^{(-)}$, H_2, H_2^+ and $H_2^{(-)}$ in order of their increasing stabilities.

➤ 6.2 Application of M.O.T. for hetero nuclear diatomic systems

In section 6.1 we have applied M.O.T on CO molecule but M.O.T does not seems to be as exact on hetero nuclear system (like NO, CO…… etc) as it is on homo nuclear system (like H_2, O_2, N_2…..) After applying M.O.T. on hetero nuclear molecule, the bond order, bond length and magnetic behavior which we get, shows different values other than experimental values. For e.g. on applying M.O.T on CO and CO$^+$, their bond orders come out to be 3 & 2.5 respectively.

$CO\,(14e^-)\quad \sigma 1s^2\ \sigma^* 1s^2,\ \sigma 2s^2\ \sigma^* 2s^2,\ \pi 2p_x^2 = \pi 2p_y^2, \sigma 2p_z^2$

$B.O. = 1/2\,(10-4) = 6/2 = 3$

If one electron is removed from BMO CO$^+$ is formed.

$CO^+\,(13e^-)\quad \sigma 1s^2\ \sigma^* 1s^2\ \sigma 2s^2\ \sigma^* 2s^2\ \pi 2p_x^2 = \pi 2p_y^2, \sigma 2p_z^1$

$B.O. = 1/2\,(9-4) = 5/2 = 2.5$

Because bond order of CO is more than CO$^+$ therefore in CO$^+$ the C–O bond length must be more than that of CO but we do not find it

Theoretically - Bond length of C–O bond in CO $<$ CO$^+$

Experimentally - Bond length of C–O bond in CO $>$ CO$^+$

Thus, Mulliken thought that when CO^+ formed out from CO then electron would emit out from ABMO rather than BMO. Then only the bond order of CO^+ must be more than CO and the experimental value of CO bond length would match with theoretical value.

He also proposed new M.O. diagram

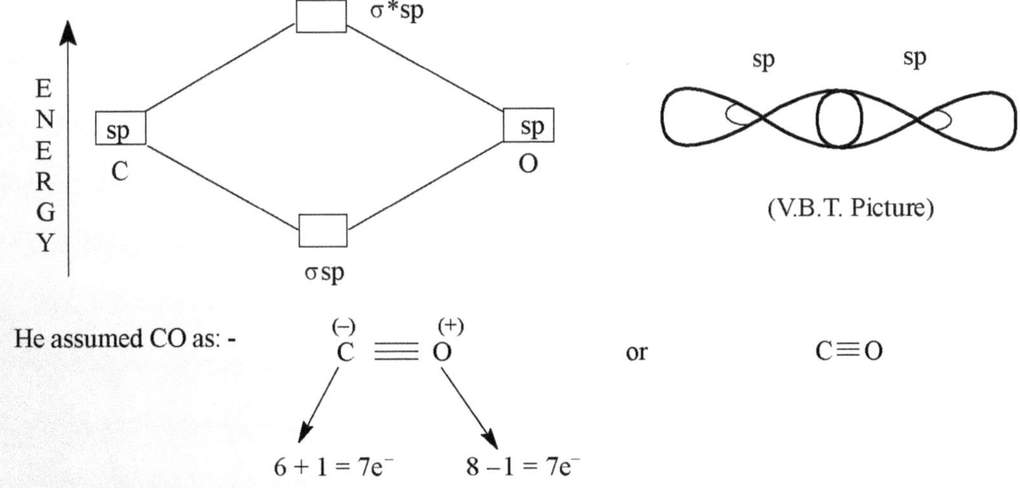

B.O. in CO $=$ $1/2\,(10-4)$ $=$ 3

B.O. in CO^+ $=$ $1/2\,(10-3)$ $=$ 3.5

But this M.O. diagram failed to describe the crystal field, ligand and coordination properties like synergic bond of CO.

➤ 6.3 M.O. diagram by Coulson

The proposed M.O. diagram by Mulliken was failed to explain ligand properties of CO hence, Coulson had presented a new M.O. diagram which was based on the principle that σ molecular orbital is formed by the mixing of hybrid orbitals rather than the mixing of pure atomic orbitals

He assumed CO as: -

We can write electronic configuration of $C^{(-)}$ and $O^{(+)}$ as

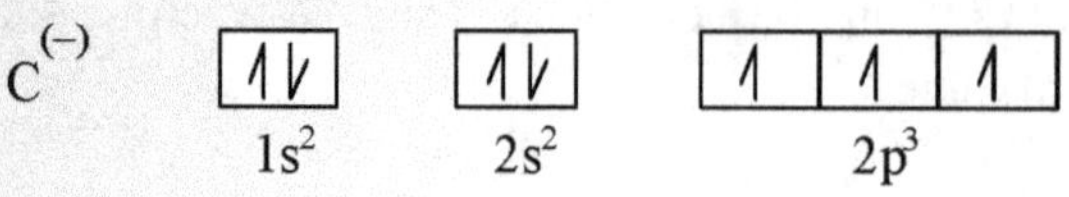

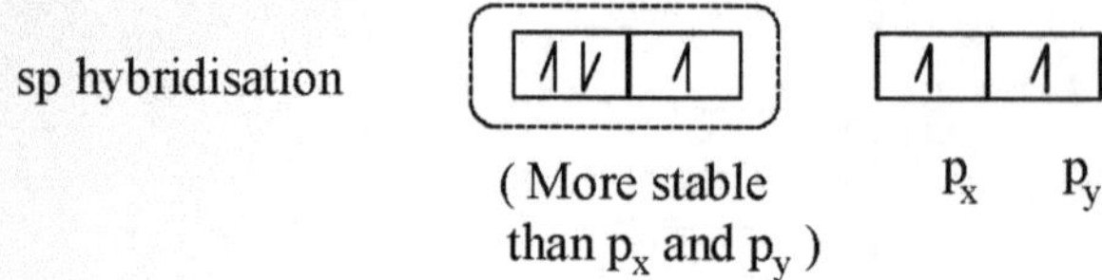

sp hybridisation

(More stable than p_x and p_y)

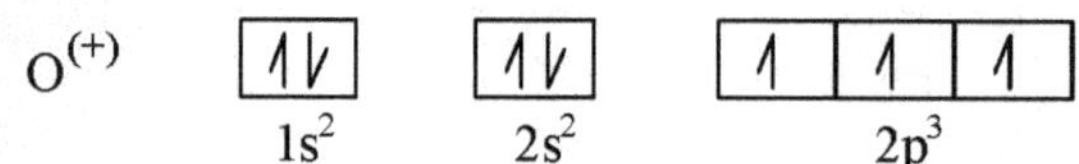

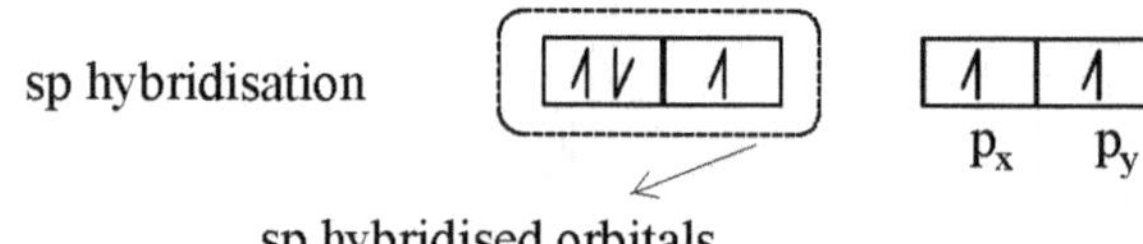

sp hybridisation

sp hybridised orbitals

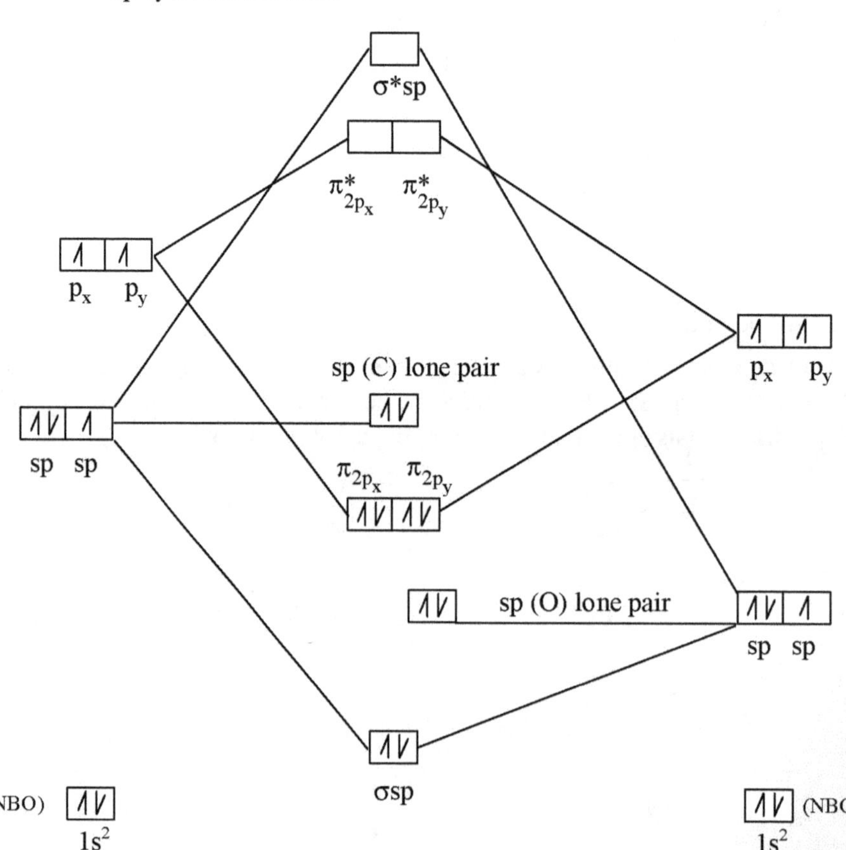

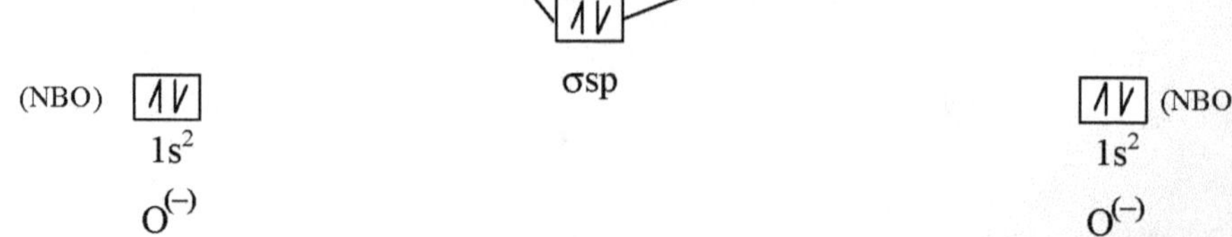

➤ 6.4 Metallic bonding

There are more than 80 metal elements in the periodic table except mercury

(m.p =$-35°C$) and gallium (mp = $29.8°$ C), rest of the metals are solid while these two are liquid.

Metals have some characteristic properties which are shown below.

➤ They are good conductor of heat and electricity.

➤ On heating metal releases e^- (thermo ionic emission) or when light of proper wavelength is allowed to fall on it's surface, it releases electron from its surface (Photo electric effect)

➤ They possess a unique lusture as their surface is good reflector of light and appears shining.

➤ They can be beaten in to sheets (malleable) and can be drawn in to wires (ductile)

➤ When reacting with non metals, they form cation.

$$\overset{}{Mg} \; + \; 1/2\,O_2 \longrightarrow \overset{+2\,-2}{MgO}$$
$$\text{(Metal)} \qquad \text{(non metal)}$$

An element is said to be metal if it looses its outer most electrons easily to form cation

These specific properties of metals can not be explained by covalent and ionic mode of linkage as, ionic bond does not form between similar elements and for the formation of covalent bond, it is necessary to have more electrons in valence shell of element so that it completes its octet. The possible of the formation of ionic and covalent bond is again ruled out in a metal because metals are good conductors of electricity where as ionic and covalent compounds are bad conductor of electricity in their solid state.

Several theories are put forward to explain metallic bonding and unique properties of metals. Amongst several theories, two theories are commonly discussed.

(1) Electron sea model

(2) Band theory

1. FREE ELECTRON THEORY OR ELECTRON SEA MODEL:-

Classical electron sea theory was proposed by Drude and late it was developed by Lorentz. Some important features of this theory are as follows.

➤ Atoms present in metal hold many vacant orbital in their valence shell for e.g. Li ($1s^2, 2s^1\,2p^0$) has vacant 2p sub shell and Mg($1s^2\,2s^2\,2p^6\,3p^0\,3d^0$) has vacant 3p & 3d sub shells.

The ionization energy of these atoms is low so that some of these atoms easily drop electrons from their outermost shell and form cation. These cations are called kernels. For e.g. Li forms Li^+ (Kernel) and Mg forms Mg^{+2} (Kernel)

➤ Because nucleus is present in these Kernels, therefore they are heavy and hence, occupy fixed position in metal. The electrons which are lost by atoms do not attach with kernel but they are free to move in the space present between Kernels just like the molecules of gas. Presence of large number of vacant orbital helps these electrons to move freely. Thus, this model is called electron sea model or electron gas model.

"The simultaneous force of attraction between kernels and mobile electrons is known as metallic bond".

➤ Metallic bond is non-directional and weaker than covalent bond.

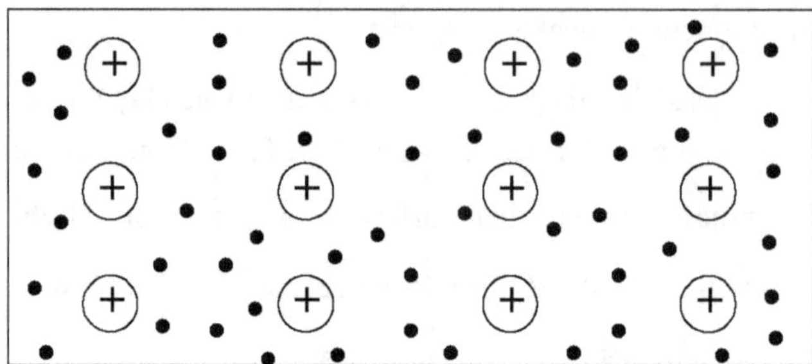

By the help of this model we can explain some physical properties of metals.

➤ If the number of mobile electron increases the strength of metallic bond also increases. This is why alkali metals are softer than alkaline earth metals because in alkali metals atom can loose only one electron form their outer most shell whereas alkaline earth metals can loose two electrons from their outermost shell. Therefore, in alkaline earth metal mobile electrons are more as comparative to alkali metals and the result is that, in alkaline earth metals the strength of metallic bond is more than alkali metals.

➤ Because of the presence of mobile electrons these electrons carry electric current from one place to another in a metal. Thus, metal is a good conductor of electricity.

➤ When a part of metal is subjected to heat, the kinetic energy of mobile electrons in that part increases. These electrons transfer their kinetic energy to the electrons of cooler part of metal by means of collision which in turn get energetic and move farther. Thus heat gets conducted from one part of metal to the other.

➤ Since mobile electrons are not bound by the help of particular bond so they can absorb and re emit light of all wavelengths a metal thus becomes a good reflector (Metallic luster).

➤ Metals exhibit properties like malleability and ductility due to non directional nature of metallic bond. The position of kerenels altered when stress is applied on metal but there is no distortion of crystals. The adjacent layers of kerenels slip one over another but the electronic environment remains the same. Thus, crystal lattice gets deformed because kerenels move from one site to other. This is the way a metal can be beaten in to thin sheets and can be drawn in to thin wires.

Limitations of free electron theory:-

(a) It can not explain that why the molar heat capacity of metals is not considerably higher than that of non metals. The mobile electrons are expected to make a significant contribution to the heat capacity.

(b) This theory can not explain why certain metals behave as semi conductor in solid state.

2. **BAND THEORY: -** This theory is an extension of the molecular orbital theory to metallic structure. We know from M.O.T that when two atomic orbitals (A.O) combine, we get two molecular orbitals (M.O), out of it one is B.M.O and other is A.B.M.O. Similarly if 'n' atomic orbitals combine with each other, they produce 'n' M.O's, out of it half are bonding type and the remaining anti bonding type. In metallic crystals 'n' may be equal to 6×10^{23} (Avogadro number). Therefore, 3×10^{23} bonding and 3×10^{23} anti bonding molecular orbitals come out of it. These molecular orbitals are closely spaced and involves in the formation of bond.

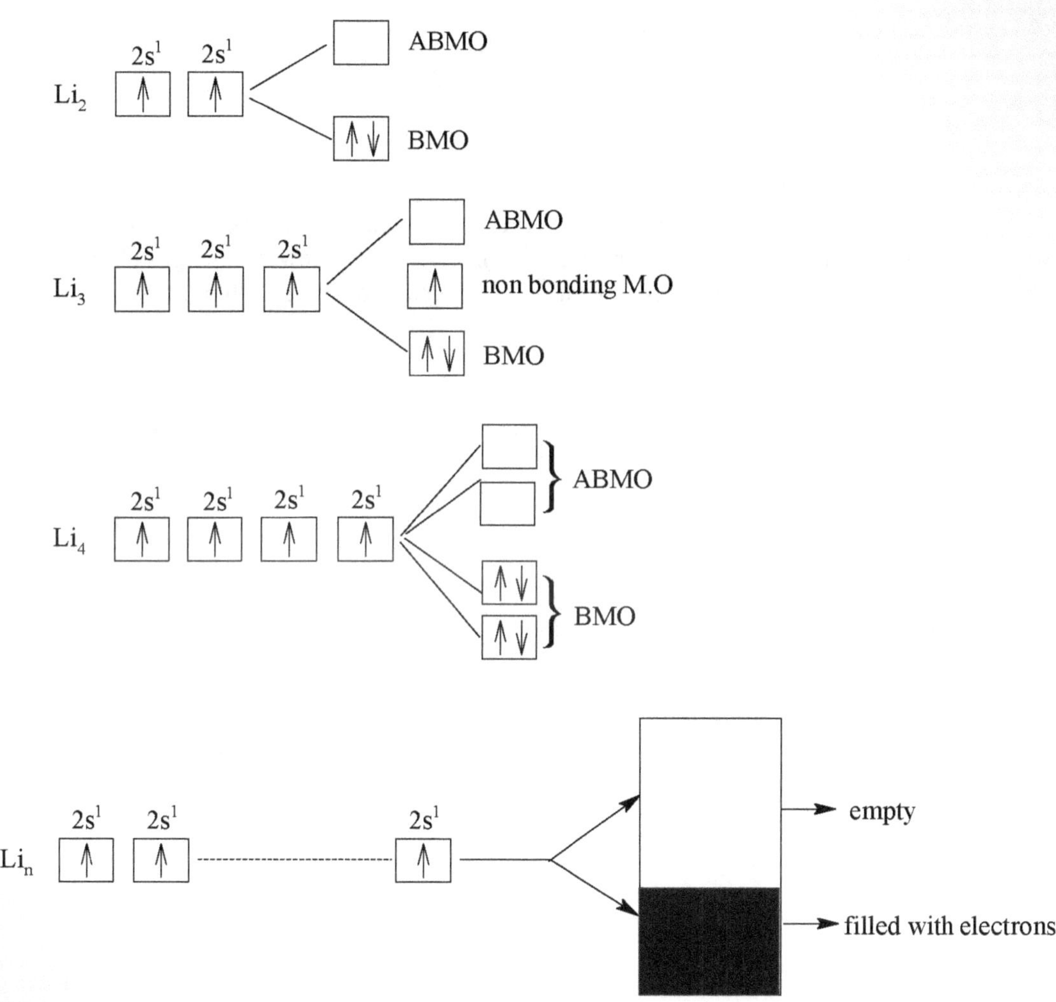

We remember that each M.O can accommodate only two electrons. The lower half of the levels that is B.M.O. is occupied by electrons, whereas the upper half i.e. A.B.M.O remain unfilled. For example when lithium crystal is placed in an electric field, a few electrons acquire enough energy to move in to higher unoccupied anti bonding orbitals. These high energy electrons carry the current.

In alkaline earth metal like Mg 's' sub shell is fulfilled, therefore, the band form with the 3s orbitals of Mg atoms are fulfilled & Mg does not conduct electricity at room temperature. But in Mg, 3s band overlaps with 3p band as shown is figure.

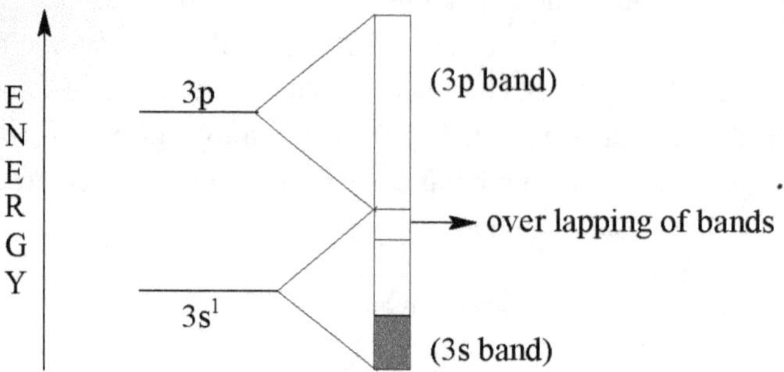

Therefore, it is easy for highest energy electron to jump in empty band and thus, Mg conducts electricity.

The lower energy bands where electrons are present are called valence band (V.B) & the bands in which electrons jump are called conduction band. (C.B). It is seen that, lower is energy difference between V.B and C.B more is the electrical conductance. On the basis of energy difference between V.B and C.B substance can be classified as:-

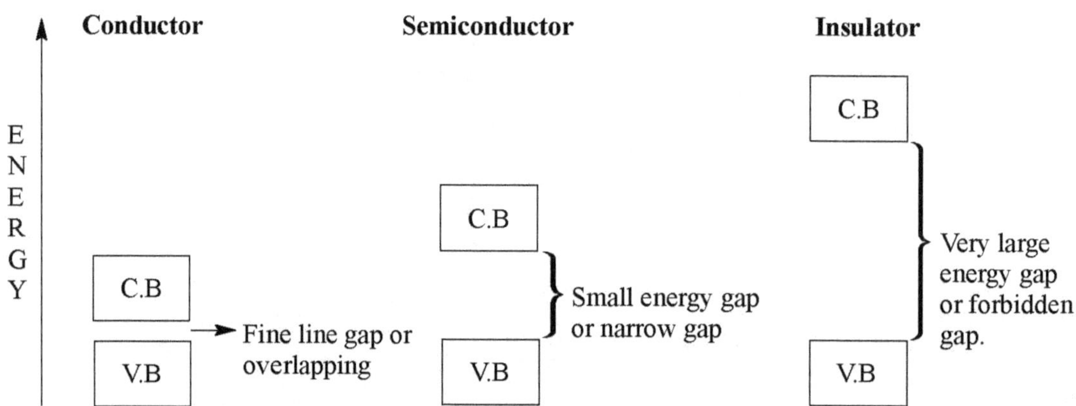

Subjective Exercise

Q.1 Suggest the type of molecular orbital formed in the following combinations assuming 'y' is bonding axis

(a) $2p_x + 2p_x$

(b) $2p_y - 2p_y$

(c) $2p_z - 2p_z$

(d) $2p_y + 2p_y$

Q.2 Explain why Be_2 does not exist.

Q.3 Explain why O_2 in found in the lower layer of atmosphere & O_3 is found in the upper layer of atmosphere however O_3 is heavier than O_2.

Q.4 O_2 appears coloured in liquid state explain.

Q.5 What happens with respect to $N - O$ bond length when NO is ionized to NO^+.

Q.6 Out of N_2^+ & N_2^- which will require more bond dissociation energy & why?

Objective Exercise

Q.1 Which among the following has node?

(a) $\sigma 2s$

(b) $2s$

(c) $\sigma^* 2s$

(d) both (b) & (c)

Q.2 Which of the following has fractional bond order?

(a) O_2^{2-}

(b) O_2^{2+}

(c) H_2^-

(d) CO

Q.3 Which is not true about the following four species?

CN^-, CO, NO^+, N_2

(a) all are linear

(b) all are iso electronic

(c) all are paramagnetic

(d) Except N_2 rest all have non zero μ

Q.4 Correct order of energy is:-

(a) BMO < non bonding orbital < ABMO

(b) non bonding orbital > BMO > ABMO

(c) BMO > ABMO > non bonding orbital

(d) BMO = non bonding orbital > ABMO

Q.5 Which of the following pairs have identical values of bond order?

(a) H_2 & He_2

(b) $H_2^{(+)}$ & $H_2^{(-)}$

(c) $CN^{(-)}$ & O_2

(d) $O_2^{2(+)}$ & $H_2^{(+)}$

Q.6   Which of the following is correct about CO?

(a)   Energy of BMO is close to the atomic orbital of oxygen.

(b)   Energy of ABMO is close to the A.O of oxygen

(c)   Energy of BMO is close to the A.O of carbon

(d)   During CO^+ formation, one electron is removed from π_{2p_x}

Q.7   Fe is harder than Na because

(a)   Size of Na atoms is smaller than Fe atoms

(b)   Na can loose only one e^- & hence in Na metallic bonds are weaker than Fe.

(c)   Size of Fe atoms is smaller than Na & hence atoms of Fe are more closely packed

(d)   E.A. of Na is smaller than Fe

Q.8   Which is an example of p - type semi conductor?

(a)   Silicon is doped with P   (b)   Al is doped with silicon

(c)   Ge is doped with Ga   (d)   Tl is doped with Pb

Q.9   Diamagnetic species is:-

(a) O_2^{2-} (b) C_2

(c) F_2 (d)   all of these

Q.10   Increasing order of 'C– O' bond length in CO, CO_2 and CO_3^{2-} is

(a) $CO > CO_2 > CO_3^{2-}$ (b) $CO_2 > CO > CO_3^{2-}$

(c) $CO_3^{2-} > CO_2 > CO$ (d) $CO_3^{2-} = CO_2 > CO$

Q.11   Which among the following can not be treated by MOT for bond order determination?

(a)   HF   (b)   NO

(c)   LiF   (d)   both (a) & (c)

Q.12   Among the oxides of nitrogen N_2O, NO and NO_2, the molecules having unpaired electrons are

(a) N_2O, NO   (b)   NO, NO_2

(c) N_2O, NO_2 (d) N_2O, NO, NO_2

Q.13   Out of CN^-, NO^+, CN^+ & $O_2^{(-)}$ the species having same bond orders are

(a) $CN^{(-)}$ & $O_2^{(-)}$ (b) $CN^{(+)}$ & $O_2^{(-)}$

(c) $NO^{(+)}$ & $CN^{(-)}$ (d) $NO^{(+)}$ & $O_2^{(-)}$

Q.14   If 'y' is bonding axis then shape of the orbital formed by $2p_x + 2p_x$ will be?

(a) 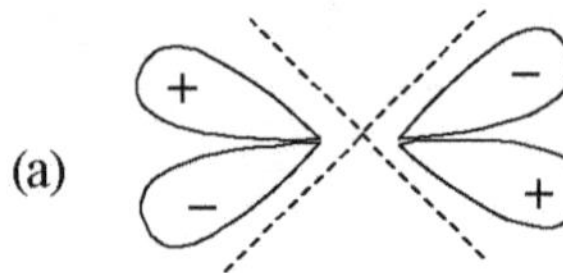   (b) 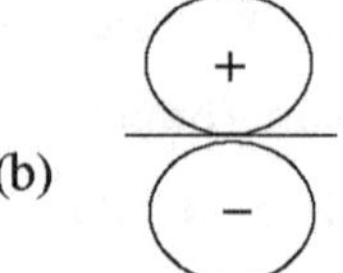

(c) 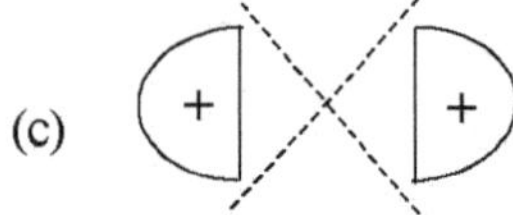   (d) 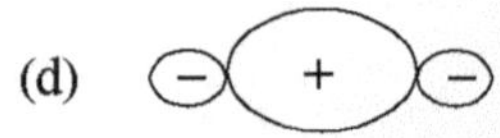

Q.15 If 'x' in bonding axis then the shape of the orbital formed by $2p_x + 2p_x$ will be?

(a) 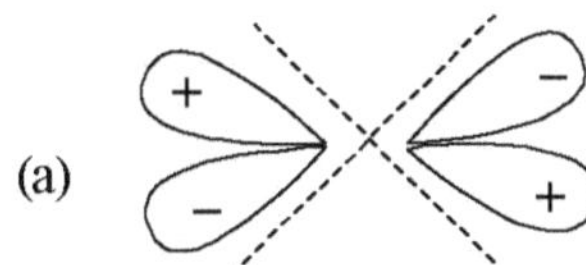

(b) 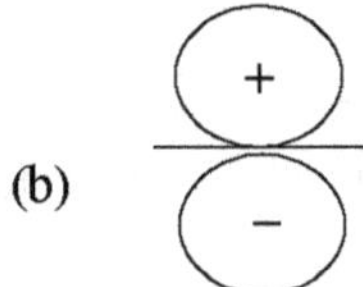

(c) 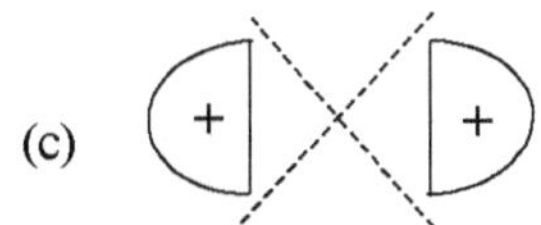

(d) 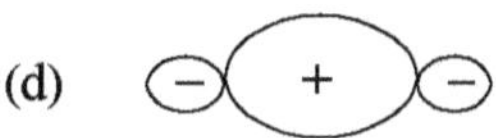

Q.16 If 'z' is bonding axis then the shape of the orbital formed by $2p_x + 2p_y$ will be?

(a) 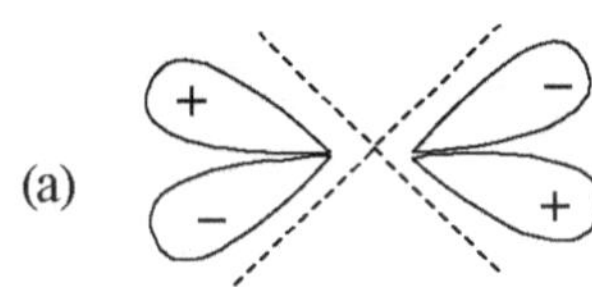

(b) 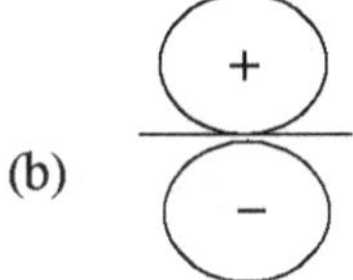

(c) 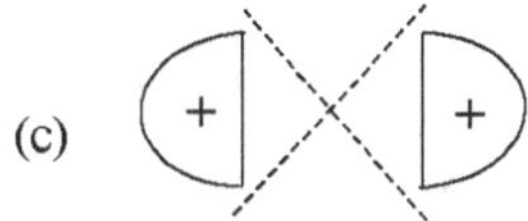

(d) no bond formation takes place.

Q.17 Correct order of bond dissociation energy is:-

(a) $N_2 > N_2^+ = N_2^-$

(b) $N_2^+ = N_2^- > N_2$

(c) $N_2 > N_2^+ > N_2^-$

(d) $N_2 > N_2^- > N_2^+$

Q.18 Correct order of bond dissociation energy is:-

(a) $O_2 > N_2 > CO$

(b) $O_2 > CO > N_2$

(c) $CO > N_2 > O_2$

(d) $N_2 > CO > O_2$

Q.19 The molecular orbital shown in the diagram is

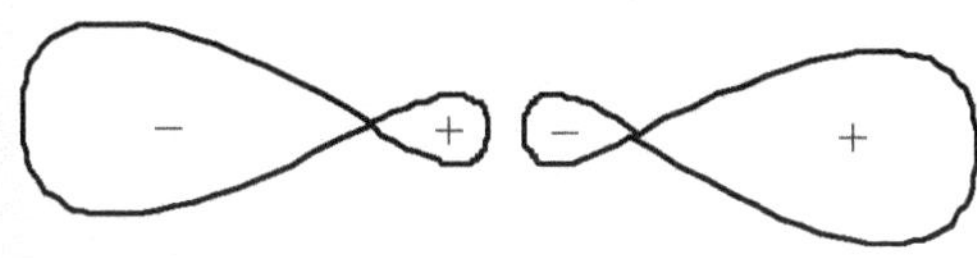

(a) $\pi 2p_y$

(b) $\pi^* 2p_x$

(c) $\pi 2p_z$

(d) $\sigma^* 2p_z$

Q.20 In a homonuclear diatomic molecule, higher the bond order, larger will be

(a) Bond length

(b) Bond strength

(c) Paramagnetic nature

(d) Ionic character

Q.21 In which set of molecules all the species are paramagnetic?

(a) C_2^{2+}, O_2, N_2

(b) C_2^{2+}, O_2, NO

(c) C_2^{2+}, F_2, O_2

(d) C_2^{2+}, O_2, Li_2

Q.22 In the formation of $NO^{(+)}$ from NO, the electron is removed from

(a) a σ orbital

(b) a π orbital

(c) a σ^* orbital

(d) a π^* orbital

Q.23 Which one of the following does not exhibit paramagnetism?

(a) NO

(b) NO_2

(c) ClO_2

(d) $ClO_2^{(-)}$

Q.24 Which of the following is non-existent according to molecular orbital theory?

(a) $H_2^{(-)}$

(b) $O_2^{(-)}$

(c) He_2

(d) $O_2^{(+)}$

Q.25 The species having highest bond order is

(a) O_2

(b) $O_2^{(-)}$

(c) $O_2^{(+)}$

(d) $O_2^{2(-)}$

Q.26 Which of the following theory provides explanation about paramagnetic nature of oxygen?

(a) Electronic theory of valency

(b) Valency bond theory

(c) Molecular orbital theory

(d) All of the above

Q.27 Which of the following species is paramagnetic?

(a) CO_2

(b) NO

(c) $O_2^{2(-)}$

(d) $CN^{(-)}$

Q.28 Paramagnetism is exhibited by molecules which

(a) are not attracted by magnetic field

(b) contain only paired electrons

(c) contain unpaired electrons

(d) carry positive charge

Q.29 Which of the following M.O. has two nodal planes per-pendicular to each other?

(a) σ_{2s}

(b) π_{2p_x}

(c) $\pi^*_{2p_y}$

(d) $\sigma^*_{2p_z}$

Q.30 Which of the following is not paramagnetic ?

(a) NO

(b) $S^{2(-)}$

(c) $O_2^{(-)}$

(d) N_2

Q.31 The number of electrons that are paired in oxygen molecule is:

(a) 16

(b) 12

(c) 7   (d) 14

Q.32   Which of the following species should be most stable?

(a) $H_2^{(+)}$ (b) $H^{(+)}$

(c) H (d) $H^{(-)}$

Q.33   The bond order in NO is 2.5 while that in $NO^{(+)}$ is 3. Which statement is true for these two species

(a) Bond length is unpredictable

(b) Bond length in NO is greater than that in $NO^{(+)}$

(c) Bon length is $NO^{(+)}$ is equal to that in NO

(d) Bond length in $NO^{(+)}$ is greater than that in NO.

Q.34   The bond order in $O_2^{(+)}$ is the same as in:-

(a) $N_2^{(+)}$ (b) $CN^{(-)}$

(c) CO (d) $NO^{(+)}$

Q.35   The bond strength increases:-

(a) With increasing bond order

(b) With increasing extent of overlapping of orbitals

(c) With decreasing difference between energies of overlapping orbitals

(d) All of the above

Q.36   Among KO_2, $AlO_2^{(-)}$, BaO_2 and $NO_2^{(+)}$, unpaired electron is present in:-

(a) $NO_2^{(+)}$ and BaO_2 (b) KO_2 and $AlO_2^{(-)}$

(c) KO_2 only   (d) BaO_2 only

Q.37   Among the following, the paramagnetic compounds is:-

(a) Na_2O_2 (b) O_3

(c) N_2O (d) RbO_2

Q.38   The species having bond order different from that in CO is:-

(a) $NO^{(-)}$ (b) $NO^{(+)}$

(c) $CN^{(-)}$ (d) N_2

Q.39   The theory related to metallic bond is

(a) Band theory   (b) Lorentz's electron gas model

(c) Ruchell model   (d) Both (a) and (b)

Q.40   Which one of the following is paramagnetic?

(a) $O_2^{(-)}$ (b) $CN^{(-)}$

(c) CO (d) $NO^{(+)}$

Q.41 The correct order in which the $O - O$ bond length increases in the following is:-

(a) $H_2O_2 < O_2 < O_3$ (b) $O_3 < H_2O_2 < O_2$

(c) $O_2 < H_2O_2 < O_3$ (d) $O_2 < O_3 < H_2O_2$

Q.42 **Matrix Match**

Column - I		**Column - II**
(A) O_2^+	(p)	Colourless
(B) NO^+	(q)	Coloured
(C) NO^-	(r)	Diamagnetic
(D) N_2	(s)	Paramagnetic

Q.43

Column - I		**Column - II**
(A) B_2	(p)	Paramagnetic
(B) N_2	(q)	Undergoes oxidation
(C) O_2^-	(r)	Undergoes reduction
(D) O_2	(s)	Bond order > 2

Q.44

Molecule / Species		**Bond order**
(A) H_2^{2-}	(p)	0
(B) Ne_2	(q)	1
(C) N_2	(r)	2
(D) O_2^-	(s)	3
	(t)	1.5

Q.45

Column - I		**Column - II**
(A) H_2^+	(p)	Diamagnetic
(B) CO	(q)	Paramagnetic
(C) N_2	(r)	B.O. $= 2$
(D) O_2^{2-}	(s)	B.O. $= 3$

SUBJECTIVE EXERCISE

1.   (a) $\pi 2p_x$ (b) $\sigma^* 2p_y$ (c) $\pi^* 2p_z$ (d) $\sigma 2p_y$

3. O_2 is paramagnetic & thus, attracted by earth's magnetic field

5.   Decreases

OBJECTIVE EXERCISE

1.   (d)   2.   (c)   3.   (c)   4.   (a)   5.   (b)

6.   (a)   7.   (b)

8.   (c)   When Ge is doped with Ga then Ga forms 3 covalent bonds with three Ge but it is unable to form 4th covalent bond & a hole is generated which makes the solid p- type semiconductor (See figure given below)

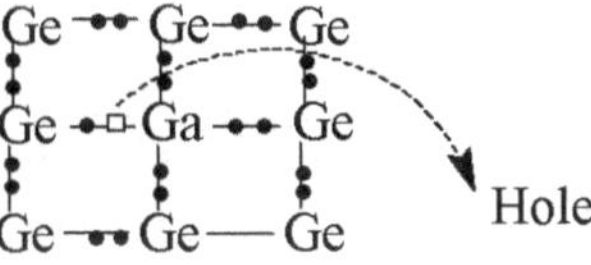

9.   (d)

10.   (c)   carbonate ion, carbon dioxide & CO have bond orders 1.33, 2 and 3 respectively.

11.   (c)   12. (b)   13. (c)   14. (b)   15. (d)

16.   (d)   17. (d)   18. (d)   19. (d)   20. (b)

21.   (b)   22. (d)   23. (d)   24. (c)   25. (c)

26.   (c)   27. (b)   28. (c)   29. (c)   30. (b)

31.   (d)   32. (d)   33. (b)   34. (a)   35. (d)

36.   (c) RbO_2, KO_2 & CsO_2 are superoxides & contains unpaired electrons & thus, these are paramagnetic

37.   (d)   38. (a)   39. (d)   40. (a)

41.   (d)   due to resonance in O_3 bond order is 1.5 while in dioxygen & hydrogen peroxide bond orders are 2 & 1 respectively

42.   A — q,s   B — p,r   C — q,s   D — p,r

43.   A—p,r   B—s   C—p,q   D—p,q

44.   A — p   B — p   C — s   D—t

45.   A — q   B — p,s   C — p,s   D — p

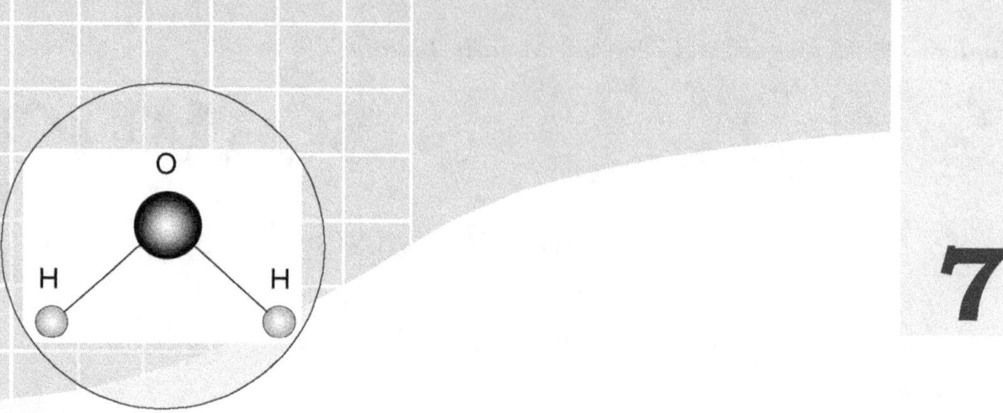

Hydrogen Bond & Inter Molecular Forces of Attractions

➤ 7.1 Hydrogen bond

1. When two dipoles come towards each other then the negative end of one dipole is attracted by the positive end of the other dipole. This is known as dipole - dipole attraction.

$$O^{\delta^-} \overset{\delta^+}{\underset{CH_3 \quad CH_3}{C}} \cdots \cdots \cdots \overset{\delta^-}{O} = \overset{\delta^+}{C} \overset{CH_3}{\underset{CH_3}{<}}$$

   However, hydrogen contains one electron in its 1s orbital but it forms covalent bond with other elements. If hydrogen forms covalent bonds with any strong electronegative element, such bonds are strongly dipolar and the dipole - dipole attraction between this dipole is known as hydrogen bond

$$\cdots \cdots \overset{\delta^+}{H} - \overset{\delta^-}{F} \cdots \cdots \cdots \overset{\delta^+}{H} - \overset{\delta^-}{F} \cdots \cdots$$

2. Hydrogen bonding is mainly shown by N, O and F. Except in some organic compounds Cl does not show hydrogen bonding because of its large size.

3. The strength of hydrogen bond lies between 8 KJ/mol to 42 KJ/mol.

4. Hydrogen bond can be classified as -

   (a) Intermolecular - H - bond

   (b) Intramolecular - H - bond

(a) **Intermolecular hydrogen bond:** - It is formed between two different molecules of the same or different substances. For e.g.

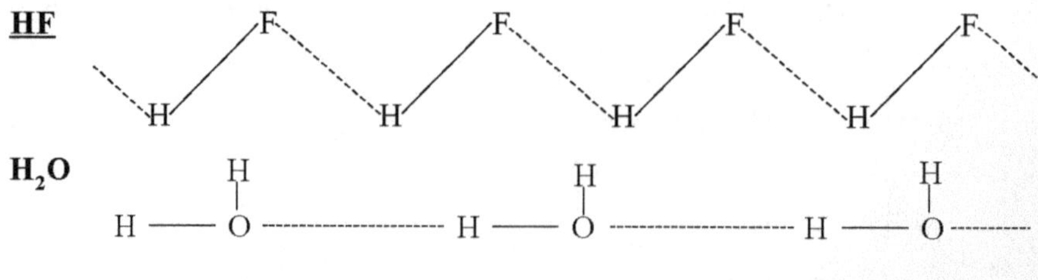

(b)   Intramolecular hydrogen bond: - It is formed between the hydrogen atom and F,N. or 'O' atoms present in the same molecule

(Ortho hydroxy benzaldehyde)
or
Salicyldehyde

(Ortho nitro phenol)

Intermolecular hydrogen bond results in to association of molecules. Thus molecules come close to one another & consequently melting point, boiling point, viscosity and surface tension increase. In intramolecular hydrogen bond in place of association, cyclisation of the molecule takes place, consequently, the effect of intramolecular hydrogen bond on the physical properties is negligible. Due to the presence of hydrogen boding in the molecules, they come close to each other and thus viscosity increase. Presence of hydrogen bonding restricts the conversion of liquid molecules in vapour state and the vapour pressure decreases and more temperature is required to boil such liquids, therefore, the boiling point increases. If any compound forms hydrogen bond with the molecules of H_2O then it dissolves in water.

To understand above facts some examples are given below.

1.   Glucose, sucrose fructose and ethyl alcohol are soluble in water due to the formation of hydrogen bond because in these compounds O - H bond is present which forms hydrogen bond with O - H bond of water.

2.   Due to the presence of hydrogen bond in water its molecules are found close to each other. Thus, it exists in liquid state whereas the big size of sulphur and low electro negativity restricts hydrogen bonding in H_2S. This inability of forming hydrogen bond keeps away all the molecules of H_2S resulting in the gaseous state of H_2S. Hence H_2O is liquid whereas H_2S is gas.

3.   Conditions for the formation of hydrogen bond

➢   Hydrogen should be bonded with highly electronegative element such as N.F. and O

➢   The size of electronegative element must be small and it must have lone pair of electrons.

(no. H - bonding as 'N' does not has lone pair of electrons)

H – C ≡ C – H   H – C ≡ C – H

(no - H - bonding as size of 'C' is large and it does not contain lone pair of electrons)

(50% 's' character highly electronegative)

➢   The strength of H - bond lies between 8 kJ/mol to 42 kJ/mol, so these bonds easily break at high temperature, therefore, temperature should be less

➤ 7.2 Influence of hydrogen bonding on physical properties

Hydrogen bonding $\propto$ 1 / vapour pressure

$\propto$ Boiling point

$\propto$ Melting point

$\propto$ Solubility $\propto$ viscosity

1. One carbon atom does not bear two OH groups and readily looses water

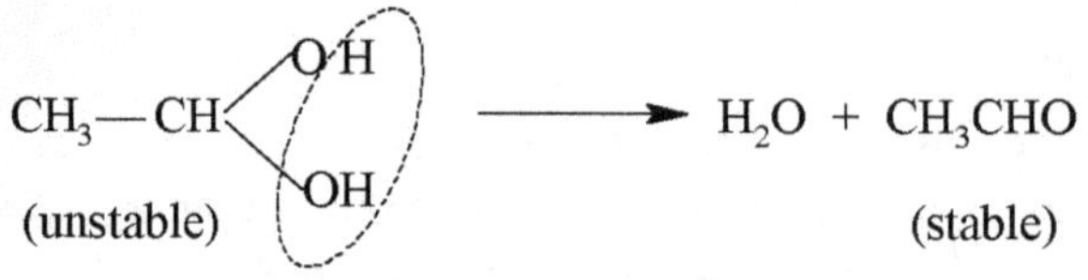

$$CH_3-CH\begin{smallmatrix}O-H\\[2pt]O-H\end{smallmatrix} \longrightarrow H_2O + CH_3CHO$$

(unstable)   (stable)

When two OH groups are present on single carbon then intra molecular hydrogen bonding takes place as follows

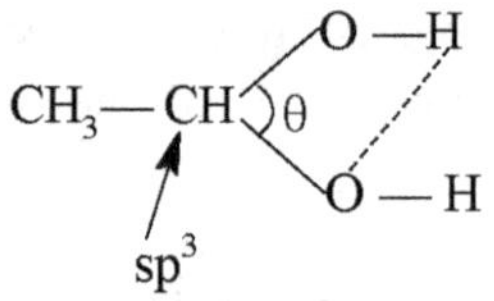

$$CH_3-CH\begin{smallmatrix}O-H\\[2pt]O-H\end{smallmatrix}\ \theta \qquad\qquad \theta < 109° 28'$$

sp^3

Thus, the OH groups come close to each other, this reduces bond angle ($\theta < 109° 28'$) and develops strain on sp^3 hybridized carbon atom. In order to reduce the strain compound release H_2O molecule and comes in to stable state.

If there is a possibility to form hydrogen bond on the adjacent carbon atom then in those conditions compound does not release H_2O. For e.g. Chloral hydrate $CCl_3CH(OH)_2$ is a stable compound and does not loose water at room temperature.

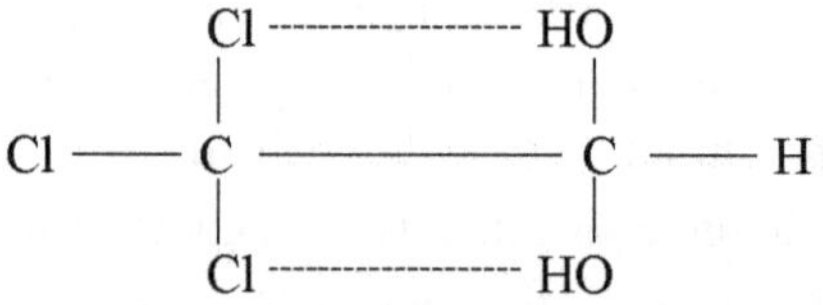

$$\begin{array}{ccccc} Cl & \cdots\cdots & HO & & \\ | & & | & & \\ Cl - C & - & C & - & H \\ | & & | & & \\ Cl & \cdots\cdots & HO & & \end{array}$$

2. Solubility of bicarbonates of alkali and alkaline earth metals increase on moving down in a group in periodic table. To clear this concept one should know about the structure of bicarbonate.

In bicarbonate ion, intramolecular H - bond is present which is shown below.

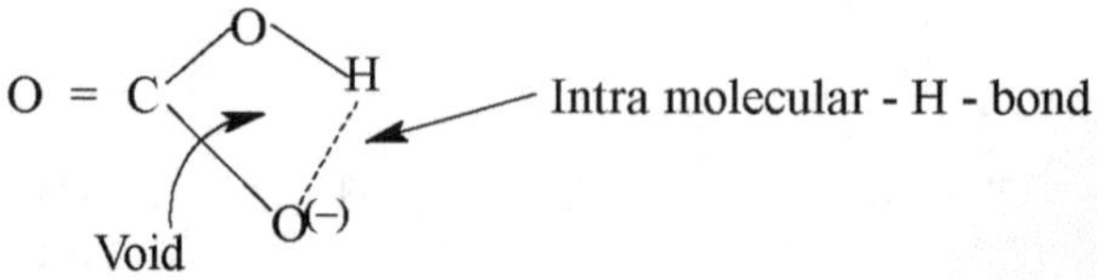

$$O = C\begin{smallmatrix}O\\ \\O^{(-)}\end{smallmatrix}H \qquad \text{Intra molecular - H - bond}$$

Void

Due to this H – bond, a void develops in bicarbonate ion which is occupied by metal cation. Now as the size of metal cation increase, the H – bond begins to weaken and hydration of bicarbonate, becomes easy resulting in increasing solubility

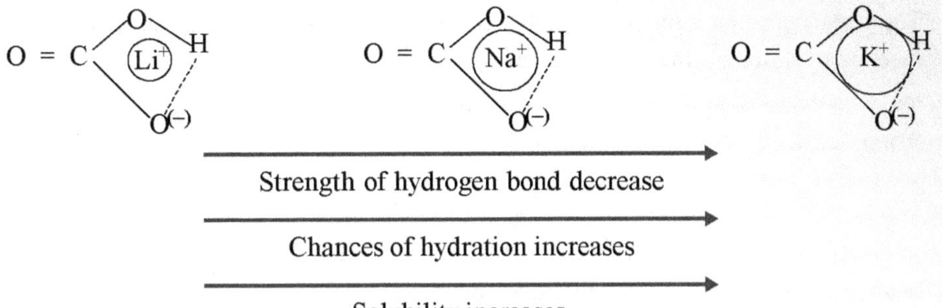

Strength of hydrogen bond decrease

Chances of hydration increases

Solubility increases.

3. **Density of ice is lesser than water**

The H_2O molecules of water are attached with hydrogen bonding and forms structures like honey comb. All oxygen forms four bonds, two covalent bonds with hydrogen and two hydrogen bonds with two H_2O molecules. Due to the cage like structure of ice, its volume increases and density decreases. $(d = m/v)$

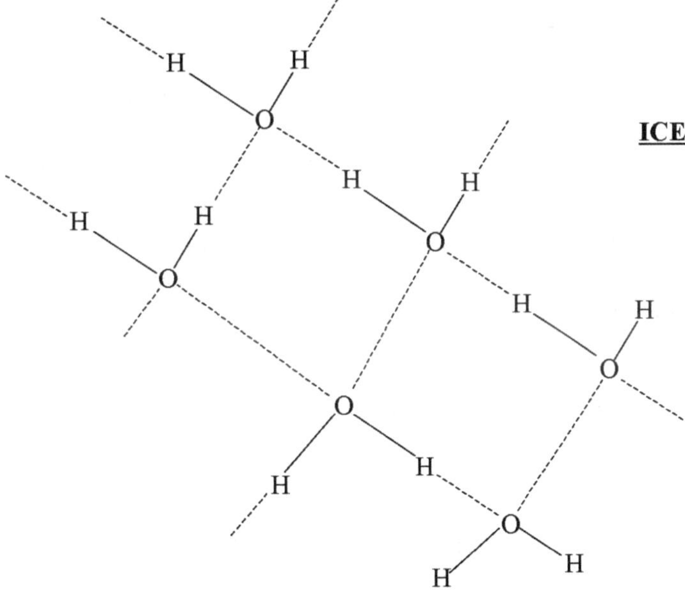

On heating ice, some hydrogen bonds break up and H_2O molecules go in to cage which decrease volume and density increases

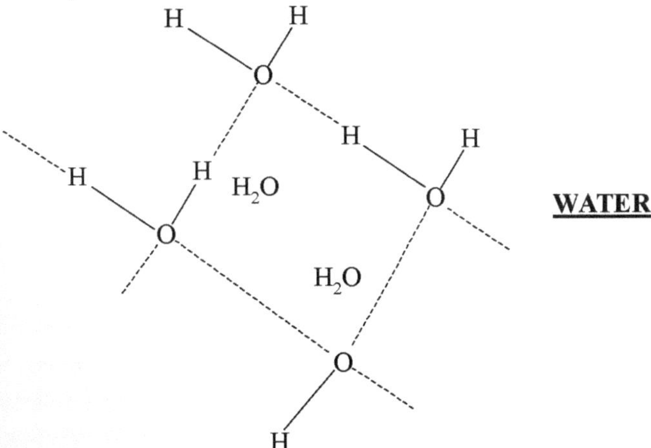

The density of water is maximum at 4°C because beyond 4°C more thermal expansion occurs which increases volume of water and decrease density (d = m/v)

Ice   ⟶ 4 hydrogen bonds (as shown above)

Water ⟶ 2 hydrogen bonds

$$------ H ---- O -------- H ---- O -------- H ---- O ---------$$

Water vapours ⟶ no hydrogen bond

4. **Hydrogen bond two also influences the acidic strength. In ortho nitro phenol intra molecular hydrogen bond is present in between OH and NO$_2$ groups**

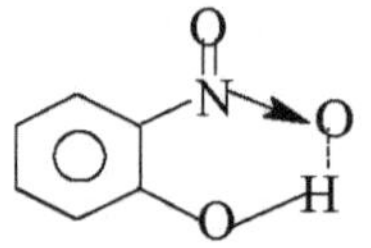

(ortho nitrophenol) 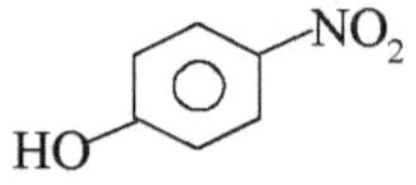   (para nitrophenol)

Thus, presence of hydrogen bonding reduces the ability of OH group to release H^+ ion and consequently **ortho nitro phenol becomes less acidic than para nitro phenol.**

5. **Viscosity of ethyl alcohol is less than glycerine** because there is only one hydrogen bond between the two molecules of ethyl alcohol whereas there are three hydrogen bonds between the two molecules of glycerine, Therefore, the molecules of glycerine are much closer to each other than the molecules of alcohol. Thus, glycerine is more viscous than ethyl alcohol.

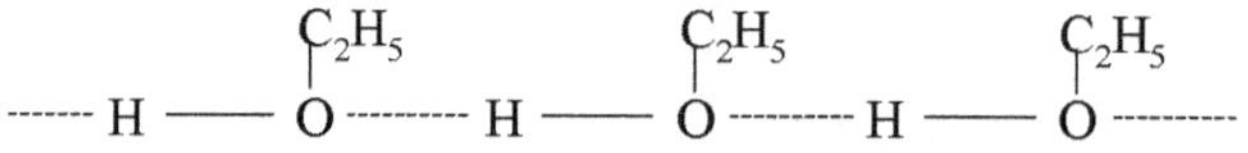

Ethyl alcohol

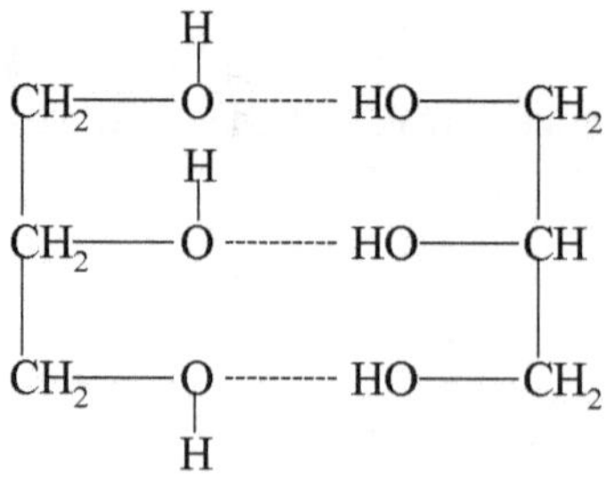

Glycerine

(Ethyl alcohol)   (Ethylene glycol)   (Glycerine)

C_2H_5OH

CH_2OH
CH_2OH

CH_2OH
$CHOH$
CH_2OH

→ Number of hydrogen bonds increases

→ Viscosity increases

→ Boiling point increases

6. **Acid strength of hydrogen halides**

   HF < HCl < HBr < HI

   On moving from HF to HI, the size of halogen increase and bond length of H — X bond increase Thus, when we move from HF to HI covalent bond becomes longer and weaker and breakes easily, consequently HI is better acid than HBr which is further more acidic than HCl and HF. Along with this acid strength is also influenced by hydrogen bonding because the molecules of HF attach with one another by the help of hydrogen bonding therefore, HF does not release H^+ easily even on breaking of H —F bond. Thus HF is least acidic among all hydrogen halides because in successive halides hydrogen bonding is absent.

7. **Hydrogen bonding also influences dipole moment.**

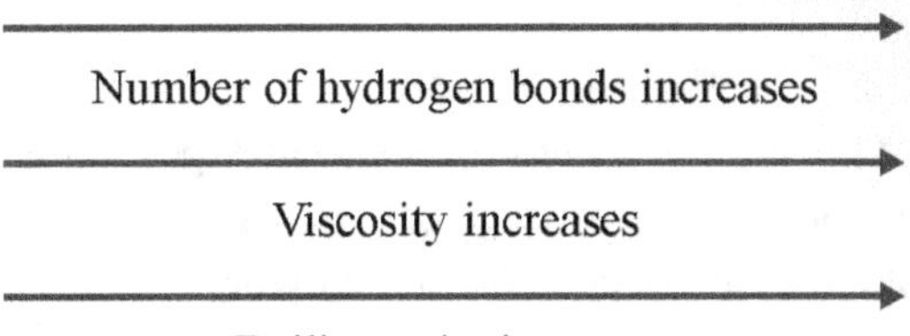

   (i)   (ii)

   In (i) case, OH and F come closer to each other due to intra molecular hydrogen bond which reduces the angle between μ_1 & μ_2 (less than 60°) and because

   $$\mu_{Res} \propto \cos\theta \propto 1/\theta$$

   Therefore, the dipole moment of (i) is greater than (ii)

8. On adding KF in HF, KHF_2 forms but HBr and HI do not form $KHBr_2$ and KHI_2

   $$KF + HF \longrightarrow KHF_2$$
   $$KBr + HBr \longrightarrow KHBr_2 \text{ (not possible)}$$
   $$KI + HI \longrightarrow KHI_2 \text{ (not possible)}$$

   Hydrogen boding is responsible for the formation of KHF_2

   $$K^{(+)} \left[F\text{–}H \cdots\cdots F \right]^{(-)}$$

➤ 7.3 Intermolecular forces of attractions

Besides the primary forces responsible for the formation of covalent, ionic and coordinate bonds there are secondary forces that operates between molecules. These forces are present in all states of matter and are responsible for structural features as well as physical properties of matter. These forces are called intermolecular forces. These are discovered by the Dutch scientist Van - der - waal therefore, these intermolecular forces are also called Van - der - waal forces of attractions. These forces of attractions are very weak. Their strength is less than 8 kJ/mol. These are mainly of three types.

(a) Dipole - dipole attraction (Keesom forces)

(b) Dipole - induce dipole attractions (Debye forces)

(c) Dispersion forces or London forces or instantaneous dipole attraction.

(a) **Dipole - dipole attraction** - When two dipoles come close to each other then the negative end of one dipole is attracted by the positive end of the other dipole. This attraction is known as dipole - dipole attraction.

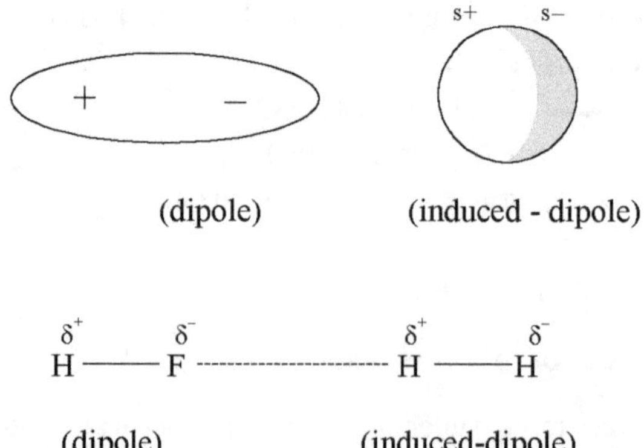

(dipole-dipole attraction in acetone)

Hydrogen bonding is also a type of this class.

| Strength of H – bond   >   Strength of other dipole – dipole attraction. |

Due to more electropositive nature and small size of hydrogen the strength of hydrogen bond is more than other dipole - dipole attraction. Thus, the boiling point of acetone is 56°C where as the boiling point of CH_3OH is 65°C because in acetone CH_3OH dipole – dipole attraction and H – bonding are present respectively.

(b) **Dipole - induce dipole attraction** - This type of forces exist when one molecule has permanent dipole and other molecule or atom has no dipole. Polar molecule distorts the electron density of non-polar species towards its +ve or –ve end, due to which a dipole is induced on non-polar molecule.

(dipole)   (induced - dipole)

(dipole)   (induced-dipole)

These forces are responsible for the formation of noble gas hydrates.

(c) **Dispersion forces or London forces or instantaneous dipole** or **induced dipole interactions** - Since permanent dipoles do not exist in homonuclear diatomic molecules H_2, N_2, O_2, Cl_2 etc a different type of attractive force must be postulated to explain the liquid and solid state of such substances.

Over a period of time the two bonding electrons in H_2 molecules are as close to one nucleus as to the other. The molecule therefore does not possess any permanent dipole. But any given moment the electron density may be concentrated at one end of the molecule and fraction of a second later this may be concentrated at the other end of the molecule. Thus instantaneous dipoles are generated. These instantaneous dipole induce similar dipoles in neighboring molecules. These instantaneous dipoles lead to an attractive force between the molecules.

The strength of such induced dipoles interaction depends on the polarizability of the molecule. The ease of polarization again depends on the size of the molecule.

Polarizing tendency $\propto$ size of molecule

$\propto$ number of electrons

$\propto$ molecular weight

This in why F_2 and Cl_2 are gases (less polarization & less magnitude of London forces) and I_2 is solid (more polarization and more magnitude of London forces)

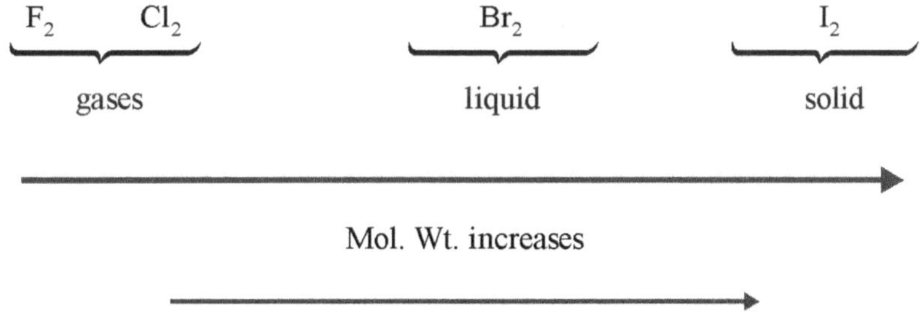

These forces of attractions are responsible for the liquefaction of gases.

Consider some more examples of this class

$CH_3F \; < \; CH_3Cl \; < \; CH_3Br \; < \; CH_3I$

(less b.p)   (More b.p)

$CH_3Cl \; < \; CH_3Cl_2 \; < \; CHCl_2 \; < \; CCl_4$

(less b.p)   (More b.p)

$CH_3F \; > \; CH_2F_2 \; > \; CHF_3 \; > \; CF_4$ (Exceptional case)

(less b.p)   (More b.p)

In addition to these inter molecular forces, ion dipole and **ion - induce dipole attractions** are also observed. But these forces of attractions are not Van - der - waal forces of attractions. Here we are doing a small discussion on these forces of attractions.

(1)   **Ion - dipole attraction:**-These forces of attractions exist between ion (Cation or anion) and polar molecule. The cation is attracted by the -ve end of dipole while the anion is attracted by the positive end of dipole.

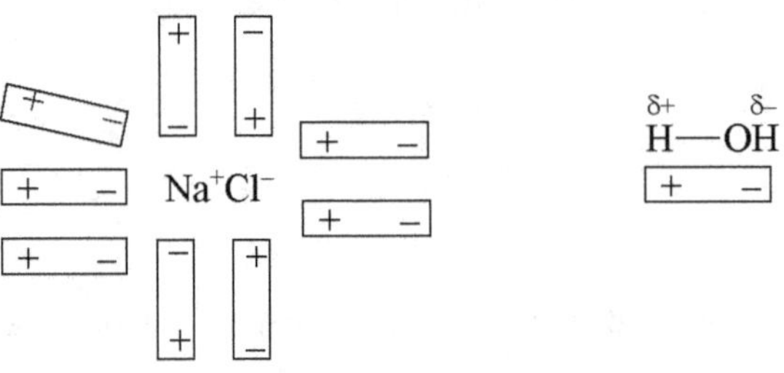

These forces are responsible for the solvation of ionic compound in polar medium like water.

(2)   **Ion - induced dipole: -** These forces of attractions exist between ion and non polar molecule. When non polar molecules come closer to the ion, ion distorts the electron density of non polar molecule and induces dipole moment in it. These forces are responsible for the solubility of ionic compound in non polar.

Solvents: - For example $F^{(-)}$ and CCl_4, $NO_3^{(-)}$ and CS_2

Descending order of forces of attractions is given below.

ion - ion > ion - dipole > dipole - dipole > ion - induced dipole > dipole - induced dipole > London forces

Objective Exercise

Q.1 Which will have highest critical temperature?

(a) HF (b) HCl

(c) H_2O (d) NH_3

Q.2 Basicity of HF is

(a) 1 (b) 2

(c) 3 (d) Zero

Q.3 Which of the following compounds would have significant intermolecular H - bonding?

H_2S,	CH_3COOH,	HCl,	CH_3CH_2F
1	2	3	4

(a) 1, 2, 3, 4 (b) 2, 3, 4

(c) 2, 4 (d) 2

Q.4 Compound with highest dipole moment is:-

(a) 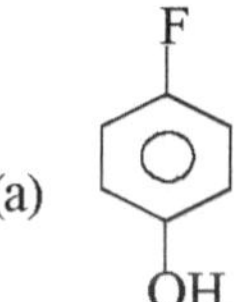

(b)

(c)

(d)

Q.5 The order of strength of H – bond is

(a) NH …..N > ClH…..Cl > OH…….O > FH ……F

(b) ClH ……Cl > NH …..N > OH…..O > FH ……F

(c) ClH ……Cl < NH …..N < OH…..O > FH…….F

(d) FH ……..F > OH ……O > NH…..N > ClH ……Cl

Q.6 Which of the following reaction is possible?

(a) $KCl + HCl \longrightarrow KHCl_2$

(b) $KBr + HBr \longrightarrow KHBr_2$

(c) $KF + HF \longrightarrow KHF_2$

(d) $KI + HI \longrightarrow KHI_2$

Q.7 Which of the following intermolecular forces of attractions are responsible for the liquefaction of N_2?

(a) Dipole - dipole attraction (b) London forces

(c) H - Bonding (d) Dipole - induce dipole attraction

Q.8 Which is not correctly matched?

(a) NO_3^- & $CHCl_3$ ion - dipole attraction

(b) HF & NH_3 dipole - dipole attraction

(c) CF_4 & HF   dipole - dipole attraction

(d) H_2 & HF   dipole - induce dipole attraction

Q.9 In which case intra molecular H – Bonding is present

(a) H_3BO_3 (b) $CH_3CHOHCHCOCH_3$

(c) CH_3OH (d) CH_3COOH

Q.10 Which is unstable at room temperature?

(a) 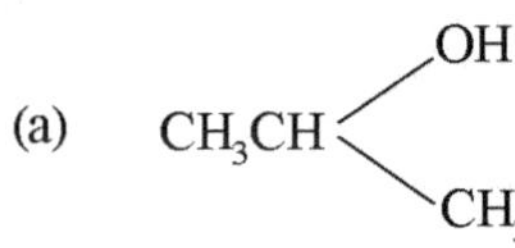   (b) $CH_3 - \overset{\overset{\textstyle OH}{|}}{C}H - OCH_3$

(c) $NaHCO_3$ (d) KHF_2

Q.11 Correct order of boiling point is:-

(a) $HF > HCl > HBr > HI$ (b) $HI > HBr > HCl > HF$

(c) $HF > HI > HBr > HCl$ (d) $HI > BHr > HF > HCl$

Q.12 Correct order of boiling point is?

(a) $BiH_3 > SbH_3 > NH_3 > AsH_3 > PH_3$

(b) $NH_3 > BiH_3 > SbH_3 > AsH_3 > PH_3$

(c) $NH_3 > PH_3 > AsH_3 > SbH_3 > BiH_3$

(d) $BiH_3 = NH_3 > SbH_3 > AsH_3 > PH_3$

Q.13 Cl does not exhibit H – bonding significantly because

(a) Cl is less electronegative   (b) Cl is more electronegative

(c) Cl has large size   (d) Cl has small size

Q.14 Correct order of vapour pressure is:-

(a) $C_6H_6 > CH_3COCH_3 > H_2O$ (b) $H_2O > C_6H_6 > CH_3COCH_3$

(c) $CH_3COCH_3 > H_2O > C_6H_6$ (d) $CH_3COCH_3 > C_6H_6 > H_2O$

Q.15 The forces of attraction which are responsible for liquefaction of inert gases are:-

(a) Keesom forces   (b) London forces

(c) H - bonding   (d) Covalent bond

Q.16   Arrange the following molecules in order of strength of London forces

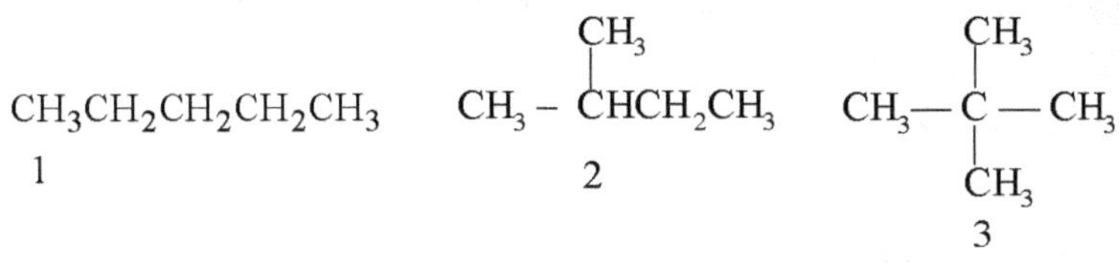

    (a) $1 > 2 > 3$ (b) $2 > 3 > 1$

    (c) $3 > 2 > 1$ (c) $1 = 2 = 3$

Q.17   Which is highly soluble in water?

    (a) CH_3OH (b) CH_3NH_2

    (c) CH_3F (d) CH_3OCH_3

Q.18   The strongest hydrogen bonding is present:-

    (a) NH_3 (b) N_2O

    (c) CH_3NH_2 (d)   HF

Q.19   The pair of compounds which likely to form the strongest hydrogen bond is:-

    (a) SiH_4 and $SiCl_4$ (b) CH_3COOH and CH_3COCH_3

    (c) CH_3COOH and $HCOOH$ (d) H_2 and H_2O

Q.20   Among H_2O, H_2Se and H_2Te, the one with highest boiling point is

    (a) H_2O because of hydrogen bonding

    (b) H_2Te because of high molecular mass

    (c) H_2S because of hydrogen bonding

    (d) H_2Se because of lower molecular mass

Q.21   In which of the following substances, the intermolecular forces are hydrogen bonds?

    (a)   Hydrogen chloride   (b)   Hydrogen sulphide

    (c)   Dry ice   (d)   Ice

Q.22   Which of the following is a non-directional bond?

    (a)   Dative bond   (b)   Covalent

    (c)   Hydrogen bond   (d)   None of these

Q.23   In which of the following species, the O-atom constitutes the positive end of electrical dipole?

    (a) CH_3CONH_2 (b) C_2H_5OH

    (c) OF_2 (d) $HO - CH_2CH_2F$

Q.24 $CuSO_4.5H_2O$ contains which type of bonds?

    (a)   Covalent only

    (b)   Covalent and co-ordinate

    (c)   Covalent, coordinate, ionic and H-bonds

    (d)   Ionic and covalent only

Q.25   Which one of the following molecules will form a linear polymeric structure due to hydrogen bonding?

    (a)   Urea   (b) H_2O

    (c) H_2O_2 (d)   HF

Q.26 H_2O is dipolar, whereas BeF_2 is not. It is because

(a)   Both have same structures but electronegativity of 'F' is greater than that of 'O'

(b) H_2O involves hydrogen bonding whereas BeF_2 is a discrete molecule

(c) H_2O is linear and BeF_2 is angular

(d) H_2O is angular and BeF_2 is linear

Q.27   Which type of bond is not present in liq HNO_2?

(a)   covalent   (b)   coordinate & H – Bond

(c)   H – Bond   (d)   coordinate

Q.28   Naphthalene is an organic compound containing two fused benzene rings. It is solid, the force of attraction which is responsible for its physical appearance is:-

(a)   van der Waal's forces   (b)   Electrostatic forces

(c)   Hydrogen bonding   (d)   None of these

Q.29   The higher values of latent heat of water than other liquids have been accounted in terms of:-

(a)   High dielectric constant   (b)   Polarity

(c)   H - bonding   (d)   None of these

Q.30   H - bonding is not present in:-

(a)   Glycerine   (b)   Water

(c) NH_4OH (d)   Urea

Matrix Match

Q.31   **Molecule**   **No. of H - Bonds**

(A) H_3BO_3 (p)   0

(B) $H_2O\,(0°C)$ (q)   1

(C) $H_2O\,(100°C)$ (r)   2

(D) CH_3COOH (s)   3

                                                         (t)   4

Q.32   **Mixture**   **Forces of attraction**

(A) $CCl_4 + HF$ (p)   London force

(B) $HF + NO_3^{(-)}$ (q)   Dipole - dipole

(C) $CCl_4 + CO_2$ (r)   Ion - dipole

(D) $CO_2 + CHCl_3$ (s)   Ion - induce dipole

                                                         (t)   Dipole - induce dipole

Q.33   **Column - I**   **Column - II**

(Decreasing order)   **(Physical properties)**

(A) $H_2O > H_2S > H_2Se > H_2Te$ (p)   Acid character

(B) $NH_3 > PH_3 > AsH_3 > SbH_3$ (q)   Thermal stability

(C) $H_2O > H_2Te > H_2Se > H_2S$ (r)   Boiling point

(D) $HI > HBr > HCl > HF$ (s)   Reducing character

HINTS & SOLUTIONS

OBJECTIVE EXERCISE

1.   (a)   critical temperature $\propto$ intermolecular forces of attraction

2.   (b)   3.   (d)

4.   (c)   due to intermolecular -H-bonding angle between μ_1 & μ_2 reduces (less than 60°) which increases dipole moment of molecule

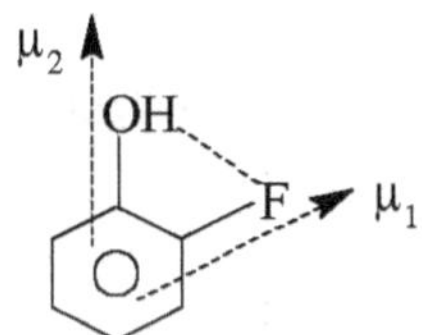

5.   (d)   6.   (c) $K^{(+)}\left[\,F\text{–}H\text{-----}\,F\,\right]^{(-)}$ 7.   (b)

8.   (c)   dipole induce dipole attraction   9.   (b)

10.   (b)   due to intramolecular –H–bonding bond angle becomes less than 109° 28' & thus, it releases CH_3OH as follows

$$CH_3\!-\!CH\!\begin{smallmatrix}OH\\[2pt]\\OCH_3\end{smallmatrix} \longrightarrow CH_3OH + CH_3CHO$$

$$\theta < 109°\,28'$$

11.   (c)   In HF hydrogen bonding takes place while in HI, HBr & HCl Van-der-waal forces of attractions are present . Since strength of hydrogen bond is more in comparison to Van-der-waal forces hence, HF has highest boiling point.

12.   (a)   13.   (c)

14.   (a)   vapour pressure $\propto$ 1 / intermolecular forces of attraction

15.   (b)   16.   (a)   London forces $\propto$ surface area   17.   (b)

18.   (d)   19.   (c)

20.   (a)   in water H-bond is present while in rest hydrides weak van-der-waal forces are present

21.   (d)   22.   (c)   23.   (c)   24.   (c)

25.   (d)   26.   (d)   27.   (d)   28.   (a)

29.   (c)   30.   (c)

31.   A—s   B—t   C—p   D—r

32.   A—s   B—r   C—p   D—t

33.   A—q   B—q   C—r   D—r, s

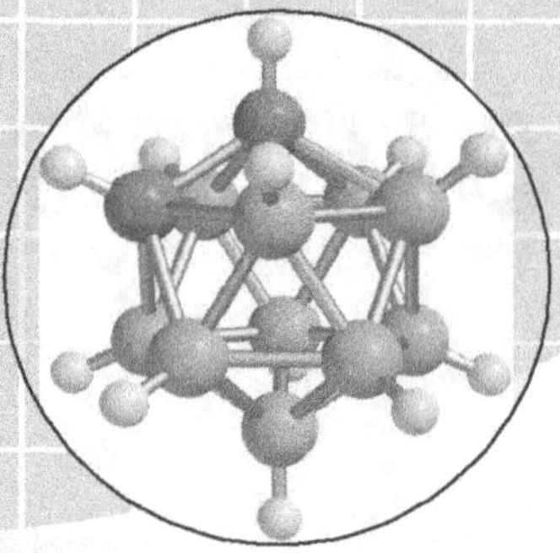

Hydrolysis of Inorganic Covalent Compounds

8

Following three conditions are required for the hydrolysis of inorganic covalent compounds:

- One atom should carry partial positive charge.

- Positively charged atom should have vacant 'p' or 'd' orbital of suitable energy so that it can receive electron pair from water molecules.

- Absence of steric crowding around positively charged atom.

Consider the following examples –

Example 1

CCl_4 does not undergo hydrolysis at room temperature though carbon atom is positively charged but it can not receive electron from H_2O molecules as carbon belongs to second period of periodic table and does not carry 'd' orbital.

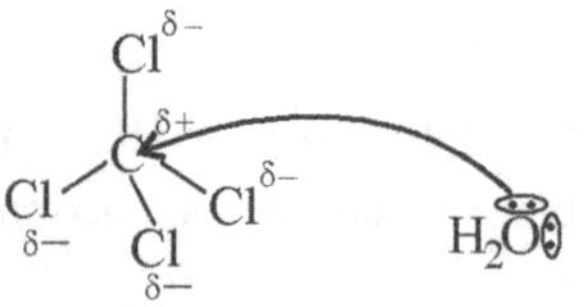

(Not possible)

But under super heated conditions hydrolysis occurs as follows:

$$CCl_4 \xrightarrow{\text{strong heat}} Cl^- + \overset{+}{C}Cl_3$$

$$\overset{+}{C}Cl_3 + H_2O \xrightarrow{S_N1} Cl_3C\!-\!\overset{+}{O}H_2$$

$$COCl_2 + HCl \longleftarrow Cl_3C\!-\!OH \longleftarrow \quad -H^+$$
(Phosgene gas)   (Unstable)

Example 2

$SiCl_4$ undergoes hydrolysis easily at room temperature because silicon atom possesses 'd' orbital of suitable energy to receive electrons from H_2O molecules as silicon belongs to third period of periodic table

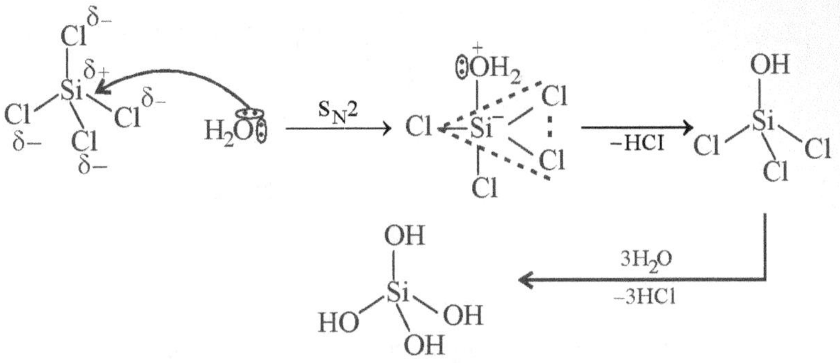

Example 3

In case of NCl_3, chlorine atoms carry partial positive charge as nitrogen is more electronegative than chlorine and since chlorine belongs to third period of periodic table hence it also possesses 'd' orbital of suitable energy to receive electrons from water molecules

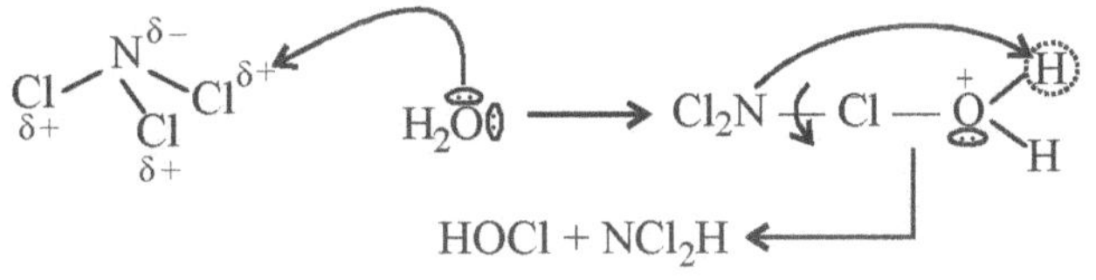

$$HOCl + NCl_2H$$

Further,

$$NCl_2H + 2H_2O \rightarrow NH_3 + 2HOCl$$

Hydrolysis of NCl_3 looks complicated so, the easiest way to perform these hydrolysis is given below –

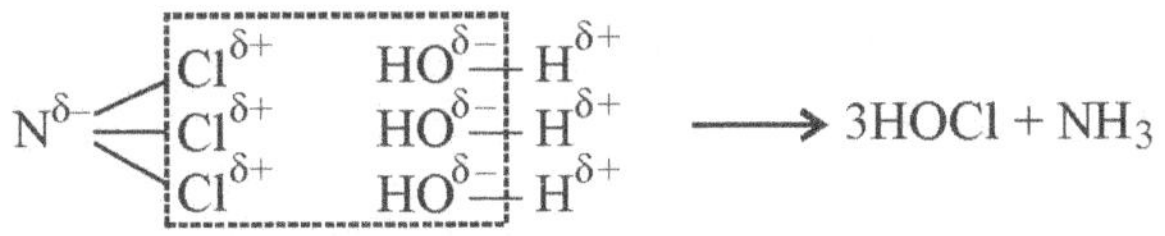

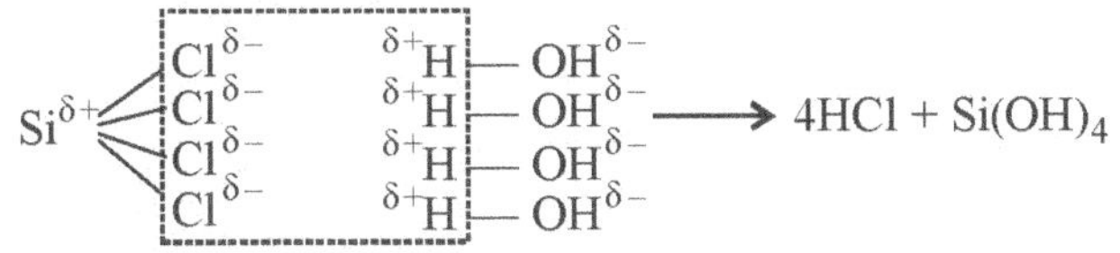

$$\longrightarrow 3HOCl + NH_3$$

$$\longrightarrow 4HCl + Si(OH)_4$$

Similarly PCl_3 on hydrolysis gives H_3PO_3 along with HCl but in $P(OH)_3$ an exceptional rearrangement occurs as shown below

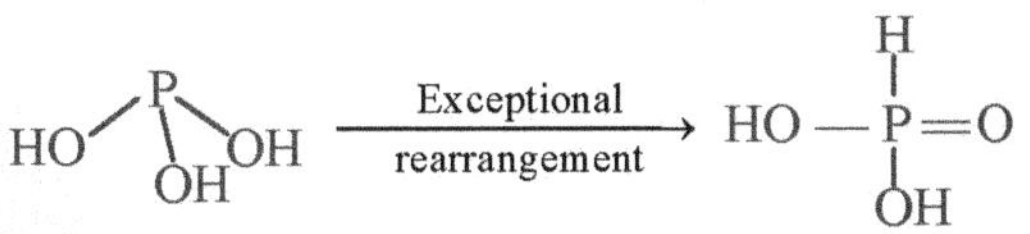

$$HO-\overset{\overset{\displaystyle H}{|}}{\underset{\underset{\displaystyle OH}{|}}{P}}=O$$

(H_3PO_3)

Example 4

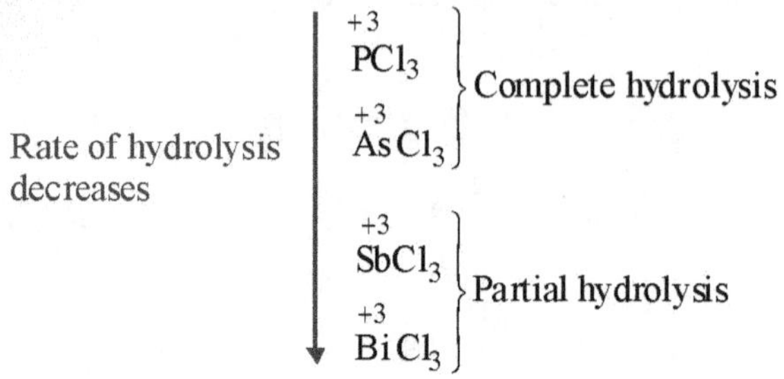

$$\text{Rate of hydrolysis decreases} \; \left\downarrow \; \begin{cases} \overset{+3}{P}Cl_3 \\ \overset{+3}{As}Cl_3 \end{cases} \text{Complete hydrolysis} \atop \begin{cases} \overset{+3}{Sb}Cl_3 \\ \overset{+3}{Bi}Cl_3 \end{cases} \text{Partial hydrolysis}$$

When we move from PCl_3 to $BiCl_3$ rate of hydrolysis decreases because size of central atom increases and hence positive charge density on central atom decreases.

This is why, $SbCl_3$ and $BiCl_3$ show partial hydrolysis as –

$$SbCl_3 + H_2O \; \rightleftharpoons \; \underset{\substack{\text{Antimonyl chloride} \\ \text{(white turbidity)}}}{SbOCl} + 2HCl$$

$$BiCl_3 + H_2O \; \rightleftharpoons \; \underset{\text{(white turbidity)}}{BiOCl} + 2HCl$$

Example 5

Marshall's acid ($H_2S_2O_8$) forms sulphuric acid on full hydrolysis as shown below –

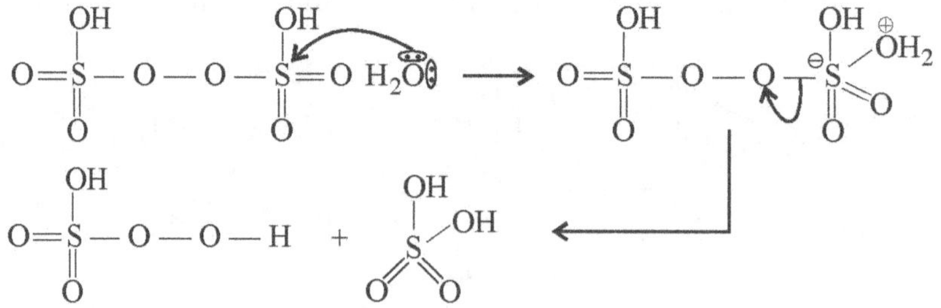

Further H_2SO_5 (caro's acid) on hydrolysis produces sulphuric acid

$$H_2SO_5 + H_2O \rightarrow H_2SO_4 + H_2O_2$$

Overall reaction: $H_2S_2O_8 + 2H_2O \rightarrow 2H_2SO_4 + H_2O_2$

Example 6

Hydrolysis of SF_4 gives sulphurous acid (H_2SO_3)

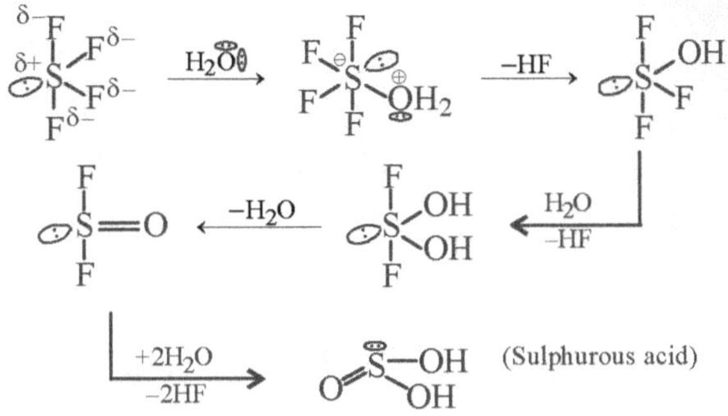

Example 7

Hydrolysis of BCl_3 and $BeCl_2$

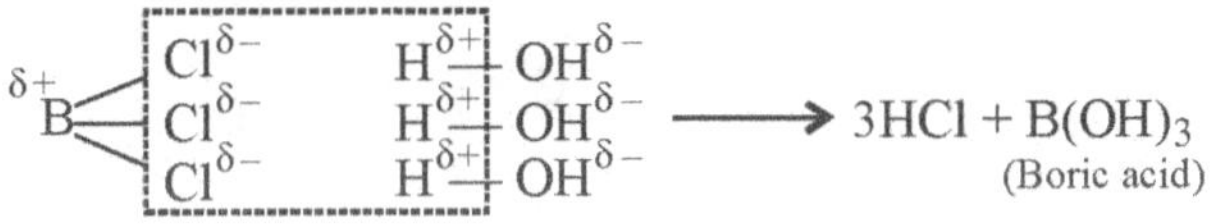

$$3HCl + B(OH)_3 \quad \text{(Boric acid)}$$

In boric acid 'B' is electron deficient and hence it further takes one electron pair from water molecule to complete its octet

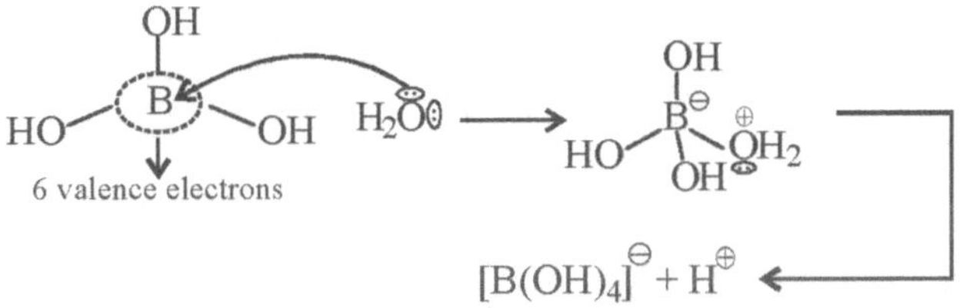

$$[B(OH)_4]^{\ominus} + H^{\oplus}$$

Similarly, $BeCl_2$ on hydrolysis forms beryllate ion

$$BeCl_2 + 2H_2O \rightarrow 2HCl + Be(OH)_2$$

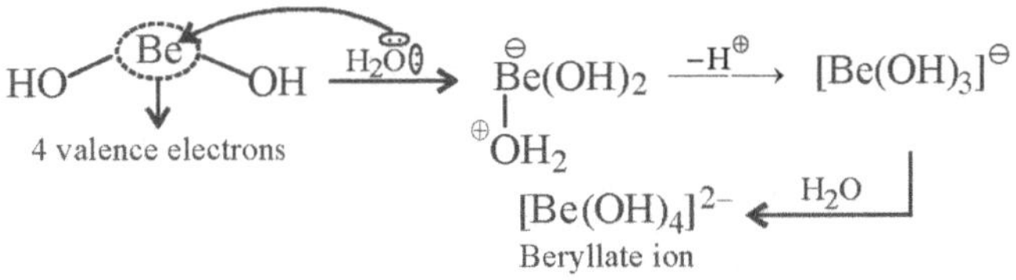

$$[Be(OH)_4]^{2-} \quad \text{Beryllate ion}$$

Example 8

SF_6 does not show hydrolysis under ordinary conditions because sulphur atom is sterically hindered from six fluorine atoms and hence water molecules cannot approach to 'S' atom.

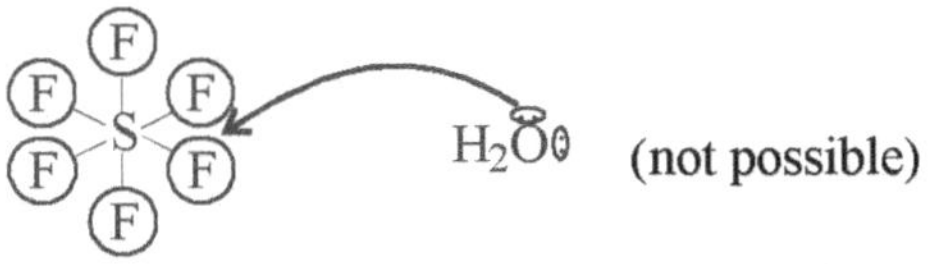

H_2O (not possible)

But when we move from SF_6 to TeF_6 size of central atom increases and steric crowding decreases, so, water molecules can easily approach to central atom and hydrolysis becomes easy

$$\underrightarrow{\quad SF_6 \quad SeF_6 \quad TeF_6 \quad}$$
Rate of hydrolysis increases

$$TeF_6 + 6H_2O \rightarrow 6HF + Te(OH)_6$$

Example 9

Hydrolysis of P_4O_{10} is shown below –

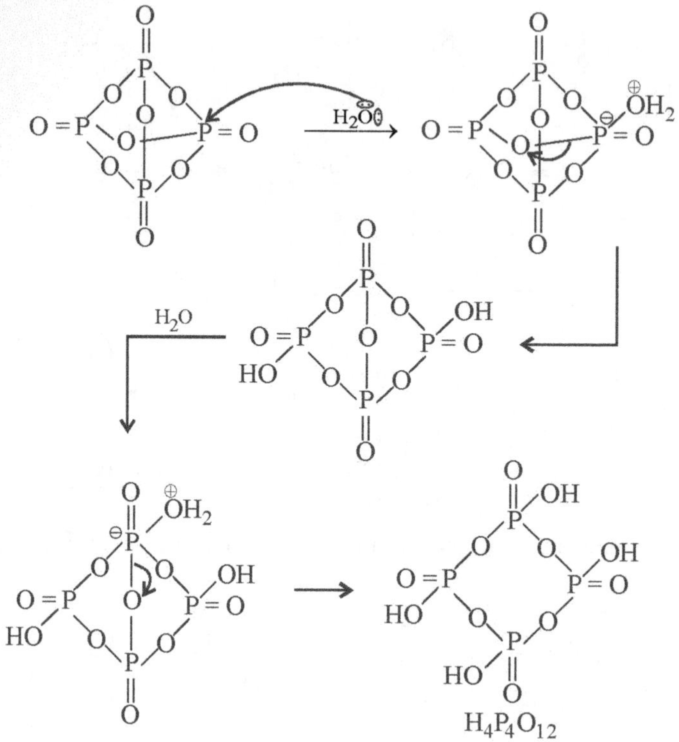

$H_4P_4O_{12}$

Tetramer of cyclic meta
phosphoric acid

Further

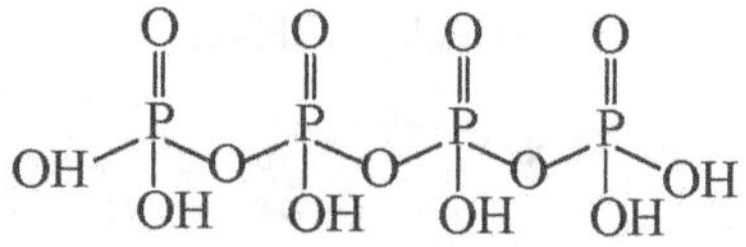

$H_6P_4O_{13}$

Tetra polyphosphoric acid

$$H_6P_4O_{13} + 3H_2O \rightarrow 4H_3PO_4$$

Like P_4O_{10}, P_4O_6 after complete hydrolysis gives H_3PO_3

$$P_4O_6 + 6H_2O \rightarrow 4H_3PO_3$$

Other important hydrolysis

$$NF_3 + H_2O \rightarrow \text{No reaction}$$

$$2NF_3 + 3H_2O \xrightarrow{\text{high T}} N_2O_3 + 6HF$$

$$3SiF_4 + 4H_2O \rightarrow Si(OH)_4 + 2H_2(SiF_6)$$

$$PCl_5 + 4H_2O \rightarrow 5HCl + H_3PO_4$$

Objective Exercise

Q.1 Which can not be hydrolysed at room temperature?

(a) PCl_5 (b) $BiCl_3$

(c) CCl_4 (d) PCl_3

Q.2 Which is correct about the hydrolysis of CCl_4?

(a) It occurs at room temperature

(b) It favours S_N2 mechanism

(c) The gas obtained by this reaction is similar to the product obtained by air oxidation of $CHCl_3$

(d) After hydrolysis, CCl_4 gives carbonic acid

Q.3 Arrange the following chlorides in order of decreasing order of rate of hydrolysis.

$$\underset{(1)}{SF_6} \quad \underset{(2)}{MgCl_2} \quad \underset{(3)}{SiCl_4} \quad \underset{(4)}{AlCl_3}$$

(a) $1 > 2 > 3 > 4$ (b) $3 > 4 > 2 > 1$

(c) $1 > 3 > 4 > 2$ (d) $4 > 2 > 3 > 1$

Q.4 Select the correct statement regarding following reaction.

$$SiCl_4 + H_2O \rightarrow SiOHCl_3 + HCl$$

(a) It favours S_N1 mechanism

(b) In intermediate hybridisation of 'Si' is sp^3d

(c) H_2O donates its electron pair to Cl atom

(d) It occurs only in super heated conditions

Q.5 In which of the following, HCl will be the by product?

(a) $NCl_3 + H_2O$ (b) $BiOCl + H_2O$

(c) $NaCl + H_2O$ (d) $AsCl_3 + H_2O$

Q.6 Which among the following will show hydrolysis at room temperature?

(a) Na_2SO_4 (b) $CuSO_4$

(c) SF_6 (d) CCl_4

Q.7 $PCl_3 + H_2O \longrightarrow x + HCl$

Which statement is correct about 'x'?

(a) Its basicity is 3

(b) Equivalent weight of 'x' is half of its molecular weight

(c) It will not show disproportionation

(d) It is stronger acid than H_3PO_2

Q.8 Which among the following is not the preparation of H_2O_2?

(a) $BaO_2 \cdot xH_2O + H_2SO_4$

(b) Hydrolysis of Marshall's acid

(c) Electrolysis of concentrated H_2SO_4 followed by hydrolysis

(d) 2-Ethyl anthraquinol $+ H_2 \xrightarrow[\Delta]{Pd}$

Q.9 Which among the following will show partial hydrolysis only?

(a) PCl_3 (b) $AsCl_3$

(c) $SbCl_3$ (d) NCl_3

Q.10 Out of NF_3, CCl_4, SF_6, NCl_3, BCl_3 and SF_4, number of halides which can undergo hydrolysis at room temperature is/are

(a) 1 (b) 2

(c) 3 (d) 4

Q.11 Consider the following statements

I. Bond length of $B-O$ bond in H_3BO_3 is greater than in $\left[B_{(OH)_4}\right]^{\ominus}$

II. $SbCl_3$ on hydrolysis produces white turbidity

III. NF_3 on hydrolysis gives nitrous acid

IV. One mole of P_4O_{10} on reaction with three moles of water gives tetra polyphosphoric acid

Correct statements are :-

(a) I, II and IV (b) II, III and IV

(c) II and IV (d) I, II and III

Q.12 $BeCl_2 + \underset{(Excess)}{NaOH} \longrightarrow x + NaCl$

Select correct statement about 'x' which is a compound of beryllium.

(a) Hybridisation on central atom is sp^2

(b) It's vant Hoff's factor is three

(c) It has pyramidal shape

(d) Coordination number of Be is three

Q.13 SF_6 and CCl_4 do not undergo hydrolysis under ordinary condition because

(a) Both possess steric crowding around central atom and hence water can not attack on central atom

(b) In both cases 'd' orbital is not available on central atom

(c) In SF_6 sulphur is sterically crowded and in CCl_4 carbon atom does not have 'd' orbital

(d) In SF_6, sulphur is sterically crowded and in CCl_4 carbon atom does not contain 'd' orbital of appropriate energy

Q.14 Which sequence of rate of hydrolysis is correct?

(a) $SF_6 > SeF_6 > TeF_6$ (b) $PCl_3 > AsCl_3 > SbCl_3 > BiCl_3$

(c) $MgCl_2 > SiCl_4 > CCl_4$ (d) $TeF_6 > SiCl_4 > SF_6 > AlCl_3$

Matrix match: -

Q.15   **Column - I**   **Column - II**

          (Hydrolysis)   **(Possible product)**

     (A) $NF_3 + H_2O$ (p) H_3PO_4

     (B) $P_4O_{10} + H_2O$ (q) One of the product is blue solid

     (C) $PCl_3 + H_2O$ (r) $H_4P_4O_{12}$

     (D) $P_4O_6 + H_2O$ (s) $H_6P_4O_{13}$

                                     (t) H_3PO_3

Q.16   **Column - I**   **Column - II**

     (A) $SF_6 + H_2O$ (p) Hydrolysis at very high T

     (B) $SF_4 + H_2O$ (q) H_2SO_3 as a product

     (C) $BCl_3 + H_2O$ (r) H_3BO_3 as a product

     (D) $BeCl_2 + H_2O$(Excess)   (s) $\left[B_{(OH)_4}\right]^{\ominus}$ as a product

                                     (t) $Be(OH)_2$ as a product

Q.17   **Column - I**   **Column - II**

     (A) $PCl_5 + H_2O$ (p) HOCl is by product

     (B) $SbCl_3 + H_2O$ (q) Show partial hydrolysis

     (C) $BiCl_3 + H_2O$ (r) White turbidity

     (D) $NCl_3 + H_2O$ (s) HCl is by product

                                     (t) H_3PO_4 is one of the product

HINTS & SOLUTIONS

OBJECTIVE EXERCISE

1. (c)	2. (c)	3. (b)	4. (b)	5. (d)	6. (b)	7. (b)
8. (d)	9. (c)	10. (c)	11. (b)	12. (b)	13. (d)	14. (b)

15. $A \rightarrow q;\ B \rightarrow p, r, s;\ C \rightarrow t;\ D \rightarrow t$

16. $A \rightarrow p;\ B \rightarrow q;\ C \rightarrow r, s;\ D \rightarrow t$

17. $A \rightarrow s, t;\ B \rightarrow q, r, s;\ C \rightarrow q, r, s;\ D \rightarrow p$

9

Miscellaneous Problems

Q.1 In which C — C bond, the mean percentage 'p' character of sigma bond is 58.5% ?

(a) $sp^2 - sp$ (b) $sp^3 - sp^2$

(c) $sp^3 - sp$ (d) $sp^3 - sp^3$

Q.2 What will be C — C bond length in propane if distance between two terminal 'C' is 2.53 Å and $\sin 54.75° = 0.82$?

(a) 1.54 Å   (b) 1.265 Å

(c) 3.08 Å   (d) 5.06 Å

Q.3 In SO_3 two $p\pi$ - $d\pi$ bonds are present. The 'd' orbitals of sulphur taking part in these π bonds are:-

(a) d_{z^2}, d_{xy} (b) $d_{x^2-y^2}, d_{z^2}$

(c) d_{xy}, d_{yz} (d) $d_{xy}, d_{x^2-y^2}$

Q.4 In which of the following these is maximum chances of $p\pi - d\pi$ bonding?

(a) BCl_3 (b) NBr_3

(c) $NH_2^{(-)}$ (d) BF_3

Q.5 There are twelve electrons in the valence shell of central atom in a molecule. These electrons are arranged in such a way that 66.67% of total electron forms bond while remaining electrons is non bonding electrons. The actual shape of molecule will be:-

(a) Square planar   (b) 'T' shape

(c) Linear   (d) Octahedral

Q.6 Which contains 33.33% d character.

(a) $PF_6^{(-)}$ (b) AlF_6^{3-}

(c) XeF_6 (d) both (a) & (b)

Q.7 C_2H_2 is isostructural with

(a) C_3O_2 (b) CO_2

(c) $ICl_2^{(-)}$ (d) all of these

Q.8

Compounds	**Boiling point**
(A) CH_3OH	(P) 65°C
(B) CH_3COOH	(Q) 118°C
(C) CH_3COCH_3	(R) 56°C

Correct matching is:-

(a) A→R, B→P, C→Q

(b) A→P, B→Q, C→R

(c) A→R, B→Q, C→P

(d) A→Q, B→P, C→R

Q.9 Which will distill at last?

(a) liquid CO_2

(b) liquid F_2

(c) liquid N_2

(d) liquid O_2

Q.10 In which case bonds are non directional

(a) $NH_2^{(-)}$

(b) $SrCl_2$

(c) $BeCl_2$

(d) $CH_3^{(-)}$

Q.11 Weakest pi bond will be present in:-

(a) $CH_3\,Si\,O\,CH_3$

(b) $POCl_3$

(c) $HO-Cl=O$

(d) CH_3COCH_3

Q.12 AB_2C_2 can exist in two forms

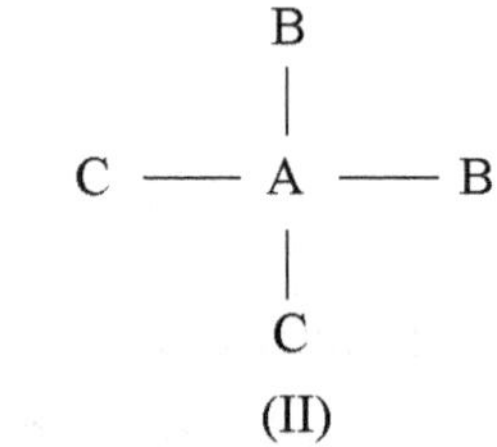

(I)   (II)

In these forms A exhibits dsp^2 hybridization. If A – C distance is 2.32 Å thus C – C distance in I & II respectively are:-

(a) 3.28 Å, 4.64 Å

(b) 5.64 Å, 4.64 Å

(c) 4.64 Å, 3.28 Å

(d) 3.28 Å, 5.64 Å

Q.13 Consider the two covalent compounds AB & XY

AB , $\mu = 8.98$ D, bond length = 2.98 Å

XY, $\mu = 7.45$ D, bond length = 2.3 Å

Select the correct statement:-

(a) AB is more ionic than XY

(b) XY is more ionic than AB

(c) Both are equally ionic

(d) AB is more ionic than XY but XY is more soluble in polar solvents in comparison to AB

Q.14 In which case maximum lp - bp repulsions are present

(a) 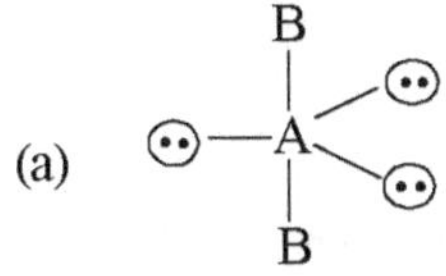

(b) *(structure with A bonded to three B and one lone pair)*

(c) *(structure with A bonded to four B and one lone pair)*

(d) $\ddot{N}H_3$

Q.15 Among NO_2, $AlO_2^{(-)}$, BaO_2 and KO_2, unpaired electron is present in:-

(a) KO_2 & NO_2

(b) $AlO_2^{(-)}$, KO_2

(c) BaO_2, NO_2 & KO_2

(d) KO_2, NO_2, $AlO_2^{(-)}$

Q.16 If a molecule MX_3 has zero dipole moment, the sigma bonding orbitals used by M (atomic number < 21) are

(a) Pure p

(b) sp hybrid

(c) sp^2 hybrid

(d) sp^3 hybrid

Q.17 The ion which is isoelectronic with CO & has same bond order as well as magnetic behaviours is:-

(a) CN^-

(b) O_2^+

(c) O_2^-

(d) N_2^+

Q.18 $CH_3CHO \xrightarrow{\text{[H]}} CH_3CH_2OH$

In the above reduction process the % of s character change in the hybrid orbital of bold carbon atom is:-

(a) 24.99%

(b) 33.33%

(c) 66.67%

(d) 50%

Q.19 The luster of metal is due to:-

(a) High polish of metal

(b) Reflection of light due to the presence of free electrons

(c) Absorption of light by Kernels

(d) Chemical inertness of metals

Q.20 Consider the following reaction:-

$$X_2 + Y_2 \longrightarrow X_2^{(+)} + Y_2^{(-)}$$
$$\text{(16e) (14e)}$$

Which of the following statement is wrong:-

(a) In $X_2^{(+)}$, X – X bond weakens

(b) In $Y_2^{(-)}$, Y – Y bond weakens

(c) In $X_2^{(+)}$, X – X bond order increases

(d) $Y_2^{(-)}$, becomes paramagnetic

Q.21 Lowest degree of paramagnetism per mol at 298 K will be shown by

(a) $CuSO_4, 5H_2O$ (b) $FeSO_4, 6H_2O$

(c) $NiSO_4, 6H_2O$ (d) $MnSO_4, 6H_2O$

Q.22 Which statement is true?

(a) Dipole moment is a measure of ionic character in covalent compound and a molecule with polar bonds will always have some dipole moment

(b) Dipole moment is a vector quantity and a molecule having polar bonds can have zero dipole moment

(c) A molecule can have a dipole moment even in the absence of polar covalent bonds

(d) AB_2 ($\mu = 0$) and AB_2 ($\mu \neq 0$) will have same geometries

Q.23 Least bond angle around central atom will be in:-

(a) SbH_3 (b) $CO_3^{2(-)}$

(c) H_2O (d) $I_3^{(-)}$

Q.24 Which among the following possess highest covalency:-

(a) $CaCl_2$ (b) $ZnCl_2$

(c) $NaCl$ (d) $CsCl$

Q.25 In which case metal - metal bond is present:-

(a) Green vitriol   (b) Calomel

(c) Chilli salt peter   (d) Plaster of pairs

Q.26 The nodal plane in the π bond of ethane is located in:-

(a) The molecular plane

(b) A plane parallel to the molecular plane

(c) A plane perpendicular to the molecular plane which bisects the carbon - carbon sigma bond at 90°

(d) A plane perpendicular to the molecular plane which contains the carbon - carbon bond

Q.27 The shape of the product 'X' will be:-

$$KI\,(aq) + I_2 \longrightarrow \text{'X'}$$

(a) Linear   (b) Angular

(c) 'T'   (d) Triangular

Q.28 Out of AgI, CdI_2, $RbCl$ & Ag_2S, the coloured compounds are :-

(a) All of these   (b) None of these

(c) AgI & CdI_2 (d) AgI, CdI_2 & Ag_2S

Q.29 Least C – C bond length will be found in:-

(a) $CCl_3 - CCl_3$ (b) $CCl_3 - CH_3$

(c) $CH_3 - CH_3$ (d) $CF_3 - CF_3$

Q.30 Which among the following species will favour reduction process:-

$$N_2, \quad O_2, \quad O_2^{(+)}, \quad CO, \quad CN^{(-)}$$

(a) $O_2^{(+)}$ (b) N_2 & O_2

(c) CO, $CN^{(-)}$ & $O_2^{(+)}$ (d) None of these

Q.31 Hybrid state of nitrogen in $(SiH_3)_3N$ is:-

(a) sp

(b) sp^2

(c) sp^3

(d) May be sp or sp^2

Q.32 In which case most stable H – bond will form?

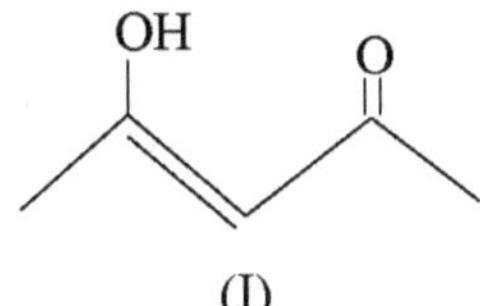
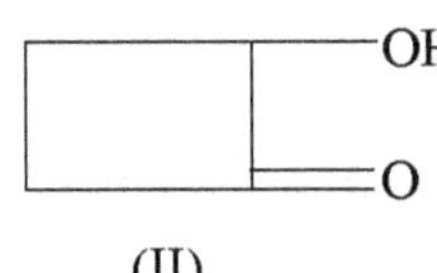
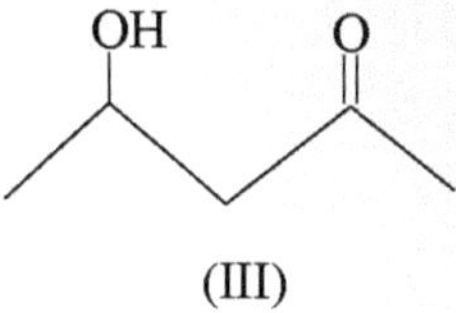

(I)   (II)   (III)

(a) I

(b) II

(c) III

(d) II & III

Q.33 In which case bold carbon atom is sp^3 hybridised:-

(a) $\overset{\bullet}{C}H_3$

(b) $\overset{\bullet}{C}F_3$

(c) $\overset{(+)}{C}H_3$

(d) $CH_3\overset{\bullet}{C}H_2$

Q.34 Which ion has higher polarizing power:-

(a) Pb^{+2}

(b) Mg^{+2}

(c) Zn^{+2}

(d) $Na^{(+)}$

Q.35 In which case, two nodal planes are present:-

(a) $\sigma 2p_z$

(b) $\pi 2p_x$

(c) σ^*2s

(d) None of these

Q.36 Highest bond order will be found in:-

(a) $ClO_4^{(-)}$

(b) $PO_4^{3(-)}$

(c) $SO_3^{2(-)}$

(d) $NO_3^{(-)}$

Q.37 Which of the following species have non linear geometry:-

(1) $SnCl_2$

(2) $ICl_2^{(-)}$

(3) XeF_2

(4) C_3O_2

Select the correct answer using the codes given below:-

(a) 1

(b) 1 & 2

(c) 2, 3 & 4

(d) 3

Q.38 Which will conduct electricity:-

(a) Na_2SO_4 in benzene

(b) Solid NaCl

(c) RbCl in molten state

(d) AgCl in molten state

Q.39 The pair of species / molecules having pyramidal geometry is:-

(a) $H_3O^{(+)}$ & $NH_4^{(+)}$

(b) ClF_3 & NH_3

(c) XeO_3 & $H_3O^{(+)}$

(d) ClF_3 & XeO_3

Q.40 A compound is made up of three elements X, Y & Z having oxidation states +4, +5 & –2 respectively. Possible formula of the compound will be:-

(a) $X_4(YZ_4)_4$

(b) $X_2(YZ_3)_2$

(c) $X(YZ_2)_2$

(d) $X_3(YZ_2)_3$

Q.41 Match list I (Molecules) with the list-II (bond angles) and select the correct answer if $x > y > z > t$

	List - I		List - II
A	NH_3	1	x
B	CH_4	2	y
C	H_2S	3	z
D	H_2O	4	t

	A	B	C	D
(a)	4	3	1	2
(b)	1	2	4	3
(c)	3	4	1	2
(d)	2	1	4	3

Q.42 A di atomic molecule has a dipole moment of 1.2 D. If its bond distance is 1.0 $\overset{\circ}{A}$ what fraction of an electronic charge exists on each atom?

(a) 25%

(b) 50%

(c) 66.67%

(d) 33.33%

Q.43 Select the correct reaction

(a) $BCl_3 + 3H_2O \longrightarrow H_3BO_3 + 3HCl$

(b) $NCl_3 + 3H_2O \longrightarrow H_3NO_3 + 3HCl$

(c) $BCl_3 + 3H_2O \longrightarrow BH_3 + 2HOCl$

(d) BCl_3 undergoes hydrolysis but NCl_3 does not.

Q.44 The correct order of increasing %s character in C–H bond will be:-

(1) $CHCl_3$

(2) CHF_3

(3) $CHBr_3$

(4) CH_4

(a) $4 > 1 > 2 > 3$

(b) $1 > 2 > 3 > 4$

(c) $4 > 3 > 2 > 1$

(d) $2 > 3 > 1 > 4$

Q.45 Carbon and silicon belong to 14th group & both of them oxides of the type MO_2 select the correct statements about CO_2 & SiO_2.

I. CO_2 is linear while SiO_2 has 3D network.

II. CO_2 is covalent while SiO_2 is ionic.

III. In CO_2, C forms double bonds with oxygen while in SiO_2 silicon forms single bonds with oxygen.

IV.   Both CO_2 & SiO_2 have linear geometry.

V.   Si can not form stable π bond with oxygen.

(a) I, II & IV

(b) I, II, III & IV

(c) I, III & V

(d) I & IV

Q.46   Out of 1, 2, 3 & 4 thermally unstable compounds are:-

(1) $PbCl_4$ (2) $SrCO_3$

(3) $BiCl_5$ (4) $PbBr_2$

(a)   1, 2 & 3   (b)   2 , 3 & 4

(c)   Only 2   (d)   1, 3 & 5

Q.47   In BiI_3 iodine is present as:-

(a) $I^{(-)}$ (b) $I_3^{(-)}$

(c) $I_3^{\,3(-)}$ (d) $I_2 .... I^{(-)}$

Q.48   Correct order of acidity of oxides will be:-

(a) $ZnO > PbO > MgO > CaO > SrO$

(b) $PbO > ZnO > MgO > CaO > SrO$

(c) $MgO > CaO > SrO > ZnO > PbO$

(d) $ZnO > CaO > SrO > PbO > MgO$

Q.49   Out of BeO, MnO_2 and Cr_2O_3 amphoteric oxides are:-

(a)   BeO only   (b) MnO_2 only

(c)   BeO and MnO_2 (d)   All of these

Q.50   Correct sequence of ionic mobility in aqueous medium will be:-

(a) $Li^+ > Na^+ > K^+ > Rb^+ > Cs^+$ (b) $Cs^+ > Rb^+ > K^+ > Na^+ > Li^+$

(c) $Li^+ Cs^+ < Rb^+ < K^+ < Na^+$ (d) $Li^+ > Na^+ K^+ > Rb^+ > Cs^+$

Q.51   Which will have highest electrical conductance at room temperature?

(a) $LiHCO_3$ (b) $NaHCO_3$

(c) $RbHCO_3$ (d) $CsHCO_3$

Q.52   Which among the following can be crystallized?

(a) $MgHCO_3$ (b) $LiHCO_3$

(c) $Ca(HCO_3)_2$ (d) $Cs(HCO_3)_2$

Q.53   When CO^+ is produced from CO electron is lost from

(a) $\pi 2p_x$ (b) $\sigma 2p_z$

(c) $\sigma^* 2s$ (d) $\pi^* 2p_x$

Q.54   Match list - I (species) with the list - II (bond order) and select the correct answer if $x > y > z > t$

List - I		List - II	
A	N_2	1	x
B	CO^+	2	y
C	O_2^+	3	z
D	H_2^+	4	t

	A	B	C	D
(a)	1	2	4	3
(b)	2	1	3	4
(c)	1	4	3	2
(d)	2	3	4	1

Q.55 In CO molecule direction of dipole moment will be from

(a) 'C' to 'O'

(b) 'O' to 'C'

(c) may be 'C' to 'O' or from 'O' to 'C

(d) It is non polar molecule

Q.56 The molecules which do not exist in nature are

SH_6	PH_5	BrF_7	HN_3	$C_3Cl_2H_2$
(1)	(2)	(3)	(4)	(5)

(a) 1, 2, 3 & 5

(b) 1, 2 & 5

(c) 1, 2 & 4

(d) 1, 2 & 3

Q.57 The C = C bond dissociation energy of olefins is 146 Kcal / mole whereas C – C bond dissociation energy of paraffins is 83 Kcal / mol. Pick out the correct statement.

(a) Olefins are more reactive than paraffins

(b) Paraffins are more reactive than olefins

(c) Both are equally reactive

(d) At room temperature oleffins are reactive in comparison to paraffins but above 50° C paraffins are more reactive than oleffins

Q.58 Which among the following is non polar?

(a) SO_3

(b) SO_2

(c) CO

(d) H_2O

Q.59 SO_3 on trimerization gives $(SO_3)_3$ or S_3O_9.

The number of S – S bonds in this trimer will be:-

(a) 1

(b) 2

(c) 3

(d) zero

Q.60 The $p\pi$ - $d\pi$ bonding is present in

SO_3	N_2O_5	P_4O_{10}	$XeOF_4$
(1)	(2)	(3)	(4)

(a) 1 & 4

(b) 1, 2 & 4

(c) 4th only

(d) 1, 2, 3 & 4

Q.61 The hybridization of the central atom will change when

(a) NH_3 combines with $H^{(+)}$

(b) AlH_3 combines $H^{(-)}$

(c) NH_3 forms $NH_2^{(-)}$

(d) H_2O forms $H_3O^{(+)}$ on reaction with $H^{(+)}$

Q.62 Which among the following will have largest size?

(a) Fe^{+3}(aq)

(b) Al^{+3}(aq)

(c) Mn^{+2}(aq)

(d) K^+(aq)

Q.63 Largest bond angle will be found in

(a) $NO_2^{(+)}$

(b) $NO_2^{(-)}$

(c) $NO_3^{(-)}$

(d) NO_2

Q.64 Softness of gypsum is due to

(a) Ionic bonding

(b) Covalent boding

(c) Hydrogen bonding

(d) London forces

Q.65 The number of π^* electrons in O_2^{2-} is

(a) 2   (b) 1

(c) 4   (d) 3

Q.66 Hybridization of N in solid N_2O_5 is

(a) sp^2 & sp^2 (b) sp^3 & sp^2

(c) sp^2 & sp^3 (d) sp & sp^2

Q.67 Which among the following will attach more number of H_2O molecules around itself?

(a) Zn^{+2} (b) Fe^{+2}

(c) Mg^{+2} (d) Ca^{+2}

Q.68 Maximum number of $p\pi$ - $d\pi$ bonds are present in:-

(a) SO_3 (b) XeO_4

(c) $HClO_3$ (d) XeO_2F_2

Q.69 Which of the following statement is correct?

(a) When a covalent bond is formed, transfer of electron takes places.

(b) Ordinary water does not contain any ion.

(c) A bond is formed when attractive forces over come repulsive forces.

(d) HF is less polar molecule than HBr

Q.70 The graph between energy and distance between atoms in the formation of molecule can be shown as :

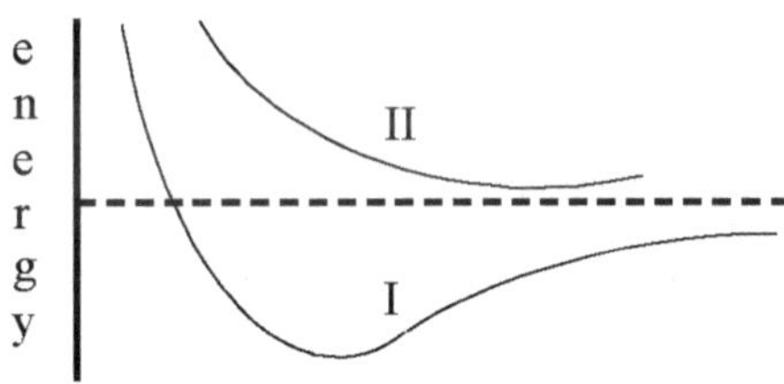

Pick out the correct statement about I & II

(a) II represents BMO   (b) I represents asymmetric BMO

(c) I represents symmetric BMO   (d) I represents ABMO while II represents BMO

Q.71 In solid $BeCl_2$ hybrid state of Be is:-

(a) sp (b) sp^2

(c) sp^3 (d) sp^3d

Q.72 In which of the following case bond order increases and magnetic moment decreases?

(a) $CO^{(+)} \xrightarrow{+e} CO$ (b) $NO \xrightarrow{-e} NO^{(+)}$

(c) $H_2 \xrightarrow{-e} H_2^{(+)}$ (d) $O_2 \xrightarrow{-e} O_2^{(+)}$

Q.73 The ratio of % of s and % d character in the hybrid orbital of central atom in a molecule is 1 : 1.

The molecule is :-

(a) SF_4 (b) XeF_4

(c) PCl_5 (d) XeF_6

ASSERTION & REASON TYPE QUESTIONS

(a) Both Assertion & Reason are correct but Reason is correct explanation of Assertion

(b) Both Assertion & Reason are correct but Reason is not correct explanation of Assertion

(c) Assertion is correct & Reason is incorrect

(d) Assertion is incorrect & Reason is correct

Q.74 **Assertion (A) :** Coordinate bond is semi ionic in nature

Reason (R) : It is formed by the formation of ionic bond followed by covalent bond

Q.75 **Assertion (A) :** Bond order of CO is greater than CO^+

Reason (R) : In the formation of CO^+ from CO electron is lost from σ^*2s

Q.76 **Assertion (A) :** Some times ionic solids conduct electricity in little amount at room temperature.

Reason (R) : At room temperature defects are present in the crystal.

Q.77 **Assertion (A) :** $2NO_2 \longrightarrow N_2O_4$

        Coloured   Colourless

Reason (R) : On dimerisation NO_2 releases unpaired electrons

Q.78 **Assertion (A) :** Bond angle in F_2O is $110°$, while it is $103°$ in Cl_2O

Reason (R) : In Cl_2O back bonding takes place

Q.79 **Assertion (A) :** $Al(OH)_3$ is amphoteric in nature

Reason (R) : $Al-O$ and $O-H$ bond strengths are almost equal there exist almost equal probability of their breaking

Q.80 **Assertion (A) :** PCl_5 exists but PH_5 does not

Reason (R) : Chlorine is an electronegative element and can transfer electron of 'P' from 3s to 3d orbital

Q.81 **Assertion (A) :** Solubility of sulphates of alkaline earth metals in water decreases on moving down the group

Reason (R) : Decrease in hydration energy is more prominent than decrease in lattice energy

Q.82 **Assertion (A) :** In B_2H_6 all $B-H$ bonds are identical

Reason (R) : It contains two banana bonds

Q.83 **Assertion (A) :** Hybridization of carbon in $\overset{\bullet}{C}H_3$ is sp^2

Reason (R) : The orbital in which unshared electron is present has high energy and does not takes part in hybridization

Q.84 **Assertion (A) :** $PbCl_4$ is thermally unstable

Reason (R) : Polarizing power of Pb^{+2} is greater than Pb^{+4}

Q.85 **Assertion (A) :** K_2SO_4 is soluble in water but $BaSO_4$ is not

Reason (R) : Lattice energy of $BaSO_4$ exceeds its hydration energy

Q.86 **Assertion (A) :** Hybridization on 'N' is sp^3 in $CH_2 = CH-\overset{\bullet\bullet}{N}H_2$

Reason (R) : Lone pair of electron present on nitrogen undergoes resonance

Q.87   **Assertion (A) :** NaI will be more soluble in acetone in comparison to NaF

   Reason (R) : NaI is more covalent than NaF

Q.88   **Assertion (A) :** In $KMnO_4$ no unpaired electron is present in Mn but it has pink appearance

   Reason (R) : O^{-2} ions transfer their charge to Mn^{+7}

Q.89   **Assertion (A) :** $XeF_5^{(-)}$ has planar geometry

   Reason (R) : Xe is sp^3d^3 hybridized and non bonding electrons occupy equatorial positions

Q.90   **Assertion (A) :** BCl_3 on hydrolysis forms HCl and H_3BO_3

   Reason (R) : Water attacks on Cl atom of BCl_3

Q.91   **Assertion (A) :** NCl_3 on hydrolysis form NH_3 and HOCl

   Reason (R) : H_2O attacks on Cl atom of NCl_3

Q.92   **Assertion (A) :** $(CH_3)_3N$ is a weaker base than $(SiH_3)_3N$

   Reason (R) : In $(SiH)_3N$ back bonding takes place

Q.93   **Assertion (A) :** $NH_3 + BF_3 \longrightarrow \overset{(+)}{NH_3} \longrightarrow \overset{(-)}{BF_3}$ in this reaction hybrid state of nitrogen and B does not change

   Reason (R) : Dative bond will be considered as sigma bond

Q.94   **Assertion (A) :**

$$\mu = x \text{ debye} \qquad \mu \neq 3 \text{ x debye}$$

   Reason (R) : In 2nd case resulting dipole moment is found to be zero

Q.95   **Assertion (A) :** C_3O_2 is linear while $SnCl_2$ is bent

   Reason (R) : In $SnCl_2$ lone pair of electron is present

Q.96   **Assertion (A) :** ICl is more reactive than Cl_2

   Reason (R) : Iodine has large size

Q.97   **Assertion (A) :** $LiHCO_3$ is liquid while $NaHCO_3$ is solid

   Reason (R) : $LiHCO_3$ has more lattice energy than $NaHCO_3$

Q.98   **Assertion (A) :** BF_3 does not undergo dimerisation to produce B_2F_6

   Reason (R) : In BF_3 back bonding occurs which reduces the electron deficiency of 'B' atom

MORE THAN ONE MAY CORRECT TYPE

Q.99   Molecules with zero dipole moments are:-

   (a) CCl_4 (b) $NH_4^{(+)}$

   (c) NH_3 (d) BF_3

Q.100   Inter molecular H – bonding will be present in:-

   (a) CH_3NH_2 (b) N_2O_4

   (c) $NH_4^{(+)}$ (d) H_3BO_3

Q.101 Which of the following has linear structure?

(a) KI_3 (b) $HgCl_2$

(c) C_2H_2 (d) $H-F$ (gas)

Q.102 Which is not correct about ionic compounds?

(a) They are less soluble in benzene but more soluble in water

(b) They have directional bonds

(c) They have low melting points

(d) Their thermal stabilities are lesser than that of covalent compounds

Q.103 Pick out the correct statement about the following reactions

(1) $SiCl_4 + 4H_2O \longrightarrow Si(OH)_4 + 4HCl$

(2) $CCl_4 + 4H_2O \longrightarrow C(OH)_4 + 4HCl$

(a) 2nd reaction is not possible while 1st reaction is possible

(b) 2nd reaction is possible while reaction is not possible

(c) 2nd reaction is not possible because 'C' can not receive electrons from water as it does not contain empty 'd' orbital

(d) 1st reaction is not possible because $Si(OH)_4$ is an unstable compound and loose water to form $(OH)_2 SiO$

Q.104 Paramagnetic species are:-

(a) $CN^{(+)}$ (b) $CN^{(-)}$

(c) $NO^{(+)}$ (d) $NO^{(-)}$

Q.105 Thermally unstable oxides are:-

(a) HgO (b) AgO

(c) ZnO (d) Li_2O

Q.106 The hybridization in which dz^2 orbital is involved will be:-

(a) dsp^2 (b) sp^3d

(c) sp^3d^2 (d) d^2sp^3

Q.107 The ion in present resonance takes is:-

(a) CO_3^{2-} (b) $HCO_3^{(-)}$

(c) SO_3^{2-} (d) $ClO_4^{(-)}$

Q.108 Compounds with $\mu = 0$ are

(a) PF_3Cl_2 (b) PCl_3F_2

(c) $\underset{Cl}{\overset{H}{>}}C=C=C=C\underset{H}{\overset{Cl}{<}}$ (d) $\underset{Cl}{\overset{H}{>}}C=C=C\underset{H}{\overset{Cl}{<}}$

Q.109 The type of bonds present in NH_4Cl is:-

(a) Ionic (b) Covalent

(c) Dative bond (d) back bonding

Q.110 Which of the following has bond order 2.5?

(a) $N_2^{(-)}$ (b) $N_2^{(+)}$

(c) $NO^{(+)}$ (d) $O_2^{(+)}$

Q.111 Which of the following has tetrahedral shape?

(a) SO_4^{2-}

(b) $ClO_4^{(-)}$

(c) SOF_4

(d) $NH_4^{(+)}$

Q.112 Pick out the correct statement:-

(a) $NO^{(+)}$ is more stable than NO towards dissociation in to its ions

(b) $NO^{(-)}$ is more stable than NO towards dissociation in to its ions

(c) $CO^{(+)}$ is more stable than CO

(d) $O_2^{(+)}$ is more stable than $O_2^{(-)}$

Q.113 Peroxide linkages are present in:-

(a) CrO_5

(b) H_2SO_5

(c) P_2O_5

(d) BaO_2

Q.114 The compounds which have least solubility in water are:-

(a) $BaSO_4$

(b) $BaCl_2$

(c) $CsNO_3$

(d) $AgCl$

Q.115 Which combination of the compounds and their geometry are correct?

(a) $ICl_4^{(-)}$ - Square planar

(b) $CHCl_3$ - Tetrahedral

(c) $XeF_5^{(-)}$ - Pentagonal planar

(d) $H_3O^{(+)}$ - Triangular planar

Q.116 In which case vacant orbital hybridization takes place:-

(a) $B_3N_3H_6$

(b) B_2O_3

(c) B_2H_6

(d) Al_2Cl_6

Q.117 Which of the following is true about hybridized orbitals?

(a) Size of hybridized orbitals follow the order $sp > sp^2 > sp^3$

(b) Longitivity of sp^2 hybridized orbitals is greater than sp^3 hybridized orbital

(c) Angle between two sp^3 hybridized orbitals is greater than that of sp^2 and sp hybridized orbitals

(d) As we move from sp to sp^3 hybridized orbitals % p character increases

Q.118 Correct order of boiling point is:-

(a) $HF > HCl > HBr$

(b) $H_2O > H_2Se > H_2S$

(c) $HBr > HCl > HF$

(d) $HF > HBr > HCl$

Q.119 Correct order of reducing nature is:-

(a) $HI > HBr > HCl > HF$

(b) $H_2S > H_2Se > H_2O$

(c) $HF > HCl > HBr > HI$

(d) $H_2Se > H_2S > H_2O$

Q.120 Species in which central atom has two lone pair is / are:-

(a) XeF_2

(b) $SnCl_2$

(c) XeO_3

(d) SO_2

Q.121 The H –bond in solid HF can be best represented as?

(a) HF --------HF

(b) [figure: zig-zag H and F chain]

(c) [figure: H, F, H arrangement]

(d) [figure: F, F, H arrangement]

Q.122 Which of the following attraction are the types of van - der - waal's forces
(a) Ion - dipole
(b) Ion - induces dipole
(c) Dipole - induces dipole
(d) Dipole - dipole

Q.123 H - bonds are not present in:-
(a) KHF_2
(b) CH_3COCH_3
(c) [benzene ring]–COOH
(d) DNA (double helix structure)

SINGLE INTEGER TYPE

The answer to each question of this section is a single digit integer, ranging from 0 to 9

Q.124 How many equatorial P –F bonds are there in PF_3Cl_2

Q.125 How many $p\pi - d\pi$ bonds are present in XeO_2F_2

Q.126 How many - H – bonds are present in water in vapour state?

Q.127 How many S – S linkages are present in S_3O_9.

Q.128 How many resonating structures are possible for $ClO_4^{(-)}$

Q.129 How many nodal planes are present in $\sigma 2p_z$

Q.130 Among the following compounds the number of compounds which are water soluble is.......

$(CH_3)_2 NH$, CH_3OH, C_6H_6, $C_6H_5NH_2$, CH_3NH_2, Na_2SO_4, $BaSO_4$

Q.131 Total number of electrons presents in BMO of N_2^{2+} are..........

Q.132 Total numbers of π bonds in the given compound are............

$NC – CH = CHCOCOOH$

Q.133 Total numbers of thermally unstable carbonates among the following are............

Li_2CO_3, $MgCO_3$, Na_2CO_3, Rb_2CO_3, $CaCO_3$, K_2CO_3, $FeCO_3$, $ZnCO_3$, $PbCO_3$

Q.134 Total number of pairs in which 1st compound has higher boiling point than 2nd are...........

NH_3 & HF, HF & HCl, H_2S & H_2Se, $AlCl_3$ & BCl_3, CH_3OH & CH_3COOH

Q.135 Total number of paramagnetic species is ....

NO, KO_2, RbO_2, $O_2^{(+)}$, $O_2^{(-)}$, $N_2^{(+)}$, O_2, $N_2^{(-)}$, $CN^{(-)}$

Q.136 Total number of molecules in which peroxide linkage is present is.......

Na_2O_2, BaO_2, $H_2S_2O_8$, $H_2S_2O_7$, CrO_5

Q.137 Total numbers of acidic hydrogens in H_3PO_2 are...........

Q.138 Total number of species in which back bonding takes place is...............

$[CH_2Cl]^{(-)}$, S_2Cl_2, OCl_2, SiH_3NH_2, BI_3

MATRIX MATCH TYPE

Q.139

Column - I		**Column - II**	
(A)	$H_3O^{(+)}$	(p)	$\mu = 0$
(B)	BF_3	(q)	Tetrahedral
(C)	$CO_3^{2(-)}$	(r)	Pyramidal
(D)	$NH_4^{(+)}$	(s)	Bond angle close to $120°$

Q.140

Column - I		**Column - II**	
(A)	Na_2SO_4	(p)	Covalent bond
(B)	$CuSO_4.5H_2O$	(q)	Coordinate bond
(C)	Cu / Zn	(r)	Hydrogen bond
(D)	H_2O	(s)	Metallic bond

Q.141

Molecules		**No. of H - bonds formed by one molecule**	
(A)	water	(p)	1
(B)	ice	(q)	2
(C)	H_3BO_3	(r)	3
(D)	CH_3COOH	(s)	4

Q.142

Species		**Shape**	
(A)	S_8	(p)	Crown
(B)	$NH_2^{(-)}$	(q)	Tetrahedral
(C)	$:\ddot{A}B_2$	(r)	V shape
(D)	$NCl_2^{(-)}$	(s)	Linear

Q.143

Species		**Bond angle**	
(A)	$NO_2^{(+)}$	(p)	$180°$
(B)	$NCl_2^{(-)}$	(q)	$120°$
(C)	$NO_3^{(-)}$	(r)	$109°$
(D)	H_2O	(s)	$104.5°$

Q.144

Column - I (Decreasing order)		**Column - II** (Properties)	
(A)	$CsCl > RbCl > KCl > NaCl$	(p)	Bond order
(B)	$N_2 > O_2^{(+)} > O_2$	(q)	Magnetic moment
(C)	$AgI > AgBr > AgCl$	(r)	Intensity of colour
(D)	$O_2 > O_2^{(+)} > N_2$	(s)	Solubility in water

Q.145

Column - I		**Column - II**	
(A)	$BrF_2^{(-)}$	(p)	sp^3
(B)	$ClF_4^{(-)}$	(q)	sp^3d
(C)	$ICl_2^{(-)}$	(r)	sp^3d^2
(D)	IF_5	(s)	sp^3d^3

Q.146

Column - I		Column - II	
(A) $FeSO_3$ & $MgSO_4$		(p)	Isomorphous
(B) $NaNO_3$ & $NaClO_3$		(q)	soluble in water
(C) K_2SO_4 & $KMnO_4$		(r)	same geometry of anion
(D) $BaSO_4$ & $BaCO_3$		(s)	Water insoluble

Q.147

Species		No. of axial bonds	
(A) $XeF_5^{(-)}$		(p)	0
(B) PCl_3		(q)	1
(C) XeO_2F_2		(r)	2
(D) ClF_3		(s)	3

Q.148

Decreasing order		Physical Properties	
(A) $SbH_3 > AsH_3 > PH_3 > NH_3$		(p)	Boiling point
(B) $BiH_3 > SbH_3 > NH_3 > PH_3$		(q)	Reducing property
(C) $HI > HBr > HCl > HF$		(r)	Geometry
(D) $SF_2 > SF_4 > SF_6$		(s)	Acid character

COMPREHENSION TYPE QUESTIONS

PASSAGE - I

The energy released in the formation of 1 g mole electrovalent compound from isolated gaseous ions is called lattice energy (U_o)

$$M^{(+)} + X^{(-)} \longrightarrow MX + U_o$$

The electric field of ions is uniformly distributed around the ion and so each ion is surrounded by oppositely charged ions and thus crystal lattice is formed iva the release of energy called lattice energy. It can be calculated by the help of Born - Lande equation

$$U_o = -N_o AZ^+Z^-e^2 / 4\pi \, e_o r_o \, (1 - 1/n)$$

Where r_o = equilibrium distance between cation and anion.

Lattice energy affects the stability and melting point of ionic solids. If lattice energy of an ionic solid is lesser than hydration energy compound is soluble in water.

Answer the question from 149 to 152

Q.149 Decreasing order of lattice energy of FeO, Fe_2O_3 & $NaCl$ is

    (a) $NaCl > FeO > Fe_2O_3$ (b) $Fe_2O_3 > FeO > NaCl$

    (c) $NaCl = FeO > < Fe_2O_3$ (d) $Fe_2O_3 > NaCl = FeO$

Q.150 Correct order of solubility in water will be :-

    (a) $KI > RbI > CsI$ (b) $RbI > KI > CsI$

    (c) $CsI > RbI > KI$ (d) All are equally soluble in water

Q.151 Correct order of solubility in water will be :

(a) $Na_2S > Rb_2S > Cl_2S > K_2S$

(b) $Cs_2S > Rb_2S > K_2S > Na_2S$

(c) $Na_2S > K_2S > Rb_2S > Cs_2S$

(d) $Na_2S > Cs_2S > K_2S > Rb_2S$

Q.152 Correct order of melting point will be:-

(a) $MgF_2 > Mg_3N_2 > MgO$

(b) $Mg_3N_2 > MgO > MgF_2$

(c) $Mg_3N_2 > MgF_2 > MgO$

(d) $MgF_2 > MgO > Mg_3N_2$

PASSAGE - II

The attraction together the constituent atoms or an ion of chemical species is called chemical bond. An atom has tendency to occupy 8 electrons in its valence shell, which is stable arrangement. Thus, to complete the octet, atom forms bonds with other atoms. But a number of molecules are known in which either octet is not complete (Hypovalent molecules) or there are more than 8 electrons in the valence shell of central atom (Hypervalent molecules)

Answer the questions from 153 to 155

Q.153 Impossible species is:-

(a) $I_3^{(-)}$

(b) $AlH_3^{(-)}$

(c) O_2^{2-}

(d) none of these

Q.154 Molecules with super octet are:-

(a) XeF_2

(b) XeO_3

(c) ClF_3

(d) All of these

Q.155 For the formation of hypervalent molecules:-

(a) Central atom should have small size and low electronegativity

(b) Central atom should have empty d orbital

(c) Central atom should have small size and high electron affinity

(d) All of these

PASSAGE - III

According to Bent's rule in trigonal bipyramidal geometry lone pair prefers to stay at equatorial positions while more electronegative element prefers to stay at axial position

Answer the questions from 156 to 158

Q.156 Correct representation of SF_4 is:-

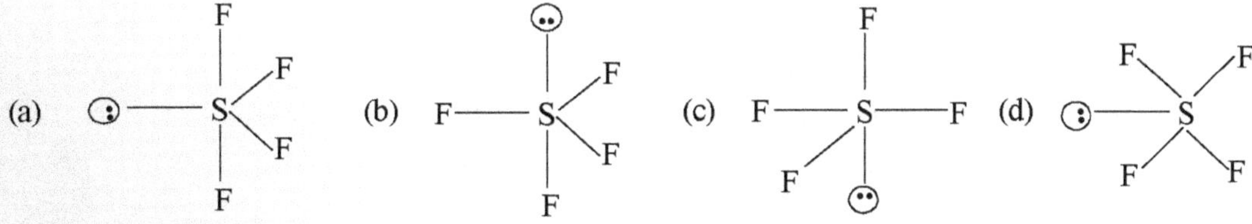

Q.157 Shape of $ICl_4^{(-)}$ is:-

    (a) Square Planar   (b) Trigonal bipyramidal

    (c) See saw   (d) Tetrahedral

Q.158 In sp^3d hybridization % s character in axial bonds is:-

    (a) 0%   (b) 25%

    (c) 33.33%   (d) 20%

PASSAGE - IV

Elements of group 15, 16 & 17 form hydrides of the type MH_3, MH_2 & MH respectively. Their boiling points depend upon the strength of intermolecular forces of attraction existing between them. Strength of $M - H$ bond decreases as the size of M increase.

Answer the questions from 159 to 163

Q.159 Compound with least boiling point is:-

    (a) HI   (b) H_2S

    (c) NH_3 (d) HF

Q.160 Which among the following is highly volatile?

    (a) HF   (b) HBr

    (c) HCl   (d) HI

Q.161 Which among the following has highest boiling point?

    (a) NH_3 (b) BiH_3

    (c) PH_3 (d) AsH_3

Q.162 Strong reducing agent is:-

    (a) H_2O (b) H_2S

    (c) H_2Se (d) H_2Te

Q.163 Highly acidic compound is:-

    (a) HF   (b) NH_3

    (c) H_2O (d) HI

TRUE AND FALSE TYPE QUESTIONS

Q.164 The size of negative ion decreases with increasing magnitude of negative charge.

Q.165 The presence of polar bonds in a poly-atomic molecule suggests that the molecule has non-zero dipole moment.

Q.166 The higher the lattice energy of an ionic solid, the greater will be its stability.

Q.167 Linear overlap of two atomic p-orbitals leads to a σ-bond.

Q.168 All molecules with polar bonds have dipole moment.

Q.169 The $H - N - H$ bond angle in NH_3 is greater than the $H - As - H$ bond angle in AsH_3

Q.170 Ca^{+2} is smaller in size than K^+ because the effective nuclear charge is greater.

Q.171 sp^2 hybrid orbitals have equal s and p - character.

Q.172 Linear overlap of atomic p & s orbitals leads to a sigma bond.

Q.173 The tetrahedral geometry in SiF_4 is due to sp^3 hybridization of Si atom.

Q.174 In benzene, carbon uses all the three p-orbitals for hybridization.

Q.175 There are seven electron bond pairs in IF_7 molecules.

Q.176 The dipole moment of CH_3F is greater than that of CH_3Cl.

Q.177 All molecules with polar bonds have dipole moment.

Q.178 Dipole of CHF_3 is greater than $CHCl_3$.

Q.179 Dipole moment of NF_3 is lesser than NH_3.

Q.180 $SnCl_2$ is a non-linear molecule.

Q.181 Among HF, HCl, HBr and HI, HF has highest dipole moment.

Q.182 The presence of polar bonds in a polytomic molecule suggests that the molecule has non zero dipole moment.

Q.183 Molten sodium chloride conducts electricity due to the presence of free ions.

Q.184 AgCl is more covalent than NaCl.

Q.185 $MgCl_2$ is a non linear molecule.

Q.186 sp^3d^3 hybrid orbitals have equal 'd' and 'p' character.

# HINTS & SOLUTIONS

MISCELLANEOUS EXERCISE

1.	(a)	2.	(a)	3.	(c)	4.	(d)	5.	(a)	6.	(d)	7.	(d)
8.	(b)	9.	(a)	10.	(b)	11.	(a)	12.	(c)	13.	(b)	14.	(a)
15.	(a)	16.	(c)	17.	(a)	18.	(a)	19.	(b)	20.	(a)	21.	(a)
22.	(b)	23.	(a)	24.	(b)	25.	(b)	26.	(a)	27.	(a)	28.	(d)
29.	(d)	30.	(d)	31.	(b)	32.	(a)	33.	(b)	34.	(c)	35.	(d)
36.	(a)	37.	(a)	38.	(c)	39.	(c)	40.	(a)	41.	(d)	42.	(a)
43.	(a)	44.	(d)	45.	(c)	46.	(a)	47.	(b)	48.	(a)	49.	(d)
50.	(b)	51.	(a)	52.	(b)	53.	(c)	54.	(b)	55.	(b)	56.	(d)
57.	(a)	58.	(a)	59.	(d)	60.	(d)	61.	(b)	62.	(b)	63.	(a)
64.	(c)	65.	(c)	66.	(d)	67.	(a)	68.	(b)	69.	(c)	70.	(c)
71.	(c)	72.	(b)	73.	(c)	74.	(a)	75.	(d)	76.	(a)	77.	(c)
78.	(d)	79.	(a)	80.	(a)	81.	(a)	82.	(d)	83.	(a)	84.	(b)
85.	(a)	86.	(d)	87.	(a)	88.	(a)	89.	(c)	90.	(c)	91.	(a)
92.	(d)	93.	(d)	94.	(a)	95.	(a)	96.	(b)	97.	(b)	98.	(b)

MORE THAN ONE, INTEGER TYPE & COMPREHENSIONS

99.	(a,b,d)	100.	(a,d)	101.	(a,b,c,d)	102.	(c,d)	103.	(a,c)	104.	(d)	105.	(a,b)
106.	(a,b,d)	107.	(a,b,c,d)	108.	(b,c)	109.	(a,b,c)	110.	(a,b,d)	111.	(a,b,d)	112.	(a,c,d)
113.	(a,b,d)	114.	(a,c,d)	115.	(a,b,c)	116.	(c,d)	117.	(a,d)	118.	(b,d)	119.	(a,d)
120.	(b,d)	121.	(c)	122.	(c,d)	123.	(b)	124.	1	125.	2	126.	0
127.	0	128.	4	129.	2	130.	4	131.	8	132.	5	133.	6
134.	2	135.	8	136.	4	137.	1	138.	3				

139. A – r   B – p, s   C – p, s   D – p, q

140. A – p, q   B – p, q, r   C – s   D – p, r

141. A – q   B – s   C – r   D – q

142. A – p   B – r   C – r   D – s

143. A – r   B – p   C – q   D – s

144. A – s   B – p   C – r   D – q

145. A – q   B – r   C – q   D – r

146. A – q   B – q   C – p, q, r   D – s

147. A – p   B – p   C – r   D – r

148. A – q, r, s   B – p, r   C – q, r, s   D – q

149. (b)   150. (a)   151. (b)   152. (b)   153. (d)   154. (d)   155. (b)
156. (a)   157. (c)   158. (a)   159. (b)   160. (b)   161. (b)   162. (d)
163. (d)

TRUE AND FALSE

164. F   165. F   166. T   167. T   168. F   169. T   170. T

171. F   172. T   173. T   174. F   175. T   176. F   177. F

178. T   179. T   180. T   181. T   182. F   183. T   184. T

185. F   186. F

ANSWERS TO MISCELLANEOUS PROBLEMS

1. (a) In sp^2 & sp hybridization %p character is 66.67 & 50% respectively thus, mean of these values will be $(66.67 + 50)/2 = 58.5\%$

2. (a)

$$\theta = \frac{109°28'}{2} = 54.75°$$

$$\sin\theta = \frac{1.265}{x}$$

$$x = \frac{1.265}{\sin 54.75}$$

$$x = 1.54 \text{ Å}$$

3. (c)

4. (d) filled 2p of 'F' can easily overlap with empty 2p of 'B'

5. (a) 66.67 % of twelve electrons = $8e^-$

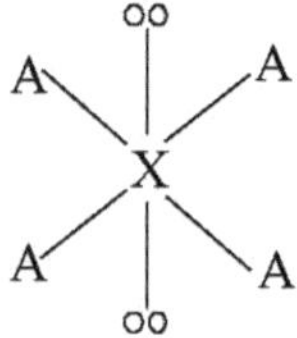

e^- of bond pair = 8 thus, bond pair = 4

e of lone pair = 12 – 8 = 4 thus, lone pair = 2

Thus central atom should have sp^3d^2 (4 + 2) hybridization & square planar shape.

6. (d)

7. (d) All are linear

8. (b) Extent of hydrogen bonding $\propto$ boiling point

9. (a) Due to more vander waal forces

10. (b) $SrCl_2$ is an ionic compound

11. (a) $3p\pi – 2p\pi$ bond

12. (a) In 1st case C – C distance = $2 \times 2.32 = 4.64$Å

While in 2nd case C – C = $\sqrt{(AC)^2 + (AC)^2} = 3.28$ Å

13. (b) Calculate 'q' on atoms by $q = \mu / d$

14. (a) 15. (a)

16. (c) $sp^2 ; \mu = 0$

17.   (a)

18.   (a)   In CH_3CHO & CH_3CH_2OH bold carbons are sp^2 and sp^3 hybridized respectively, thus, change in % 's' character will be $(33.33 - 25) \times 100 / 33.33$

19.   (b)   20. (a)

21.   (a)   22. (b)

23.   (a) SbH_3 (almost 90°) $CO_3{}^{2-}$ (almost 120°), H_2O (104.5°), $I_3{}^{(-)}$ (180°)

24.   (b)   Except $ZnCl_2$ rest all are ionic compounds

25.   (b) Hg_2Cl_2 is called calomel $Hg_2{}^{2+}$ ion possesses Hg – Hg bond

26.   (a)

27.   (a) $KI + I_2 \longrightarrow KI_3$ & $I_3{}^{(-)}$ has linear geometry

28.   (d)   29. (d)   30. (d)

31.   (b)   N donates its lone pair to empty 'd' orbital of Si (back bonding) and makes double bond.

$$H_3Si \; = \; \overset{(+)}{N} - SiH_3 \quad sp^2$$
$$\hspace{3.5cm} | $$
$$\hspace{3.5cm} SiH_3 $$

32.   (a)   33. (b)

34.   (c)   35. (d)

36.   (a)   B.O. = No. of bonds participating in resonance / No. of resonating structure.

37.   (a)

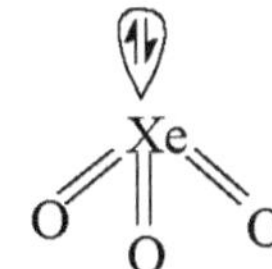

38.   (c)   ion are mobile

39.   (c)

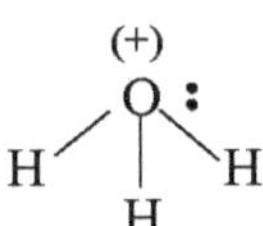

40.   (a)   Net charge on molecule should be zero

41.   (d)

42.   (a)   see Q 11 in chapter – 05

43.   (a)

44. (d)   45. (c)   46. (a)

47. (b)   Because due to inert pair effect Bi forms Bi^+ & not Bi^{+3}

48. (a)

49. (d)   50. (b)

51. (a) $LiHCO_3$ is liquid while rest are solid.

52. (d)   Except $Cs(HCO_3)_2$ rest all exist in liquid state (see polarization in chapter – 05)

53. (c)   See section - 6.2   54. (b)

55. (b)   Because of coordinate bond direction of dipole moment is from O to C ; $\overset{(-)}{C} \Longleftarrow \overset{(+)}{O}$

56. (d)   57. (a)

58. (a) SO_3 has zero dipole moment

59. (d)

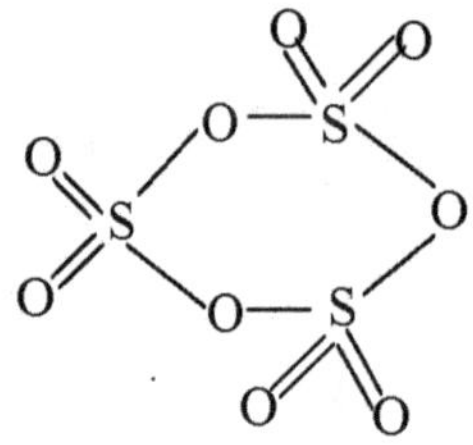

60. (b)

61. (b) $AlH_3 (sp^2) + H^{(-)} \longrightarrow AlH_4^{(-)}(sp^3)$

62. (b)   Hydration $\propto$ 1 / size of ion $\propto$ size of hydrated ion.

63. (a) $O = N^{(+)} = O$ (sp hybridization an N, bond angle is 180°)

64. (c)   65. (c)

66. (d) N_2O_5 in solid state exists as $NO_2^{(+)}$ & $NO_3^{(-)}$.

67. (a) $[Zn(H_2O)_6]^{+2}$

68. (b)   Four $p\pi – d\pi$ bonds are present in XeO_4

69. (c)   70. (c)

71. (c)

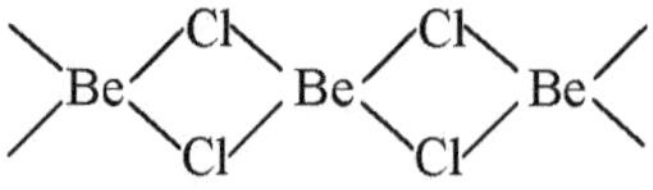

72. (b)

73. (c) sp^3d hybridization is present in PCl_5

74. (a)   See coordinate bond in chapter – 02

75. (d)   See text in chapter – 06

76. (a)

77. (c)   In NO_2 unpaired electron is present on nitrogen which gets paired up on dimerisation

78. (d)   79. (a)

80. (a)   81. (a)

82. (d)

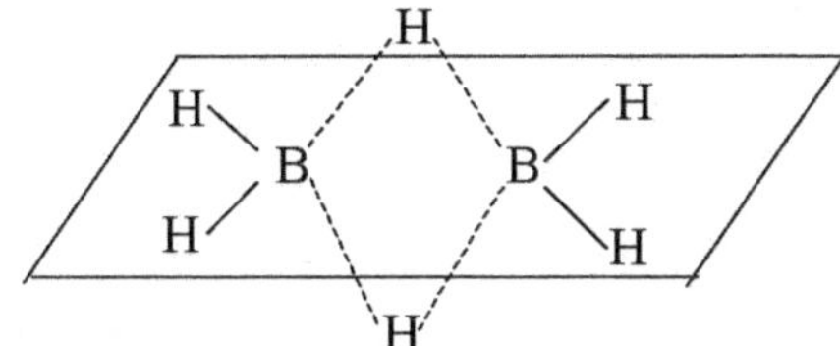

Four B – H bonds are present on a plane and two – H – bonds are not present in plane, one is on above plane & other is on below the plane. These two bonds are called banana bonds.

83. (a) See text chapter – 04, section – 4.8.

84. (b) Due to inert pair effect

85. (a)

86. (d) Delocalized electron pair (electron pair take part in resonance) are not considered in hybridization.

87. (a) Due to polarization NaI is covalent and thus, soluble in less polar solvent like acetone.

88. (a)

89. (c) See section

90. (c) See question – 43   91. (a)

92. (d) See question no. 28   93. (d)

94. (a) Resulting dipole moment will be zero.   95. (a)

96. (b) I – Cl bond is polar & needs less dissociation energy in comparison to Cl – Cl bond.

97. (b) See polarization

98. (b) 'B' Can not adjust more than 3 – fluorine around it self.

MORE THAN ONE MAY CORRECT

99. NH_3 has pyramidal shape and hence it has non zero dipole moment.

100. In NH_4^+, N does not contains lone pair & hence can not form H – bond.

102. Ionic bonds are non directional bond.

103. Hydrolysis of CCl_4 is not possible as 'C' does not contain empty 'd' orbitals.

105. Oxides of native metals like Pt, Ag, Hg, A_4 are thermally unstable.

108. (d) is not planar while PF_3Cl_2 has following geometry.

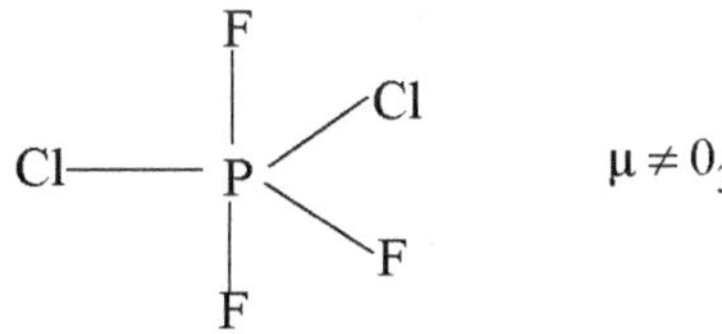

109.

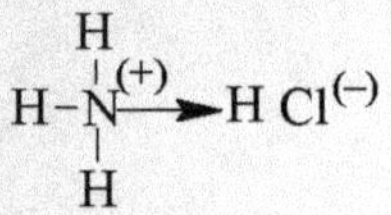

111. In a, b & d central atom has sp^3 hybridization

115. $H_3O^{(+)}$ has pyramidal shape

117. See section – 4.1

118. In H_2O, H – bonding is present while in H_2Se and H_2S van– der– waal forces of attraction are present.

119. As length of M – H bond increases, stability decreases & M – H bond dissociates easily to produce $H^{(+)}$ consequently reducing nature increases.

123.

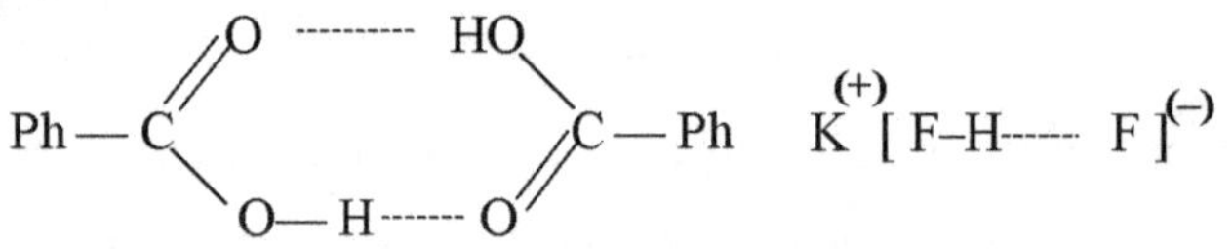

COMPREHENSION TYPE QUESTIONS

Passage – I

149. (b) L.E. $\propto q_1 q_2$

150. (a) Check it by polarization

151. (b) Check it by L.E. & H.E

152. (b) M.P $\propto$ L.E. $\propto q_1 q_2$

Passage – II

153. (d)

154. (d) In all cases central atom possesses more than 8 e in outermost shell

155. (b)

Passage – III

156. (a) least bp – lp repulsions are present

157. (c) due to sp^3d hybridization

158. (a) axial bonds have pd hybridization, thus, 0% 's' character

Passage – IV

159. (b) less extent of inter molecular forces are present

160. (b) same as previous

161. (b) More extent of London forces

162. (d) as it is least thermally stable

163. (d) same as previous

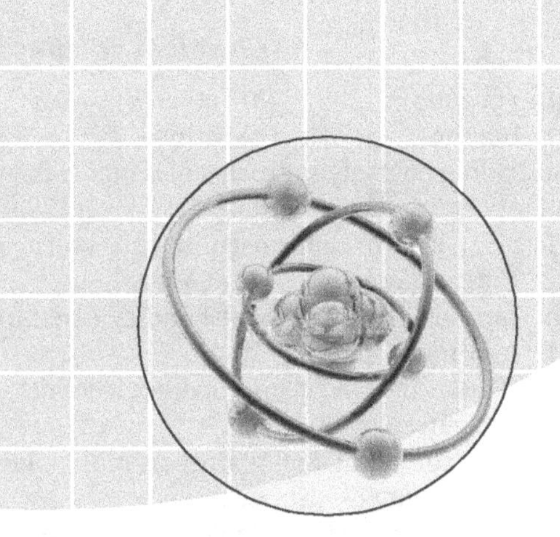

10

Past Year NEET/AIPMT Questions

1. The angle between the overlapping of one s-orbital and one p-orbital is *[1988]*
   (a) $180°$ (b) $120°$
   (c) $109°28'$ (d) $120°, 60°$

2. Equilateral shape has *[1988]*
   (a) sp hybridisation (b) sp^2 hybridisation
   (c) sp^3 hybridisaiton (d) sp^3 hybridisation

3. Which of the following molecule does not have a linear arrangement of atoms ? *[1989]*
   (a) H_2S (b) C_2H_2
   (c) BeH_2 (d) CO_2

4. In which one of the following molecules the central atom said to adopt sp^2 hybridization?
   (a) BeF_2 (b) BF_3 *[1989]*
   (c) C_2H_2 (d) NH_3

5. H_2O has a non zero dipole moment while BeF_2 has zero dipole moment because *[1989]*
   (a) H_2O molecule is linear while BeF_2 is bent
   (b) BeF_2 molecule is linear while H_2O is bent
   (c) Fluorine has more electronegativity than oxygen
   (d) Beryllium has more electronegativity than oxygen.

6. Which of the following does not apply to metallic bond ? *[1989]*
   (a) Overlapping valence orbitals
   (b) Mobile valency electrons
   (c) Delocalized electrons
   (d) Highly directed bonds.

7. Which statement is NOT correct ? *[1990]*
   (a) A sigma bond is weaker than a π-bond.
   (b) A sigma bond is stronger than a π-bond.

   (c) A double bond is stronger than a single bond.
   (d) A double bond is shorter than a single bond.

8. Which one shows maximum hydrogen bonding?
   (a) H_2O (b) H_2Se *[1990]*
   (c) H_2S (d) HF.

9. Which one of the following formulae does not correctly represent the bonding capacities of the two atoms involved ? *[1990]*

   (a) $\left[\begin{array}{c} H \\ | \\ H-P-H \\ | \\ H \end{array} \right]^+$ (b) $\underset{O}{F \diagdown \diagup F}$

   (c) $O \leftarrow N \underset{O-H}{\overset{O}{\diagup\diagdown}}$ (d) $H-C=C \underset{O-H}{\overset{O}{\diagup\diagdown}}$

10. Among $LiCl, BeCl_2 BCl_3$ and CCl_4, the covalent bond character follows the order *[1990]*
    (a) $LiCl < BeCl_2 > BCl_3 > CCl_4$
    (b) $BeCl_2 < BCl_3 < CCl_4 < LiCl$
    (c) $LiCl < BeCl_2 < BCl_3 < CCl_4$
    (d) $LiCl > BeCl_2 > BCl_3 > CCl_4$

11. Linear combination of two hybridized orbitals belonging to two atoms and each having one electron leads to a *[1990]*
    (a) Sigma bond
    (b) Double bond
    (c) Co-ordinate covalent bond
    (d) Pi bond.

12. In compound X, all the bond angles are exactly $109°28$; X is *[1991]*
    (a) Chloromethane (b) Carbon tetrachloride
    (c) Iodoform (d) Chloroform.

13. Which one of the following has the shortest carbon carbon bond length ? *[1992]*
(a) Benzene   (b) Ethene
(c) Ethyne   (d) Ethane

14. Which structure is linear ? *[1992]*
(a) SO_2 (b) CO_2
(c) CO_3^{2-} (d) SO_4^{2-}

15. Which of the following bonds will be most polar? *[1992]*
(a) $N-Cl$ (b) $O-F$
(c) $N-F$ (d) $N-N$

16. Strongest hydrogen bond is shown by *[1992]*
(a) Water
(b) Ammonia
(c) Hydrogen fluoride
(d) Hydrogen sulphide.

17. Which of the following statements is not correct ? *[1993]*
(a) Double bond is shorter than a single bond
(b) Sigma bond is weaker than a π (pi) bond
(c) Double bond is stronger than a single bond
(d) Covalent bond is stronger than hydrogen bond.

18. Which one of the following is the correct order of interactions ? *[1993]*
(a) Covalent < hydrogen bonding < vander Waals < dipole-dipole
(b) vander Waals < hydrogen bonding < dipole < covalent
(c) vander Waals < dipole-dipole < hydrogen bonding < covalent
(d) Dipole-dipole < vander Waals < hydrogen bonding < covalent.

19. Among the following which compound will show the highest lattice energy ? *[1993]*
(a) KF   (b) NaF
(c) CsF   (d) RbF

20. Strongest bond is in between *[1993]*
(a) CsF   (b) NaCl
(c) Both (a) and (b)   (d) None of above

21. Which of the following does not have a tetrahedral structure ? *[1994]*
(a) BH_4^- (b) BH_3
(c) NH_4^+ (d) H_2O.

22. Among the following orbital bonds, the angle is minimum between *[1994]*
(a) sp^3 bonds   (b) p_x and p_y orbitals
(c) $H-O-H$ in water   (d) sp bonds.

23. The distance between the two adjacent carbon atoms is largest in *[1994]*
(a) benzene   (b) ethene
(c) butane   (d) ethyne

24. The boiling point of *p*-nitrophenol is higher than that of *o*-nitrophenol because *[1994]*
(a) NO_2 group at *p*-position behave in a different way from that at *o*-position.
(b) intramolecular hydrogen bonding exists in *p*-nitrophenol
(c) there is intermolecular hydrogen bonding in *p*-nitrophenol
(d) *p*-nitrophenol has a higher molecular weight than *o*-nitrophenol.

25. The weakest among the following types of bonds is *[1994]*
(a) ionic   (b) covalent
(c) metallic   (d) H–bond.

26. Which of the following pairs will form the most stable ionic bond ? *[1994]*
(a) Na and Cl   (b) Mg and F
(c) Li and F   (d) Na and F

27. Linus Pauling received the Nobel Prize for his work on *[1994]*
(a) atomic structure   (b) photosynthesis
(c) chemical bonds   (d) thermodynamics

28. Mark the incorrect statement in the following *[1994]*
(a) The bond order in the species O_2, O_2^+ and O_2^- decreases as $O_2^+ > O_2 > O_2^-$
(b) The bond energy in a diatomic molecule always increases when an electron is lost
(c) Electrons in antibonding M.O. contribute to repulsion between two atoms.
(d) With increase in bond order, bond length decreases and bond strength increases.

29. Which of the following species is paramagnetic? *[1995]*
(a) O_2^{2-} (b) NO
(c) CO   (d) CN^-

30. The ground state electronic configuration of valence shell electrons in nitrogen molecule (N_2) is written as KK $\sigma 2s^2, \sigma * 2s^2, \pi 2p_x^2, \pi 2p_y^2 \sigma 2p_z^2$
Bond order in nitrogen molecule is *[1995]*
(a) 0   (b) 1
(c) 2   (d) 3

31. The BCl_3 is a planar molecule whereas NCl_3 is pyramidal because *[1995]*
(a) B-Cl bond is more polar than N-Cl bond
(b) N-Cl bond is more covalent than B-Cl bond
(c) nitrogen atom is smaller than boron atom
(d) BCl_3 has no lone pair but NCl_3 has a lone pair of electrons

32. The correct order of N–O bond lengths in NO, NO_2^-, NO_3^- and N_2O_4 is *[1996]*

(a) $N_2O_4 > NO_2^- > NO_3^- > NO$

(b) $NO > NO_3^- > N_2O_4 > NO_2^-$

(c) $NO_3^- > NO_2^- > N_2O_4 > NO$

(d) $NO > N_2O_4 > NO_2^- > NO_3^-$

33. Which of the following compounds has a 3-centre bond? *[1996]*

(a) Diborane   (b) Carbon dioxide

(c) Boron trifluroide   (d) Ammonia

34. N_2 and O_2 are converted into Mono-anions, N_2^- and O_2^- respectively. Which of the following statements is wrong ? *[1997]*

(a) In N_2, the N—N bond weakens

(b) In O_2, the O—O bond order increases

(c) In O_2, bond length decreases

(d) N_2^- becomes diamagnetic

35. The cylindrical shape of an alkyne is due to the fact that it has *[1997]*

(a) three sigma C – C bonds

(b) two sigma C – C and one 'π' C – C bond

(c) three 'π' C – C bonds

(d) one sigma C– C and two 'π' C – C bonds

36. The AsF_5 molecule is trigonal bipyramidal. The hybrid orbitals used by the As atom for bonding are

(a) $d_{x^2-y^2}, d_z^2, s, p_x, p_y$ *[1997]*

(b) d_{xy}, s, p_x, p_y, p_z

(c) s, p_x, p_y, p_z, d_z^2

(d) $d_{x^2-y^2}, s, p_x, p_y, p_z$

37. The low density of ice compared to water is due to *[1997]*

(a) hydrogen-bonding interactions

(b) dipole-dipole interactions

(c) dipole-induced dipole interactions

(d) induced dipole-induced dipole interactions

38. The number of anti-bonding electron pairs in O_2^{2-} molecular ion on the basis of molecular orbital theory is, (Atomic number of O is 8)

(a) 5   (b) 2   *[1998]*

(c) 3   (d) 4

39. Among the following which one is not paramagnetic? [Atomic numbers : Be = 4, Ne = 10, As = 33, Cl = 17] *[1998]*

(a) Cl^- (b) Be^+

(c) Ne^{2+} (d) As

40. Which of the following molecules is planar?

(a) SF_4 (b) XeF_4 *[1998]*

(c) NF_3 (d) SiF_4

41. In PO_4^{3-} ion, the formal charge on each oxygen atom and P—O bond order respectively are *[1998]*

(a) $-0.75, 0.6$ (b) $-0.75, 1.0$

(c) $-0.75, 1.25$ (d) $-3, 1.25$

42. Which one of the following arrangements represents the increasing bond orders of the given species? *[1999]*

(a) $NO^+ < NO < NO^- < O_2^-$

(b) $O_2^- < NO^- < NO < NO^+$

(c) $NO^- < O_2^- < NO < NO^+$

(d) $NO < NO^+ < O_2^- < NO^-$

43. Which one of the following has the pyramidal shape? *[1999]*

(a) CO_3^{2-} (b) SO_3

(c) BF_3 (d) PF_3

44. The dipole moments of diatomic molecules AB and CD are 10.41D and 10.27 D, respectively while their bond distances are 2.82 and 2.67 Å, respectively. This indicates that *[1999]*

(a) bonding is 100% ionic in both the molecules

(b) AB has more ionic bond character than CD

(c) AB has lesser ionic bond character than CD

(d) bonding is nearly covalent in both the molecules

45. The relationship between the dissociation energy of N_2 and N_2^+ is : *[2000]*

(a) Dissociation energy of N_2^+ > dissociation energy of N_2

(b) Dissociation energy of N_2 = dissociation energy of N_2^+

(c) Dissociation energy of N_2 > dissociation energy of N_2^+

(d) Dissociation energy of N_2 can either be lower or higher than the dissociation energy of N_2^+

46. Among the following ions the pπ–dπ overlap could be present in *[2000]*

(a) NO_2^- (b) NO_3^-

(c) PO_4^{3-} (d) CO_3^{2-}

47. Which one of the following molecules will form a linear polymeric structure due to hydrogen bonding? *[2000]*

(a) NH_3 (b) H_2O

(c) HCl (d) HF

48. Among the following the electron deficient compound is : *[2000]*

  (a) BCl_3 (b) CCl_4

  (c) PCl_5 (d) $BeCl_2$

49. Cation and anion combines in a crystal to form following type of compound. *[2000]*

  (a) ionic   (b) metallic

  (c) covalent   (d) dipole-dipole

50. In which of the following the bond angle is maximum? *[2001]*

  (a) NH_3 (b) SCl_2

  (c) NH_4^+ (d) PCl_3

51. Which of the following two are isostructural?

  (a) NH_3, BF_3 (b) PCl_5, ICl_5 *[2001]*

  (c) XeF_2, IF_2^- (d) CO_3^{2-}, SO_3^{2-}

52. Main axis of a diatomic molecule is z, molecular orbital p_x and p_y overlap to form which of the following orbital? *[2001]*

  (a) π - molecular orbital

  (b) σ - molecular orbital

  (c) δ - molecular orbital

  (d) No bond will be formed

53. In X — H --- Y, X and Y both are electronegative elements

  (a) Electron density on X will increase and on H will decrease *[2001]*

  (b) In both electron density will decrease

  (c) In both electron density will increase

  (d) Electron density will decrease on X and will increase on H

54. In NO_3^- ion number of bond pair and lone pair of electrons on nitrogen atom respectively are

  (a) 2, 2   (b) 3, 1   *[2002]*

  (c) 1, 3   (d) 4, 0

55. Which of the following has $p_\pi - d_\pi$ bonding?

  (a) NO_3^- (b) SO_3^{2-} *[2002]*

  (c) BO_3^{3-} (d) CO_3^{2-}

56. Which of the following statements is not correct for sigma and pi-bonds formed between two carbon atoms? *[2003]*

  (a) Sigma-bond determines the direction between carbon atoms but a pi-bond has no primary effect in this regard

  (b) Sigma-bond is stronger than a pi-bond

  (c) Bond energies of sigma- and pi-bonds are of the order of 264 kJ/mol and 347 kJ/mol, respectively

  (d) Free rotation of atoms about a sigma-bond is allowed but not in case of a pi-bond

57. Among the following the pair in which the two species are **not** isostructural is *[2004]*

  (a) SiF_4 and SF_4 (b) IO_3^- and XeO_3

  (c) BH_4^- and NH_4^+ (d) PF_6^- and SF_6

58. In a regular octahedral molecule, MX_6 the number of X - M - X bonds at $180°$ is *[2004]*

  (a) three   (b) two

  (c) six   (d) four

59. In an octahedral structure, the pair of d orbitals involved in d^2sp^3 hybridization is *[2004]*

  (a) $d_{x^2-y^2}, d_{z^2}$ (b) $d_{xz}, d_{x^2-y^2}$

  (c) d_{z^2}, d_{xz} (d) d_{xy}, d_{yz}

60. In BrF_3 molecule, the lone pairs occupy equatorial positions to minimize *[2004]*

  (a) lone pair - bond pair repulsion only

  (b) bond pair - bond pair repulsion only

  (c) lone pair - lone pair repulsion and lone pair - bond pair repulsion

  (d) lone pair - lone pair repulsion only

61. H_2O is dipolar, whereas BeF_2 is not. It is because *[2004]*

  (a) the electronegativity of F is greater than that of O

  (b) H_2O involves hydrogen bonding whereas BeF_2 is a discrete molecule

  (c) H_2O is linear and BeF_2 is angular

  (d) H_2O is angular and BeF_2 is linear

62. Which of the following molecules has trigonal planar geometry? *[2005]*

  (a) BF_3 (b) NH_3

  (c) PCl_3 (d) IF_3

63. The correct order of the O–O bond length in O_2, H_2O_2 and O_3 is *[1995, 2005]*

  (a) $O_2 > O_3 > H_2O_2$

  (b) $O_3 > H_2O_2 > O_2$

  (c) $O_2 > H_2O_2 > O_3$

  (d) $H_2O_2 > O_3 > O_2$

64. Which of the following would have a permanent dipole moment? *[2005]*

  (a) SiF_4 (b) SF_4

  (c) XeF_4 (d) BF_3

65. Which of the following is the electron deficient molecule? *[2005]*

  (a) C_2H_6 (b) B_2H_6

  (c) SiH_4 (d) PH_3

66. The correct sequence of increasing covalent character is represented by *[2005]*
(a) $LiCl < NaCl < BeCl_2$
(b) $BeCl_2 < LiCl < NaCl$
(c) $NaCl < LiCl < BeCl_2$
(d) $BeCl_2 < NaCl < LiCl$

67. The number of unpaired electrons in a paramagnetic diatomic molecule of an element with atomic number 16 is *[2006]*
(a) 3   (b) 4
(c) 1   (d) 2

68. In which of the following molecules all the bonds are not equal? *[2006]*
(a) BF_3 (b) AlF_3
(c) NF_3 (d) ClF_3

69. Which of the following species has a linear shape ?
(a) SO_2 (b) NO_2^+ *[2006]*
(c) O_3 (d) NO_2^-

70. Which of the following is not isostructural with $SiCl_4$? *[2006]*
(a) SO_4^{2-} (b) PO_4^{3-}
(c) NH_4^+ (d) SCl_4

71. The electronegativity difference between N and F is greater than that between N and H yet the dipole moment of NH_3 (1.5 D) is larger than that of NF_3 (0.2D). This is because *[2006]*
(a) in NH_3 the atomic dipole and bond dipole are in the same direction whereas in NF_3 these are in opposite directions
(b) in NH_3 as well as NF_3 the atomic dipole and bond dipole are in opposite directions
(c) in NH_3 the atomic dipole and bond dipole are in the opposite directions whereas in NF_3 these are in the same direction
(d) in NH_3 as well as in NF_3 the atomic dipole and bond dipole are in the same direction

72. Which of the following is not a correct statement? *[2006]*
(a) The canonical structures have no real existence
(b) Every AB_5 molecule does in fact have square pyramidal structure
(c) Multiple bonds are always shorter than corresponding single bonds
(d) The electron-deficient molecules can act as Lewis acids

73. The correct order of C–O bond length among CO, CO_3^{2-}, CO_2 is *[2007]*
(a) $CO < CO_3^{2-} < CO_2$ (b) $CO_3^{2-} < CO_2 < CO$
(c) $CO < CO_2 < CO_3^{2-}$ (d) $CO_2 < CO_3^{2-} < CO$

74. In which of the following pairs, the two species are isostructural? *[2007]*
(a) SO_3^{2-} and NO_3^- (b) BF_3 an NF_3
(c) BrO_3^- and XeO_3 (d) SF_4 and XeF_4

75. The angular shape of ozone molecule (O_3) consists of : *[2008]*
(a) 1 sigma and 2 pi bonds
(b) 2 sigma and 2 pi bonds
(c) 1 sigma and 1 pi bonds
(d) 2 sigma and 1 pi bonds

76. The correct order of increasing bond angles in the following triatomic species is : *[2008]*
(a) $NO_2^- < NO_2^+ < NO_2$
(b) $NO_2^- < NO_2 < NO_2^+$
(c) $NO_2^+ < NO_2 < NO_2^-$
(d) $NO_2^+ < NO_2^- < NO$

77. According to MO theory which of the following lists ranks the nitrogen species in terms of increasing bond order? *[2009]*
(a) $N_2^{2-} < N_2^- < N_2$ (b) $N_2 < N_2^{2-} < N_2^-$
(c) $N_2^- < N_2^{2-} < N_2$ (d) $N_2^- < N_2 < N_2^{2-}$

78. In which of the following molecules / ions BF_3, NO_2^-, NH_2^- and H_2O, the central atom is sp^2 hybridized ? *[2009]*
(a) NH_2^- and H_2O (b) NO_2^- and H_2O
(c) BF_3 and NO_2^- (d) NO_2^- and NH_2^-

79. What is the dominant intermolecular force or bond that must be overcome in converting liquid CH_3OH to a gas? *[2009]*
(a) Dipole-dipole interaction
(b) Covalent bonds
(c) London dispersion force
(d) Hydrogen bonding

80. Which one of the following species does not exist under normal conditions? *[2010]*
(a) Be_2^+ (b) Be_2
(c) B_2 (d) Li_2

81. In which of the following pairs of molecules/ ions, the central atoms have sp^2 hybridization? *[2010]*
(a) NO_2^- and NH_3 (b) BF_3 and NO_2^-
(c) NH_2^- and H_2O (d) BF_3 and NH_2^-

82. In which one of the following species the central atom has the type of hybridization which is not the same as that present in the other three?
(a) SF_4 (b) I_3^- *[2010]*
(c) $SbCl_5^{2-}$ (d) PCl_5

83. Some of the properties of the two species, NO_3^- and H_3O^+ are described below. Which one of them is correct? *[2010]*
   (a) Similar in hybridization for the central atom with different structures.
   (b) Dissimilar in hybridization for the central atom with different structures.
   (c) isostructural with same hybridization for the central atom.
   (d) Isostructural with different hybridization for the central atom.

84. In which of the following molecules the central atom does not have sp^3 hybridization? *[2010]*
   (a) NH_4^+ (b) CH_4 (c) SF_4 (d) BF_4^-

85. Which of the following has the minimum bond length ? *[2011]*
   (a) O_2^+ (b) O_2^- (c) O_2^{2-} (d) O_2

86. The pairs of species of oxygen and their magnetic behaviours are noted below. Which of the following presents the correct description ?
   (a) O_2^-, O_2^{2-} – Both diamagnetic *[2011 M]*
   (b) O^+, O_2^{2-} – Both paramagnetic
   (c) O_2^+, O_2 – Both paramagnetic
   (d) O, O_2^{2-} – Both paramagnetic

87. Considering the state of hybridization of carbon atoms, find out the molecule among the following which is linear ? *[2011]*
   (a) $CH_3 - CH = CH - CH_3$
   (b) $CH_3 - C \equiv C - CH_3$
   (c) $CH_2 = CH - CH_2 - C \equiv CH$
   (d) $CH_3 - CH_2 - CH_2 - CH_3$

88. Which of the two ions from the list given below that have the geometry that is explained by the same hybridization of orbitals, NO_2^-, NO_3^-, NH_2^-, NH_4^+, SCN^-? *[2011]*
   (a) NO_2^- and NO_3^- (b) NO_4^+ and NO_3^-
   (c) SCN^- and NH_2^- (d) NO_2^- and NH_2^-

89. Which of the following structures is the most preferred and hence of lowest energy for SO_3? *[2011 M]*

90. Bond order of 1.5 is shown by : *[2012]*
   (a) O_2^+ (b) O_2^-
   (c) O_2^{2-} (d) O_2

91. The pair of species with the same bond order is :
   (a) O_2^{2-}, B_2 (b) O_2^+, NO^+ *[2012]*
   (c) NO, CO (d) N_2, O_2

92. During change of O_2 to O_2^- ion, the electron adds on which one of the following orbitals ? *[2012 M]*
   (a) π^* orbital (b) π orbital
   (c) σ^* orbital (d) σ orbital

93. Four diatomic species are listed below. Identify the correct order in which the bond order is increasing in them: *[2008, 2012 M]*
   (a) $NO < O_2^- < C_2^{2-} < He_2^+$
   (b) $O_2^- < NO < C_2^{2-} < He_2^+$
   (c) $C_2^{2-} < He_2^+ < O_2^- < NO$
   (d) $He_2^+ < O_2^- < NO < C_2^{2-}$

94. Which one of the following pairs is isostructural (i.e., having the same shape and hybridization)?
   (a) $\left[BCl_3 \text{ and } BrCl_3^- \right]$ *[2012]*
   (b) $\left[NH_3 \text{ and } NO_3^- \right]$
   (c) $\left[NF_3 \text{ and } BF_3 \right]$
   (d) $\left[BF_4^- \text{ and } NH_4^+ \right]$

95. Which of the following species contains three bond pairs and one lone pair around the central atom ? *[2012]*
   (a) H_2O (b) BF_3
   (c) NH_2^- (d) PCl_3

96. Which one of the following molecules contains no π bond? *[2013]*
   (a) H_2O (b) SO_2
   (c) NO_2 (d) CO_2

97. Which of the following is paramagnetic ?
   (a) O_2^- (b) CN^- *[2013]*
   (c) NO^+ (d) CO

98. In which of the following ionisation processes the bond energy increases and the magnetic behaviour changes from paramagnetic to diamagnetic? *[2013]*
   (a) $N_2 \rightarrow N_2^+$ (b) $O_2 \rightarrow O_2^+$
   (c) $C_2 \rightarrow C_2^+$ (d) $NO \rightarrow NO^+$

99. The outer orbitals of C in ethene molecule can be considered to be hybridized to give three equivalent sp^2 orbitals. The total number of sigma (σ) and pi (π) bonds in ethene molecule is
   (a) 1 sigma (σ) and 2 pi (π) bonds *[2013]*
   (b) 3 sigma (σ) and 2 pi (π) bonds
   (c) 4 sigma (σ) and 1 pi (π) bonds
   (d) 5 sigma (σ) and 1 pi (π) bonds

100. XeF_2 is isostructural with **[2013]**
  (a) ICl_2^- (b) $SbCl_3$
  (c) $BaCl_2$ (d) TeF_2

101. In which of the following pair both the species have sp^3 hybridization? **[2013]**
  (a) H_2S, BF_3 (b) SiF_4, BeH_2
  (c) NF_3, H_2O (d) NF_3, BF_3

102. The pair of species that has the same bond order in the following is: **[2013]**
  (a) O_2, B_2 (b) CO, NO^+
  (c) NO^-, CN^- (d) O_2, N_2

103. Which of the following is a polar molecule ?
  (a) SF_4 (b) SiF_4 **[2013]**
  (c) XeF_4 (d) BF_3

104. Which of the following is electron - deficient?
  (a) $(SiH_3)_2$ (b) $(BH_3)_2$ **[2013]**
  (c) PH_3 (d) $(CH_3)_2$

105. Which one of the following species has plane triangular shape ? **[2014]**
  (a) N_3^- (b) NO_3^-
  (c) NO_2^- (d) CO_2

106. Be^{2+} is isoelectronic with which of the following ions? **[2014]**
  (a) H^+ (b) Li^+
  (c) Na^+ (d) Mg^{2+}

107. Which of the following molecules has the maximum dipole moment ? **[2014]**
  (a) CO_2 (b) CH_4
  (c) NH_3 (d) NF_3

108. The hybridization involved in complex $[Ni(CN)_4]^{2-}$. is (At. No. Ni $= 28$) **[2015 RS]**
  (a) dsp^2 (b) sp^3
  (c) d^2sp^2 (d) d^2sp^3

109. Decreasing order of stability of O_2, O_2^-, O_2^+ and O_2^{2-} is : **[2015 RS]**
  (a) $O_2^+ > O_2 > O_2^- > O_2^{2-}$
  (b) $O_2^{2-} > O_2^- > O_2 > O_2^+$
  (c) $O_2 > O_2^+ > O_2^{2-} > O_2^-$
  (d) $O_2^- > O_2^{2-} > O_2^+ > O_2$

110. Which of the following species contains equal number of σ- and π-bonds : **[2015]**
  (a) XeO_4 (b) $(CN)_2$
  (c) $CH_2(CN)_2$ (d) HCO_3^-

111. Which of the following options represents the correct bond order ? **[2015]**
  (a) $O_2^- < O_2 < O_2^+$ (b) $O_2^- > O_2 < O_2^+$
  (c) $O_2^- < O_2 > O_2^+$ (d) $O_2^- > O_2 > O_2^+$

112. The correct bond order in the following species is: **[2015]**
  (a) $O_2^{2+} < O_2^- < O_2^+$ (b) $O_2^+ < O_2^- < O_2^{2+}$
  (c) $O_2^- < O_2^+ < O_2^{2+}$ (d) $O_2^{2+} < O_2^+ < O_2^-$

113. In which of the following pairs, both the species are not isostructural ? **[2015 RS]**
  (a) $SiCl_4, PCl_4^+$
  (b) diamond, silicon carbide
  (c) NH_3, PH_3
  (d) XeF_4, XeO_4

114. Maximum bond angle at nitrogen is present in which of the following ? **[2015]**
  (a) NO_2^- (b) NO_2^+
  (c) NO_3^- (d) NO_2

115. Which of the following pairs of ions are isoelectronic and isostructural ? **[2015]**
  (a) ClO_3^-, CO_3^{2-} (b) SO_3^{2-}, NO_3^-
  (c) ClO_3^-, SO_3^{2-} (d) CO_3^{2-}, SO_3^{2-}

116. Predict the correct order among the following : **[2016]**
  (a) lone pair- lone pair > lone pair - bond pair > bond pair - bond pair
  (b) lone pair - lone pair > bond pair - bond pair > lone pair - bond pair
  (c) bond pair - bond pair > lone pair - bond pair > lone pair - lone pair
  (d) lone pair - bond pair > bond pair - bond pair > lone pair - lone pair

117. Consider the molecules CH_4, NH_3 and H_2O. Which of the given statements is false? **[2016]**
  (a) The H–C–H bond angle in CH_4, the H–N–H bond angle in NH_3, and the H–O–H bond angle in H_2O are all greater than $90°$
  (b) The H–O–H bond angle in H_2O is larger than the H–C–H bond angle in CH_4.
  (c) The H–O–H bond angle in H_2O is smaller than the H–N–H bond angle in NH_3.
  (d) The H–C–H bond angle in CH_4 is larger than the H–N–H bond angle in NH_3.

118. The species, having bond angles of $120°$ is :-
  (a) ClF_3 (b) NCl_3 **[2017]**
  (c) BCl_3 (d) PH_3

119. Which of the following pairs of compounds is isoelectronic and isostructural ? **[2017]**
  (a) TeI_2, XeF_2 (b) IBr_2^-, XeF_2
  (c) IF_3, XeF_2 (d) $BeCl_2, XeF_2$

120. Which of the following pairs of species have the same bond order ? **[2017]**
  (a) O_2, NO^+ (b) CN^-, CO
  (c) N_2, O_2^- (d) CO, NO

1. **(a)**

The overlap between s- and p-orbitals occurs along internuclear axis and hence the angle is 180°.

2. **(b)** Equilateral or triangular planar shape involves sp^2 hybridization.

3. **(a)** For linear arrangement of atoms the hybridisation should be sp(linear shape, 180° angle). Only H_2S has sp^3-hybridization and hence has angular shape while C_2H_2, BeH_2 and CO_2 all involve sp - hybridization and hence have linear arrangement of atoms.

4. **(b)** BF_3 involves sp^2-hybridization.

5. **(b)** BeF_2 is linear and hence has zero dipole moment while H_2O, being a bent molecule, has a finite or non-zero dipole moment.

6. **(d)** In metallic bonds each ion is surrounded by equal no. of oppositely charged ions hence have electrostatic attraction on all sides and hence do not have directional characteristics.

7. **(a)** A σ–bond is stronger than a π-bond hence option (a) is not correct. Sigma (σ) bonds are formed by head on overlap of unhybridised s–s, p–p or s–p orbitals and hybridised orbitals (sp, sp^2, sp^3, sp^3d and sp^3d^2) hence σ bonds are strong bonds where as Pi (π)-bonds are formed by side ways overlap of unhybridised p- and d-orbitals hence π bonds are weak bonds.

8. **(d)** With the increase of electronegativity and decrease in size of the atom to which hydrogen is covalently linked, the strength of hydrogen bond increases. As F is most electronegative thus HF shows maximum strength of hydrogen bond.

9. **(d)**
$$H-C=\overset{O\ ||}{C^*}-O-H$$
The star marked carbon has a valency of 5 and hence this formula is not correct.

10. **(c)** As we move in period from Li → Be → B → C, the electronegativity (EN) increases and hence the EN difference between the element and Cl decreases and accordingly the covalent character increases. Thus $LiCl < BeCl_2 < BCl_3 < CCl_4$ is correct.

11. **(a)** Linear combination of two hybridized orbitals leads to the formation of sigma bond.

12. **(b)** CCl_4 has sp^3 hybridisation, tetrahedral geometry and all bond angles of 109° 28′.

13. **(c)** The bond length decreases in the order $sp^3 > sp^2 > sp$.
Because of the triple bond, the carbon-carbon bond distance in ethyne is shortest.

14. **(b)** CO_2 has sp-hybridization and is linear. SO_2 and CO_3^{2-} are planar (sp^2) while SO_4^{2-} is tetrahedral (sp^3).

15. **(c)** Polarity of the bond depends upon the electronegativity difference of the two atoms forming the bond. Greater the electronegativity difference, more is the polarity of the bond.

N – Cl	O – F	N – F	N – N
3.0–3.0	3.5–4.0	3.0–4.0	3.0–3.0

As the electronegativity difference between N and F is maximum hence this bond is most polar.

16. **(c)** H – F shows strongest H-bonds. (see Ans. 9)

17. **(b)** Sigma bond is stronger than π-bond. The electrons in the π bond are loosely held. The bond is easily broken and is more reactive than σ-bond. Energy released during sigma bond formation is always more than π bond because of greater extent of overlapping.

18. **(b)** The strength of the interactions follows the order vander Waal's < hydrogen – bonding < dipole-dipole < covalent.

19. **(b)** For compounds containing ions of same charge, lattice energy increases as the size the ions decrease. Thus, NaF has highest lattice energy. The size of cation is in the order $Na^+ < K^+ < Rb^+ < Cs^+$.

20. **(a)** According to Fajan rules, ionic character increases with increase in size of the cation and decrease in size of the anion. Thus, CsF has higher ionic character than NaCl and hence bond strength of CsF is stronger than NaCl.

21. **(b)** BH_3 has sp^2 hybridization and hence does not have tetrahedral structure while all others have tetrahedral structures.

22. **(b)** The angle between the bonds formed by p_x and p_y orbitals is the minimum i.e. 90°.

23. **(c)** The C–C bond distance decreases as the multiplicity of the bond increases. Thus, bond distance decreases in the order: butane (1.54 Å) > benzene (1.39 Å) > ethene (1.34) Å > ethyne (1.20 Å). Thus in butane, C – C bond distance is the largest.

24. **(c)** The b.p. of p-nitrophenol is higher than that of o-nitrophenol because in p-nitrophenol there is intermolecular H-bonding but in o-nitrophenol it is intramolecular H-bonding.

25. **(d)** H-bond is the weakest.

26. **(b)** The stability of the ionic bond depends upon the lattice energy which is expected to be more between Mg and F due to +2 charge on Mg atom.

27. **(c)** Chemical bonds.

28. **(b)** The removal of an electron from a diatomic molecule may increase the bond order as in the conversion $O_2 (2) \longrightarrow O_2^+ (2.5)$ or decrease the bond order as in the conversion, $N_2 (3.0) \longrightarrow N_2^+ (2.5)$, As a result, the bond energy may increase or decrease. thus, statement (b) is incorrect.

29. **(b)** Paramagnetism is caused by the presence of atoms, ions or molecules with unpaired electrons. In NO the presence of unpaired electron is clear. Therefore it is paramagnetic.

30. **(d)** In this configuration, there are four completely filled bonding molecular orbitals and one completely filled antibonding molecular orbital. So that $N_b = 8$ and $N_a = 2$.

$\therefore$ Bond order $= \dfrac{1}{2}(N_b - N_a) = \dfrac{1}{2}(8-2) = 3$.

31. **(d)** As there is no lone pair on boron in BCl_3 therefore no repulsion takes place. But there is a lone pair on nitrogen in NCl_3. Therefore repulsion takes place. Thus BCl_3 is planar molecule but NCl_3 is a pyramidal molecule.

32. **(c)** The N–O bond length decreases in the order

33. **(a)**

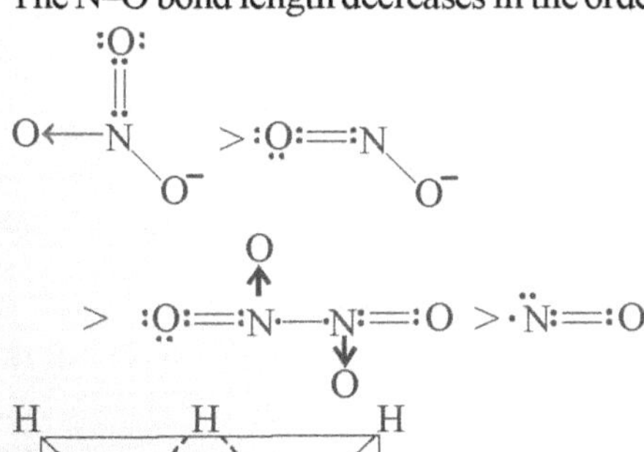

The bond represented by dots form the 3-centred electron pair bond. The idea of three centred electron pair bond B–H–B bridges is necessary because diborane does not have sufficient electrons to form normal covalent bonds. It has only 12 electrons instead of 14 that are required to give simple ethane like structure.

34. **(b)** We know that in O_2 bond, the order is 2 and in O_2^- bond, the order is 1.5. Therefore the wrong statements is (b).

35. **(d)** In alkynes the hybridisation is sp i.e each carbon atom undergoes sp hybridisation to form two sp-hybrid orbitals. The two 2p-orbitals remain unhybridised. Hybrid orbitals form one sigma and two unhybridised orbitals form π-bonds.

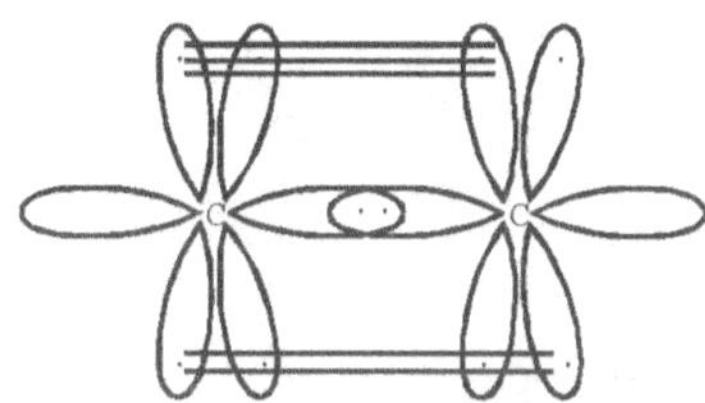

Hence two π bond and one sigma bond between C — C lead to cylindrical shape.

36. **(c)** The electronic configuration of As is

$$As = 1s^2, 2s^2, 2p^6, \underbrace{3s^1\, 3p_x^1\, 3p_y^1\, 3p_z^1\, 3d^1}_{\downarrow sp^3 d \text{ hybridisation}}$$

So, the hybrid orbitals used by As atom in AsF_5 molecule are s, p_x, p_y, p_z, d_z^2.

37. **(a)** We know that due to polar nature, water molecules are held together by intermolecular hydrogen bonds. The structure of ice is open with large number of vacant spaces, therefore the density of ice is less than water.

38. **(d)** Total no. of electrons in $O_2^{2-} = 16 + 2 = 18$

Distribution of electrons in molecular orbital

$$\sigma 1s^2, \sigma^* 1s^2, \sigma 2s^2, \sigma^* 2s^2, \sigma 2p_x^2, \pi 2p_y^2$$

$$\pi 2p_z^2, \pi^* 2p_x^2\, \pi^* 2p_y^2$$

Anti bonding electron = 8 (4 pairs)

39. **(a)** Paramagnetic character is based upon presence of unpaired electron
$Cl^- = 1s^2, 2s^2\, 2p^6, 3s^2\, 3p_x^2\, 3p_y^2\, 3p_z^2$
$Be^+ = 1s^2, 2s^1$
$Ne^{2+} = 1s^2, 2s^2\, 2p_x^2\, 2p_y^1\, 2p_z^1$
$As^+ = 1s^2, 2s^2\, 2p^6, 3s^2\, 3p^6\, 3d^{10},$
$4s^2\, 4p_x^1\, 4p_y^1\, 4p_z^0$
Hence only Cl^- do not have unpaired electrons.

40. **(b)**

41. (c) Bond order between P – O

$$= \frac{\text{no. of bonds in all possible direction}}{\text{total no. of resonating structures}} = \frac{5}{4} = 1.25$$

or Formal charge on oxygen $= -\dfrac{3}{4} = -0.75$

42. (b) $NO^+ = \sigma 1s^2 \; \sigma^* 1s^2 \; \sigma 2s^2 \sigma^* 2s^2 \; \sigma 2p_x{}^2$

$$\pi 2p_y{}^2 = \pi 2p_z{}^2$$

Bond order of $NO^+ = \dfrac{1}{2}(N_b - N_a)$

$$= \frac{1}{2}(10 - 4) = \frac{1}{2} \times 6 = 3$$

Similarly, Bond order of $NO = \dfrac{1}{2}(10 - 5)$

$$= \frac{1}{2}(5) = 2.5$$

Bond order of $NO^- = \dfrac{1}{2}(10 - 6) = \dfrac{1}{2}(4) = 2$

Bond order of $O_2^- = \dfrac{1}{2}(10 - 7) = \dfrac{1}{2}(3) = 1.5$

By above calculation, we get
Decreasing bond order

$$NO^+ > NO > NO^- > O_2^-$$

43. (d) PF_3 has pyramidal shape
Phosphorus exist in sp^3 hybridiation state hence it exist in tetrahedral shape. But due to presence of lone pair its shape is pyramidal.

44. (c) As dipole moment = electric charge × bond length D. M. of AB molecules

$$= 4.8 \times 10^{-10} \times 2.82 \times 10^{-8} = 13.53D$$

D.M. of CD molecules

$$= 4.8 \times 10^{-10} \times 2.67 \times 10^{-10} = 12.81D$$

now % ionic character

$$= \frac{\text{Actual dipole moment of the bond}}{\text{Dipole moment of pure ionic compound}}$$

% ionic character in

$$AB = \frac{10.41}{13.53} \times 100 = 76.94\%$$

% ionic character in

$$CD = \frac{10.27}{12.81} \times 100 = 80.23\%$$

45. (c) Dissociation energy of any molecules depends upon bond order. Bond order in N_2 molecule is 3 while bond order in N_2^+ is 2.5. Further we know that more the Bond order, more is the stability and more is the BDE.

46. (c) In P–O bond, π bond is formed by the sidewise overlapping of d-orbital of P and p-orbital of oxygen. Hence it is formed by $p\pi$ and $d\pi$ overlapping.

47. (d) F—H----F—H----F—H----F
HF form linear polymer structure due to hydrogen bonding.

48. (a) Boron in BCl_3 has 6 electrons in outer most shell. Hence BCl_3 is an electron pair deficient compound.

49. (a) We know that the electrostatic force that binds the oppositely charged ions which are formed by transfer of electron from one atom to another is called ionic bond. We also know that cation and anion are oppositely charged particles therefore they form ionic bond in crystal.

50. (c) We know that bond angles of $NH_3 = 107°$, $NH_4^+ = 109.5°$, $PCl_3 < 109°$. Therefore bond angle of NH_4^+ is maximum.

51. (c) In XeF_2 and IF_2^-. Both XeF_2 and IF_2^- are sp^3d hybridized and have planar shape.

52. (a) For π-overlap the lobes of the atomic orbitals are perpendicular to the line joining the nuclei.

53. (a) In $X — H - - - Y$, X and Y both are electronegative elements (i.e attracts the electron pair) then electron density on X will increase and on H will decrease.

54. (d) N :

To form NO_3^-, nitrogen uses one p-electron for π-bond formation and two p-electrons for σ-bond formation. 2s electrons are used for coordinate bond formation. Thus there is no lone pair on nitrogen and four bond pairs are present.

55. **(b)** In SO_3^{2-}

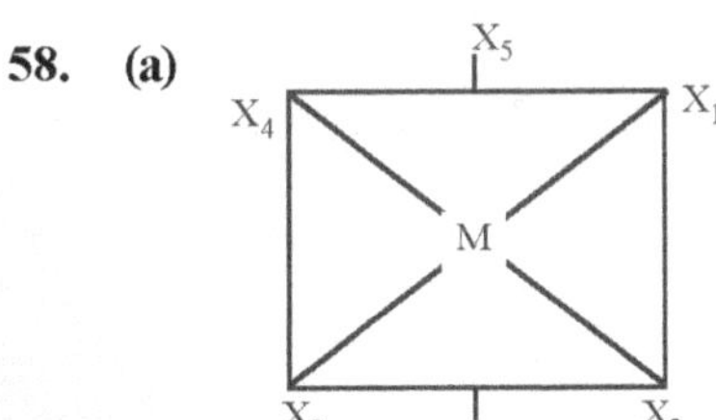

S is sp^3 hybridised, so

$$_{16}S = 1s^2, 2s^2 2p^6, \underbrace{3s^2 3p_x^1 3p_y^1 3p_z^1}_{sp^3 \text{hybridisation}} \; \underbrace{3d_{xy}^1}_{\text{unhybrid}}$$

In 'S' unhybride d- orbital is present, which will involved in π bond formation with oxygen atom.

$$_8O = 1s^2, \; 2s^2 \, 2p_x^2 \, 2p_y^1 \, 2p_z^1$$

In oxygen two unpaired p- orbital is present in these one is involved in σ bond formation while other is used in π bond formation

Thus in SO_3^{2-} , p_π and d_π orbitals are involved

for $p_\pi - d_\pi$ bonding.

56. **(c)** As sigma bond is stronger than the π (pi) bond, so it must be having higher bond energy than π (pi) bond.

57. **(a)** SiF_4 has symmetrical tetrahedral shape which is due to sp^3 hybridisation of silicon atom in its excited state while SF_4 has distorted tetrahedral or sea-saw geometry which arises due to sp^3d hybridisation of sulphur atom and one lone pair of $e^- s$ in one of the equatorial hybrid orbital.

58. **(a)**

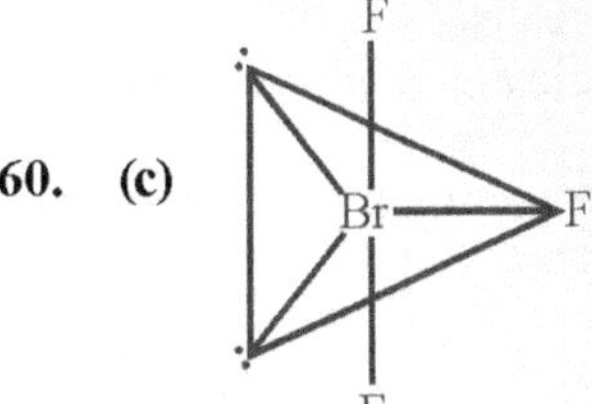

Thus here bond angles between

$$X_4 - M - X_2 = 180°$$

$$X_1 - M - X_3 = 180°$$

$$X_5 - M - X_6 = 180°$$

59. **(a)** Only those d orbitals whose lobes are directed along X, Y and Z directions hybridise with s and p orbitals. In other three d orbitals namely d_{xy}, d_{yz} and d_{xz}, the lobes are at an angle of 45° from both axis, hence the extent of their overlap with s and p orbitals is much lesser than $d_{x^2-y^2}$ and d_{z^2} orbitals.

60. **(c)**

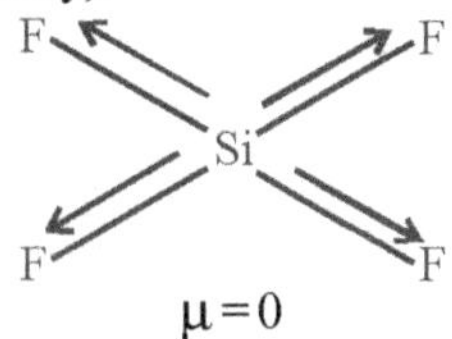

In BrF_3, both bond pairs as well as lone pairs of electrons are present. Due to the presence of lone pairs of electrons (lp) in the valence shell, the bond angle is contracted and the molecule takes the T-shape. This is due to greater repulsion between two lone pairs or between a lone pair and a bond pair than between the two bond pairs.

61. **(d)** In a linear symmetrical molecule like BeF_2, the bond angle between three atoms is $180°$, hence the polarity due to one bond is cancelled by the equal polarity due to other bond. Also it is not angular H_2O.

62. **(a)** BF_3 is sp^2 hybridised. So, it is trigonal planar. NH_3, PCl_3 has sp^3 hybridisation hence has trigonal bipyramidal shape, IF_3, has sp^3d hydridization and is T-shaped.

63. **(d)** The bond length of $O-O$ in O_2 is 1.21 Å, in H_2O_2 it is 1.48 Å and in O_3 it is 1.28 Å.
$\therefore$ correct order of bond length is $H_2O_2 > O_3 > O_2$.
In a linear symmetrical molecule like BeF_2, the bond angle between three atoms is $180°$, hence the polarity due to one bond is cancelled by the equal polarity due to other bond. Also it is not angular H_2O.

64. **(b)** SF_4 has permanent dipole moment. SF_4 has sp^3d hybridization and see saw shape (irregular geometry).

F   F
Si
F   F
$\mu = 0$

Whereas XeF_4 shows squre planar geometry SiF_4 has tetrahedral shape and BF_3 has Trigonal planar shape. All these are symmetric molecules. Hence $\mu = 0$.

65. **(b)** The compound, of which central atom is octetless known as electron deficient compound. Hence B_2H_6 is electron deficient compound.

66. **(c)** As difference of electronegativity increases % ionic character increases and covalent character decreases i.e., electronegativity difference decreases covalent character increases.

Further greater the charge on the cation more will be its covalent character. Be has maximum (+2) charge.

67. **(d)** Electronic configuration of the molecule according to molecular orbital theory, is

$$\sigma 1s^2 \sigma^* 1s^2 \sigma 2s^2 \sigma^* 2s^2 \sigma 2p_z^2 (\pi 2p_x^2 = \sigma 2p_y^2)$$
$$(\pi^* 2p_x^2 = \pi 2p_y^2)\, \sigma^* 2p_z^2 \sigma 3s^2 \sigma^* 3s^2 \sigma 3p_z^2$$
$$(\pi 3p_x^2 = \pi 3p_y^2)(\pi^* 3p_x^1 = 3p_y^1)$$

Last two electrons are unpaired. So no. of unpaired electron is 2.

68. **(d)** In BF_3, AlF_3 & NF_3 all fluoride atoms are symmetrically oriented with respect to central metal atom but in ClF_3 three fluorine atoms are arranged as follows :

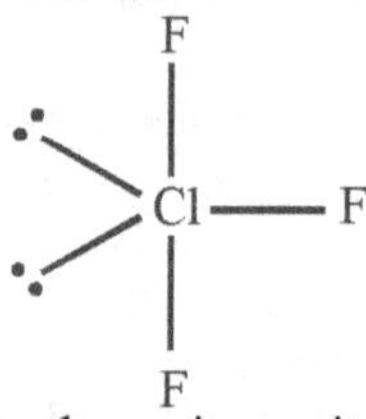

Here two bonds are in equitorial plane & one bond is in axial plane.

69. **(b)** NO_2^+ will have linear shape as it will have sp hybridisation.

70. **(d)** In $SiCl_4$ there is sp^3 hybridisation so the structure is tetrahedral. In SO_4^{2-}, PO_4^{3-}, NH_4^+ the structure is tetrahedral with sp^3 hybridisation. But in SCl_4, sp^3d hybridisation is present so its shape is different i.e., see saw.

71. **(a)** In NH_3 the atomic dipole and bond dipole are in the same direction whereas in NF_3 these are in opposite direction so in the former case they are added up whereas in the latter case net result is reduction of dipole moment. It has been shown in the following figure :

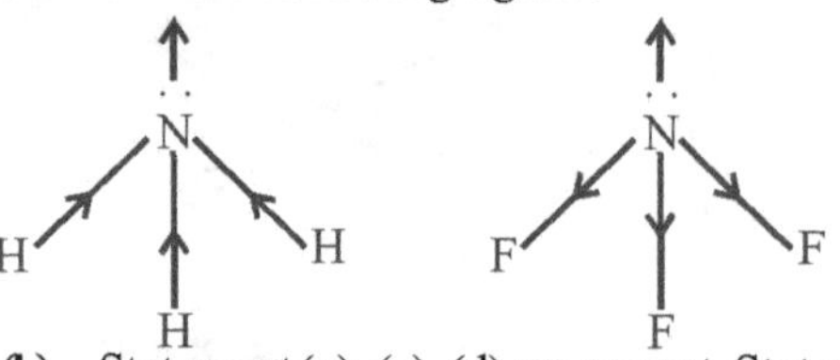

72. **(b)** Statement (a), (c), (d) are correct. Statement (b) is incorrect statement.

AB_5 may have two structures as follows :

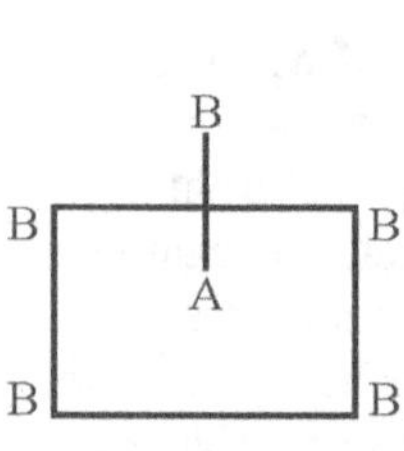

Square Pyramidal

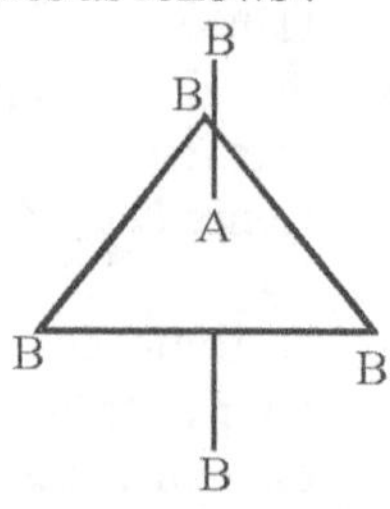

Trigonal Bipyramidal

73. **(c)** All these structures exhibits resonance and can be represented by the following resonating structures.

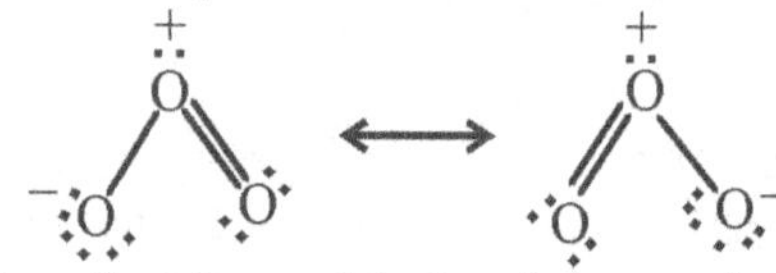

(i) $:\overset{-}{C} \equiv \overset{+}{O}: \longrightarrow\ :C = \overset{..}{O}:$

(ii)   (resonance structures of carbonate)

(iii) $:\overset{..}{O} = C = \overset{..}{O}: \longrightarrow :\overset{+}{O} - C \equiv \overset{-}{O}:$

$$\longrightarrow\ \overset{-}{:}\overset{..}{O} \equiv C - \overset{+}{O}:$$

More is the single bond character. More will be the bond length. Hence, the corret order is :
$$CO < CO_2 < CO_3^{2-}$$

74. **(c)**

75. **(d)** The shape of ozone molecule is

In it we find 2 σ and 1π bond, i.e., option (d) is correct.

76. **(b)** From the structure of three species we can determine the number of lone pair electrons on central atom (i.e. N atom) and thus the bond angle.

$$\left[\,\overset{\cdot\cdot}{N}\ \text{with } O,\,O\,\right]^{-}\quad NO_2^- \qquad \overset{\cdot}{N}\ \text{with } O,\,O \quad NO_2 \qquad \left[O \leftarrow N = O\right]^{+}\ NO_2^+$$

We know that higher the number of lone pair of electron on central atom, greater is the lp – lp repulsion between Nitrogen and oxygen atoms. Thus smaller is bond angle.

The correct order of bond angle is

$$NO_2^- < NO_2 < \overset{+}{N}O_2$$

77. **(a)** Molecular orbital configuration of

$$N_2^{2-} = \sigma 1s^2\, \sigma^* 1s^2 \sigma 2s^2\, \sigma^* 2s^2\ -$$
$$\begin{cases}\pi 2p_y^2 \\ \pi 2p_z^2\end{cases}\sigma 2p_x^2\ \begin{cases}\pi^* 2p_y^1 \\ \pi^* 2p_z^1\end{cases}$$

$$\text{Bond order} = \frac{10-6}{2} = 2$$

$$N_2^- = \sigma 1s^2\, \sigma^* 1s^2\, \sigma 2s^2 \sigma^* 2s^2$$
$$\begin{cases}\pi 2p_y^2 \\ \pi 2p_z^2\end{cases}\sigma 2p_x^2\ \begin{cases}\pi^* 2p_y^1 \\ \pi^* 2p_z^0\end{cases}$$

$$\text{Bond order} = \frac{10-5}{2} = 2.5$$

$$N_2 = \sigma 1s^2\, \sigma^*1s^2\, \sigma 2s^2 \sigma^*2s^2 \begin{cases} \pi 2p_y^2 \\ \pi 2p_z^2 \end{cases},\ \sigma 2p_x^2$$

Bond order $= \dfrac{10-4}{2} = 3$

$\therefore$ The correct order is $= N_2^{2-} < N_2^- < N_2$

78. **(c)**

79. **(d)** Due to intermolecular hydrogen bonding in methanol, it exist as assosiated molecule.

80. **(b)** Bond order of $Be_2 = 0$, hence Be_2 cannot exist.

81. **(b)** **82.** **(c)**

83. **(b)** In NO_3^-, nitrogen is in sp^2 hybridisation, thus planar in shape. In H_3O^+, oxygen is in sp^3 hybridisation, thus tetrahedral in shape.

84. **(a)** $NH_4^+ : sp^3$ hybridisation
  (b) CH_4: sp^3 hybridisation
  (c) SF_4: sp^3 d hybridisation
  (d) $BF_4^- : sp^3$ hybridisation

85. **(a)** O_2 (16) : $KK\,(\sigma 2s)^2\,(\sigma^*2s)^2\,(\sigma 2p_z)^2\,(\pi 2p_x)^2$ $(\pi 2p_y)^2$, B.O.: 2

O_2^+ (15) : Remove one electron from π^*2p_y from O_2, B.O.: 2.5

O_2^- (17) : $KK\,(\sigma 2s)^2\,(\sigma^*2s)^2\,(\sigma 2p_z)^2\,(\pi 2p_x)^2$ $(\pi 2p_y)^2$, B.O.: 1.5

O_2^{2-} (18) : $KK\,(\sigma 2s)^2\,(\sigma^*2s)^2\,(\sigma 2p_z)^2\,(\pi 2p_x)^2$ $(\pi 2p_y)^2$, B.O.: 1

Since, the bond length decreases as the bond order increases, hence, O_2^+ have least bond length.

86. **(c)** MOT configurations of O_2 and O_2^+ :
$O_2^+ : (\sigma 1s)^2\,(\sigma^*1s)^2\,(\sigma 2s)^2\,(\sigma^*2s)^2\,(\sigma 2p_z)^2$ $(\pi 2p_x^2 = \pi 2p_y^2)\,(\pi^*2p_x^1 = \pi^*2p_y^1)$
Number of unpaired electrons $= 2$, so paramagnetic.
$O_2 : (\sigma 1s)^2\,(\sigma^*1s)^2\,(\sigma 2s)^2\,(\sigma^*2s)^2\,(\sigma 2p_z)^2$ $(\pi 2p_x^2 = \pi 2p_y^2)\,(\pi^*2p_x^1 = \pi^*2p_y^0)$
Number of unpaired electrons $= 1$, so paramagnetic.

87. **(b)** $\overset{sp^3}{H_3C} - \overset{sp}{C} \equiv \overset{sp}{C} - \overset{sp^3}{CH_3}$
  linear

88. **(a)**

89. **(d)** Formal charges help in the selection of the lowest energy structure from a number of possible Lewis structures for a given compound. The lowest energy structure means the structure with the smallest formal charge on each atom of the compound. A Lewis dot structure is preferable when all formal charges are zero.

90. **(b)** $(O_2) = \sigma 1s^2\, \sigma^*1s^2\, \sigma 2s^2 \sigma^*2s^2\, \sigma 2p_z^2\, \pi 2p_x^2$
$= \pi 2p_y^2\, \pi^*2p_x^1 = \pi^*2p_y^1$

Bond order $= \dfrac{N_b - N_a}{2} = \dfrac{10-6}{2} = \dfrac{4}{2} = 2$

$\left(O_2^+ \text{ion}\right) = \sigma 1s^2\, \sigma^*1s^2\, \sigma 2s^2\, \sigma^*2s^2$
$\sigma 2p_z^2\, \pi 2p_x^2 = \pi 2p_y^2\, \pi^*2p_x^1$

Bond order $= \dfrac{N_b - N_a}{2} = \dfrac{10-5}{2} = \dfrac{5}{2} = 2\dfrac{1}{2}$

$\left(O_2^-\right) = \sigma 1s^2\, \sigma^*1s^2\, \sigma 2s^2\, \sigma^*2s^2\, \sigma 2P_z^2$
$\pi 2p_x^2 = \pi 2p_y^2\, \pi^*2p_x^2\, \pi^*2p_y^1$

Bond order $= \dfrac{(N_b - N_a)}{2} = \dfrac{10-7}{2} = \dfrac{3}{2} = 1\dfrac{1}{2}$

$\left(O_2^{2-}\right) = \sigma 1s^2 \sigma^*1s^2\, \sigma 2s^2\, \sigma^*2s^2 \sigma 2p_z^2\, \pi 2p_x^2$
$= \pi 2p_y^2\, \pi^*2p_x^2 = \pi^*2p_y^2$

Bond order $\dfrac{N_b - N_a}{2} = \dfrac{10-8}{2} = \dfrac{2}{2} = 1$

91. **(a)** Both O_2^{2-} and B_2 has bond order equal to 1.
$B_2 (10) = [\sigma 1s^2 \sigma^*1s^2 \sigma 2s^2 \sigma^*2s^2 \pi 2p^1_y \pi 2p_z^1]$

Bond order $= \dfrac{N_b - N_a}{2} = \dfrac{6-4}{2} = \dfrac{2}{2} = 1$

B_2 is known to be in the gas phase.
$O_2^{2-} = \sigma 1s^2 \sigma^*1s^2 \sigma 2s^2 \sigma^*2s^2 \sigma 2p_z^2$
$\pi 2p_x^2 \pi 2p_y^2 \pi^*2p_x^2 \pi^*2p_y^2$

Bond order $= \dfrac{1}{2}(10-8) = 1$

92. **(a)** $O_2 = KK\,(\sigma\,2s)^2\,(\sigma^*\,2s)^2\,(\sigma\,2p_z)^2$
$(\pi\,2p_x)^2\,(\pi\,2p_y)^2\,(\pi^*\,2p_x)^1\,(\pi^*\,2p_y)^1$

$O_2^- = KK\,(\sigma\,2s)^2\,(\sigma^*\,2s)^2\,(\sigma\,2p_z)^2$
$(\pi\,2p_x)^2\,(\pi\,2p_y)^2\,(\pi^*\,2p_x)^2\,(\pi^*\,2p_y)^1$

93. **(d)** Calculating the bond order of various species.

$O_2^- : kk\, \sigma\, 2s^2\, \sigma^*\, 2s^2 \sigma 2p_z^2$

$\pi 2p_x^2\, \pi 2p_y^2\, \pi^*2p_x^2\, \pi^*2p_y^1$

$$\text{B.O.} = \frac{\text{Number of electrons in bonding} - \text{Number of electrons in non-bonding}}{2}$$

$$= \frac{8-5}{2} \text{ or } 1.5$$

$NO : kk\,\sigma 2s^2\,\sigma^*2s^2\,\pi 2p_x^2 \approx \pi 2p_y^2\,\sigma 2p_z^2\,\pi^*2p_x^1$

$B.O. = \dfrac{N_b - N_a}{2} = \dfrac{8-3}{2}$ or 2.5

$C_2^{2-} : kk\,\sigma 2s^2\,\sigma^*2s^2\,\pi 2p_x^2\,\pi 2p_y^2\,\sigma 2p_z^2$

$B.O. = \dfrac{N_b - N_a}{2} = \dfrac{8-3}{2}$ or 3

$He_2^+ = \sigma 1s^2\,\sigma^*1s^1$

$B.O. = \dfrac{N_b - N_a}{2} = \dfrac{2-1}{2}$ or 0.5

From these values we find the correct order of increasing bond order is

$He_2^{2+} < O_2^- < NO < C_2^{2-}$

94. **(d)** BF_4^- hybridisation sp^3, tetrahedral structure.
NH_4^+ hybridisation sp^3, tetrahedral structure.

95. PCl_3

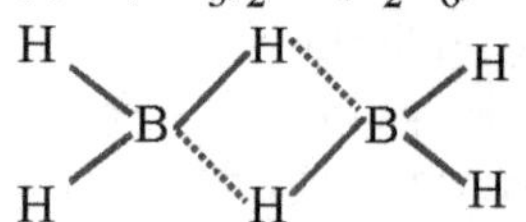

96. **(a)**

$O \leftarrow S = O \quad O \leftarrow N = O \quad O = C = O$

97. **(a)** Molecular orbital configuration of O_2^- is

$O_2^- (17) = \sigma 1s^2, \sigma^*1s^2, \sigma 2s^2, \sigma^*2s^2,$
$\sigma 2p_z^2, \pi 2p_x^2 = \pi 2p_y^2, \pi^*2p_x^2 = \pi^*2p_y^1$

98. **(d)** (a) $\quad N_2 \longrightarrow N_2^+$
         B.O.   3   2.5
Bond energy decreases
Magnetic behaviour changes from diamagnetic to paramagnetic

(b) $\quad O_2 \longrightarrow O_2^+$
         B.O.   2   2.5
Bond energy increases
Magnetic behaviour does not change.

(c) $\quad C_2 \longrightarrow C_2^+$
         B.O.   2   2.5
Bond energy decreases
Magnetic behaviour changes from diamagnetic to paramagnetic

(d) $\quad NO \longrightarrow NO^+$
         B.O.   2   2.5
bond energy increases
Magnetic behaviour changes from paramagnetic to diamagnetic

99. **(d)**

100. **(a)**   F—$\ddot{\underset{\cdot\cdot}{Xe}}$:—F sp^3d and Linear

           Cl—$\ddot{\underset{\cdot\cdot}{\overset{\cdot\cdot}{I}}}^-$—Cl sp^3d and Linear

101. **(c)** Applying VSEPR theory, both NF_3 and H_2O are sp^3 hybridized.

102. **(b)** No. of electrons in CO = $6 + 8 = 14$
No. of electrons in $NO^+ = 7 + 8 - 1 = 14$
$\therefore$ CO and NO^+ are isoelectronic species.
Isoelectronic species have identical bond order.

103. **(a)** SF_4 has 4 bond pairs and 1 lone pair of electrons, sp^3d hybridisation leads to irregular

shape :S$\Big\langle$ and resultant $\mu \neq 0$.

104. **(b)** $(BH_3)_2$ or (B_2H_6)

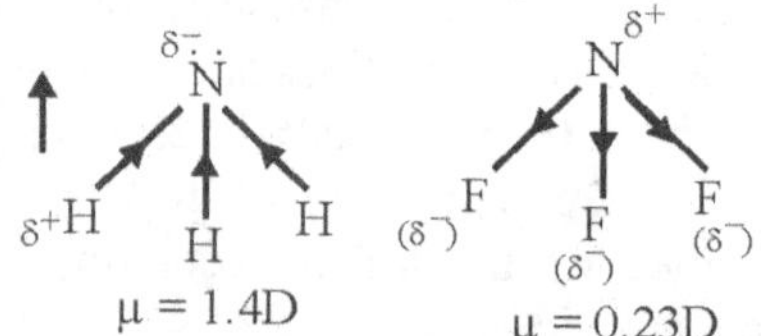

It contains two 3 centre - 2 electron bonds and present above and below the plane of molecules compounds which do not have sufficient number of electrons to form normal covalent bonds are called electron deficient molecules.

105. **(b)**

106. **(b)** $Be^{2+} = (4-2) = 2$
is isoelectronic with $Li^+ (3 - 1 = 2)$
Since both have same number of electrons in their outermost shell.

107. **(c)** Dipole moment of $NH_3 > NF_3$

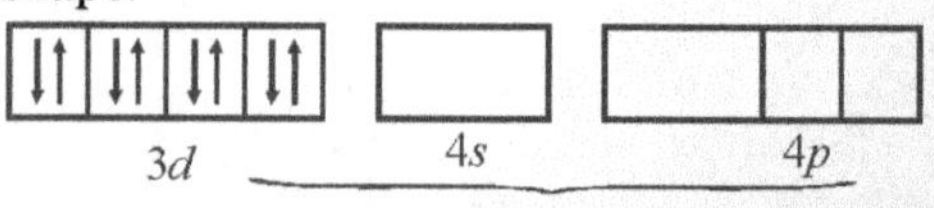

(F is more electronegative than N)

108. **(a)** $Ni^{2\oplus} = [Ar]^{18}\,4s^0\,3d^8$
Valence bond theory can be used to predict shape.

$\uparrow\downarrow$	$\uparrow\downarrow$	$\uparrow\downarrow$	$\uparrow\downarrow$				

      $3d$ $4s$ $4p$

dsp^2 hybridization
(In presence of ligand, pairing of electron occurs)
$\therefore$ Square planar.

109. **(a)** According to molecular orbital theory as bond order decreases stability of the molecule decreases

Bond order $= \dfrac{1}{2}(N_b - N_a)$

Bond order for $O_2^+ = \dfrac{1}{2}(10-5) = 2.5$

Bond order for $O_2 = \dfrac{1}{2}(10-6) = 2$

Bond order for $O_2^- = \dfrac{1}{2}(10-7) = 1.5$

Bond order for $O_2^{2-} = \dfrac{1}{2}(10-8) = 1.0$

hence the correct order is

$O_2^+ > O_2 > O_2^- > O_2^{2-}$

110. **(a)**

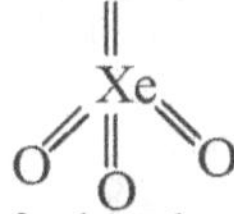

Number of σ bonds = 4
Number of π bonds = 4

111. **(a)** Oxygen molecule (O_2) – Total number of electrons = 16 and electronic configuration is

$\sigma 1s^2 < \sigma^* 1s^2 < \sigma 2s^2 < \sigma^* 2s^2 < \sigma 2p_x^2$
$< \pi 2p_y^2 = \pi 2p_z^2 < \pi^* 2p_y^1 = \pi^* 2p_z^1$

Bond order $= \dfrac{N_b - N_a}{2} = \dfrac{10-6}{2} = \dfrac{4}{2} = 2$

O_2^+ ion - Total number of electrons $(16-1) = 15$.
Electronic configuration

$\sigma 1s^2 < \sigma^* 1s^2 < \sigma 2s^2 < \sigma^* 2s^2 < \sigma 2p_x^2$
$< \pi 2p_y^2 = \pi 2p_z^2 < \pi^* 2p_y^1$

Bond order $= \dfrac{N_b - N_a}{2} = \dfrac{10-5}{2} = \dfrac{5}{2} = 2\dfrac{1}{2}$

O_2^- (Super oxide ion) Total number of electrons $(16+1) = 17$. Electronic configuration

$\sigma 1s^2 < \sigma^* 1s^2 < \sigma 2s^2 < \sigma^* 2s^2 < \sigma 2p_x^2$
$< \pi 2p_y^2 = \pi 2p_z^2 < \pi^* 2p_y^2 = \pi^* 2p_z^1$

Bond order $= \dfrac{(N_b - N_a)}{2} = \dfrac{10-7}{2} = \dfrac{3}{2} = 1\dfrac{1}{2}$

112. **(c)** O_2^+ ion - Total number of electrons $(16-1) = 15$.
Electronic configuration

$\sigma 1s^2 < \sigma^* 1s^2 < \sigma 2s^2 < \sigma^* 2s^2 < \sigma 2p_x^2$
$< \pi 2p_y^2 = \pi 2p_z^2 < \pi^* 2p_y^1$

Bond order $= \dfrac{N_b - N_a}{2} = \dfrac{10-5}{2} = \dfrac{5}{2} = 2\dfrac{1}{2}$

O_2^- (Super oxide ion): Total number of electrons $(16+1) = 17$.

Electronic configuration

$\sigma 1s^2 < \sigma^* 1s^2 < \sigma 2s^2 < \sigma^* 2s^2 < \sigma 2p_x^2$
$< \pi 2p_y^2 = \pi 2p_z^2 < \pi^* 2p_y^1 = \pi^* 2p_z^1$

Bond order $= \dfrac{(N_b - N_a)}{2} = \dfrac{10-7}{2} = \dfrac{3}{2} = 1\dfrac{1}{2}$

O_2^{2+} ion: Total number of electrons
$= (16-2) = 14$ Electronic configuration
$\sigma 1s^2 < \sigma^* 1s^2 < \sigma 2s^2 < \sigma^* 2s^2 < \sigma 2p_x^2 < \pi 2p_y^2$
$= \pi 2p_z^2$

Bond order $= \dfrac{(N_b - N_a)}{2} = \dfrac{10-4}{2} = \dfrac{6}{2} = 3$

So bond order: $O_2^- < O_2^+ < O_2^{2+}$

113. **(d)** XeF_4, XeO_4

(Square planar)   [Tetrahedral]

114. **(b)** NO_2^+ has sp hybridisation so it is linear with bond angle = 180°.

115. **(c)** ClO_3^- and SO_3^{2-} both have same number of electrons (42) and central atom in each being sp^3 hybridised. Both are having one lone pair on central atom hence they are pyramidal.

116. **(a)** According to VSEPR theory order of repulsion in between lp – lp, lp – bp and bp – bp is as under
lp – lp > lp – bp > bp – bp

117. **(b)**

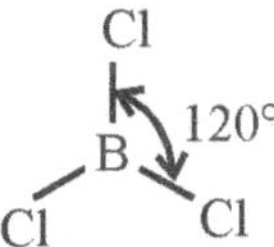

Tetrahedral;   Trigonal   Bent
          pyramidal

Note: The geometry of H_2O should have been tetrahedral if there are all bond pairs. But due to presence of two lone pairs the shape is distorted tetrahedral. Hence bond angle reduced to 104.5° from 109.5°.

118. **(c)** BCl_3 is trigonal planar and hence the bond angle is 120°.

119. **(b)** IBr_2^-, XeF_2
Total number of valence electrons are equal in both the species and both the species exhibit linear shape.

120. **(b)** CN^- and CO have same no. of electrons and have same bond order equal to 3.

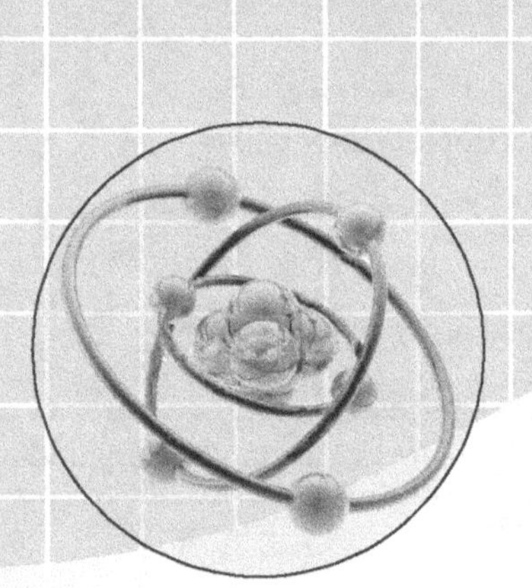

11

Past Year JEE Mains/ AIEEE Questions

1. Which of the following are arranged in an increasing order of their bond strengths?
   (a) $O_2^- < O_2 < O_2^+ < O_2^{2-}$ *[2002]*
   (b) $O_2^{2-} < O_2^- < O_2 < O_2^+$
   (c) $O_2^- < O_2^{2-} < O_2 < O_2^+$
   (d) $O_2^+ < O_2 < O_2^- < O_2^{2-}$

2. Hybridisation of the underline atom changes in:
   (a) $\underline{A}lH_3$ changes to AlH_4^- *[2002]*
   (b) $H_2\underline{O}$ changes to H_3O^+
   (c) $\underline{N}H_3$ changes to NH_4^+
   (d) in all cases

3. In which of the following species the interatomic bond angle is 109° 28'?   *[2002]*
   (a) NH_3, BF_4^- (b) NH_4^+, BF_3
   (c) NH_3, BF_4 (d) NH_2^-, BF_3.

4. The pair of species having identical shapes for molecules of both species is   *[2003]*
   (a) XeF_2, CO_2 (b) BF_3, PCl_3
   (c) PF_5, IF_5 (d) CF_4, SF_4

5. Which one of the following compounds has the smallest bond angle in its molecule ?   *[2003]*
   (a) OH_2 (b) SH_2
   (c) NH_3 (d) SO_2

6. Which one of the following pairs of molecules will have permanent dipole moments for both members ?   *[2003]*
   (a) NO_2 and CO_2 (b) NO_2 and O_3
   (c) SiF_4 and CO_2 (d) SiF_4 and NO_2

7. An ether is more volatile than an alcohol having the same molecular formula. This is due to   *[2003]*
   (a) alcohols having resonance structures
   (b) intermolecular hydrogen bonding in ethers
   (c) intermolecular hydrogen bonding in alcohols
   (d) dipolar character of ethers

8. The maximum number of 90° angles between bond pair-bond pair of electrons is observed in
   (a) dsp^2 hybridization   *[2004]*
   (b) sp^3d hybridization
   (c) dsp^3 hybridization
   (d) sp^3d^2 hybridization

9. Which one of the following has the regular tetrahedral structure ?   *[2004]*
   (a) BF_4^- (b) SF_4
   (c) XeF_4 (d) $[Ni(CN)_4]^{2-}$
   (Atomic nos.: B = 5, S = 16, Ni = 28, Xe = 54)

10. The states of hybridization of boron and oxygen atoms in boric acid (H_3BO_3) are respectively
        [2004]
    (a) sp^3 and sp^2 (b) sp^2 and sp^3
    (c) sp^2 and sp^2 (d) sp^3 and sp^3

11. The correct order of bond angles (smallest first) in H_2S, NH_3, BF_3 and SiH_4 is   *[2004]*
    (a) $H_2S < NH_3 < SiH_4 < BF_3$
    (b) $NH_3 < H_2S < SiH_4 < BF_3$
    (c) $H_2S < SiH_4 < NH_3 < BF_3$
    (d) $H_2S < NH_3 < BF_3 < SiH_4$

12. The bond order in NO is 2.5 while that in NO^+ is 3. Which of the following statements is true for these two species ?   *[2004]*
    (a) Bond length in NO^+ is equal to that in NO
    (b) Bond length in NO is greater than in NO^+
    (c) Bond length in NO^+ is greater than in NO
    (d) Bond length is unpredictable

13. Which of the following species is diamagnetic in nature?   *[2005]*

(a) H_2^- (b) H_2^+

(c) H_2 (d) He_2^+

14. Lattice energy of an ionic compound depends upon   *[2005]*
   (a)   Charge on the ion and size of the ion
   (b)   Packing of ions only
   (c)   Size of the ion only
   (d)   Charge on the ion only

15. Which of the following molecules/ions does not contain unpaired electrons?   *[2006]*

   (a) N_2^+ (b) O_2

   (c) O_2^{2-} (d) B_2

16. The decreasing values of bond angles from NH_3 (106°) to SbH_3 (101°) down group-15 of the periodic table is due to   *[2006]*
   (a)   decreasing lp-bp repulsion
   (b)   decreasing electronegativity
   (c)   increasing bp-bp repulsion
   (d)   increasing p-orbital character in sp^3

17. In which of the following molecules/ions are all the bonds **not** equal?   *[2006]*
   (a) XeF_4 (b) BF_4^-
   (c) SF_4 (d) SiF_4

18. In which of the following ionization processes, the bond order has increased and the magnetic behaviour has changed?   *[2007]*

   (a) $N_2 \rightarrow N_2^+$ (b) $C_2 \rightarrow C_2^+$

   (c) $NO \rightarrow NO^+$ (d) $O_2 \rightarrow O_2^+$.

19. Which of the following species exhibits the diamagnetic behaviour ?   *[2007]*
   (a) NO (b) O_2^{2-}
   (c) O_2^+ (d) O_2.

20. The charge/size ratio of a cation determines its polarizing power. Which one of the following sequences represents the increasing order of the polarizing power of the cationic species, K^+, Ca^{2+}, Mg^{2+}, Be^{2+}?   *[2007]*
   (a) $Ca^{2+} < Mg^{2+} < Be^+ < K^+$
   (b) $Mg^{2+} < Be^{2+} < K^+ < Ca^{2+}$
   (c) $Be^{2+} < K^+ < Ca^{2+} < Mg^{2+}$
   (d) $K^+ < Ca^{2+} < Mg^{2+} < Be^{2+}$.

21. Which of the following hydrogen bonds is the strongest?   *[2007]*
   (a) $O-H---F$ (b) $O-H---H$
   (c) $F-H---F$ (d) $O-H---O$.

22. Using MO theory, predict which of the following species has the shortest bond length?   *[2008]*

   (a) O_2^+ (b) O_2^-

   (c) O_2^{2-} (d) O_2^{2+}

23. The bond dissociation energy of $B-F$ in BF_3 is 646 kJ mol^{-1} whereas that of $C-F$ in CF_4 is 515 kJ mol^{-1}. The correct reason for higher $B-F$ bond dissociation energy as compared to that of $C-F$ is   *[2008]*
   (a)   stronger σ bond between B and F in BF_3 as compared to that between C and F in CF_4.
   (b)   significant $p\pi - p\pi$ interaction between B and F in BF_3 whereas there is no possibility of such interaction between C and F in CF_4.
   (c)   lower degree of $p\pi - p\pi$ interaction between B and F in BF_3 than that between C and F in CF_4.
   (d)   smaller size of B– atom as compared to that of C– atom.

24. Which one of the following pairs of species have the same bond order?   *[2008]*
   (a) CN^- and NO^+ (b) CN^- and CN^+
   (c) O_2^- and CN^- (d) NO^+ and CN^+

25. The number of types of bonds between two carbon atoms in calcium carbide is :   *[2011RS]*
   (a)   One sigma, One pi   (b) Two sigma, one pi
   (c)   Two sigma, two pi   (d) One sigma, two pi

26. Among the following species which two have trigonal bipyramidal shape?
                              [Online May 26, 2012]

   (I) NI_3 (II) I_3^-

   (III) SO_3^{2-} (IV) NO_3^-
   (a)   I and III   (b)   III and IV
   (c)   I and IV   (d)   II and III

27. Which of the following has the square planar structure?   *[Online May 19, 2012]*

   (a) XeF_4 (b) NH_4^+

   (c) BF_4^- (d) CCl_4

28. The formation of molecular complex $BF_3 - NH_3$ results in a change in hybridization of boron   *[Online May 12, 2012]*
   (a)   from sp^2 to dsp^2 (b)   from sp^2 to sp^3
   (c)   from sp^3 to sp^2 (d)   from sp^3 to sp^3d

29. In which of the following pairs the two species are not isostructural ?   *[2012]*

   (a) CO_3^{2-} and NO_3^- (b) PCl_4^+ and $SiCl_4$

   (c) PF_5 and BrF_5 (d) AlF_6^{3-} and SF_6

30. Although CN^- ion and N_2 molecule are isoelectronic, yet N_2 molecule is chemically inert because of   *[Online May 12, 2012]*
   (a)   presence of more number of electrons in bonding orbitals
   (b)   lone bond energy
   (c)   absence of bond polarity
   (d)   uneven electron distribution.

31. Among the following chloro-compound having the lowest dipole moment is

[Online May 12, 2012]

(a) CH_3Cl

(b)   [structure: Cl and H_3C on one carbon, $C=C$, with H and Cl on other carbon]

(c) CH_2Cl_2

(d)   [structure: Cl and H_3C on one carbon, $C=C$, with Cl and H on other carbon]

32. Among the following, the species having the smallest bond is   *[Online May 7, 2012]*

(a) NO^- (b) NO^+

(c) O_2 (d) NO

33. Ortho-nitrophenol is less soluble in water than *p*- and *m*- Nitrophenols because :   *[2012]*

(a)   *o*-nitrophenol is more volatile steam than those of *m*- and *p*-isomers.

(b)   *o*-nitrophenol shows intramolecular H-bonding

(c)   *o*-nitrophenol shows intermolecular H-bonding

(d)   Melting point of *o*-Nitrophenol is lower than those of *m*- and *p*-isomers.

34. The internuclear distances in O – O bonds for O_2^+, O_2, O_2^- and O_2^{2-} respectively are :

[Online April 25, 2013]

(a)   1.30 Å, 1.49 Å, 1.12 Å, 1.21 Å

(b)   1.49 Å, 1.21 Å, 1.12 Å, 1.30 Å

(c)   1.21 Å, 1.12 Å, 1.49 Å, 1.30 Å

(d)   1.12 Å, 1.21 Å, 1.30 Å, 1.49 Å

35. Bond order normally gives idea of stability of a molecular species. All the molecules viz. H_2, Li_2 and B_2 have the same bond order yet they are not equally stable. Their stability order is

[Online April 22, 2013]

(a) $H_2 > B_2 > Li_2$ (b) $Li_2 > H_2 > B_2$

(c) $Li_2 > B_2 > H_2$ (d) $B_2 > H_2 > Li_2$

36. In which of the following ionization processes the bond energy has increased and also the magnetic behaviour has changed from paramagnetic to diamagnetic ?   *[Online April 9, 2013]*

(a) $NO \rightarrow NO^+$ (b) $N_2 \rightarrow N_2^+$

(c) $C_2 \rightarrow C_2^+$ (d) $O_2 \rightarrow O_2^+$

37. Stability of the species Li_2, Li_2^- and Li_2^+ increases in the order of :   *[2013]*

(a) $Li_2 < Li_2^+ < Li_2^-$ (b) $Li_2^- < Li_2^+ < Li_2$

(c) $Li_2 < Li_2^- < Li_2^+$ (d) $Li_2^- < Li_2 < Li_2^+$

38. Which of the following is the wrong statement

[2013]

(a) $ONCl$ and ONO^- are not isoelectronic.

(b) O_3 molecule is bent

(c)   Ozone is violet-black in solid state

(d)   Ozone is diamagnetic gas.

39. Which one of the following molecules is expected to exhibit diamagnetic behaviour ?

(a) C_2 (b) N_2 *[2013]*

(c) O_2 (d) S_2

40. In which of the following pairs of molecules/ions, both the species are not likely to exist ?

(a) H_2^+, He_2^{2-} (b) H_2^-, He_2^{2-} *[2013]*

(c) H_2^{2+}, He_2 (d) H_2^-, He_2^{2+}

41. In which of the following sets, all the given species are isostructural ?   *[Online April 25, 2013]*

(a) CO_2, NO_2, ClO_2, SiO_2

(b) $PCl_3, AlCl_3, BCl_3, SbCl_3$

(c) BF_3, NF_3, PF_3, AlF_3

(d) $BF_4^-, CCl_4, NH_4^+, PCl_4^+$

42. The shape of IF_6^- is :   *[Online April 23, 2013]*

(a)   Trigonally distorted octahedron

(b)   Pyramidal

(c)   Octahedral

(d)   Square antiprism

43. Bond distance in HF is 9.17×10^{-11} m. Dipole moment of HF is 6.104×10^{-30} Cm. The percentage ionic character in HF will be : (electron charge $= 1.60 \times 10^{-19}$ C) *[Online April 23, 2013]*

(a)   61.0%   (b)   38.0%

(c)   35.5%   (d)   41.5%

44. Which one of the following molecules is polar ?

[Online April 9, 2013]

(a) XeF_4 (b) IF_5

(c) SbF_5 (d) CF_4

45. Which one of the following molecules is paramagnetic?   *[Online April 19, 2014]*

(a) N_2 (b) NO (c) CO (d) O_3

46. Which of the following has unpaired electron(s)?

[Online April 9, 2014]

(a) N_2 (b) O_2^- (c) N_2^{2+} (d) O_2^{2-}

47. Which one of the following properties is **not** shown by NO?   *[2014]*

(a)   It is diamagnetic in gaseous state

(b)   It is neutral oxide

(c)   It combines with oxygen to form nitrogen dioxide

(d)   It's bond order is 2.5

48. Which of the following molecules has two sigma (σ) and two pi (π) bonds?

[Online April 12, 2014]

(a) C_2H_4 (b) N_2F_2

(c) $C_2H_2Cl_2$ (d) HCN

49. The number and type of bonds in C_2^{2-} ion in CaC_2 are: *[Online April 9, 2014]*
(a) One σ bond and one π-bond
(b) One σ bond and two π-bond
(c) Two σ bond and two π-bond
(d) Two σ bond and one π-bond

50. The correct order of bond dissociation energy among N_2, O_2, O_2^- is shown in which of the following arrangements? *[Online April 11, 2014]*

(a) $N_2 > O_2^- > O_2$ (b) $O_2^- > O_2 > N_2$

(c) $N_2 > O_2 > O_2^-$ (d) $O_2 > O_2^- > N_2$

51. Which of these statements is not true?
[Online April 19, 2014]
(a) NO^+ is not isoelectronic with O_2
(b) B is always covalent in its compounds
(c) In aqueous solution, the Tl^+ ion is much more stable than Tl (III)
(d) $LiAlH_4$ is a versatile reducing agent in organic synthesis.

52. Amongst $LiCl$, $RbCl$, $BeCl_2$ and $MgCl_2$ the compounds with the greatest and the least ionic character, respectively are:
[Online April 19, 2014]
(a) LiCl and RbCl
(b) RbCl and $BeCl_2$
(c) $MgCl_2$ and $BeCl_2$
(d) RbCl and $MgCl_2$

53. After understanding the assertion and reason, choose the correct option.
[Online April 10, 2015]
Assertion : In the bonding molecular orbital (MO) of H_2, electron density is increased between the nuclei.
Reason : The bonding MO is $\Psi_A + \Psi_B$, which shows destructive interference of the combining electron waves.
(a) Assertion is incorrect, reason is correct.
(b) Assertion is correct, reason is incorrect.
(c) Assertion and reason are correct and reason is the correct explanation for the assertion.
(d) Assertion and reason are correct, but reason is not the correct explanation for the assertion.

54. Molecular AB has a bond length of 1.61Å and a dipole moment of 0.38 D. The fractional charge on each atom (absolute magnitude) is : ($e_0 = 4.802 \times 10^{-10}$ esu)
[Online April 11, 2015]
(a) 0.5   (b) 0.05   (c) 0   (d) 1.0

55. Which compound exhibits maximum dipole moment among the following ?
[Online April 11, 2015]

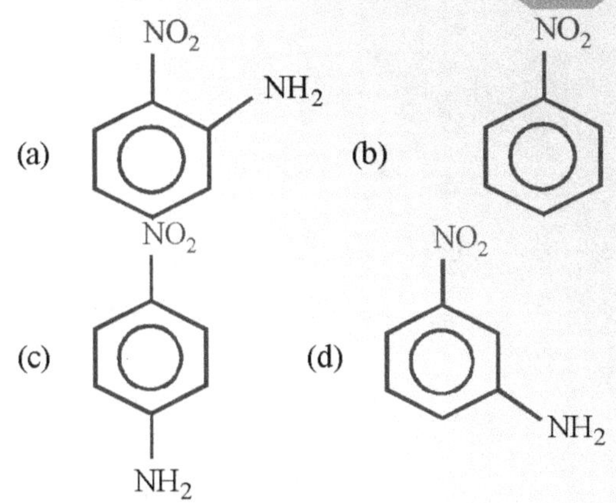

56. The intermolecular interaction that is dependent on the inverse cube of distance between the molecules is : *[2015]*
(a) London force
(b) hydrogen bond
(c) ion - ion interaction
(d) ion - dipole interaction

57. The bond angle H–X–H is the greatest in the compound : *[Online April 10, 2016]*
(a) PH_3 (b) CH_4
(c) NH_3 (d) H_2O

58. The group of molecules having identical shape is : *[Online April 9, 2016]*
(a) PCl_5, IF_5, XeO_2F_2
(b) BF_3, PCl_3, XeO_3
(c) SF_4, XeF_4, CCl_4
(d) ClF_3, $XeOF_2$, XeF_3^+

59. The species in which the N atom is in a state of sp hybridization is : *[2016]*
(a) NO_3^- (b) NO_2
(c) NO_2^+ (d) NO_2^-

60. Which of the following species is not paramagnetic ? *[2017]*
(a) NO   (b) CO
(c) O_2 (d) B_2

61. Which of the following is paramagnetic ?
[Online April 8, 2017]
(a) NO^+ (b) CO
(c) O_2^{2-} (d) B_2

62. The group having triangular planar structures is *[Online April 9, 2017]*

(a) BF_3, NF_3, CO_3^{2-} (b) CO_3^{2-}, NO_3^-, SO_3

(c) NH_3, SO_3, CO_3^{2-} (d) NCl_3, BCl_3, SO_3

63. sp^3d^2 hybridization is not displayed by :
[Online April 8, 2017]
(a) BrF_5 (b) SF_6
(c) $[CrF_6]^{3-}$ (d) PF_5

HINTS & SOLUTIONS

1. **(b)** $O_2^+ (15) = KK\, \sigma 2s^2, \sigma^* 2s^2, \sigma 2p_x^2,$

$\{\pi 2p_y^2 = \pi 2p_z^2, \{\pi^* 2p_y^1 = \pi 2p_z^0$

$$\text{Bond order} = \frac{1}{2}(8-3) = \frac{5}{2} = 2.5$$

$O_2 (16) = KK\, \sigma 2s^2, \sigma^* 2s^2, \sigma 2p_x^2,$

$\{\pi 2p_y^2 = \pi 2p_z^2, \{\pi^* 2p_y^1 = \pi^* 2p_z^1$

$$\text{Bond order} = \frac{1}{2}(8-4) = 2$$

$O_2^- (17) = KK\, \sigma 2s^2, \sigma^* 2s^2, \sigma 2p_x^2,$

$\{\pi 2p_y^2 = \pi 2p_z^2, \{\pi^* 2p_y^2 = \pi^* 2p_z^1$

$$\text{Bond order} = \frac{1}{2}(8-5) = 1.5$$

$O_2^{2-} (18) = KK\, \sigma 2s^2\, \sigma^* 2s^2\, \sigma 2p_x^2,$

$\{\pi 2p_y^2 = \pi 2p_z^2, \{\pi^* 2p_y^2 = \pi^* 2p_z^2$

$$\text{Bond order} = \frac{1}{2}(8-6) = 1$$

 **NOTE** As we know that as the bond order decreases, stability also decreases and hence the bond strength also decreases. Hence the correct order of their increasing bond strength is

$$O_2^{2-} < O_2^- < O_2 < O_2^+$$

2. **(a)**

3. **(a)**   In NH_3 and BF_4^- the hybridisation is sp^3 and the bond angle is almost $109° 28'$.

4. **(a)**   Both XeF_2 and CO_2 have a linear structure.

5. **(b)**   In H_2S, due to low electronegativity of sulphur the L.P. - L. P. repulsion is more than B. P. - B. P. repulsion and hence the bond angle is minimum.

	SO_2	H_2O	H_2S	NH_3
Bond angle	119.5°	104.5°	92.5°	106.5°

6. **(b)**   Both NO_2 and O_3 have angular shape and hence will have net dipole moment.

7. **(c)**   In ether, there is no H-bonding while alcohols have intermolecular H-bonding

8. **(d)**

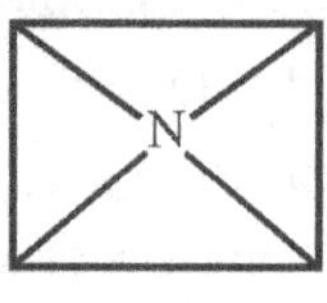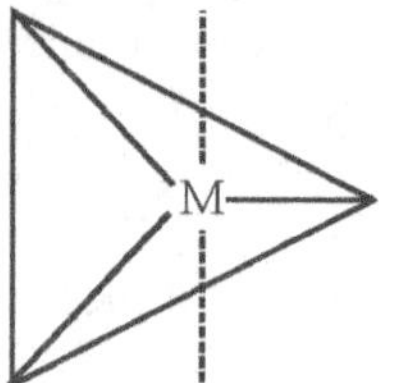

dsp^2 hybridisation sp^3d or dsp^3 hybridisation
Number of 90° angle   Number of 90° angle
between bonds = 4   between bonds = 6

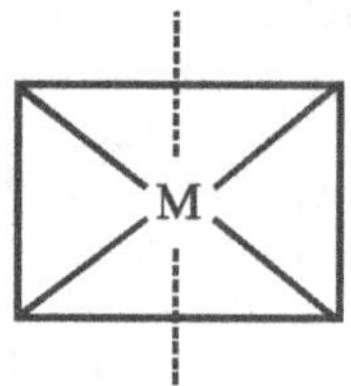

sp^3d^2 hybridisation
Number of 90° angle
between bonds = 12

9. **(a)** XeF_4 (sp^3d^2 square planar),
$[Ni(CN)_4]^{2-}$ (dsp^2 square planar),
BF_4^- (sp^3 tetrahedral), SF_4 (sp^3d see saw shaped)

10. **(b)**

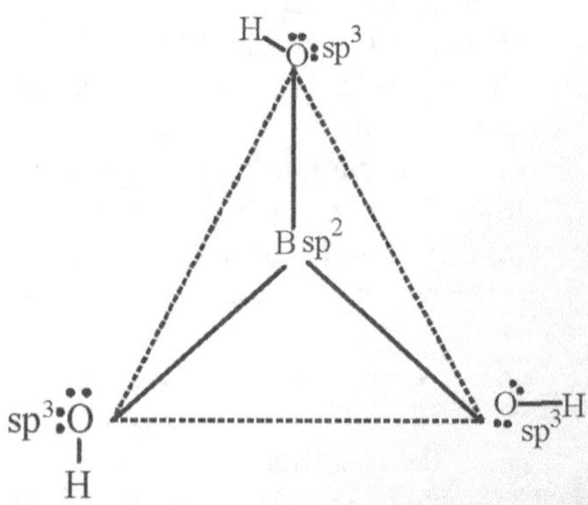

11. **(a)**   The order of bond angles

$$\underset{120°}{BF_3} > \underset{109°28'}{SiH_4} > \underset{107°}{NH_3} > \underset{92.5°}{H_2S}$$

12. **(b)**   Now since bond order of NO^+ given (3) is higher than that of NO (2.5). Thus bond length of NO^+ will be shorter.

13. (c) **TIPS / Formulae**

A diamagnetic substance contains no unpaired electron.

H_2 is diamagnetic as it contains all paired electrons

$$H_2 = \sigma_b^2 , \quad H_2^+ = \sigma_b^1, \quad H_2^- = \sigma_b^2,$$
(diamagnetic) (paramagnetic) (paramagnetic)

$$\sigma_a^{*1}; \ He_2^+ = \sigma_b^2, \sigma_a^{*1}$$
(paramagnetic) (paramagnetic)

14. (a) The value of lattice energy depends on the charges present on the two ions and the distance between them.

15. (c) The distribution of electrons in MOs is as follows :

N_2^+(electrons 13) $\sigma^2 \sigma^{*2} \sigma^2 \sigma^{*2}$

$$\begin{matrix} \pi^2 \\ \pi^2 \end{matrix} \sigma^1 \begin{matrix} \pi^* \\ \pi^* \end{matrix} \sigma^*$$

O_2 (electrons 16) $\sigma^2 \sigma^{*2} \sigma^2 \sigma^{*2} \sigma^2 \begin{matrix} \pi^2 \\ \pi^2 \end{matrix}$

$$\begin{matrix} \pi^{*1} \\ \pi^{*1} \end{matrix} \sigma^*$$

O_2^{2-} (electrons 18) $\sigma^2 \sigma^{*2} \sigma^2 \sigma^{*2} \sigma^2 \begin{matrix} \pi^2 \\ \pi^2 \end{matrix}$

$$\begin{matrix} \pi^* \\ \pi^* \end{matrix} \sigma^*$$

B_2 (electrons 10) $\sigma^2 \sigma^{*2} \sigma^2 \sigma^{*2} \begin{matrix} \pi^1 \\ \pi^1 \end{matrix}$

Only O_2^{2-} does not contain any unpaired electron.

16. (b) The bond angle decreases on moving down the group due to decrease in bond pair-bond pair repulsion.

NH_3	PH_3	ASH_3	SbH_3	BiH_3
107°	94°	92°	91°	90°

NOTE This can also be explained by the fact that as the size of central atom increases sp^3 hybrid orbital becomes more distinct with increasing size of central atom i.e. pure p- orbitals are utilized in M–H bonding

F—Xe—F   O=C=O

17. (d) In SF_4 the hybridisation is sp^3d and the shape of molecule is

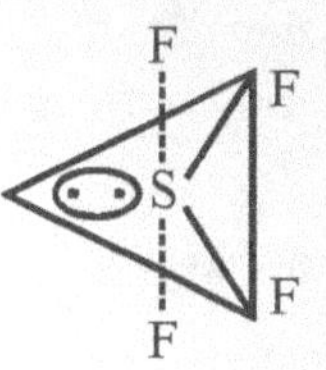

18. (c) (a) N_2 : bond order 3, paramagnetic

N_2^+ : bond order, 2.5, paramagnetic

(b) C_2 : bond order 2, diamagnetic

C_2^+ : bond order 1.5, paramagnetic

(c) NO : bond order 2.5, paramagnetic

NO^+ : bond order 3, diamagnetic

(d) O_2 : bond order 2, paramagnetic

O_2^+ : bond order 2.5, paramagnetic

19. (b) Diamagnetic species have no unpaired electrons

$$O_2^{2-} \Rightarrow \sigma 1s^2, \sigma*1s^2, \sigma 2s^2, \sigma*2s^2, \sigma 2p_x^2,$$
$$\{\pi 2p_y^2 = \pi 2p_z^2, \{\pi*2p_y^2 = \pi*2p_z^2$$

Whereas paramagnetic species has one or more unpaired electrons as in

$$O_2 \to \sigma 1s^2, \sigma^*1s^2, \sigma 2s^2, \sigma^*2s^2, \sigma 2p_x^2,$$
$$\{\pi 2p_y^2 = \pi 2p_z^2,$$

$$\{ \pi^* 2p_y^1 = \pi^* 2p_z^1 - 2 \text{ unpaired electrons}$$

$$O_2^+ \to \sigma 1s^2, \sigma^*1s^2, \sigma 2s^2, \sigma^*2s^2, \sigma 2p_x^2,$$

$$\{ \pi 2p_y^2 = \pi 2p_z^2 \{\pi^* 2p_y^1 = \pi^* 2p_z^0 - 1$$

unpaired electron

$$NO \to \sigma 1s^2, \sigma^*1s^2, \sigma 2s^2, \sigma^*2s^2, \sigma 2p_x^2,$$

$$\pi 2p_z^2, \{\pi^* 2p_y^1 = \pi^* 2p_z^0 \ -1 \text{ unpaired electron}$$

20. (d) Smaller the size and higher the charge more will be polarising power of cation. Since the order of the size of cation is $K^+ > Ca^{++} > Mg^{++} > Be^{++}$. So the correct order of polarising power is $K^+ < Ca^{2+} < Mg^{2+} < Be^{2+}$

21. (c) **NOTE** Greater the difference between electro-negativity of bonded atoms, stronger will be bond. Since F is most electronegative hence F – H ...... F is the strongest bond.

22. (d) Bond order

$$\frac{\text{No. of bonding electrons} - \text{No. of antibonding electrons}}{2}$$

$$\text{Bond order in } O_2^+ = \frac{10-5}{2} = 2.5$$

$$\text{Bond order in } O_2^- = \frac{10-7}{2} = 1.5$$

$$\text{Bond order in } O_2^{2-} = \frac{10-8}{2} = 1$$

$$\text{Bond order in } O_2^{2+} = \frac{10-4}{2} = 3$$

$$\text{Since Bond order} \propto \frac{1}{\text{Bond length}}$$

$\therefore$ Bond length is shortest in O_2^{2+}.

23. (b) 📓 **NOTE** The delocalised $p\pi - p\pi$ bonding between filled p-orbital of F and vacant p-orbital of B leads to shortening of B–F bond length which results in higher bond dissociation energy of the B–F bond.

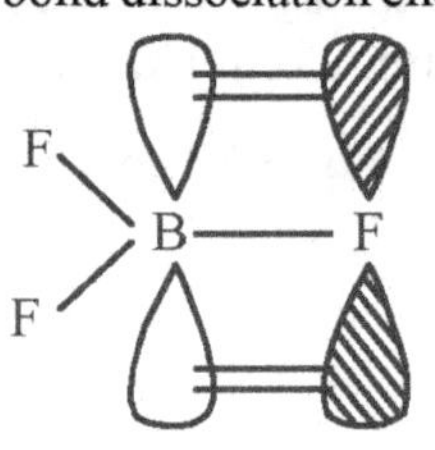

24. (a) For any species to have same bond order we can expect them to have same number of electrons. Calculating the number of electrons in various species.

$O_2^- (8+8+1=17)$; $CN^- (6+7+1=14)$

$NO^+(7+8-1=14)$; $CN^+ (6+7-1=12)$

We find CN^- and NO^+ both have 14 electrons so they have same bond order. Correct answer is (a).

$$N_2 > O_2 > O_2^-$$

25. (d) Calcium carbide exists as Ca^{2+} and C_2^{2-}. According to the molecular orbital model, C_2^{2-} should have molecular orbital configuration :

$$\sigma 1s^2\, \sigma^* 1s^2\, \sigma 2s^2\, \sigma^* 2s^2$$
$$\{\pi 2p_y^2 = \pi 2p_z^2\}\sigma\, 2p_x^2$$

Thus M.O. configuration suggests that it contains one σ & 2π bonds.

26. (a)

27. (a) XeF_4 has square pyramidal structure, while NH_4^+, BF_4^- and CCl_4 have tetrahedral structure.

28. (b) In BF_3, B is sp^2 hybridized with one empty p_z orbital. The empty p_z orbital of BF_3 can be filled by lone pair of molecules such as NH_3. When this occurs a tetrahedral molecule or ion is formed which is sp^3 hybridized.

29. (c) PF_5 trigonal bipyramidal

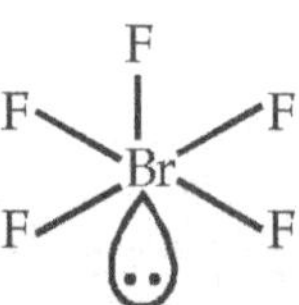

BrF_5 square pyramidal (distorted)

30. (c) In nitrogen molecule, both the nitrogen atoms have same electronegativity. So it has zero polarity and hence less tendency to break away and form ions.

31. (c) Dipole moment $(\mu) = 0$

32. (b) $NO^-(16)$ – B.O. – 2 $\quad O_2(16)$ – B.O. – 2

$NO^+(14)$ – B.O. – 3 $\quad NO(15)$ – B.O. – 2.5

Higher the bond order lower is the bond length. Hence NO^+ will have smallest bond.

33. (b) Compounds involved in chelation become non-polar. Consequently such compounds are soluble in non-polar solvents like ether, benzene etc. and are only sparingly soluble in water whereas meta and para isomers are more soluble in water & less soluble in non-polar solvents.

O intramolecular H-bonding

34. **(d)**   The bond length follows the order

$$O_2^+ < O_2 < O_2^- < O_2^{2-}$$

According to this the possible values are 1.12Å, 1.21Å, 1.30Å, 1.49Å

35. **(None)** None of the given option is correct. The molecular orbital configuration of the given molecules is
$H_2 = \sigma 1s^2$ (no electron anti-bonding)
$Li_2 = \sigma 1s^2 \; \sigma^* 1s^2 \; \sigma 2s^2$ (two anti-bonding electrons)
$B_2 = \sigma 1s^2 \; \sigma^* 1s^2 \; \sigma 2s^2 \; \sigma^* 2s^2$

$$\{\pi 2p_y^1 = \pi 2p_z^1\}$$

(4 anti-bonding electrons)
Though the bond order of all the species are same (B.O = 1) but stability is different. This is due to difference in the presence of no. of anti-bonding electron.
Higher the no. of anti-bonding electron lower is the stability hence the correct order is $H_2 > Li_2 > B_2$

36. **(a)**   For NO
Total no. of electrons = 15
B.O = 2.5
Mag. Behaviour = Paramagnetic
For NO^+
Total no. of electrons = 14
B.O = 3
Mag. Behaviour = Diamagnetic

37. **(b)** $Li_2 = \sigma 1s^2 \; \sigma^* 1s^2 \; \sigma 2s^2$

$$\therefore \text{Bond order} = \frac{1}{2}(4-2) = 1$$

$Li_2^+ = \sigma 1s^2 \; \sigma^* 1s^2 \; \sigma 2s^1$

$$\text{B.O.} = \frac{1}{2}(3-2) = 0.5$$

$Li_2^- = \sigma 1s^2 \; \sigma^* 1s^2 \sigma 2s^2 \sigma^* 2s^1$

$$\text{B.O.} = \frac{1}{2}(4-3) = 0.5$$

The bond order of Li_2^+ and Li_2^- is same but Li_2^+ is more stable than Li_2^- because Li_2^+ is smaller in size and has 2 electrons in antibonding orbitals whereas Li_2^- has 3 electrons in antibonding orbitals. Hence Li_2^+ is more stable than Li_2^-.

38. **(None).**   All options are correct,

(a) $ONCl = 8 + 7 + 17 = 32e^-$ ⎱ not
      $ONO^- = 8 + 7 + 8 + 1 = 24e^-$ ⎰ isoelectronic

(b)   The central atom is sp^2 hybridized with one lone pair. (1.278Å, 116.8°, 1.278Å)

(c)   It is a pale blue gas. At $-249.7°$, it forms violet black crystals.

(d)   It is diamagnetic in nature due to absence of unpaired electrons.

39. **(a,b)**   The molecular orbital structures of C_2 and N_2 are

$$N_2 = \sigma 1s^2 \sigma^* 1s^2 \sigma 2s^2 \sigma^* 2s^2 \sigma 2p_x^2 \pi 2p_y^2 \pi 2p_z^2$$

$$C_2 = \sigma 1s^2 \sigma^* 1s^2 \sigma 2s^2 \sigma^* 2s^2 \pi 2py^2 \pi 2P_z^2$$

Both N_2 and C_2 have paired electrons, hence they are diamagnetic.

40. **(c)** $H_2^{2+} = \sigma 1s^0 \sigma^* 1s^0$

$$\text{Bond order for } H_2^{2+} = \frac{1}{2}(0-0) = 0$$

$$He_2 = \sigma 1s^2 \sigma^* 1s^2$$

$$\text{Bond order for } He_2 = \frac{1}{2}(2-2) = 0$$

so both H_2^{2+} and He_2 does not exist.

41. **(d)**   All have tetrahedral structure.

42. **(a)**   The structure of IF_6^- is distorted octahedral
This is due to presence of a "weak" lone pair.

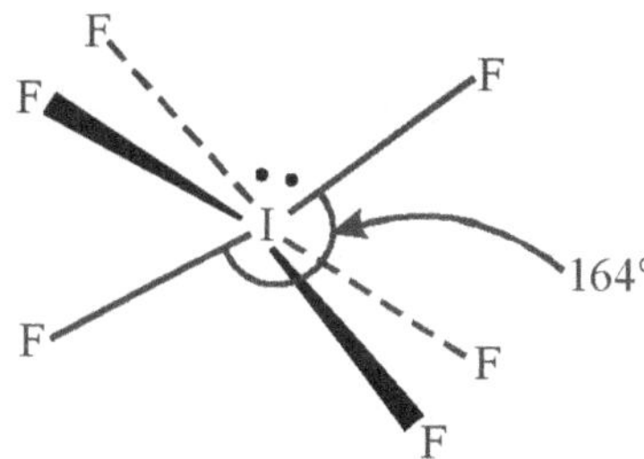

43. **(d)**   Given $e = 1.60 \times 10^{-19}$ C
$$d = 9.17 \times 10^{-11} \text{ m}$$
From $\mu = e \times d$

$$\mu = 1.60 \times 10^{-19} \times 9.17 \times 10^{-11}$$
$$= 14.672 \times 10^{-30}$$

% ionic character

$$= \frac{\text{Observed dipole moment}}{\text{Dipole moment for 100\% ionic bond}}$$

$$= \frac{6.104 \times 10^{-30}}{14.672 \times 10^{-30}} \times 100$$

$$= 41.5\%$$

44. (b) The geometry of IF_5 is square Pyramide with an unsymmetric charge distribution therefore this molecule is polar.

45. (b) The molecular orbital configuration of the molecules given is

Total no. of electrons in NO
$$= 7(N) + 8(O) = 15$$

Hence E.C. of NO

$$= KK[\sigma(2s)]^2[\sigma*(2s)]^2[\sigma 2p_z]^2$$
$$[\pi(2p_x)]^2[\pi(2p_y)]^2[\pi*(2p_x)]^1$$

Due to presence of one unpaired electron NO is paramagnetic.

Except NO all are diamagnetic due to absence of unpaired electrons.

46. (b) $$O_2^-(17) = KK(\sigma 2s)^2(\sigma^* 2s^2)(\sigma 2p_x)^2$$
$$(\pi 2p_y)^2(\pi 2p_z)^2(\pi^* 2p_y)^2(\pi^* 2p_z)^1$$

one unpaired electron - Paramagnetic.

47. (a) Nitric oxide is paramagnetic in the gaseous state because of the presence of one unpaired electron in its outermost shell. The electronic configuration of NO is

$$\sigma_{1s}^2 \, \sigma_{1s}^{*2} \, \sigma_{2s}^2 \sigma_{2s}^{*2} \sigma_{2p_z}^2 \, \pi_{2p_x}^2 = \pi_{2p_y}^2 \, \pi_2^{*1}{}_{p_x}$$

48. (d) $$H \underset{\sigma}{-\!\!\!-} C \overset{\pi,\,\sigma}{\underset{\pi}{\equiv\!\!\!\equiv}} N$$

49. (d) The structure of CaC_2 is $Ca^{2+}[:C \equiv C:]^2$

i.e, one π and two σ bonds

i.e $2\,\pi$ and $2\,\sigma$ bonds.

50. (c) The bond order of N_2, O_2, and O_2^- are respectively 3, 2 and 1.5

Since higher bond order implies higher bond dissociation energy hence the correct order will be

51. (a) $NO^+ = 7 + 8 - 1 = 14 \, e^-$.
$O_2 = 16 \, e^-$
i.e not isoelectric

(b) Boron forms only covalent compounds. This is due to its extremely high ionisation energy.

(c) Compounds of Tl^+ are much more stable than those of Tl^{3+}.

(d) $LiAlH_4$ is a versatile reducing agent in organic synthesis

52. (b) According to Fajan's rules smaller, highly charged cation has greatest covalent character while large cation with smaller charge has greatest ionic character.

53. (b) Assertion is correct but reason is incorrect. Bonding MO shows constructive interference of the combining electron waves.

54. (b) $1\,e = 1.602 \times 10^{-19} C$
$1\,esu = 3.33 \times 10^{-10} C$

$$\frac{1e}{1esu} = \frac{1.602 \times 10^{-19} C}{3.33 \times 10^{-10} C}$$

$1\,e = 4.802 \times 10^{-10}$ esu
Dipole moment $= q \times$ distance
$\Rightarrow 1\,D \approx 10^{-18}$ esu cm
0.38×10^{-18} esu cm $= q \times (1.61 \times 10^{-8} \text{cm})$
$q = 2.36 \times 10^{-11}$ esu

$$q = \frac{2.36 \times 10^{-11} \text{ esu}}{4.802 \times 10^{-10} \text{ esu}}$$

$q = 0.049$
$q \approx 0.05$ fractional charge

55. (c)

Dipole moment = (Distance between opposite charges) $\times$ (charge, q)
$$\mu = q \times d$$

So, greater the distance between the opposite charges higher the dipole. Due to the resonance the greater charge separation occurs between charges due to linearity.

$$CO \Rightarrow KK \cdot \sigma(2s)^2 \sigma*(2s)^2 \cdot (\pi 2p_x)^2$$

$$= (\pi 2p_y)^2 \cdot (\sigma 2p_z)^2 \quad \text{diamagnetic}$$

$$O_2^{2-} \Rightarrow KK \cdot \sigma(2s)^2 \sigma*(2s)^2 \cdot \sigma(2p_z)^2 (\pi 2p_x)^2$$

$$= (\pi 2p_y)^2 \cdot \pi*(2p_x)^2 = \pi*(2p_y)^2$$

$$\text{diamagnetic}$$

$$B_2 \Rightarrow KK \cdot \sigma(2s)^2 \sigma*(2s)^2 \cdot \pi(2p_x)^1 = \pi(2p_y)^1$$

$$\text{paramagnetic}$$

56. (b) Hydrogen bond is a type of strong electrostatic dipole-dipole interaction and dependent on the inverse cube of distance between the molecular ion-dipole interaction $\propto \dfrac{1}{r^3}$.

57. (b) More the number of lone pairs on central atom, the greater is the contraction caused in the angle between bond pairs. In CH_4 there is no lone pair of electrons hence bond angle is greatest.

58. (d)

59. (c)

60. (b)

1. $NO \rightarrow$ one unpaired electron is present in $\pi*$ molecular orbit hence paramagnetic.

2. $CO \rightarrow \sigma_{1s}^2, \sigma_{1s}^{*2}, \sigma_{2s}^2, \sigma_{2s}^{*2}, \pi_{2p_x}^2, \pi_{2p_y}^2, \sigma 2pz^2$
   no unpaired electron hence diamagnetic.

3. $O_2 \rightarrow \sigma_{1s}^2, \sigma_{1s}^{*2}, \sigma_{2s}^2, \sigma_{2s}^{*2}, \sigma_{2p_z}^2, \pi_{2p_x}^2, \pi_{2p_y}^2, \pi_{2p_x}^{*1}, \pi_{2p_y}^{*1}$
   two unpaired electron hence paramagnetic.

4. $B_2 \rightarrow \sigma_{1s}^2, \sigma_{1s}^{*2}, \sigma_{2s}^2, \sigma_{2s}^{*2}, \pi_{2p_x}^1, \pi_{2p_y}^1$
   B_2 contains two unpaired electrons hence paramagnetic

61. (d)

	Total electron
NO^+	14
CO	14
O_2^{2-}	18
B_2	10

$$NO^+ \Rightarrow KK \cdot \sigma(2s)^2 \sigma*(2s)^2 \cdot (\pi 2p_x)^2$$

$$= (\pi 2p_y)^2 \cdot (\sigma 2p_z)^2 \quad \text{diamagnetic}$$

62. (b)

Group	Hybridi-zation	Shape	
(1) BF_3	sp^2	Triangular Planar (TP)	
NF_3	sp^3	Tetrahedral (T)	
CO_3^{2-}	sp^2	T.P.	
(2) CO_3^{2-}	sp^2	T.P.	
NO_3^-	sp^2	T.P.	All have same hybridization
SO_3	sp^2	T.P.	
(3) NH_3	sp^3	T	
SO_3	sp^2	T.P.	
CO_3^{2-}	sp^2	T.P.	
(4) NCl_3	sp^3	T	
BCl_3	sp^2	T.P.	
SO_3	sp^2	T.P.	

63. (d)

(a) BrF_5 — $sp^3 d^2$

(b) SF_6 — $sp^3 d^2$

(c) $[CrF_6]^{3-}$ — $sp^3 d^2$

(d) PF_5 — $sp^3 d$

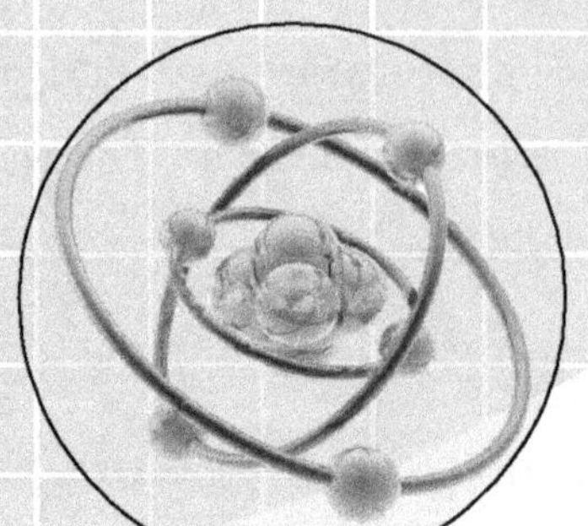

Past Year JEE Advanced Questions

12

1. The compound which contains both ionic and covalent bonds is *[1979]*
   - (a) CH_4
   - (b) H_2
   - (c) KCN
   - (d) KCl

2. The octet rule is not valid for the molecule
   - (a) CO_2
   - (b) H_2O *[1979]*
   - (c) O_2
   - (d) CO

3. Element X is strongly electropositive and element Y is strongly electronegative. Both are univalent. The compound formed would be
   - (a) X^+Y^-
   - (b) X^-X^+ *[1980]*
   - (c) X–Y
   - (d) $X \rightarrow Y$

4. Which of the following compounds are covalent? *[1980]*
   - (a) H_2
   - (b) CaO
   - (c) KCl
   - (d) Na_2S

5. The total number of electrons that take part in forming the bond in N_2 is *[1980]*
   - (a) 2
   - (b) 4
   - (c) 6
   - (d) 10

6. Which of the following is soluble in water
   - (a) CS_2
   - (b) C_2H_5OH *[1980]*
   - (c) CCl_4
   - (d) $CHCl_3$

7. If a molecule MX_3 has zero dipole moment, the sigma bonding orbitals used by M (atomic number < 21) are *[1981]*
   - (a) pure p
   - (b) sp hybrid
   - (c) sp^2 hybrid
   - (d) sp^3 hybrid

8. The ion that is isoelectronic with CO is
   - (a) CN^-
   - (b) O_2^+ *[1982]*
   - (c) O_2^-
   - (d) N_2^+

9. Among the following, the molecule that is linear is *[1982]*
   - (a) CO_2
   - (b) NO_2
   - (c) SO_2
   - (d) ClO_2

10. The compound with no dipole moment is
   - (a) methyl chloride *[1982]*
   - (b) carbon tetrachloride
   - (c) methylene chloride
   - (d) chloroform

11. Carbon tetrachloride has no net dipole moment because of *[1983]*
   - (a) its planar structure
   - (b) its regular tetrahedral structure
   - (c) similar sizes of carbon and chlorine
   - (d) similar electron affinities of carbon and chlorine

12. Which one among the following does not have the hydrogen bond? *[1983]*
   - (a) phenol
   - (b) liquid NH_3
   - (c) water
   - (d) liquid HCl

13. The types of bonds present in $CuSO_4.5H_2O$ are only *[1983]*
   - (a) electrovalent and covalent
   - (b) electrovalent and coordinate covalent
   - (c) electrovalent, covalent and coordinate covalent
   - (d) covalent and coordinate covalent

14. On hybridization of one s and one p orbitals we get : *[1984]*
- (a) two mutually perpendicular orbitals
- (b) two orbitals at 180°
- (c) four orbitals directed tetrahedrally
- (d) three orbitals in a plane

15. The molecule having one unpaired electron is :
- (a) NO
- (b) CO *[1985]*
- (c) CN^-
- (d) O_2

16. The bond between two identical non-metal atoms has a pair of electrons : *[1986]*
- (a) unequally shared between the two
- (b) transferred fully from one atom to another
- (c) with identical spins
- (d) equally shared between them

17. The hydrogen bond is strongest in : *[1986]*
- (a) O–H..........S
- (b) S–H..........O
- (c) F–H..........F
- (d) F–H..........O

18. The hybridisation of sulphur in sulphur dioxide is : *[1986]*
- (a) sp
- (b) sp^3
- (c) sp^2
- (d) dsp^2

19. Hydrogen bonding is maximum in *[1987]*
- (a) Ethanol
- (b) Diethyl ether
- (c) Ethyl chloride
- (d) Triethylamine

20. The species in which the central atom uses sp^2 hybrid orbitals in its bonding is *[1988]*
- (a) PH_3
- (b) NH_3
- (c) CH_3^+
- (d) SbH_3

21. The molecule that has linear structure is
- (a) CO_2
- (b) NO_2 *[1988]*
- (c) SO_2
- (d) SiO_2

22. The molecule which has zero dipole moment is : *[1989]*
- (a) CH_2Cl_2
- (b) BF_3
- (c) NF_3
- (d) ClO_2

23. The molecule which has pyramidal shape is :
- (a) PCl_3
- (b) SO_3 *[1989]*
- (c) CO_3^{2-}
- (d) NO_3^-

24. The compound in which $\overset{*}{C}$ uses its sp^3 hybrid orbitals for bond formation is : *[1989]*
- (a) $H\overset{*}{C}OOH$
- (b) $(H_2N)_2\overset{*}{C}O$
- (c) $(CH_3)_3\overset{*}{C}OH$
- (d) $CH_3\overset{*}{C}HO$

25. Which of the following is paramagnetic?
- (a) O_2^-
- (b) CN^- *[1989]*
- (c) CO
- (d) NO^+

26. The type of hybrid orbitals used by the chlorine atom in ClO_2^- is *[1992]*
- (a) sp^3
- (b) sp^2
- (c) sp
- (d) none of these

27. The maximum possible number of hydrogen bonds a water molecule can form is *[1992]*
- (a) 2
- (b) 4
- (c) 3
- (d) 1

28. The cyanide ion, CN^- and N_2 are isoelectronic. But in contrast to CN^-, N_2 is chemically inert, because of *[1992]*
- (a) low bond energy
- (b) absence of bond polarity
- (c) unsymmetrical electron distribution
- (d) presence of more number of electrons in bonding orbitals

29. Pick out the isoelectronic structures from the following: *[1993]*

I. CH_3^+ II. H_3O^+

III. NH_3 IV. CH_3^-

- (a) I and II
- (b) III and IV
- (c) I and III
- (d) II, III and IV

30. Which one is most ionic : *[1995S]*
- (a) P_2O_5
- (b) CrO_3
- (c) MnO
- (d) Mn_2O_7

31. Number of paired electrons in O_2 molecule is : *[1995S]*
- (a) 7
- (b) 8
- (c) 16
- (d) 14

32. Among the following species, identify the isostructural pairs. NF_3, NO_3^-, BF_3, H_3O^+, HN_3 *[1996]*
- (a) $[NF_3, NO_3^-]$ and $[BF_3, H_3O^+]$
- (b) $[NF_3, HN_3]$ and $[NO_3^-, BF_3]$
- (c) $[NF_3, H_3O^+]$ and $[NO_3^-, BF_3]$
- (d) $[NF_3, H_3O^+]$ and $[HN_3, BF_3]$

33. The number and type of bonds between two carbon atoms in CaC_2 are : *[1996]*
(a) one sigma (σ) and one pi (π) bonds
(b) one sigma (σ) and two pi (π) bonds
(c) one sigma (σ) and one and a half pi (π) bonds
(d) one sigma (σ) bond.

34. Which contains both polar and non-polar bonds? *[1997]*
(a) NH_4Cl
(b) HCN
(c) H_2O_2
(d) CH_4

35. The critical temperature of water is higher than that of O_2 because the H_2O molecule has *[1997]*
(a) fewer electrons than O_2
(b) two covalent bonds
(c) V-shape
(d) dipole moment.

36. Which one of the following compounds has sp^2 hydridization? *[1997]*
(a) CO_2
(b) SO_2
(c) N_2O
(d) CO

37. The geometry and the type of hybrid orbital present about the central atom in BF_3 is *[1998]*
(a) linear, sp
(b) trigonal planar, sp^2
(c) tetrahedral, sp^3
(d) pyramidal, sp^3.

38. The correct order of increasing $C — O$ bond length of CO, CO_3^{2-}, CO_2, is *[1999]*
(a) $CO_3^{2-} < CO_2 < CO$
(b) $CO_2 < CO_3^{2-} < CO$
(c) $CO < CO_3^{2-} < CO_2$
(d) $CO < CO_2 < CO_3^{2-}$

39. The geometry of H_2S and its dipole moment are *[1999]*
(a) angular and non-zero
(b) angular and zero
(c) linear and non-zero
(d) linear and zero

40. Molecular shapes of SF_4, CF_4 and XeF_4 are *[2000S]*
(a) the same, with 2, 0 and 1 lone pairs of electrons respectively
(b) the same, with 1, 1 and 1 lone pairs of electrons respectively
(c) different, with 0, 1 and 2 lone pairs of electrons respectively
(d) different, with 1, 0 and 2 lone pairs of electrons respectively

41. The hybridisation of atomic orbitals of nitrogen in NO_2^+, NO_3^- and NH_4^+ are *[2000S]*
(a) sp, sp^3 and sp^2 respectively
(b) sp, sp^2 and sp^3 respectively
(c) sp^2, sp and sp^3 respectively
(d) sp^2, sp^3 and sp respectively

42. The common features among the species CN^-, CO and NO^+ are *[2001S]*
(a) bond order three and isoelectronic
(b) bond order three and weak field ligands
(c) bond order two and $\pi-$acceptors
(d) isoelectronic and weak field ligands

43. The correct order of hybridization of the central atom in the following species NH_3, $[PtCl_4]^{2-}$, PCl_5 and BCl_3 is *[2001S]*
(a) dsp^2, dsp^3, sp^2 and sp^3
(b) sp^3, dsp^2, dsp^3, sp^2
(c) dsp^2, sp^2, sp^3, dsp^3
(d) dsp^2, sp^3, sp^2, dsp^3

44. Specify the coordination geometry around and hybridisation of N and B atoms in a 1 : 1 complex of BF_3 and NH_3 *[2002S]*
(a) N : tetrahedral, sp^3; B : tetrahedral, sp^3
(b) N : pyramidal, sp^3; B : pyramidal, sp^3
(c) N : pyramidal, sp^3; B : planar, sp^2
(d) N : pyramidal, sp^3; B : tetrahedral, sp^3

45. Identify the least stable ion amongst the following : *[2002S]*
(a) Li^-
(b) Be^-
(c) B^-
(d) C^-

46. Which of the following molecular species has unpaired electron(s) ? *[2002S]*
(a) N_2
(b) F_2
(c) O_2^-
(d) O_2^{2-}

47. Which of the following are isoelectronic and isostructural? $NO_3^-, CO_3^{2-}, ClO_3^-, SO_3$ *[2003S]*

(a) NO_3^-, CO_3^{2-} (b) SO_3, NO_3^-

(c) ClO_3^-, CO_3^{2-} (d) CO_3^{2-}, SO_3

48. According to molecular orbital theory which of the following statement about the magnetic character and bond order is correct regarding O_2^+ *[2004S]*

(a) Paramagnetic and Bond order $< O_2$

(b) Paramagnetic and Bond order $> O_2$

(c) Diamagnetic and Bond order $< O_2$

(d) Diamagnetic and Bond order $> O_2$

49. Which species has the maximum number of lone pair of electrons on the central atom?   *[2005S]*

(a) $[ClO_3]^-$ (b) XeF_4

(c) SF_4 (d) $[I_3]^-$

50. Among the following, the paramagnetic compound is   *[2007]*

(a) Na_2O_2 (b) O_3

(c) N_2O (d) KO_2

51. The species having bond order different from that in CO is   *[2007]*

(a) NO^- (b) NO^+

(c) CN^- (d) N_2

52. Assuming that Hund's rule is violated, the bond order and magnetic nature of the diatomic molecule B_2 is   *[2010]*

(a) 1 and diamagnetic

(b) 0 and dimagnetic

(c) 1 and paramagnetic

(d) 0 and paramagnetic

53. The species having pyramidal shape is : *[2010]*

(a) SO_3 (b) BrF_3

(c) SiO_3^{2-} (d) OSF_2

54. Geometrical shapes of the complexes formed by the reaction of Ni^{2+} with Cl^-, CN^- and H_2O, respectively, are   *[2011]*

(a) octahedral, tetrahedral and square planar

(b) tetrahedral, square planar and octahedral

(c) square planar, tetrahedral and octahedral

(d) octahedral, square planar and octahedral

55. Assuming $2s$-$2p$ mixing is **NOT** operative, the paramagnetic species among the following is   *[2014]*

(a) Be_2 (b) B_2

(c) C_2 (d) N_2

56. The geometries of the ammonia complexes of Ni^{2+}, Pt^{2+} and Zn^{2+} respectively, are   *[2016]*

(a) octahedral, square planar and tetrahedral

(b) square planar, octahedral and tetrahedral

(c) tetrahedral, square planar and octahedral

(d) octahedral, tetrahedral and square planar

Topic 2: MCQs with One More Than One Correct

1. CO_2 is isostructural with :   *[1986]*

(a) $HgCl_2$ (b) $SnCl_2$

(c) C_2H_2 (d) NO_2

2. The linear structure is assumed by :   *[1991]*

(a) $SnCl_2$ (b) NCO^-

(c) CS_2 (d) NO_2^+

3. Which of the following have identical bond order?   *[1992]*

(a) CN^- (b) O_2^-

(c) NO^+ (d) CN^+

4. The molecules that will have dipole moment are   *[1992]*

(a) 2, 2-dimethylpropane

(b) trans-2-pentene

(c) cis-3-hexene

(d) 2,2,3,3-tetramethylbutane

5. The compound(s) with TWO lone pairs of electrons on the central atom is(are)   *[2016]*

(a) BrF_5 (b) ClF_3

(c) XeF_4 (d) SF_4

6. According to Molecular Orbital Theory,   *[2016]*

(a) C_2^{2-} is expected to be diamagnetic

(b) O_2^{2+} is expected to have a longer bond length than O_2

(c) N_2^+ and N_2^- have the same bond order

(d) He_2^+ has the same energy as two isolated He atoms

Topic 3: Match the Following

1. Match the orbital overlap figures shown in List-I with the description given in List-II and select the correct answer using the code given below the lists. *[2014]*

List-I		List-II

P. 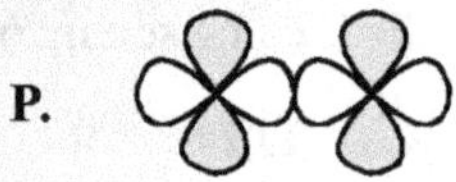   1. $p - d\,\pi$ antibonding

Q. 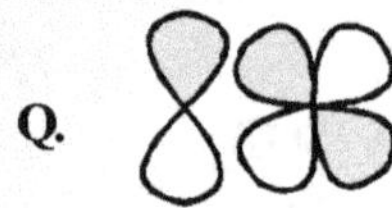   2. $d - d\,\sigma$ bonding

R. 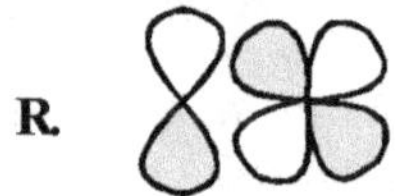   3. $p - d\,\pi$ bonding

S. 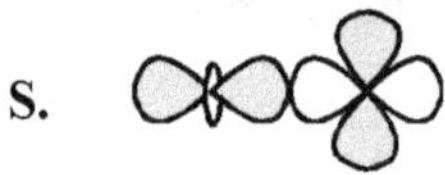   4. $d - d\,\sigma$ antibonding

Code:

	P	Q	R	S
(a)	2	1	3	4
(b)	4	3	1	2
(c)	2	3	1	4
(d)	4	1	3	2

Topic 4: Assertion & Reason Type Questions

1. Read the following Assertion and Reason and answer as per the options given below :

   [1998]

   Assertion : The electronic structure of O_3 is

   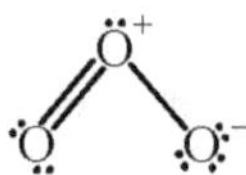

   Reason : structure is not allowed because octet around O cannot be expanded.

(a) If both *assertion* and *reason* are correct, and *reason* is the correct explanation of the *assertion*.

(b) If both *assertion* and *reason* are correct, but *reason* is not the correct explanation of the *assertion*.

(c) If *assertion* is correct but *reason* is incorrect.

(d) If *assertion* is incorrect but *reason* is correct.

2. Read the following Assertion and Reason and answer as per the options given below : *[1998]*

   Assertion : LiCl is predominantly a covalent compound.

   Reason : Electronegativity difference between Li and Cl is too small.

(a) If both *assertion* and *reason* are correct, and *reason* is the correct explanation of the *assertion*.

(b) If both *assertion* and *reason* are correct, but *reason* is not the correct explanation of the *assertion*.

(c) If *assertion* is correct but *reason* is incorrect.

(d) If *assertion* is incorrect but *reason* is correct.

Topic 5: Integer Value Correct Type

1. Based on VSEPR theory, the number of 90 degree F–Br–F angles in BrF_5 is *[2010]*

2. The total number of lone-pairs of electrons in melamine is *[2013]*

3. A list of species having the formula XZ_4 is given below.

   XeF_4, SF_4, SiF_4, BF_4^-, BrF_4^-, $[Cu(NH_3)_4]^{2+}$, $[FeCl_4]^{2-}$, $[CoCl_4]^{2-}$ and $[PtCl_4]^{2-}$.

   Defining shape on the basis of the location of X and Z atoms, the total number of species having a square planar shape is *[2014]*

4. Among the triatomic molecules/ions, $BeCl_2$, N_3^-, N_2O, NO_2^+, O_3, SCl_2, ICl_2^-, I_3^- and XeF_2, the total number of linear molecule(s)/ion(s) where the hybridization of the central atom does not have contribution from the d-orbital(s) is [Atomic number : S = 16, Cl = 17, I = 53 and Xe = 54] *[2015]*

HINTS & SOLUTIONS

Topic 1: MCQs with One Correct Answer

1. (c) In KCN, ionic bond is present between K^+ and CN^- and covalent bonds are present between carbon and nitrogen $C \equiv N$.

2. (d) $\because$ after forming the bonds, C has only $6\,e^-$ in its valence shell.

3. (a) X^+Y^-

$\because$ Electropositive elements forms cation and electronegative elements forms anion. Except this all compounds are ionic.

4. (a) H_2 $H - H$

5. (c) $N \equiv N$ $:N::N:$

6. (b) $\because$ It forms hydrogen bonds with water

7. (c) **NOTE :** Dipole moment is vector quantity In trigonal planar geometry (for sp^2 hybridisation), the vector sum of two bond moments is equal and opposite to the dipole moment of third bond.

8. (a) **NOTE :** Isoelectronic species have same number of electrons.

Electrons in $CO = 6 + 8 = 14$

Electrons in $CN^- = 6 + 7 + 1 = 14$

Electrons in $O_2^- = 8 + 8 + 1 = 17$

Electrons in $O_2^+ = 8 + 8 - 1 = 15$

$\therefore$ CO and CN^- are isoelectronic.

9. (a) **TIPS/Formulae :**

(i) CO_2, sp hybridisation

(ii) SO_2

     $\therefore$ sp^2 hybridisation

(iii) NO_2 has V shaped structure.

(iv) ClO_2 has V shaped structure.

     $\therefore$ CO_2 having sp hybridation has linear shape.

10. (b) **TIPS/Formulae :**

(i)   Dipole moment is vector quantity. When vector sum of all dipoles in molecule will be zero, then molecule will not have net dipole moment.

(ii)   **NOTE :** For net dipole moment to be equal to zero, all the atoms attached to central atom must be identical and geometry must be regular.

Methyl chloride   Carbon tetrachloride

Methylene chloride   Chloroform

$\therefore$ Carbon tetrachloride having regular geometry and identical atoms attached to bonds has zero dipole moment.

11. (b) In regular tetrahedral structure, dipole moment of one bond is cancelled by opposite dipole moment of the other bonds.

12. (d) **TIPS/Formulae :** Hydrogen bonding is formed in those compounds in which F or O or N atoms are attached to hydrogen atom.

$\because$ HCl does not have F or N or O

$\therefore$ It does not form hydrogen bond.

13. (c) Ionic bond or electrovalent between Cu^{2+} and SO_4^{2-}, covalent and coordinate in

$$SO_4^{2-}; \left[O \leftarrow \underset{\underset{O}{\parallel}}{\overset{\overset{O}{\parallel}}{S}} \rightarrow O \right]^{2-} \text{ion.}$$

14. (b) **TIPS/Formulae :** sp type of hybridization involves the intermixing of one s and one p (say p_x) orbitals to give two equivalent hybrid orbitals, known as sp hybrid orbitals.

The two sp hybrid orbitals are directed diagonally, i.e., in a straight line with an angle of $180°$ (**collinear orbitals**). The other two p orbitals (say p_y and p_z) remain pure.

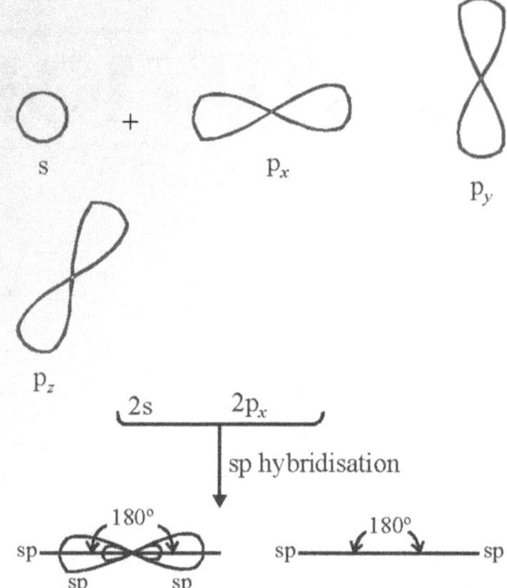

15. (a) **NOTE THIS STEP :** Write the electronic configuration of each species according to molecular orbital theory.

NO $(15e^-)-\sigma 1s^2, \sigma^* 1s^2, \sigma 2s^2, \sigma^* 2s^2, \sigma 2p_x^2,$
$\{\pi 2p_y^2 = \pi 2p_z^2, \{\pi^* 2p_y^1 = \pi^* 2p_z^0$

1 unpaired electron.

CO $(14e^-)-\sigma 1s^2, \sigma^* 1s^2, \sigma 2s^2, \sigma^* 2s^2,$
$\{\pi 2p_y^2 = \pi 2p_z^2, \sigma 2p_x^2$

no unpaired electron

CN$^-$ $(14e^-)-\sigma 1s^2, \sigma^* 1s^2, \sigma 2s^2, \sigma^* 2s^2,$
$\{\pi 2p_y^2 = \pi 2p_z^2, \sigma 2p_x^2$

O$_2$ $(16e^-)-\sigma 1s^2, \sigma^* 1s^2, \sigma 2s^2,$
$\sigma^* 2s^2, \sigma 2p_x^2, \{\pi 2p_y^2 = \pi 2p_z^2,$
$\{\pi^* 2p_y^1 = \pi^* 2p_z^1 ;$

Two unpaired electrons.

16. (d) In covalent bonds between two identical non-metal atoms share the pair of electrons equally between them, e.g. : F_2, O_2, N_2.

17. (c) **NOTE :** Greater the difference between electro-negativities of two covalently bonded atoms more will be strength of hydrogen bond.

∴ F – H ....F bond is strongest due to largest difference in electronegativity of atoms and smallest size of F atom.

18. (c)

19. (a) **NOTE :** Compounds having F or O or N attached to H form hydrogen bond.

CH$_3$CH$_2$OH   C$_2$H$_5$– O –C$_2$H$_5$ CH$_3$CH$_2$Cl
ethanol   diethyl ether   ethyl chloride

CH$_3$
|
CH$_3$ – N – CH$_3$
Trimethyl amine

∴ Ethanol having H attached to O atom will form hydrogen bond. Rest of the compounds do not hydrogen bonds.

20. (c) From amongst given species PH$_3$, NH$_3$ and SbH$_3$ are all sp^3 hybridised. Their central atom has both bond pair as well as lone pair of electrons. The lone pair occupy the fourth orbital. CH$_3^+$ has only three pairs of electrons so it is sp^2 hybridised.

21. (a) **TIPS/Formulae :** Compound having sp hybridisation will have linear shape.

∴ CO$_2$ or (O=C=O) which has C in sp hybrid state has linear shape.

22. (b) **TIPS/Formulae :** Dipole moment of compound having regular geometry and same type of atoms is zero. It is vector quantity.

The zero dipole moment of BF$_3$ is due to its symmetrical (triangular planar) structure. The three fluorine atoms lie at the corners of an equilateral triangle with boron at the centre.

NOTE : The vectorial addition of the dipole moments of the three bonds gives a net sum of zero because the resultant of any two dipole moments is equal and opposite to the third. The dipole moment of NH$_3$ is 1.46 D indicating its unsymmetrical structure. The dipole moment of CH$_2$Cl$_2$ (the molecule uses sp^3 hybridisation but is not symmetric) is 1.57D.

23. (a) **TIPS/Formulae :**

Molecule having sp^3 hybridisation and one lone pair of electron will have pyramidal structure.

(i)   CO$_3^{2-}$ and NO$_3^-$ have tetrahedron structure.

(ii) In PCl$_3$, P is sp^3 hybridised and has one lone pair of electrons, hence it is pyramidal in shape.

24. (c) **TIPS/Formulae :**

4σ bonds – sp^3 hybridisation
2σ and 2π bonds – sp^2 hybridisation
1σ and 3π bonds – sp hybridisation

[For hybridization only σ-bonds are considered]

O
‖
H – C – OH
*
(a)

NH$_2$
|
H$_2$N – C = O
*
(b)

CH$_3$
|
CH$_3$ – C* – OH
|
CH$_3$
(c)

O
‖
CH$_3$ – C – H
*
(d)

(a) 3σ, 1π (b) 3σ, 1π (c) 4σ (d) 3σ, 1π
∴ (CH$_3$)$_3$COH has 4σ bonds and thus it has sp^3 hybridisation.

25. **(a)** O_2^- $(17e^-) - KK \sigma 2s^2 \sigma^* 2s^2 \sigma 2p_x^2,$

$\{\pi 2p_y^2 = \pi 2p_z^2, \{\pi^* 2p_y^2 = \pi^* 2p_z^1$

Thus, O_2^- has one unpaired electron; hence it is paramagnetic. Other species have no unpaired electron. All of them have 14 electrons.

26. **(a)**

27. **(b)** H$_2$O molecule can form four hydrogen bonds per molecule, two via lone pairs and two via hydrogen atoms.

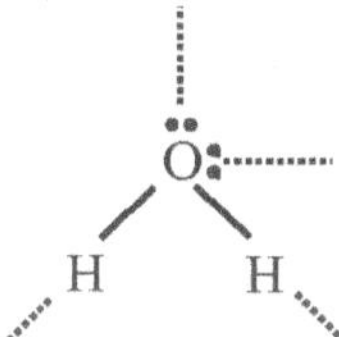

28. **(b)** In N$_2$, similar atoms are linked to each other and thus there is no polarity.

29. **(d)** No. of e^- in CH$_3^+$ = 6 + 3 – 1 = 8
No. of e^- in H$_3$O$^+$ = 3 + 8 – 1 = 10
No. of e^- in NH$_3$ = 7 + 3 = 10
No. of e^- in CH$_3^-$ = 6 + 3 + 1 = 10
∴ H$_3$O$^+$, NH$_3$ and CH$_3^-$ are isoelectronic.

30. **(c)** **TIPS/Formulae :**
(i) Non metallic oxides are more covalent (or less ionic) as compared to metallic oxides.
(ii) Higher the polarising power of cation (higher for higher oxidation state of similar size cations) more will be covalent character.
(i) P$_2$O$_5$ will be more covalent than other metallic oxides.

(ii) Oxidation state of Mn is + 7 in Mn$_2$O$_7$, oxidation state of Cr in CrO$_3$ is + 6 and oxidation state of Mn is + 2 in MnO.
∴ MnO is most ionic.

NOTE : P$_2$O$_5$, being a non-metallic oxide will definitely be more covalent than the other metallic oxides. Further, we know that higher the polarising power of the cation (higher for higher oxidation state of the similar size cations) more will be the covalent character. Here Mn is in +7 O.S in Mn$_2$O$_7$, Cr in +6 in CrO$_3$ and Mn in +2 in MnO. So MnO is the most ionic and Mn$_2$O$_7$ is the most covalent.

31. **(d)** O$_2$ = Oxygen (Z = 8) has following molecular orbital configuration of O$_2$.
O$_2$ $(16e^-)$ = σ 1s^2, σ* 1s^2, σ 2s^2, σ* 2s^2, σ2p$_x^2$, $\{\pi 2p_y^2$
= π 2p$_z^2$, $\{\pi^* 2p_y^1 = \pi^* 2p_z^1$ i.e., 2 unpaired and 14 paired electrons.

32. **(c)**

33. **(b)** Calcium carbide is an ionic compound (Ca^{2+} C^{2-}) which produces acetylene on reacting with water. Thus the structure of C^{2-} is [C ≡ C]$^{2-}$. It has one σ and two π bonds. [∵ A triple bond consists of one σ and two π-bonds]

34. **(c)** (a)

$$\left[\begin{array}{c} H \\ | \\ H - N - H \\ | \\ H \end{array} \right]^+ [Cl]^-$$ – It has ionic and non-polar covalent bond

(b) H – C ≡ N - It has ionic and polar covalent bonds.

(c)
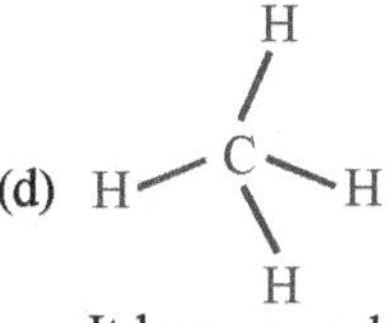

It has polar and non polar both type of covalent bonds.

(d)
H
|
H – C – H
|
H

It has non polar covalent bonds only.

35. **(d)** Critical temperature of water is higher than O$_2$ because H$_2$O molecule has dipole moment which is due to its V-shape.

36. **(b)**

37. **(b)** $\therefore$ Boron, in BF_3, is sp^2 hybridised leading to trigonal planar shape.

38. **(d)** **KEY CONCEPT**

(i) Bond length $\propto \dfrac{1}{\text{Bond order}}$

(ii) Bond order is calculated by either the help of molecular orbital theory or by resonance.

(i) Bond order of CO as calculated by molecular orbital theory = 3

$$\left\{ b.o. = \frac{1}{2}[N_b - N_a] \right\}$$

(ii) Bond order of CO_2 (by resonance method)

$$= \frac{\text{No. of bonds in all possible sides}}{\text{No. of resonating structure}}$$

$$= \frac{4}{2} = 2$$

(iii) Bond order in CO_3^{2-} (by resonance method)

$$= \frac{4}{3} = 1.33$$

$\therefore$ Order of bond length of C – O is CO < CO_2 < CO_3^{2-}

39. **(a)** $\therefore$ It has angular geometry and so it has non-zero value of dipole moment.

40. **(d)**

41. **(b)** For NO_2^+

$\therefore sp$ hybridisation

For NO_3^-

$\therefore sp^2$ hybridisation

For NH_4^+

$\therefore sp^3$ hybridisation

42. **(a)** Number of electrons in each species are

$CN^- = 6 + 7 + 1 = 14$, $CO = 6 + 8 = 14$

$NO^+ = 7 + 8 - 1 = 14$

Each of the species has 14 electrons which are distributed in MOs as below

$$\sigma 1s^2, \sigma^* 1s^2, \sigma 2s^2, \sigma^* 2s^2, \{\pi 2p_y^2$$

$$= \pi 2p_z^2, \sigma 2p_x^2$$

$$\text{Bond order} = \frac{10 - 4}{2} = 3$$

43. **(b)**

44. **(a)** $H_3N \rightarrow BF_3$ where both N, B are attaining tetrahedral geomerty.

45. **(b)** **NOTE THIS STEP :** Write configuration of all species. Half filled and full filled orbitals are more stable as compared to nearly half filled and nearly full filled orbitals.

$Li^- = 1s^2, 2s^2$; $Be^- = 1s^2, 2s^2, 2p^1$

$B^- = 1s^2, 2s^2, 2p^2$; $C^- = 1s^2, 2s^2, 2p^3$

$\therefore$ Be^- will be least stable. It has lowest I.E.

46. **(c)** $N_2(7+7=14)$; $\sigma 1s^2, \sigma 1^* s^2, \sigma 2s^2, \sigma^* 2s^2,$

$$\begin{cases} \pi^* 2p_y^2 \\ \pi^* 2p_z^2 \end{cases}, \sigma 2p_x^2$$

$F_2(9+9=18)$; $\sigma 1s^2, \sigma^* 1s^2, \sigma 2s^2, \sigma^* 2s^2, \sigma 2p_x^2,$

$$\begin{cases} \pi 2p_y^2 \\ \pi 2p_z^2 \end{cases}, \begin{cases} \pi^* 2p_y^2 \\ \pi^* 2p_z^2 \end{cases}$$

$O_2^- (8+8+1 = 17)$; $\sigma 1s^2, \sigma^* 1s^2, \sigma 2s^2, \sigma^* 2s^2, \sigma 2p_x^2,$

$$\begin{cases} \pi 2p_y^2 \\ \pi 2p_z^2 \end{cases}, \begin{cases} \pi^* 2p_y^2 \\ \pi^* 2p_z^1 \end{cases}$$

$O_2^{2-} (8+8+2 = 18)$; $\sigma 1s^2, \sigma^* 1s^2, \sigma 2s^2, \sigma^* 2s^2, \sigma 2p_x^2,$

$$\begin{cases} \pi 2p_y^2 \\ \pi 2p_z^2 \end{cases}, \begin{cases} \pi^* 2p_y^2 \\ \pi^* 2p_z^2 \end{cases}$$

$\therefore$ O_2^- is the only species having unpaired electron.

47. **(a)** **NOTE :** Isoelectronic species have same number of electrons and isostructural species have same type of hybridisation at central atom.

NO_3^- ; No. of $e^- = 7 + 8 \times 3 + 1 = 32$, hybridisation of N in NO_3^- is sp^3

CO_3^{2-} ; No. of $e^- = 6 + 8 \times 3 + 2 = 32$, hybridisation of C in CO_3^{2-} is sp^3

ClO_3^- ; No. of $e^- = 17 + 8 \times 3 + 1 = 42$, hybridisation of Cl in ClO_3^- is sp^3

SO_3; No. of $e^- = 16 + 8 \times 3 = 40$, hybridisation of S in SO_3 is sp^2

$\therefore$ NO_3^- and CO_3^{2-} are isostructural and isoelectronic.

48. **(b)** $O_2 : \sigma 1s^2, \sigma^* 1s^2, \sigma 2s^2, \sigma^* 2s^2, \sigma 2p_x^2,$

$$\begin{cases} \pi 2p_y^2, \\ \pi 2p_z^2 \end{cases}, \begin{cases} \pi^* 2p_y^1 \\ \pi^* 2p_z^1 \end{cases}$$

Bond order $= \dfrac{10-6}{2} = 2$

(two unpaired electrons in antibonding molecular orbital)

$O_2^+ : \sigma 1s^2, \sigma^* 1s^2, \sigma 2s^2, \sigma^* 2s^2, \sigma 2p_x^2,$

$$\begin{cases} \pi 2p_y^2, \\ \pi 2p_z^2, \end{cases} \begin{cases} \pi^* 2p_y^1 \\ \pi^* 2p_z^0 \end{cases}$$

Bond order $= \dfrac{10-5}{2} = 2.5$

(One unpaired electron in antibonding molecular orbital)

Hence O_2 as well as O_2^+ is paramagnetic,

and bond order of O_2^+ is greater than that of O_2.

49. **(d)** $\underline{ClO_3^-}$
(1 lone pair)

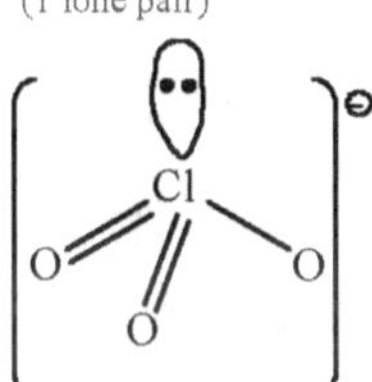

Pyramidal

$\underline{XeF_4^-}$
(2 lone pair)

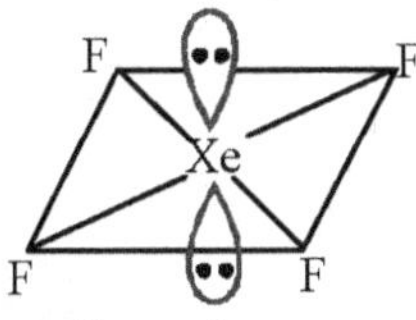

Square planar

$\underline{SF_4}$
(1 lone pair)

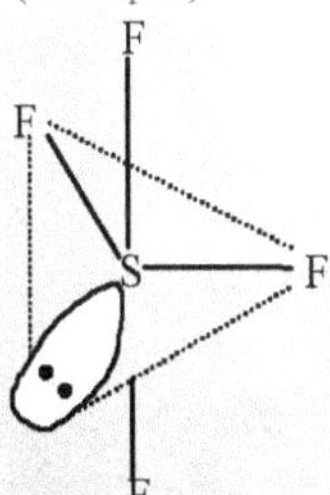

Irregular tetrahedral

$\underline{I_3^-}$
(3 lone pair)

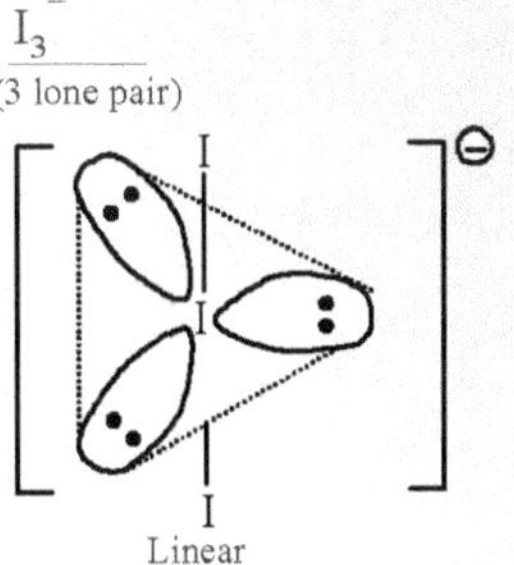

Linear

50. **(d)** (i) In Na_2O_2, we have O_2^{2-} ion. Number of valence elctrons of the two oxygen in O_2^{2-} ion $= 8 \times 2 + 2 = 18$ which are present as follows

$\sigma 1s^2, \ \sigma*1s^2, \ \sigma 2s^2, \ \sigma*2s^2, \sigma 2p_x^2,$

$\{ \pi 2p_y^2 = \pi 2p_z^2, \{ \pi*2p_y^2 = \pi*2p_z^2$

$\therefore$ Number of unpaired electrons $= 0$,

hence, O_2^{2-} is diamagnetic.

(ii) No. of valence electrons of all atoms in $O_3 = 6 \times 3 = 18$.
Thus, it also, does not have any unpaired electron, hence it is diamagnetic.

(iii) No. of valence electrons of all atom in N_2O
$= 2 \times 5 + 6 = 16$. Hence, here also all electrons are paired. So it is diamagnetic.

(iv) In KO_2, we have O_2^- No. of valence electrons of all atoms in $O_2^- = 2 \times 6 + 1$
$= 13$,
Thus it has one unpaired electron, hence it is paramagnetic.

51. **(a)** Molecular electronic configuration of

$CO : \sigma 1s^2, \sigma*1s^2, \sigma 2s^2, \sigma*2s^2, \{\pi 2p_y^2$

$= \pi 2p_z^2, \sigma 2p_x^2$

Therefore, bond order

$$= \frac{N_b - N_a}{2} = \frac{10-4}{2} = 3$$

$NO^+ : \sigma 1s^2, \sigma*1s^2, \sigma 2s^2, \sigma*2s^2, \sigma 2p_x^2, \{\pi 2p_y^2 = \pi 2p_z^2$

Bond order $= \dfrac{10-4}{2} = 3$

$$CN^- = \sigma 1s^2, \sigma^* 1s^2, \sigma 2s^2, \sigma^* 2s^2,$$
$$\{\pi 2p_y^2 = \pi 2p_z^2, \sigma 2p_x^2$$

Bond order $= \dfrac{10-4}{2} = 3$

$$N_2 : \sigma 1s^2, \sigma^* 1s^2, \sigma 2s^2, \sigma^* 2s^2, \{\pi 2p_y^2$$
$$= \pi 2p_z^2, \sigma 2p_x^2$$

Bond order $= \dfrac{10-4}{2} = 3$

$$NO^- : \sigma 1s^2, \sigma^* 1s^2, \sigma 2s^2, \sigma^* 2s^2, \sigma 2p_x^2,$$
$$\{\pi 2p_y^2 = \pi 2p_z^2, \{\pi^* 2p_y^1 = \pi^* 2p_z^1$$

Bond order $= \dfrac{10-6}{2} = 2$

$\therefore$ NO^- has different bond order from that in CO.

52. (a) Molecular orbital configuration of $B_2(10)$

as per the condition will be

$$\sigma 1s^2, \sigma^* 1s^2, \sigma 2s^2, \sigma^* 2s^2, \pi 2p_y^2$$
Bond order of $B_2 = \dfrac{6-4}{2} = 1$,

B_2 will be diamagnetic.

53. (d) $OSF_2 : \dfrac{N}{2} = \dfrac{6+2}{2} = 4$. It has 1 lone pair.

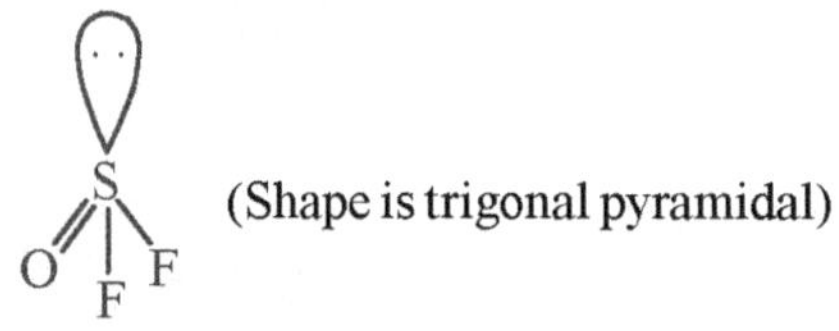

(Shape is trigonal pyramidal)

The shapes of SO_3, BrF_3 and SiO_3^{2-} are triangular planar respectively.

54. (b) $Ni^{+2} + 4Cl^- \longrightarrow [NiCl_4]^{2-}$
sp^3

$[NiCl_4]^{2-}. = 3d^8$ configuration with nickel in $+2$ oxidation state, Cl^- being weak field ligand does not compel for pairing of electrons.

So, $[NiCl_4]^{2-}$

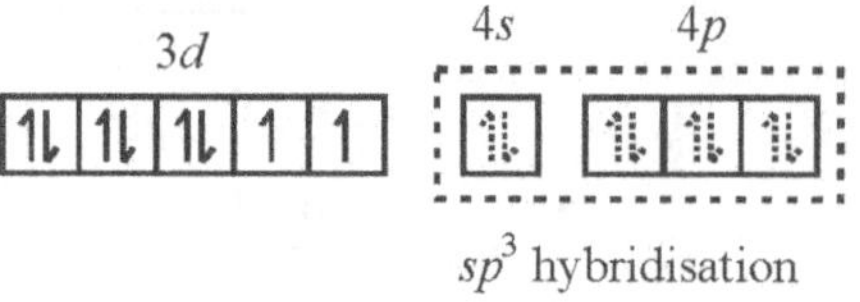

sp^3 hybridisation

Hence, complex has tetrahedral geometry

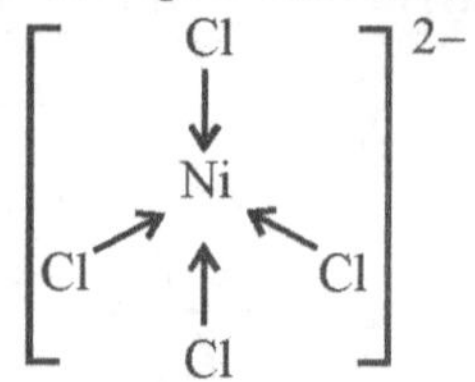

$$Ni^{+2} + 4CN^- \longrightarrow [Ni(CN)_4]^{2-}$$
$[Ni(CN)_4]^{2-} = 3d^8$ configuration with nickel in $+2$ oxidation state, CN^- being strong field ligand compels for pairing of electrons. So, $[NiCN_4]^{-2}$

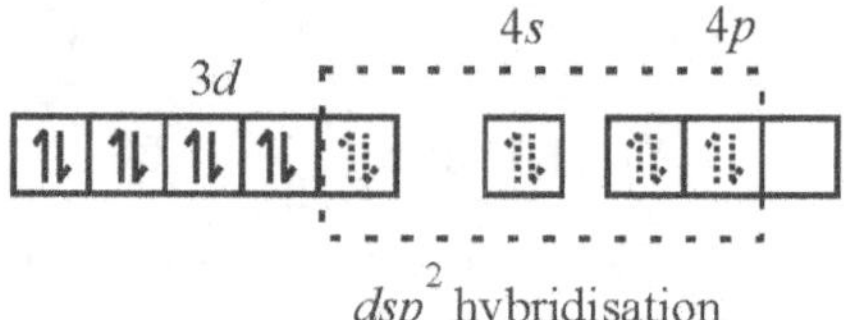

dsp^2 hybridisation

Hence, complex has square planar geometry.

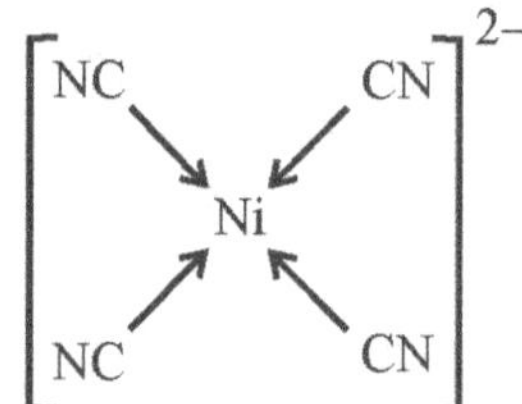

$$Ni^{+2} + 6H_2O \longrightarrow [Ni(H_2O)_6]^{2+}$$

$[Ni(H_2O)_6] = 3d^8$ configuration with nickel in $+2$ oxidation state. As with $3d^8$ configuration two d-orbitals are not available for d^2sp^3 hybridisation. So, hybridisation of Ni (II) is sp^3d^2 and Ni (II) with six co-ordination will have octahedral geometry.

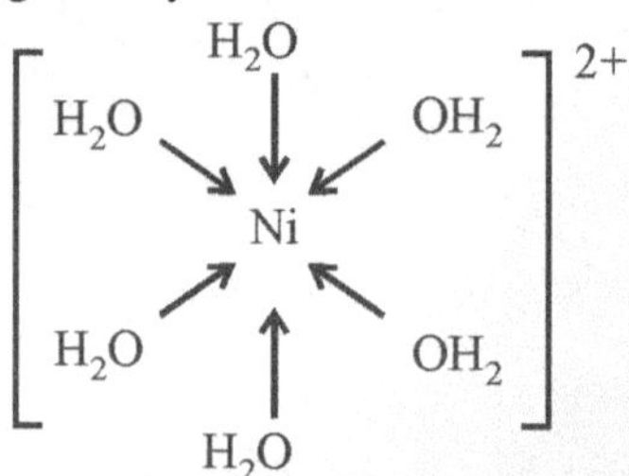

Note : With water as ligand, Ni (II) forms octahedral complexes.

55. (c) $Be_2 = \sigma 1s^2 \, \sigma^* 1s^2 \, \sigma 2s^2 \, \sigma^* 2s^2$
$B_2 = \sigma 1s^2 \, \sigma^* 1s^2 \, \sigma 2s^2 \, \sigma^* 2s^2 \, \sigma^2 p_z^2$
$C_2 = \sigma 1s^2 \, \sigma^* 1s^2 \, \sigma 2s^2 \, \sigma^* 2s^2 \, \sigma^2 p_z^2 \, \pi 2p_x^1$
$\pi 2p_y^1$

$N_2 = \sigma 1s^2\ \sigma^*1s^2\ \sigma 2s^2\ \sigma^*2s^2\ \sigma 2p_z^2\ \pi 2p_x^2\ \pi 2p_y^2$

Thus only C_2 will be paramagnetic

56. **(a)** Ni^{2+} with NH_3 shows CN = 6 forming $[Ni(NH_3)_6]^{2+}$

(Octahedral)

Pt^{2+} with NH_3 shows CN = 4 forming $[Pt(NH_3)_4]^{2+}$

(5d series CMA, square planner)

Zn^{2+} with NH_3 shows CN = 4 forming $[Zn(NH_3)_4]^{2+}$

($3d^{10}$ configuration, tetrahedral)

Topic 2: MCQs with One More Than One Correct

1. **(a,c)** CO_2, $HgCl_2$ and C_2H_2 have linear structure (*sp* hybridization), while $SnCl_2$ is trigonal planar (*sp²* hybridisation). NO_2 has angular structure (*V*-shape).

2. **(b,c,d)** $[O = N = O]^+$; $[N \equiv C - O]^-$; $S = C = S$

It can be seen from the structure shown above that CS_2 being *sp* hybridized has a linear shape and other two molecules are isoelectronic to CS_2, so they are also linear. $SnCl_2$ and SO_2 are *sp²* hybridised and are not linear.

3. **(a,c)** The outer most shells of C, N & O has 4, 5 and 6 electrons respectively. Thus CN^- and NO^+ each has 10 electrons to accommodate in the molecular orbitals.

So their bond order is same. O_2^- has 13 and CN^+ has 12 electrons in outermost orbits.

4. **(b,c)** Alkanes (a) and (d) don't have dipole moment because of symmetry in them.

$$\underset{H}{\overset{C_2H_5}{>}}C = C\underset{CH_3}{\overset{H}{<}}$$

$$\underset{H}{\overset{C_2H_5}{>}}C = C\underset{H}{\overset{C_2H_5}{<}}$$

trans 2-pentene   cis 3-hexene

These alkenes are not symmetrical and so they have dipole moment.

5. **(b,c)**

Compound		Number of lone pairs on central atom
BrF_5	→	1
ClF_3	→	2
XeF_4	→	2
SF_4	→	1

6. **(a,c)**

(A) The molecular orbital energy configuration of C_2^{2-} is

$$\sigma_{1s}^2, \sigma_{1s}^{*2}, \sigma_{2s}^2, \sigma_{2s}^{*2}, \pi_{2p_x}^2 = \pi_{2p_y}^2, \sigma_{2p_z}^2$$

In the MO of C_2^{2-} there is no unpaired electron hence it is diamagnetic

(B) Bond order of O_2^{2+} is 3 and O_2 is 2 therefore bond length of O_2 is greater than O_2^{2+}

(C) The molecular orbital energy configuration of N_2^+ is

$$\sigma_{1s}^2, \sigma_{1s}^{*2}, \sigma_{2s}^2, \sigma_{2s}^{*2}, \pi_{2p_x}^2 = \pi_{2p_y}^2, \sigma_{2p_z}^1$$

Bond order of $N_2^+ = \dfrac{1}{2}(9-4) = 2.5$

The molecular orbital energy configuration of N_2^- is

$$\sigma_{1s}^2, \sigma_{1s}^{*2}, \sigma_{2s}^2, \sigma_{2s}^{*2}, \pi_{2p_x}^2 = \pi_{2p_y}^2, \sigma_{2p_z}^2, \pi_{2p_x}^{*1} = \pi_{2p_y}^*$$

Bond order of $N_2^- = \dfrac{1}{2}(10-5) = 2.5$

(D) He_2^+ has less energy in comparison to two isolated He atoms because some energy is released during the formation of He_2^+ from 2 He atoms.

Topic 3: Match the Following

1. **(c)** P.   d – d (σ bonding)

Q.   p – d (π bonding)

R.   p – d (π antibonding)

S.   d – d (σ antibonding)

Topic 4: Assertion & Reason Type Questions

1. **(a)** Both assertion and reason are correct. The reason explains the assertion as the central O-atom cannot have more than 8 electrons (octet).

2. **(c)** LiCl is a covalent compound since due to the large size of the anion (Cl^-) its effective nuclear charge lessens and its valence shells are held less tightly towards its nucleus. Here, assertion is correct but reason is incorrect.

Topic 5: Integer Value Correct Type

1. **(0)** Its gemoetry is square pyramidal and due to lp-bp repulsion disturtion occurs due to which bond angle reduces from $90°$ to $89.8°$

2. **(6)** Structure of melamine is as follows :

Total no. of lone pairs of electron is '6'.

3. **(4)**

XeF_4 :   Square planar (sp^3d^2)

SF_4 :   See-saw (sp^3d)

SiF_4 :   Tetrahedral (sp^3)

BF_4^- :   Tetrahedral (sp^3)

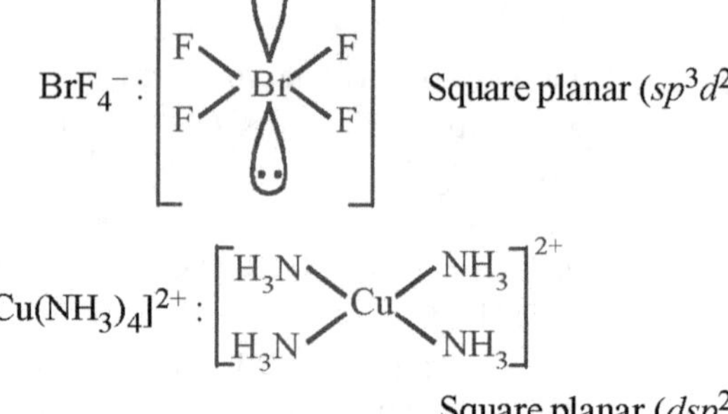

BrF_4^- :   Square planar (sp^3d^2)

$[Cu(NH_3)_4]^{2+}$:   Square planar (dsp^2)

$[FeCl_4]^{2-}$:   Tetrahedral (sp^3)

$[CoCl_4]^{2-}$:   Tetrahedral (sp^3)

$[PtCl_4]^{2-}$:   Square planar (dsp^2)

4. **(4)**

$Cl-Be-Cl$
Hybridization sp
Structure linear

$N \equiv N - \overset{..}{\underset{..}{N}}{:}^-$
Hybridisation sp
Structure linear

$O = \overset{+}{N} \to O$
Hybridisation sp
Structure Linear planar

Hybridisation sp^2
Structure Trigonal

Hybridisation sp^3
Structure Angular

$[Cl - \overset{..}{\underset{..}{I}} - Cl]^-$
Hybridisation sp^3d
Structure linear

$[I - \overset{..}{\underset{..}{I}} - I]^-$
Hybridisation sp^3d
Structure Linear

$F - \overset{..}{\underset{..}{Xe}} - F$
Hybridisation sp^3d
Structure Linear

$\overset{-}{N} = \overset{+}{N} = O$
Hybridisation sp
Structure Linear

Only $BeCl_2$, N_3^-, N_2O and NO_2 are linear with sp-hybridisation.

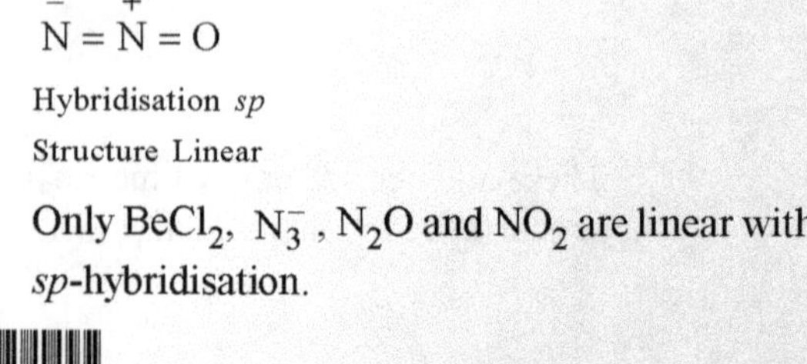

www.ingramcontent.com/pod-product-compliance
Lightning Source LLC
Chambersburg PA
CBHW081935160726
47999CB00008B/2400